Citizen Canine

Our Evolving Relationship
with Cats and Dogs

Citizen
Canine

David Grimm

PUBLICAFFAIRS
New York

Copyright © 2014 by David Grimm.

Published in the United States by PublicAffairs™,
a Member of the Perseus Books Group
All rights reserved.

Printed in the United States of America.

No part of this book may be reproduced in any manner whatsoever without
written permission except in the case of brief quotations embodied in critical
articles and reviews. For information, address PublicAffairs, 250 West 57th
Street, 15th Floor, New York, NY 10107.

PublicAffairs books are available at special discounts for bulk purchases in
the U.S. by corporations, institutions, and other organizations. For more
information, please contact the Special Markets Department at the Perseus
Books Group, 2300 Chestnut Street, Suite 200, Philadelphia, PA 19103, call
(800) 810-4145, ext. 5000, or e-mail special.markets@perseusbooks.com.

Book Design by Trish Wilkinson
Set in 11 point Goudy Old Style

Library of Congress Cataloging-in-Publication Data

Grimm, David, 1975–
    Citizen canine : our evolving relationship with cats and dogs / David
Grimm.
        pages   cm
    Includes bibliographical references and index.
    ISBN 978-1-61039-133-7 (hardcover)—ISBN 978-1-61039-134-4
(e-book) 1. Pets—History. 2. Pets—Social aspects—History. 3. Animal
rights. 4. Human-animal relationships—History. I. Title.
SF411.35.G75 2014
636.088'7—dc23   2013043916

First Edition

10 9 8 7 6 5 4 3 2

To Jasper and Jezebel,
who inspired me,
and Amy,
who put up with me

Contents

Introduction

Alex wasn't the kind of pet you'd imagine people fighting over. The thirteen-year-old golden retriever was hobbled by arthritis and kidney disease. He had to take glucosamine twice a day, swim to keep his joints limber, and visit a veterinarian multiple times a week. Yet, when his owner, a wealthy Memphis businessman named Ronald Callan Jr., took his own life on New Year's Day 2007, all his survivors wanted was the dog. Callan's divorced parents each filed for custody, as did his ex-girlfriend and his fiancée. Things got nasty. At one point, the father accused the mother of trying to kidnap Alex. So the judge appointed the animal an attorney, who represented his interests in court and eventually hammered out a four-way visitation agreement. For the first time in US history, a dog had a lawyer.

It's been a long road from campsite to courtroom. Dogs and cats were once wild animals, lurking in the shadows as our ancestors gathered around the fire pit. But over the course of thousands of years, a few individuals mustered the courage to join us. Wolves followed nomadic bands of humans across vast grassy plains, inching closer and closer until, one day, they were eating out of our hands. Wildcats slunk out of the desert, drawn to early farming villages and the rodents they attracted. Early dogs were hunting companions. The first cats protected crops. And slowly, these formerly feral creatures became our friends.

The ancient Egyptians deified cats, and the Romans mourned their fallen dogs as they would children, but the good times didn't last. Pets lost their souls in the centuries that followed. A paranoid pope linked felines to Satan, sparking a mass slaughter that nearly exterminated them in medieval Europe. A famed French philosopher declared that animals were mere machines without thought or feeling, a doctrine that helped justify canine vivisection in the seventeenth century and beyond. Yet, through it all, dogs and cats stuck with us. And we returned to them. We welcomed them into our homes; we treated them like children; we loved and pampered them like never before. They are no longer companions or even friends. They are family.

An equally dramatic transformation has taken place in the legal system. Early American laws ignored cats and dogs, dismissing them as worthless objects that didn't even warrant the meager legal status of property. They could be stolen and killed without repercussion. But as pets have become family in our homes, they've also become family in the eyes of the law. State legislatures have passed tough anticruelty acts, imposing fines of up to $125,000 and ten years in prison for anyone who harms a dog or cat. Judges have begun awarding damages for mental suffering and loss of companionship to the owners of slain pets, legal claims typically reserved for the wrongful death of a spouse or child. And the federal government, spurred by the ultimate sacrifice so many made for their animals during Hurricane Katrina, now impels rescue agencies to save pets as well as people during natural disasters. Today, cats and dogs are the most valued and legally protected animals in the country.

Pets aren't just becoming more like people in our laws and homes. They're also becoming more like people in our society. Every year, they take on more roles and more responsibilities, providing critical services in our increasingly dangerous and fractured world. A new generation of assistance animals is treating everything from high blood pressure to autism. Canine soldiers are laying down their lives in unprecedented numbers for their human counterparts. Even the dogs and cats that share our beds may be indispensable, filling the emotional void created by technology and our disintegrating human relationships.

Our pets are becoming as much a part of our world as we are. They are, in effect, becoming fellow citizens. Yet the path to citizenship is not a smooth one, and cats and dogs may not complete the journey. They'll face segregation and discrimination. They'll even be put on trial. Meanwhile, owners—now "guardians"—may have to adjust to a new reality in which pets are seen as people. Soon pet guardians could be treated like the parents of human children, getting fined or having their animals taken away by a sort of Pet Protective Services if they don't walk their dog enough or spring for their cat's chemotherapy. The impact could extend to society itself. Veterinarians worry that a flood of malpractice cases could destroy their profession, and the biomedical research and agriculture industries have fought the pet "personhood" movement tooth and claw, concerned it could bleed over to lab rats and farm animals, jeopardizing cures for human diseases and shutting down meat production. One prominent legal scholar frets for the future of humanity. "A powerful argument may be made," he writes, "that assigning rights to animals that do not possess moral responsibility represents a rejection of the foundation of human civilization."

How did we get here—and what happens next? That's what this book is all about. In the pages that follow, I'll travel the country to trace the evolution of dogs and cats from wild animals to quasi-citizens. I'll ride along with police detectives as they investigate animal cruelty in Los Angeles, tour the devastation of New Orleans in search of the pet survivors of Katrina, and come face to face with gray wolves and feral cats. I'll also take a virtual seat in the courtroom, witnessing how some of the most fascinating cases of the last century have dramatically altered the legal status of pets in society—and continue to do so. Along the way, I'll meet some of the nation's top animal thinkers and doers, including one man who wants to wipe cats and dogs from the face of the earth and another who's trying to find a compromise before it's too late.

The book is divided into three parts. The first, "Family," uncovers how pets became our virtual children, trekking the long—and often tortuous—path from feral animal to family member. The second, "Person," follows the legal evolution of dogs and cats from valueless objects to beings on the precipice of personhood. And the final section, "Citizen," explores how these social and legal revolutions are transforming society and what the future holds for both us and our pets. Each section begins with a chapter that illustrates where we are now; the remaining chapters reveal how we got here.

This is a story about more than dogs and cats. It's about what it means to be a person and what it means to be valued by society. And ultimately, it's about how the quest for inclusion defines us all, animal and man.

I

FAMILY

ONE

The Pet Republic

I never imagined that writing a book about cats and dogs would land me in jail. Yet here I am on a Friday afternoon in mid-September, surrounded by inmates in the middle of Cell Block B. At the moment, I'm more cold than afraid. The guards have cranked up the air conditioner, and I stand shivering, my arms crossed tightly against my chest. The space is two stories high, with a drab gray floor, chalky cinder block walls, and round convex mirrors hinged on every corner. The only color comes from thirty dark orange doors that line both floors, each sporting a large white number and two narrow slits for windows. A couple of minutes ago these doors swung open, and inmates poured out from their closet-sized cells. Now they're all around me. One—heavily tattooed, with a bald head, tan skin, and a long, ragged goatee—heads my way. He has something in his hand.

I'm here by choice. A month ago, I phoned Marc Bekoff, the world's foremost authority on animal emotions, to ask about his work on pets. During our conversation, he mentioned that he volunteers at the Boulder County Jail, just a few miles from his Colorado home. He teaches a class on animal behavior as part of Roots & Shoots, a community outreach program founded by his friend, renowned primatologist Jane Goodall. Sometimes, he told me, he chats with the inmates about dogs and cats. My interest was piqued. I asked if I could fly out and sit in on a class. He shot a couple of e-mails to the jail, and I was cleared for takeoff.

I met Bekoff in person earlier this morning. A wiry sixty-six-year-old with reddish-gray hair tied back in a long ponytail, he lives in a cabin in the woods about a ten-minute drive from downtown Boulder. After a short hike around his property, we hopped into his car and drove to the jail. On the way, he told me he started teaching the class eleven years ago. The inmates who take it are "in transition," meaning they're either coming from a maximum-security prison or are about to enter one. "I've had everyone from a virtuoso pianist to a guy who killed his step-parents," he told me. One inmate used to act as Bekoff's bodyguard while he was inside. "I only needed him once," he said cryptically.

After about fifteen minutes we pulled into a large asphalt parking lot surrounded by grass and trees. A small lake was just a few hundred yards away; the Rocky Mountains dominated the horizon. The view was wasted on the adobe-colored structure hunkered in the middle of the lot, a boxy behemoth of tall, windowless walls. We parked the car and headed in.

I had never been inside a jail before. On first impression, it reminded me of a doctor's office. Bekoff and I entered a modest lobby, where a receptionist handed me a clipboard heavy with paperwork. A vending machine buzzed nearby. A handful of people sat in chairs lining the perimeter of the room, seemingly waiting for their appointments. But the doctor's office vibe quickly faded when the receptionist told me to remove everything from my pockets and handed me a badge with a large black *E* on it. (I would later learn it stood for "escorted visitor.") Then, a burly guard everyone referred to as "the Commander" entered the room and led Bekoff and me into the heart of the jail. We walked a maze of narrow hallways, occasionally stopping to stare up at a security camera before a door would open. Finally, we arrived at the command center, a glass room with a couple of guards sitting in swivel chairs before a control panel of knobs and monitors. On the other side was the door to Cell Block B. Bekoff and I walked through it. The Commander closed the door behind us, remaining with the other guards. I'd never felt so vulnerable.

And now the cell doors have swung open, the inmates have streamed out, and one is heading straight for me. "Hey!" he shouts, advancing on me in blue scrubs and bright orange sneakers. "I want to show you something." He thrusts an object in my face.

It's a photo of his cats. "These are my little ones," he beams. "My wife sends me pictures of them instead of the kids." The inmate, whose name I would later learn is Richard, owns a couple of pit bulls as well, plus a turtle and three fish. He begins to tell me about them when another man approaches. This one, named George, is in his mid-sixties with short white hair and a Band-Aid slapped across his left temple. He shows me a picture of two collies standing on a stack of tires. "These are my grand dogs," he says. "The one on the left is the fastest dog west of the Mississippi." More inmates crowd around me. More pictures of pets. I feel like a judge at a proud-parent contest.

"Come on," Bekoff smiles, tugging my arm. "Help me set up." We grab some plastic chairs from the sides of the room and begin to place them in the center of the cell block. The inmates pitch in. Then Bekoff and I take a seat, and everyone else follows suit. Staring out at a motley crew of ages, temperaments, and tattoo patterns, this doesn't feel like any class I've ever been in. But as we start chatting, I find the men surprisingly attentive, gregarious, and well-spoken.

Bekoff asks if any of the guys consider their pets members of the family. He's met with an enthusiastic chorus of yeahs. "Our dogs get Christmas and birthday presents," says George, who I learn used to be a lawyer. "Our cats run our house," hollers Mark, a redhead with light crimson skin. "When one of our animals dies, it's like a death in the family," murmurs another inmate, Darren. "We cry like nobody's business." Many of the men see themselves in their animals. Russell, a muscular fellow with short black hair who has been in and out of prisons his entire life, says his dog was saved from an abusive home, just like he was. "Me, my wife, my German shepherd—we're all rescues. We've all had the same life." Matt, in his mid-forties with spiky white hair, says that in here he feels like a stray no one wants. "We're outcasts." Growing up, he says, his parents beat his pets. That's not an attitude he's inherited, at least when it comes to animals. "I'll punch a guy in the mouth, but not a cat or a dog," he says. "I'll pet my kitten and not think twice about getting into a bar fight."

We talk for an hour. The men tell me stories about their dogs experiencing separation anxiety while they're behind bars, sniffing their old clothes and whimpering; about their cats curling up with them in bed when they get out; about how their pets eat better at home than they do in here. They seem acutely aware that, over the decades, their status in society has stagnated while the status of cats and dogs has skyrocketed.

"Years ago, these guys would have said, 'They're treating me like a dog in here,'" Bekoff tells me later. "They don't say that anymore."

The Commander enters the room, and the men fall silent. Bekoff nods to me. We get up, thank the inmates for their time, and exit the cell block. On the drive back to his cabin, I tell Bekoff I had been surprised by how much the men cared for their pets. Given the low value many of them seemed to place on human life, I hadn't expected them to hold animals in high regard. He says the opposite is true. A lot of these guys come from broken or abusive homes, he notes. "For many, their best friend growing up was a cat or a dog—someone who loved them no matter what." Their pets were the only real family they had.

A Society Transformed

My journey to the Boulder County Jail didn't begin the day I phoned Marc Bekoff. It started a few years earlier in an emergency hospital. My fiancée and I had driven there late one night with a dying patient in our car: Jasper, our five-month-old gray-and-white kitten, who was in the final stages of kidney failure. We had adopted him from a shelter just three months earlier, along with his nearly identical sister, Jezebel. Both of us had grown up with cats, but these were the first we had lived with since leaving home and the first we owned together. We treated the decision to get pets the way some couples might consider having their first child. College wasn't the right time. And when we were living together in graduate school, we moved around so much and had so little money, it didn't make sense then either. So we waited. And then waited some more.

It wasn't until we moved to Baltimore, with me starting a career as a science writer and my fiancée beginning her medical residency, that we felt ready to adopt. Years of anticipation didn't do wonders for our self-control. We walked into a humane society one Saturday morning and picked the first cats we saw. Spotting Jasper and Jezebel (then "Jack" and "Jill") in a cage together—their fuzzy white bellies, their gray striped backs, their tiny heads with oversized ears staring back at us from behind the bars—we lost all sense of patience or reason. "We'll take them," I said to a slightly stunned shelter worker. They were a package deal: one cat for $85; both for $130. It was a steal. Or so we thought.

By the time my fiancée and I raced to the emergency hospital, Jasper was well on his way to costing us $3,000—and we were just getting started. This typically energetic kitten, who leaped between countertops, dove into empty soda cartons, and had even learned to fetch, had lately grown still as a stone. He sat crumpled into himself on our bed, staring into space, barely aware of our presence. We took him to the veterinarian, who drew blood, x-rayed him, and cultured his urine. The diagnosis: acute renal failure. She didn't know what had caused it. Perhaps he had gotten into an ant trap or some of my medication. Perhaps he was just born with a bum pair of kidneys. What she did know was that he might have only a few days to live. The emergency hospital was our last hope.

The location didn't inspire confidence. Situated in a dimly lit strip mall beyond the outer edge of the city, the PET+E.R. sat in a large parking lot next to a clothing warehouse and a big-screen-TV store. I felt like we were about to bargain shop, not save our kitten. But once inside, we may as well have been in a human trauma center. Assistants in light blue scrubs raced in and out of hallways. Doctor's names blared through overhead speakers. People sat nervously in the waiting room. And that's only what I could see. Behind metal double doors, the clinic opened up into a state-of-the-art intensive care unit, with surgical suites, an in-house lab, and a blood bank. On-site specialists were trained in everything from cardiology to neurology. One of the world's best hospitals, Johns Hopkins, was just a few miles away, but this place seemed to be giving it a run for its money.

We took a seat in the waiting room, with Jasper worryingly silent in a carrier at our feet. Desperate. Exhausted. Distraught. We began to have some crazy thoughts. Our veterinarian had mentioned one option we hadn't considered at the time: a $20,000 kidney transplant. We didn't have the money, but we did have something few people do: a feline sibling. As a close blood relative, Jezebel could donate a kidney to save her brother—though we'd be using the word "donate" loosely. The two didn't exactly get along. Given the choice, she'd surely refuse.

Fortunately, it never came to that. Jasper saw an internist that night, then a nephrologist the following day. He spent three days in the ICU, hooked up to a catheter and IV antibiotics while he underwent ultrasounds, urinalyses, and blood-chemistry profiles. Slowly he began to improve. The doctors never figured out why his kidneys failed. And they weren't sure why he got better. He'd have permanent damage, but he was alive—and he was coming home.

Sitting there in the reception area, waiting for the hospital to discharge him, I wondered if we had taken things too far: the crying, the sleepless nights, the damage to our bank accounts—all for a cat we had only known for a few months. But as I looked around the room, I realized we were not alone. A heavyset man sat near the exit, fingering an empty dog collar. An elderly couple stood by the register, the woman cradling an orange tabby as the man dipped into his wallet for a second credit card. A wife sobbed to her husband on the phone. We weren't the only worried parents in the room.

It wasn't a thought I spent much time on that day. But a while later, with Jasper safe at home (and Jezebel still in possession of both her kidneys), I began to think back on that week. A couple of decades ago, we would have been laughed at for doing so much for an animal. I wasn't sure that was still the case. Cats and dogs, once mere pets, had become family. Or so I thought. A journalist by trade and a scientist by training, I didn't want to base such a sweeping conclusion on a highly emotional week at a pet emergency clinic. I needed a larger sample size.

The Washington National Cathedral may be the closest thing America has to a medieval castle. Gleaming white, with limestone towers, giant stained glass windows, and more than a hundred gargoyles springing from its stone walls, the gothic structure commands a forested hillside overlooking Washington, DC. It's the highest point in the city, the sixth-largest church in the world, the site of Ronald Reagan's state funeral and Martin Luther King Jr.'s final sermon. One day a year, however, it belongs to pets.

I drove down on a bright and breezy Sunday afternoon in early October. The cathedral was hosting its annual Blessing of the Animals ceremony, an event that actually encourages congregants to bring their pets to church. I was here to find out if Christianity, the world's most popular religion, had begun to treat cats and dogs like family members. If it had, perhaps my experience in the PET+E.R. wasn't such an anomaly.

I could hear the barking as I drove up. Hundreds of people and animals had gathered on a small brick plaza near the western steps of the church. Fluffy white bichons pulled on short pink leashes. Tiny tan Chihuahuas shivered in their owners' arms. Saint Bernards drooled. Collies yapped. Cats . . . well, the cats mostly stared at the dogs. Cats in carriers. Cats on shoulders. One cat sat between a fish bowl and a birdcage. He stared at the dogs too.

The Blessing of the Animals is a celebration of St. Francis of Assisi, the patron saint of animals and the environment. St. Francis, it turns out, was an early tree hugger. The thirteenth-century Italian friar preached to the birds and called the moon his sister and the wind and air his brothers. He let a donkey have his hovel; he convinced locals to feed a ferocious wolf. For more than seven hundred years, churches around the world have honored his legacy by blessing congregants' animals. Until recently, these creatures were typically farm animals, brought to church by owners who prayed God's grace would shepherd their pigs, cows, and goats through the winter, allowing them to sire plenty of progeny in the spring. Human survival depended on it. Now we bring our pets.

The National Cathedral has held a Blessing of the Animals service since 1999. Turnout grows every year, and in the last decade, hundreds of churches (and some synagogues) have added the ceremony. The largest takes place at New York City's Cathedral of Saint John the Divine. Recent services there have hosted as many as 1,500 animals and 2,000 humans, most of whom wait in line for hours for a spot inside. During the proceedings, the church opens the central doors of its sanctuary, an event that typically happens only two other times during the year: at Christmas and Easter.

Back at the National Cathedral, I had begun to wander through the crowd. One animal in particular caught my eye: a Chesapeake Bay retriever with a faded chestnut coat and tired yellow eyes. A rickshaw-like contraption was harnessed to the lower half of her body; black straps secured her torso to an aluminum frame, and wheels replaced her back legs, which hung slightly off the ground. As I approached the dog's owners, the massive cast-bronze doors behind the church steps creaked open, wide as ten men and twice as tall. Out processed a choir in long purple robes, then a handful of clergy in white robes. I almost didn't notice that one of them was cradling a cat.

The service began. "Bless the Lord, all you creatures," boomed the officiant, Reverend Gwendolyn Tobias, a middle-aged woman with short, sandy hair. "Let us praise and exalt our Creator forever," the audience chimed back. The reverend read a passage from the Book of Job ("Ask the animals, and they will teach you"), the choir sang "All Things Bright and Beautiful," and the reverend continued her dialogue with the crowd, giving thanks for the pets in attendance and calling on the cats and dogs to live lives of purpose and serve the Lord.

Aside from the regular references to animals, I assume a lot of services go like this. But I doubt they culminate in the blessing of the church cat. It turns out the pet I had seen in the arms of the clergy member was the National Cathedral's new resident feline, an eighteen-month-old black tortoiseshell named Carmina, after the *Carmina Burana* cantata. Adopted from a local humane society, she has her run of the building. Though the benediction of pets is a relatively new phenomenon, Carmina's role goes back centuries. Records from England's famed Exeter Cathedral indicate that from 1305 to 1467, the parish paid its cat a penny a week to catch rodents; there is still a cat hole in the door of the north transept wall. Today, church cats don't get paid. They apparently get blessed—though I suspect Carmina would have traded eternal salvation for a warm spot in the sun.

The cat cringed as another reverend, the cherub-faced Samuel Lloyd III, dipped a small branch from a boxwood bush into a silver bowl of holy water and shook it over her head. "May God bless you and keep you as you grow into all the creature you were made to be," he said. A chorus of dogs barked in the audience. The reverend laughed. "There are a lot of jealous creatures out there, great and small."

Carmina's was just the first of many blessings. As the choir sang a closing hymn, the clergy fanned out into the crowd, sprinkling holy water on wagging pups and flinching felines. I caught Reverend Tobias as she finished spritzing an Old English sheepdog whose head came up to her waist. "I just blessed a cocker spaniel with hay fever," she told me. "I didn't know dogs got hay fever." I asked her if the ceremony tacitly acknowledged that cats and dogs had become family members. She said there were certainly differences between the modern services and the ones geared toward farm animals. For one thing, the relationship between people and their pets is one of love, not survival. For another, many congregants seem to believe that their dogs and cats have souls. "Last year, several people asked us to pray for animals that had died," she noted. She added that she would like to take the ceremony inside, so that pets could sit in pews with their owners. "We had a parish at home that did that, and they were all very well behaved."

I thanked the reverend for her time and continued through the crowd. There I saw the handicapped retriever I had spotted earlier. The older couple who owned her told me that the dog, Dasher, had suffered an embolism earlier that year and was paralyzed from the waist down. This was the eleven-year-old's fourth Blessing of the Animals and possibly her last. "We're asking for God's blessing for her continued life," said the husband, a retired naval officer. "However long that may be."

Next I ran into Hunter and Katie, law and journalism students, respectively, who had just moved to DC from Arkansas. "Darby brought us to church today," said Katie, referring to their two-and-a-half-year-old wheaten terrier, a medium-size, well-postured canine with the shaggy white sideburns of a Civil War general. She said she and her husband were Catholic, and the ceremony was a way to welcome the dog as a spiritual member of their household. "We don't have kids, so she's our baby." Hunter volunteered that the holy water was for washing away sin. "I don't think we're doing that with Darby," he laughed, "though she did eat my textbook." They had thought about bringing their cat as well— "She's just as important," Katie said—but the logistics were too hard.

The crowd was beginning to disperse. As I made my way out, I stopped for one last chat on the church steps. There, dragging his floppy ears against the pavement as he waddled behind his owners, was a ten-year-old basset hound named Flash. "He's my first dog," boasted Rick, a husky federal employee in his early forties. He said he'd grown up without pets; yet he and the hound had become inseparable. Owning Flash, he said, helped him and his wife, Jenny, feel like part of their community for the first time. "When you have kids or dogs, you tend to meet people." The couple has fully embraced canine culture. They fund-raise for a local basset hound rescue, and last year they marched in a St. Patrick's Day parade with sixty other dogs and their owners. "We're even thinking about getting him a Sherlock Holmes costume for Halloween," Rick said. "We view him as a member of the family," he smiled. "I guess we're sick that way."

As I drove home from the National Cathedral, I wondered how sick Rick and Jenny really were. Certainly no sicker than those of us at the PET+E.R., who had gone through so much for our dogs and cats, or the hundreds of other folks who had gathered on the cathedral steps, bringing their pets to church as they might their children. If there's something wrong with Rick and Jenny, there's something wrong with all of us.

Pets have become an integral part of our lives. Cats and dogs are everywhere. Nearly 150 million of them live with us in the United States, one for every two people. About 37 percent of homes have a dog; 30 percent have a cat. More than half of all dwellings contain either animal, five times more than have birds, horses, and fish combined. Dog and cat ownership has quadrupled since the mid-1960s, double the growth rate of the human population. More homes have cats and dogs than have kids.

As these animals have filled our homes, we've grown closer to them than ever before. Eighty-three percent of owners refer to themselves as their pet's "mom" or "dad," up from 55 percent just twenty years ago. More than 90 percent consider their dog or cat a family member. Seventy percent celebrate their pet's birthday. Half would be "very likely" to risk their life to save their pet, and another third would be "somewhat likely" to do so. And perhaps my favorite stat: if trapped on a desert island, half of all owners would rather live out their days with a cat or dog than with a human companion.

All of this talk isn't cheap. We shelled out a staggering $55 billion on our companion animals in 2013, two and half times what we spent in 2000. From 2007 to 2012 alone—a period that marks the Great Recession—pet spending jumped 28 percent. We may have tightened our belts in other areas, but we kept pulling the credit card out for our dogs and cats. In those five years, PetSmart's shares rose more than 150 percent, outperforming Walmart, Target, and Macy's. The pet industry is now the seventh-largest retail industry in the United States. We spend more on our animals than the entire economic outputs of over half the world's countries.

As we spend, society changes. It's not just the church services and the pet emergency clinics. Walk the streets of any major city, and you'll see a world transformed by cats and dogs. That's certainly the case in Baltimore. After my visit to the National Cathedral, I decided to conduct one final experiment: I wanted to see how many signs of our modern pet republic I could spot on a one-mile stroll from my house to downtown.

It didn't take long for me to hit my first stop, and it was a doozy. Just a few blocks from my neighborhood, I encountered that paragon of modern pet culture, the pet-supply superstore. This one, called PetValu, is significantly smaller than its big-box counterparts, but it's still crammed with hundreds of products. Multicolored bags of food line the shelves; toys and treats hang from hooks, curtaining entire walls; pet beds are piled high on the floor, stacked smallest to largest to create cushiony brown pyramids. There's a dog wash station with rubber smocks and three deep sinks, a cat adoption area housing felines from a local shelter in black wire cages, and a large flat-screen TV on the far wall, looping an infomercial extolling the virtues of a grain-free diet. It's like a mall, grocery store, and salon rolled into one.

The toy section alone is staggering. Gone are the days of pale rubber dog bones. There are stuffed squirrels and dragons, soft rubber Frisbees, and bright red chew cones. Plastic puzzles hide treats to boost your dog's IQ. The K9 Kannon Ball Launcher fires tennis balls into the air so you don't have to. For felines there are furry mice that feel and sound like the real thing, cigars filled with catnip, and a plastic obelisk that shoots random patterns of laser light onto the floor, guaranteed to keep your kitty busy for . . . well, at least a few minutes.

Half the store is dedicated to a seemingly infinite selection of pet food. With images of bucolic farms and brand names like Natural Balance, Harvest Moon, and Earthborn, shoppers could be forgiven for thinking they just wandered into a high-end supermarket. It isn't just the packaging; it's the ingredients: venison, rabbit, duck, and bison. And the way they're prepared: soupy, crunchy, chunky, and pâté. There's even a tube of lamb and brown rice you cut like salami. The choices are bound to overwhelm even the most experienced owner. What should I feed my pet tonight? Free-range chicken or grass-fed beef? Gluten-free or hormone-free? Organic or holistic? It's a carnivore's dilemma.

For dessert, a nearby glass case displays the latest in canine confections. Lining the shelves are cookies, cakes, and bonbons made of carob and peanut butter and topped with pastel yogurt frostings. Next to that is the supplement section, with salves for aches and pains and herbs for constipation and travel anxiety. Then there is the doggy mouthwash and waterless cat shampoo, the hoodies and sunglasses, the booster seats and life vests. There are also wee-wee pads and environmentally friendly cat litter made from naturally processed wheat (which, I'm embarrassed to say, Jasper ate when he was a kitten. Now we buy the cheap stuff). It's no wonder PetSmart's stock performance is putting Walmart's to shame.

After the pet store, I walked a bit farther south, entering the Mount Vernon neighborhood, where grand nineteenth-century brownstones mingle with museums and pricey restaurants. Here, I discovered a portrait studio that paints pets and a plaza plastered with fliers advertising a monthly "Yappy Hour," where owners can bring their dogs to meet and greet other local pooches while their humans enjoy free beer and live music. Someone seemed early to the party: parked on the street was a Honda Element, decked out with a dog-friendly package that included paw-print seat covers and a back end converted into a nylon-webbed kennel, complete with pet bed, spill-resistant water bowl, and poop bag dispenser.

As I continued to walk, the streets widened, and the buildings rose. I had reached downtown. There were hotels everywhere, but two caught my eye: one for humans and one for pets—though you might be hard-pressed to tell the difference. Charm City Dogs offers twenty-four-hour doggy day care that features orthopedic beds, agility classes, and food specially designed by a local chef. The Hotel Monaco, with its marble staircases, crystal chandeliers, and Tiffany stained glass windows, was designed for people, but today it also welcomes canine and feline guests. Upon check-in, owners receive a gift bag that includes treats, a map of doggy jogging spots, and a copy of *The Pet Times*, which lists nearby pet-friendly restaurants and canine day spas. A pet concierge can arrange everything from dog walking to kitty day care. Want your Saint Bernard to be best man at your wedding? He can take care of that too.

At this point it's probably worth mentioning that Baltimore doesn't qualify as one of the country's most pet-friendly cities, at least according to countless Internet rankings. That honor goes to places like Austin, Texas, which boasts 180 veterinarians and thirty-five pet photographers, and Portland, Oregon, home to more than a dozen pet massage therapists and thirty-three dog parks, the most per capita in the nation. Other cities offer pet taxis and dog yoga. There are even a few where you can be buried with your pet, a practice that was once illegal but which has gained acceptance in recent years. Humans can be laid to rest in some pet cemeteries and pets in some human cemeteries. If the trend continues, the distinction may disappear. They'll all just be family plots.

There was one more stop on my walk worth mentioning: Kirby insurance. Located in a gray, four-story building downtown, the company writes the traditional policies—home, car, and life—but it also offers pet insurance. In these days of CAT scans for dogs and Prozac for cats—not to mention pet acupuncture, cancer vaccines, high-tech radiation, heart surgery, eye surgery, hip replacements, knee replacements, gene therapy, and stem cell therapy—pet insurance is not the extravagance it used to be. Indeed, it's the third-most-requested employee benefit after health and dental insurance and offered by a third of Fortune 500 companies. I only wish we had known about it when we adopted Jasper. His stint at the emergency hospital put such a crimp in our savings that for the next two years, my fiancée and I didn't exchange presents; we just passed Jasper back and forth. Still, it's the best money we've ever spent.

Thinking back on that week at the PET+E.R., I didn't feel so bad for everything we had done for Jasper. The love, the pain, the financial sacrifice—they didn't make us eccentric pet owners. They made us intimately part of society. Cats and dogs really are our family. Yet I was still left with one lingering mystery: How had these animals become our family in the first place? I thought I had reached the end of my journey, but I was only at the beginning. I would spend the next two years traveling the country in search of answers to this seemingly simple question. Along the way, I'd meet some brilliant people, face some ferocious animals, and, yes, even end up in the Boulder County Jail.

But first things first. Let's start where it all begins.

TWO

Wolves and Wildcats

Seventy miles northwest of Indianapolis, at the end of a narrow road that crosses a one-lane bridge over the Wabash River, lies the faded town of Battle Ground, Indiana, a square-mile patch of grass and asphalt bisected by a railroad track and dotted with a few modest houses, a tavern, and an antiques shop. Battle Ground is home to two main attractions: Tippecanoe Battlefield, where US soldiers under William Henry Harrison dealt a crushing blow to Native American forces in the early 1800s, and Wolf Park, a seventy-five-acre oasis of forest and lake dedicated to studying the gray wolf. I had come for the wolves.

Of the millions of creatures on earth, only cats and dogs have become our true family members. They sleep in our beds; they play with our children; they love and are loved. Yet these were once wild animals, too terrified to approach, too ferocious to touch. Something remarkable must have happened to transform them into the pets we know today. I hoped that a visit to Wolf Park would shed some light on this mystery. There are no cat ancestors here—solving the riddle of where our feline pals came from would have to wait a while—but the reserve is home to gray wolves, widely accepted as the predecessor of today's mutts. So I arrived on a brisk, clear morning in late September to meet the beginnings of the dog.

When I enter the park, I'm directed to a safety-training seminar. That's my first clue that I'm not dealing with a domesticated animal. The second is the chain-link fence topped with razor wire that separates the wolves from everyone else. As I walk along a dirt path that leads from the visitor's center to the beige bunkhouse where the safety briefing will be held, I catch my first glimpse of a wolf. There, on the other side of the fence, stands a small black female, her eyes glowing yellow, her ears on alert. She's staring at me, and not in a way that makes me feel comfortable. Despite what I've heard about the similarities between wolves and dogs, there's nothing doglike about this animal. She's cold, she's tense, and she clearly doesn't want me here. Nevertheless, we will soon meet face-to-face.

The safety lecture is led by John Davis, a lean sixty-four-year-old with white stubble on his face and a baseball cap on his head. Davis is in charge of children's programs at the park, and he breezes through much of his talk with the energy and humor of someone doing it for the first time. But when it comes to how to interact with the wolves, he turns dead serious. The list of prohibitions seems endless. Don't stare at the wolves: they'll take it as a sign of aggression. Don't pat them on the head or rub their belly. Don't panic if they "muzzle" you—that is, grab your arm or face in their mouths; though they could easily crush you, they're probably just asserting dominance. Don't make any sudden movements, especially with your arms. Kneel on the ground so you don't look threatening, but don't kneel on both knees or the wolves will knock you over. And if you drop something, don't reach down to grab it; the wolves will beat you to it, and their teeth are much bigger than yours. Oh, and don't forget to sign the legal release, which includes this frightening bit of prose: "I understand that I am at some risk of being injured and that the injury may not be trivial."

"OK!" says Davis, smiling again. "Are you ready to meet the wolves?"

I enter the wolf enclosure with two other guests and six staff members, including Davis. That's a good ratio, he tells me. "When you make mistakes, they're not as forgiving as dogs," he says. "All of us have pulled wolves off each other." I instinctively shove both of my hands—the only bits of exposed skin—into my pockets. We aren't able to enter the wolf enclosure directly. First, we all huddle into a narrow gated antechamber, referred to as "the airlock," and the staff bars the door behind us. Then we open a second gate into the enclosure itself. It's a peaceful setting, with a small lake, yellow flowers, and tall grass. The wolves aren't around, so we sit on a log to make ourselves look small and vulnerable. The strategy appears to work: soon the black wolf I saw earlier emerges from behind some trees and cautiously makes her way over.

Her name is Dharma. She's about a year and a half old and seventy pounds—scrawnier than the other wolves I'd meet, but alert and agile. She has a reputation for pushing the social envelope. Wolf packs organize themselves into rigid hierarchies, with alphas at the top, betas below them, and so on. Dharma is technically near the bottom of the totem pole, but she doesn't act that way. The staff tells me that when a dominant wolf approaches her, she rolls over on her back and licks and paws the other wolf's face like she's supposed to, but she's overly zealous about it, licking and pawing so much that the other wolf gets irritated and backs off. She has elevated her social standing in the pack simply by being annoying.

Dharma is more reserved with us, and she seems to have warmed slightly since our first encounter. She approaches me cautiously and stands on my feet, her paws eclipsing my sneakers. Then, slowly, she brings her muzzle up to my face, her mouth less than an inch from mine. I freeze. She hovers there near my lips, her mouth slightly open, her hot breath sucking in. If Dharma were a dog, I would be half covered in slobber by now. But she isn't loving me; she's probing me. I gingerly reach out to pet her, but she jerks away and trots off.

Then I notice another wolf wandering over. This one, named Wotan, is much larger, with a sandy brown coat, noble golden eyes, and markings like a Siberian husky's. He's a direct descendent of the first two wolves that came to the park in 1972, and he knows it. Wotan is confident and intense, and when he circles us, I feel like a diver in a shark cage. He finally approaches and lets me touch him. I pass my hand along the coarse fur of his body. He doesn't lean into my touch like a dog would, and he doesn't look at me; instead, he stares off toward the lake. This isn't two animals forming a bond; it's one barely tolerating the attention of another.

And yet, the remarkable thing is that these wolves *are* much friendlier than their wild counterparts. They have been raised by people since they were two weeks old: they've been bottle fed, they've been played with, and they've spent more than 2,000 hours closely interacting with their caretakers. All of this, and Davis doesn't let his guard down for a second. When I walk over to chat, he keeps one eye on me and one on the wolves. "I've got five dogs at home, and we're one big family," he says. "I've been here for thirteen years, and I'm still an outsider."

I start to ask Davis a question, but he stops me. Off in the distance, Wotan has begun rapidly pacing back and forth, a sign of stress. Davis rounds us up and hustles us back through the airlock. And once again, I'm looking at a wolf through a chain-link fence, marveling at the vast gulf between it and a dog. How on earth did these wild animals end up sleeping in our beds?

Man's Oldest Friend

In 1868, a young geologist named Edouard Dupont dug up what he thought was a fairly worthless object in a cave in southern Belgium: the skull of a wolf in a lair littered with thousands of other bones. Dutifully, he brought the specimen back to his museum, where he promptly forgot about it. Lost among the archives, it would be nearly a century and a half before one scientist realized the importance of the find. The skull, she believed, didn't belong to a wolf at all—a proposition that would upend major assumptions about dog domestication.

Dupont was twenty-seven years old at the time, yet he had already racked up quite the resume. Inspired by the recent publication of Charles Darwin's theory of evolution, this handsome and headstrong son of an amateur archaeologist was determined to make his newly independent country a major player in the budding field of paleoarchaeology. At age twenty-four, he had petitioned the minister of the interior to allow him to explore Belgium's caves. Within three years, he had excavated nearly thirty sites, uncovered countless human bones and artifacts (including one of the first Neanderthal skulls in Europe), and thrown his name into the hat to become the next director of the Royal Museum of Natural History in Brussels.

But the 1868 discovery may be Dupont's lasting legacy. Here, in a rural town on the banks of a small river, he entered the Goyet Cave, a vast labyrinth of hallways and chambers tunneled into a limestone cliff. Neanderthals had lived here, then modern humans, and at various points, cave bears and hyenas. All had left bones behind. The deeper Dupont ventured into the cavern, the more he found: lion and horse bones, bones chopped by human hands and stained with ochre, ivory beads, a shell necklace, a harpoon. Distant echoes of tens of thousands of years of occupation. In a small alcove off one of the rooms, Dupont found yet more bones: beneath the ground were the remains of mammoths, lynx, and deer—and among them, the skull of a wolf.

Dupont seems not to have thought much of the skull; it barely registers in his notes. He was far more excited about a caribou bone he found. Some ancient human had etched a fish into the side and drilled a hole at one end. The mysterious object, which Dupont referred to as a *baton de commandement*, was the only one of its kind discovered in Belgium. Archaeologists would later speculate that Ice Age people had used it either to straighten arrows or hurl spears. Dupont himself had little time to analyze his finds. When he returned to the natural history museum in Brussels, he learned he had been named director. Soon, bureaucratic duties took over his life. And the artifacts and bones he'd uncovered, including the wolf skull, began collecting dust in the archives.

Then, in late 2001, a paleontologist named Mietje Germonpré began doing some excavating of her own. She had embarked on a project comparing the features of Ice Age carnivores and had been burrowing into the archives of Dupont's former museum, now the Royal Belgian Institute of Natural Sciences. After examining a few skulls belonging to bears and foxes, she set her eyes on the wolf cranium from the Goyet Cave. "I knew right away that this wasn't a wolf," she told me over the phone. Although the skull bared large, wolflike teeth, it was slender and sported a short, wide snout. This wasn't like any wolf Germonpré had ever seen. She was, she believed, staring at the head of a dog.

Like Dupont before her, Germonpré didn't think the skull was especially significant. Other ancient dog skulls had been found. The earliest specimens at that point were three craniums found in Germany dating to about 15,000 years ago. Germonpré doubted the Goyet find would be much older. But when she dated it, she had a hard time accepting her results; the skull was nearly 32,000 years old. That flew in the face of established thinking about dog domestication. Researchers had long believed that dogs first appeared somewhere between 12,000 and 16,000 years ago. The German remains supported this idea, as did a host of other archaeological evidence. Now Germonpré was saying that dogs had entered the picture as many as 20,000 years before this. "I have to admit, I was a bit disappointed when I found out the date," she said. "I thought no one would believe me."

She was nearly right. Germonpré's analysis of the Goyet skull, published in 2009, has generated considerable controversy in the field. While some researchers accept that the specimen represents the earliest evidence of dog domestication, others contend that the skull merely belonged to a wolf that evolved a short face to better scavenge carcasses left behind by human hunters. Still others say the creature was an evolutionary dead end, an early dog that did not give rise to today's canines.

Even if Germonpré is correct, the Goyet creature didn't look like any of today's dog breeds. It was a big, bulky animal with powerful jaws and a ferocious bite. If anything, it would have resembled a Siberian husky on steroids—not quite dog, but not quite wolf either. Nor would it have been a pet. The humans of this era, known as the Aurignacians, were the first modern people to inhabit Europe. Only Neanderthals had come before them. Though the Aurignacians gave us some of our earliest art—including a short, plump female figurine carved from a wooly mammoth tusk and cave paintings in southwestern France—they didn't stay put for long. Small groups of twenty or so individuals were on the move for most of the year, following the seasonal migrations of horse, reindeer, and other animals over vast grassy plains. The climate would have been dry, with short summers and long, cold winters. Any doglike creature adopted by such a society would have been put to work. "Given their size and sturdiness, people probably strapped firewood, tent poles, and even food to them," Germonpré told me. These animals would have functioned much like a donkey or mule today. As a reward, they probably got to eat a bit of whatever the people killed. And slowly, a closer relationship may have started to form.

But how did this relationship begin? That is, how was anyone able to survive strapping firewood to a husky on steroids?

Perhaps not surprisingly, Charles Darwin was one of the first scientists to ponder the origin of dogs. His 1868 book *The Variation of Animals and Plants Under Domestication*, published a decade after his tome on evolution, *On the Origin of Species*, devotes nearly its entire first chapter to the question (the rest of the chapter is dedicated to cats). Darwin wondered, for example, if dogs evolved from a single species or from several. The latter, he thought, could explain the great diversity of dog breeds. The hulky gray wolf may have given rise to large dogs like the mastiff, the skinny Ethiopian wolf to the greyhound, and so on. He even suspected that some breeds were the products of unusual hookups, like a wolf mating with a jackal. Ultimately, even the father of evolution threw up his hands on the question of where dogs came from. "We shall probably never be able to ascertain their origin with certainty," he wrote.

But scientists did get to the truth eventually. As twentieth-century researchers began to closely examine the skeletons of various species on the canine family tree, they became more and more convinced that the many dog breeds had a single ancestor: the gray wolf. Recent genetic studies have backed this up. Dogs share a whopping 99.9 percent of their DNA with the gray wolf, versus only about 99.3 percent with the coyote, their next closest relative. As a result, dogs are no longer classified according to their original scientific name, *Canis familiaris* (literally, "friendly dog"); today they are known as *Canis lupus familiaris*, a designation that recognizes them as a subspecies of the gray wolf, *Canis lupus*.

And doing Darwin one better, researchers have now traced the dog lineage back 60 million years to weasel-like creatures known as miacids. These granddaddies of all carnivores gave rise to both dogs and cats, though the dog lineage eventually split off, along with seals, bears, and raccoons, while cats branched with hyenas and mongooses. Genetic studies also suggest that dogs may have been domesticated more than once: in Europe, the Middle East, and East Asia.

Still, none of this tells us *how* dogs became dogs.

Back at Wolf Park, I asked Clive Wynne about this. Wynne, an expert on dog and wolf behavior at Arizona State University in Tempe, has been coming here for five years to figure out, among other things, how the wolf became the dog. He's not the first person I'd have thought would be interested in such a question. He's spent much of his career being, by his own admission, "the wettest of wet blankets," criticizing any study purporting to show a hint of animal emotion or self-recognition. Animals may very well experience joy, sorrow, and jealousy, Wynne says, but science hasn't proven it. He's written a book called *Do Animals Think?*, which seems to come down on the negative side, and he's railed against anthropomorphism, the tendency to ascribe human attributes to animals, as "folk psychology" and "dirty bathwater." I expected an ogre.

But Wynne is a charming fellow—a short, fifty-year-old Englishman with an easygoing disposition and dry sense of humor. His black, rectangular glasses contrast with a soft face, and he covers his balding head with an olive green cap that matches a messenger bag slung across his left shoulder. He seems genuinely perplexed that anyone would view him as a curmudgeon. "I don't really like being so negative all the time," he smiles.

When I chat with Wynne, he's in the middle of supervising an unusual experiment. A few years ago, he flew through Russia's Sheremetyevo Airport and noticed that the security guards were using dog-jackal hybrids to sniff for bombs. The thinking was that dogs' wild relatives had superior noses, but no one had ever published scientific research to prove this. So earlier in the day, Wynne had driven out to a nearby hardware store and grabbed a couple of empty paint cans. While I watch, two of his graduate students fill the cans with pine shavings and cotton balls scented with either anise or almond extract. Then, because it's too dangerous for them to work directly with the wolves, the students give the cans to a couple of staff members, who enter a small-gated enclosure with a wolf named Renki.

Renki is a large, black-and-white male named after Irenaus "Renki" Eibl-Eibesfeldt, a German scientist renowned for his study of animal behavior. Despite his namesake, this Renki displays little interest in the scientific process. He only has to show that he can distinguish between the smells in the two cans, but the staffers spend most of their time just trying to get his attention. As I chat with Wynne, calls of "Renki, Renki . . . Come on, Renki!" fill the background.

When I ask Wynne about how dogs became domesticated, he tells me that one early hypothesis, still espoused by a few scientists, is that ancient humans simply scooped up some wolf pups from a den and brought them back to their campsite. Raised among people, these animals would have grown up tame and quickly proven themselves useful hunters and guardians. If you've seen a picture of baby wolves, the idea doesn't seem so far-fetched. Tiny, fluffy balls of fur with big eyes and oversized ears, how could you not want to pick one up and take it home? That's certainly what happened to me and my fiancée when we impulsively adopted Jasper and Jezebel.

Anthropologists call this our "cute response." The theory is that, to survive in a world with scarce resources, our ancestors had to take care of each other's babies. This could only happen if we evolved to think that *all* babies were cute, not just our own. Big eyes, round foreheads, and snub noses became adorable—even when, by a sort of evolutionary accident, they didn't belong to human beings. (That may be one reason cats and dogs far outnumber snakes and fish as pets, at least in the United States. Even Mickey Mouse has co-opted the cute response; as famed evolutionary biologist Stephen Jay Gould noted in a 1980 essay, the iconic Disney character's face has become less rodent-like and more childlike over the years.)

There's just one problem with the wolf-nabbing hypothesis: it doesn't work. Dharma and Wotan—two decidedly undomesticated animals raised in the company of humans—seem to be evidence of that. In 2001, researchers in Budapest refuted the idea scientifically. They took a handful of week-old wolf and dog pups and gave them to human caretakers. Both animals were treated exactly the same. The caretakers spent twenty-four hours a day with them, bottle-feeding them, sleeping with them, and carrying them around in a pouch. Just like the dogs, the wolves were leash-trained and taught commands like "sit" and "stay." Their caretakers even brought them to Christmas parties.

At first, the wolves behaved just like domesticated dogs. They came running when their caretakers called their names. They obeyed commands. And they allowed themselves to be muzzled. But as the animals grew older, things began to change. When someone they didn't know tried to play with them, they growled and bared their teeth. Some began to bite. And unlike the dogs, the wolves didn't seem attuned to human gestures. When a researcher pointed at a bowl with food in it, the dogs came running. But the wolves just sat there; they didn't even make eye contact.

Most importantly, despite the incredible amount of work the caretakers had put into training their wolves, the offspring of these animals would have been just as feral as wolves born in the wild. The same goes for the animals at Wolf Park: it took thousands of hours of close human interaction for Dharma to even approach me; without the same socialization, her offspring would bolt at first sight. That's the difference between a tame animal and a domesticated one: almost any animal can be tamed with enough human contact, but only a domesticated one remains tame generation after generation. A dog that has never encountered a human still acts very much like a dog; a wolf born in someone's bedroom is still a wild animal.

Clearly then, turning a wolf into a dog wasn't as simple as grabbing a few pups from a den and hoping for the best. Early humans may have started out with something tame, but they'd soon have a ferocious beast on their hands. And indeed, after a few months the Budapest wolves became so unmanageable that their caretakers had to release them to a wolf sanctuary.

The pup-abduction theory has another serious flaw. It assumes that early humans had some sort of conception that one animal could be changed into another. In their 2001 book *Dogs*, Raymond and Lorna Coppinger call this the "Pinocchio Hypothesis," the idea being that early humans, like Geppetto sculpting himself a wooden son in his workshop, saw a wolf and wished it turned into a dog. The problem, the Coppingers note, is that these people had no conception of what a dog was, let alone that a wolf could be turned into one. Humans had never domesticated an animal before wolves came along.

Wynne is also skeptical. "For the [pup-abduction] argument to work, you have to imagine trying to share your dinner with a wolf. And that would show you a whole different side of its personality. Meanwhile, what's the humans' motivation? Wolves are big, bad, nasty, dangerous animals. The Big Bad Wolf story has an element of exaggeration to it, but if you kept wolves as pets, they would eat your children." And, he grins, "from a biological point of view, that's a really bad thing." Plus, he says, "these people couldn't have possibly known that domestication was a possibility. So there was no reason for them to put up with these wild animals for so long. They weren't thinking, 'You know, in a century or two, we'll create this really handy animal, the dog.'"

So what really took place? Wynne, the Coppingers, and others have argued for a more passive mode of domestication. People didn't turn the wolf into a dog—the transformation just sort of happened by itself. The idea, known as self-domestication, is based on the fact that ancient humans weren't the most sanitary people. Their campsites and early settlements would have resembled garbage dumps, littered with bones, carcasses, and half-eaten fruit. For a hungry wolf, it was a virtual buffet. Most of these animals would have been too timid to approach the dump, however, especially while people were around. And if they waited for the people to move on, the food would be rotten. But a few wolves did approach. Those least fearful of humans emerged from the shadows to grab a quick bite. And then another bite. And then another.

No longer forced to eke out a living in the wild, these braver wolves would have survived longer and produced more offspring than their skittish counterparts. Some of these offspring would have ventured closer and closer to the camp, eating more food, surviving longer, and giving birth to even more pups. Over the course of hundreds or even thousands of years, the amount of space these wolves put between themselves and humans—what the Coppingers call their "flight distance"—would have continued to shrink, until one day a wolf was eating out of a person's hand.

Wynne explains why the theory took so long to take hold. "Some people have a hard time coping with the idea that domestication, which some people have said is the single most important thing humans ever did, was just a natural process," he said. "It dethrones us as the creators. But the truth of the matter is, we're probably descended from dumpster divers ourselves."

Dogs aren't just friendly wolves, however. They come in numerous shapes, sizes, and colors; they bark; many have floppy ears and curled tails—all features wolves lack. Could such dramatic changes have happened simply because some wolves became less fearful of humans? An extraordinary experiment in Siberia showed that it could.

In 1959, a sturdy and serious Russian named Dmitri Belyaev began breeding foxes in Novosibirsk, Siberia's largest city. He wasn't a farmer or a fur trader. And he wasn't there by choice. Belyaev had studied to become a geneticist, and by the mid-1940s he was head of the somewhat redundantly named Department of Fur Animal Breeding at the Central Research Laboratory of Fur Breeding in Moscow. He had begun investigating the genetics of silver foxes, but the Soviet government cut his research short. Joseph Stalin's regime denounced genetics as a "bourgeois pseudoscience" and prosecuted anyone who practiced it. Belyaev's brother, also a prominent geneticist, was arrested by the secret police and executed.

Belyaev himself suffered a less severe fate. He lost his job at the Moscow institute and fled to Novosibirsk. There, he continued his experiments on foxes as the head of the Department of Animal Genetics at the Institute of Cytology and Genetics, the last bastion of genetic research in the Soviet Union. And that's where he came up with a revolutionary idea. He proposed that, simply by selecting for friendly behavior—not features like size or appearance—humans had domesticated a whole host of animals. To prove his point, Belyaev and colleagues would embark on a grand experiment: they would domesticate a wild animal from scratch.

Belyaev chose a creature he was familiar with: the silver fox. His team kept the animals outside, in long rows of barren, wire cages; and, unlike with the Budapest wolves, the researchers made no attempt to tame them. Instead, they simply stuck their hands into the enclosures. Most of the foxes cowered in the corner, and many tried to bite. But a few allowed themselves to be touched. These foxes got to keep breeding. And so it went, generation after generation, with only the friendliest foxes selected each time. After a mere nine years, something extraordinary happened. The tamest foxes stopped looking like foxes. Their silver-gray fur turned white and splotchy, sometimes resembling the "star" pattern seen on the faces of border collies and other dogs. Their rigid ears became floppy. Their bushy tails curled upward. Some even began to bark.

The foxes didn't just look like dogs. They began to act like dogs too. Unlike their predecessors, which flinched when humans came near, these animals wanted to be held. They wagged their tales when people, even strangers, approached their cages; they answered to nicknames the scientists gave them; and when a hand reached toward them, they didn't bite it—they licked it. Today, more than five decades after the "Farm-Fox Experiment" began, the tamest foxes are as tame as the tamest dogs. In behavior and temperament, they're similar to a golden retriever. Indeed, some of the animals are now sold as pets around the world.

What was behind such a dramatic change? When Belyaev's team looked under the hood, one of the biggest differences it found between the domesticated and the wild foxes was that the friendly foxes had far lower levels of cortisol coursing through their veins. In humans, this hormone spikes whenever we get stressed, whether from nerves related to public speaking, anxiety about a test, or fear of strangers. Like the gray wolf millennia ago, the Russian foxes had undergone a radical transformation, all because they had stopped being afraid. Belyaev had pulled on a single thread, and the entire sweater had unraveled. Of course, in the wild, without a human hand to guide the process, wolf domestication took a lot more time. But once it happened, human society would never be the same.

Dogs had an enormous impact on people right from the start. They made us more efficient, they made us safer, and they made us better hunters. Animals like the Goyet dog may have helped early people haul supplies over vast distances. Other canines, now having evolved the ability to bark, would have proven themselves useful sentries, alerting people when strangers or other animals approached a cave or campsite— and tearing them to pieces if necessary. Dogs also would have been valuable hunting companions: the first breeds may have been a mastiff-like animal that could bring large prey, like bears, to bay at close range, and a greyhound-like canine that could course for smaller creatures, like rabbits and mountain goats. Indeed, dogs may have proven such a valuable tool that people who kept them outcompeted their rivals for scarce resources. Some scientists even believe that dogs may have led to the downfall of Neanderthals, making our ancestors so successful, the thinking goes, that they left few resources behind for our closest human relatives. Just as wolves had gained an advantage by embracing people, people gained an advantage by embracing the dog.

Still, it took some time for this alliance to develop into a true friendship. And there were plenty of speed bumps along the way. A 14,000-year-old skull found near a Russian river—one of the earliest candidates for dog domestication before the Goyet find came to light— may have been a hunter and guardian, but it was also dinner. A large hole in the left side of its skull indicates that humans removed, and ate, its brain.

As early people began to give up their hunter-gatherer ways and settle down, however, their relationship with dogs changed. The most striking evidence for this comes from a find in northern Israel. In 1977, archaeologists were excavating an ancient village known as Ain Mallaha, sixteen miles north of the Sea of Galilee in the rolling Hula Valley. Here, about 12,000 years ago, people built one of the world's first permanent settlements, a community of fifty small, circular houses made of limestone and sheltered with roofs of brushwood and animal hides. The inhabitants, known as Natufians, were a sort of transitional culture between hunter-gatherers and farmers. They fished for carp in a nearby lake, hunted gazelle and deer with bow and arrow in a surrounding forest, and ground wild nuts and grains in giant stone mortars. They also buried their dead beneath their homes.

When the archaeologists dug into the floor of one of the dwellings, they hit a large limestone slab, a common grave marker at the time. Underneath lay the skeletons of an elderly human and a four-month-old puppy. Unlike earlier canine finds, this was a complete skeleton, not a skull or some other bone fragment. The animal hadn't been eaten, chopped up, or tossed away like so much garbage. This was an individual. This was a creature that mattered. And there was one more thing: the human's hand was resting on the dog's chest.

The Wildest of the Wildcats

After my visit to Wolf Park, I felt I had a pretty good idea of where dogs came from. But cats were another story. I didn't imagine that their journey into human society was quite the same. For one thing, I had no idea what kind of creature could have eventually given rise to Jasper and Jezebel. For another, I was fairly sure that ancient cats didn't follow early humans around from campsite to campsite—unless they were trying to eat them. And then there was the biggest issue: felines aren't exactly known for doing a lot of work for people; surely someone hadn't tried strapping firewood to a cat.

Alas, there is no cat version of Wolf Park. And scientists have only recently begun to untangle the origins of our feline companions. So the journey into the history of the cat doesn't begin with a trip. It begins with an odd court case.

If you live in Scotland and you like to hunt birds, chances are you spend most of the year pining for the Glorious Twelfth. That's the twelfth of August, for those in the know, the official opening of grouse-hunting season.

It's also the onset of a flood of business for grouse moors, vast expanses of hilly countryside where hunters pay big bucks to spend a day shooting at these chicken-sized, low-flying birds. When it comes to grouse killing, however, hunters have some unwelcome competition: cats.

Felines and other small carnivores like foxes and stoats can wreak havoc on a grouse moor, killing thousands of the birds every year. Game-keepers do their best to minimize the damage. They prowl the moors at night, trekking through forestry and scrub with a flashlight fastened to their rifles. Occasionally, the light picks up a pair of glowing eyes in the distance, and the gamekeepers take aim and shoot. The technique, known as lamping, has proven successful. But not every cat is fair game. One gamekeeper found that out the hard way in 1990. After a witness saw him shoot three cats on a grouse moor in northern Scotland, he was taken to court and charged with killing an endangered species. The gamekeeper claimed he had dispatched feral cats. The witness said he had killed Scottish wildcats. The two animals can look nearly identical, but as far as UK law is concerned, there's a world of difference.

The Scottish wildcat is a local variety of the European wildcat, itself a subspecies of the wildcat, an animal that arose in Europe a few hundred thousand years ago and eventually spread into Africa and Asia. Each region claims its own variety of wildcat, but you'd be hard-pressed to tell the difference. They're all gray or brown, sport dark tiger stripes, and are about the size of a common house cat. Put them in a room with a mackerel tabby, and even experts have a hard time telling them apart.

That's become a real problem in Scotland. The wildcats here were doing just fine until about 2,000 years ago, when the Romans brought domestic cats to the British Isles. Suddenly the Scottish wildcat had a competitor, and one with a big advantage. Like the skittish wolves of human prehistory, the wildcats would not venture near people. That meant they couldn't partake in the scraps left by an expanding human civilization. But domestic cats could, and they could live in the wild as well. When these house cats roamed into the countryside, they mated with the Scottish wildcat, corrupting the DNA of a creature that had been isolated for thousands of years. Slowly the wildcat began to disappear, its unique genome scrubbed from existence.

Today, there are just a few hundred wildcats left in Scotland, down from about 100,000 in pre-Roman times. And the Scots, fiercely protective of this iconic symbol of national pride (the venerable Scottish Clan Chattan is the "Clan of the Wildcat"), have enacted tough laws to keep them from vanishing altogether. It's hard to protect an animal, though, when you can't tell the difference between it and the creature that's obliterating it. When the gamekeeper went to court, the prosecutor couldn't find a single expert to testify beyond a reasonable doubt that the man had actually shot Scottish wildcats and not run-of-the-mill tabbies. The state was forced to drop the case.

To have any hope of saving the Scottish wildcat, conservationists would need a more foolproof way to distinguish it from its domestic counterpart. Enter an American graduate student named Carlos Driscoll. A compact, muscular thirty-year-old with messy brown hair, Driscoll didn't know much about the Scottish wildcat, but he did know a lot about feline genetics. He had just completed his master's degree at the National Cancer Institute in Frederick, Maryland, where he had used short, repeating segments of DNA, called "microsatellites," to track the evolutionary history of lions, pumas, and cheetahs in Africa and India. The microsatellites also helped him determine which populations of the big cats were most inbred and in need of help.

Driscoll's work caught the attention of David Macdonald, a professor of wildlife conservation at the University of Oxford who was trying to figure out a way to save the Scottish wildcat. He wondered if the American could apply his expertise to the problem. Driscoll agreed to do his PhD research in Macdonald's lab, though his reasons weren't entirely altruistic. "Oxford doesn't require classwork," he chuckled over the phone, "and I was lazy."

Nonetheless, he soon found himself working his tail off. "I realized the only way to distinguish the wildcat from the domestic cat was to genetically reconstruct the family tree of the entire species," he said—something that had never been done before. That meant traveling to every region where the wildcat lives and collecting blood and tissue samples. He'd have to venture far into the wilderness, to places he hoped the domestic cat hadn't invaded. "I was looking for the wildest of wildcats," he said.

Europe was easy. Driscoll hopped on his motorcycle and rode out to laboratories that had been collecting European wildcat specimens for conservation purposes. He also did some collecting of his own. "If I saw a dead cat on the side of the road," he said, "I'd stop and take a sample." The rest of the family tree took a lot more work. Over the course of six months, Driscoll flew to various parts of Asia, Africa, and the Middle East. He rode horses through the mosquito-infested swamps of Azerbaijan, jeeps into the desolate deserts of Israel and South Africa, and trucks into the snow-packed mountains of western Mongolia. Everywhere he went, he looked for a local guide who could take him out into the wilderness. "You go out, you talk to people, and you ask them where they've seen cats," he told me. "A lot of them laugh at you. But a few are willing to help."

In Israel's Negev Desert, Driscoll was on the trail of the Near Eastern wildcat. "We were in a place that's known in the Bible as 'The Wilderness of Zin,'" he said. "Even today, nobody lives there because the Israelis use it as a tank firing range. You never know when the shells are going to fall, which is great for wildlife because it keeps people out." Here, Driscoll set out wire box traps at night with live pigeons as bait. ("The cat knows it's a trap," he said, "but if a bird's inside it doesn't care.") Then, he'd wake up at five in the morning to check on the boxes. If one held a feline, he'd poke an anesthetic-filled syringe through the cage, draw some blood, and clip off a tiny piece of its ear.

In the bushland of southern Africa, home to a different subspecies of wildcat, Driscoll set out rubber leghold traps behind ten-foot-tall bushes. If one snared a cat, he'd throw a blanket over the animal and collect his samples. Things were a bit simpler in Mongolia: in the territory of the central Asian wildcat, Driscoll spent some time among nomadic Kazaks, who wander the land on camelback with goats, cows, and other animals in tow. Hunters would occasionally ride out on horseback with golden eagles perched on their arms. The birds were trained to catch cats and foxes for fur, said Driscoll, "so all I had to do was take a sample of the clothes the Kazaks were wearing; their jackets are made of forty cats." And not always wildcats. Even out here, in the middle of nowhere, Driscoll saw felines with white paws and black spots. "Domestic cats," he said, "are everywhere."

By the time he was done, Driscoll had sampled nearly 1,000 cats. The genetic data revealed a few surprises. Taxonomists believed that there were only three subspecies of wildcat (*Felis silvestris*): *Felis silvestris silvestris* in Europe, *Felis silvestris lybica* in the Near East, and *Felis silvestris ornata* in the Middle East and central Africa. Driscoll's data showed there were two more: *Felis silvestris cafra* in southern Africa and *Felis silvestris bieti* in China. But the biggest shock came when he analyzed the DNA of the domestic cat. Scientists thought that house cats belonged to their own subspecies, *Felis catus*, and that they had been domesticated in Egypt. But according to Driscoll's research, the domestic cat grouped squarely with the Near Eastern wildcat, a creature that calls the region encompassing Israel, Turkey, and Iraq home. Genetically, the two were nearly identical. That meant conservationists now had a simple DNA test to distinguish the Scottish wildcat from its domestic cousin. But it also meant something far more profound: the domestic cat had arisen in the Near East.

A couple of thousand years after the Natufians buried a human and a dog together in northern Israel, people in the region gave up their hunter-gatherer ways. The climate, once frigid and dry, had become wet and temperate. Gazelle, deer, and ibex roamed a landscape of forest and open parkland, and rich soil sprouted with wild barley and wheat, figs and tubers. People no longer had to follow the seasonal migrations of the animals they hunted, some theories go, so they began to settle down in permanent villages across the Fertile Crescent, a sickle-shaped Garden of Eden that wound its way up the eastern coast of the Mediterranean Sea and down through the Mesopotamian valley to the Persian Gulf. It is here, during a period called the Neolithic, that Western civilization began to take hold.

People started domesticating the world around them. They cultivated wild grains, transforming them into crops that grew faster, bigger, and easier to eat, and they corralled wild boar, cattle, and goats, selecting for traits that would reshape them into the livestock we know today. Perhaps their experience with the dog showed it could be done. With a stable supply of cereals, meat, milk, and hides, Neolithic humans were no longer roped to the whims of nature. They had time to develop new technologies and new ways of living. Early forms of writing would eventually appear, as would the wheel. Farming became a central way of life. Society stratified, long-distance trade began, and an entirely new economic system arose. It was an exciting time to be a human—and an even better time to be a cat.

The earliest evidence for cat domestication comes from a Neolithic village known as Shillourokambos, located on the southern coast of the

Mediterranean island of Cyprus. Built about 10,000 years ago, Shillourokambos sat on top of a low hill, near the intersection of two small rivers. It was a community of several hundred people who lived in circular
homes of wood and clay. Throughout the village, wood-thatched fences
penned goats, pigs, and cattle, and numerous stone silos stored grain.

All of this had disappeared by the time a French archaeologist named
Jean-Denis Vigne began excavating the site in 1992. Millennia of neglect and erosion had left behind only fire pits, post holes, and the vague
outlines of silos and wells. All that remained of the homes were foundations of clay and stone. Like the Natufians before them, the Shillou-
rokambians buried their dead beneath their houses. Still, when Vigne
dug into the floor of a 9,500-year-old dwelling, he was stunned by what
he found: underneath lay the skeletons of a human in the fetal position and an animal nearby. Unlike the Natufian grave excavated in the
1970s, however, the Shillourokambos pit was full of precious artifacts,
including polished stone axes and flint blades. And the animal wasn't a
dog—it was a cat.

The feline, about eight months old, had been placed in its own small
plot, roughly a foot from the human skeleton, and it was surrounded by
twenty-four carved seashells. It had been oriented in such a way that it
and the human appeared to be looking at each other. Vigne had found
pieces of cats before, but never a complete skeleton, and never one interred with such pomp. "This burial was special," he told me. "We're seeing a different kind of relationship between man and cat." And one that
had formed thousands of years before ancient Egypt even existed.

It makes sense for cats to have entered human society around this time.
With the advent of farming came the need to store large surpluses of
grain. And with large surpluses of grain came mice. Archaeologists
aren't sure exactly how the rodents made it to Shillourokambos, or even
to Cyprus for that matter. But they do know what the natives did about
it: they ferried in boatloads of cats from the mainland.

These early felines had already begun to diverge from their ancestor,
the Near Eastern wildcat. Like the wolves before them, only those wildcats least fearful of people would have been able to enter human settlements, feeding off garbage and gaining a selective advantage over their
skittish counterparts. Over time, they became tamer and somewhat

smaller, and they evolved slightly longer intestines, an adaptation Darwin chalked up to the need to digest a more varied diet that included table scraps. But unlike dogs, cats appear to have reached a certain point in their domestication and then just stopped.

Perhaps wildcats weren't built to be fully domesticated. Wolves are social animals, and they're most active during the day, a perfect fit for the human lifestyle; wildcats, meanwhile, are solitary, nocturnal, and territorial—traits that don't mesh well with village living. Or perhaps people just didn't try to domesticate them. When dogs started to show their utility, humans bred them to be better hunters, herders, and guardians. But cats, eager to take advantage of the human hearth, appear to have completely domesticated themselves. If Neolithic people played any role, it was likely limited to merely letting the best mousers live.

And yet cats did change. They didn't just become smaller and grow larger intestines. They eventually began to sport a wide variety of coat colors and patterns, they evolved a high-pitched purr that mimics human baby cries (the better to get the attention of their owners), and they largely shed the antisocial tendencies of their wild relatives, accepting us as friends. Sure, they're independent, aloof, and practically untrainable. But dogs may have had a 20,000-year head start.

Today, cats are the world's most popular pet, with hundreds of millions living among us. But here's a curious thought: it could have been foxes. Though the people of Shillourokambos imported cats to deal with their rodent problem, they also brought in foxes to do the same job. So why did cats take over the globe, while the only domestic foxes are found on a farm in Siberia? Maybe cats were better mousers. Maybe dogs had already filled the canine niche. Or maybe, said Carlos Driscoll, now an expert on cat domestication, there's a simpler explanation. "Kittens are playful, friendly, and huggable," he told me. "It may just come down to the fact that cats are cute."

Regardless of the reason, cats and dogs had embarked on a bold new path. In a world once divided between man and beast, they emerged as a new class of animal: the companion. These two creatures would be part of human society forever more. Yet domestication was only the beginning. In order to evolve from companion to pet, dogs and cats wouldn't just have to become friendlier. They'd have to travel to hell and back.

THREE

The Rise of the Pet

In August 1348, an English princess sailed into the port of Bordeaux, France. Her ship led a flotilla of four, their grand white sails billowing in the wind as they trailed banners bearing her family's blue-and-red crest. One vessel carried her vast collection of silk and velvet dresses, embroidered with silver and gold; the others conveyed her extensive entourage of servants, advisors, and one hundred longbow-bearing bodyguards. The princess was on her way to marry the prince of Castile—a union that would grant her father, King Edward III, a powerful Spanish ally in his war for the French throne—and she had decided to rest up in Bordeaux. The city's mayor begged her not to stay. A mysterious plague was decimating the region, he said, killing people by the thousands. Undeterred, the princess asked to be escorted to her family's castle overlooking the water. A few weeks later, she and most of her companions were dead.

Princess Joan, as she was known, would have witnessed many horrors before she died. Bordeaux's harbor, once among the busiest ports in Europe, had become a rotting necropolis. Hundreds of bodies piled up on the docks, leaving countless bales of wool and barrels of red wine unattended, destined for far-off places they would never reach. Walking among the corpses, a perfumed handkerchief pressed firmly to her nose, the princess would have noticed that many were covered in dark blotches and egg-shaped boils, some crusted with pus and blood. And everywhere scurried black rats the size of possums.

It was a scene playing out in cities and villages across the country. People became weak, burned with fever, coughed up blood, and collapsed in the street. Some died in days, others in hours. A father buried five of his sons in a single week, church cemeteries ran out of space, and bodies were poured like gravel into vast pits. Panic set in. The wrath of god, people believed, rode on the breath of friends and relatives. Husbands abandoned wives, parents deserted children, and thousands fled to the countryside seeking sanctuary that did not exist. The Black Death was everywhere.

Back in Bordeaux, members of Princess Joan's entourage began to fall ill. They may have been bitten by the fleas that infested the black rats swarming the docks. The insects harbored a deadly microbe that, when it infected people, hemorrhaged blood vessels, swelled lymph nodes, and rotted the lungs, ravaging the body from within. Baron Robert Bouchier, head of the princess's diplomatic delegation and a veteran of one of King Edward's epic battles, was among the first to fall. Then, one by one, others collapsed and gurgled their last breaths. The family castle was becoming a tomb. And soon the princess herself would succumb.

In hopes of stopping the epidemic, Bordeaux's mayor set fire to the port. The flames engulfed the castle and the body of the princess within. But it was too late. By 1351, the Black Death had consumed Europe. As many as half its people perished. Millions of lives might have been saved, however, if Europeans hadn't nearly exterminated the chief predator of the plague-carrying black rat: the domestic cat.

Gods and Devils

Several thousand years after humans took up farming and began burying their dead under their homes, people settled in the Nile River valley of northeastern Africa, a narrow oasis of lush vegetation that wound its way through an otherwise brown and barren desert. Over millennia, sleepy villages became bustling towns, and trade brought in luxury goods, stratifying society. Chiefs rose to rule over local communities, local communities became part of principalities, and in 3100 BC a pharaoh named Narmer united it all into a single nation, one of the most advanced societies the world had ever seen. This place, now known as ancient Egypt, teemed with animal life. The creatures featured prominently in the art of the day: on pottery, papyrus, and the walls of tombs, fish and crocodiles plied the Nile, birds swarmed dense marshes, and farmers herded cattle and sheep, donkeys and pigs. So it went for hundreds of years. Then, around 1950 BC, Egyptian art began to feature a curious new animal.

The creature first appears in the tomb of Baket III, a local ruler who modestly referred to himself as "the Great Overlord of the Oryx District." The chamber, a spacious rectangular room carved into a limestone cliff about 160 miles south of Cairo, is plastered with scenes of Baket's dominion. Women weave linen on looms. Butchers slaughter cattle. Farmers are beaten for tax evasion. Toward the back of the tomb, on a wall outside a shrine that once housed a statue of the ruler, are several columns of images, one depicting a field rat facing off against what appears to be a house cat. The painting of the feline—its tail vertical, its hind legs ready to pounce—is the first known of a domestic cat. The animal stands next to a man (in the sidewise pose of the time), indicating that it was a valuable member of the household. The rat is also significant: it's the reason cats would eventually overshadow every other animal in ancient Egypt.

The rise of the cat coincides with the rise of Egypt itself. As the nation grew, towns became denser and grain production boomed—perfect conditions for a rodent infestation. Indeed, as famed Egyptologist Flinders Petrie wrote of his late-nineteenth-century excavation of Kahun, a 2000 BC village of mud-brick homes populated by pyramid builders, "Nearly every room has its corners tunneled by rats, and the holes are stuffed up with stones and rubbish to keep them back." The rodents were such a problem that the villagers created one of the world's first rattraps: a small pottery box with a sliding door.

Cats, having made their way from the Near East, would have been highly valued as pest control, just as they had been thousands of years earlier in Cyprus. By protecting granaries from rodents, they allowed ancient Egypt to expand and prosper. And by killing poisonous snakes and scorpions as well, they saved lives. Houses with cats had more food and less death. As a bonus, they were easy to take care of. Cats hunted their own meals, bathed themselves, and buried their waste in the sand—qualities that made them an ideal pet for a busy civilization. It's no wonder that, over the next several centuries, the popularity of felines exploded. Images of house cats became ubiquitous in ancient Egyptian art, from alabaster sculptures in homes to gold necklaces worn by queens. In paintings and parchment, cats sat on laps, grew plump under kitchen tables, and wore jeweled collars and earrings. They even supplanted dogs in hunting scenes, flushing birds into the nets of their human owners. But cats achieved their greatest renown in the reverence the Egyptians paid to them in death.

One of the most poignant examples is a small limestone sarcophagus made for the pet of Prince Thutmose, the oldest son of Pharaoh Amenhotep III. The object, described in intricate detail in Jaromír Málek's *The Cat in Ancient Egypt*, dates to around 1350 BC and looks like a miniature house, with a rectangular base and a peaked roof. The figure of a cat is etched into the two longest sides, facing a table of flowers and offerings (including a duck), and framed by hieroglyphics. The words reveal that the animal was named Tamyt, and the prose wouldn't be out of place on the casket of any Egyptian. "On the lid," writes Málek, the cat "addresses the sky goddess Nut and wishes to become an 'imperishable star.'" Another inscription guarantees that "the limbs of Tamyt, one true voice before the great god, shall not be weary."

Ultimately, it wasn't enough that cats be honored by the gods. They had to *become* gods. One of the ancient Egyptians' most important deities, Ra, the sun god, was not originally affiliated with the cat. But as felines gained prominence, they began to accompany him on his nightly journey to the underworld. While there, Ra could even take the form of a cat, as when he did battle with his nemesis, the snake demon Apophis. If he won, a victory depicted by a feline cutting off a snake's head, the sun would rise the next morning. By 1500 BC, Ra was frequently referred to as "the Great Tomcat."

The cat's link to the goddess Bastet, however, is what ultimately sealed its fate, for good and for ill. In her original incarnation, Bastet had the head of a lion, the Egyptian symbol of strength and ferocity. But as ancient Egypt became a more civilized society—one might say a more domestic society—the cat, a creature more identified with playfulness and affection, replaced the lion. Indeed, the cat's reputation as a prolific breeder and attentive mother meshed well with the role of Bastet as the goddess of nurturing and fertility, critical concerns in a society with short lifespans and high infant mortality. This connection seems to have forever linked cats and women; it's a stereotype the Egyptians themselves embraced in their art, often depicting a cat sitting under a lady's chair while a dog sat under a man's. Other associations also took shape:

Bastet was said to have nine lives, and in some representations, she appears to be playing a musical instrument that looks a lot like a fiddle.

Bastet eventually rose to such prominence in Egyptian society that her home village of Bubastis on the eastern Nile Delta became the site of one of the nation's most popular festivals. The Greek historian Herodotus estimated that, by the mid-fifth century BC, more than 700,000 people (about half the country's adult population) attended annual celebrations in the goddess's honor. They flocked to Bubastis by foot and riverboat, clapping, singing, and playing flutes and drums. "Women . . . indecently throw aside their garments," he wrote, and "a greater quantity of wine is consumed than in all the rest of the year." The revelers eventually met at the great temple of Bastet, encircled like an island by two branches of the Nile River. Covered in sculptures, it was home to a giant statue of the goddess. There, worshippers brought mummified cats by the thousands. At first, they carried their own deceased pets. But when demand outstripped supply, they relied on priests to "prepare" felines for them. Soon, large temples sprung up just to breed cats for mummification. Most of these animals were sacrificed—an act the Egyptians could justify because the felines would be honored for eternity—but the tamest and most beautiful individuals may have been allowed to live, furthering the domestication of the cat.

The cat was now as revered as it would ever be. Herodotus wrote that if an Egyptian's house was on fire, his priorities were clear: "The Egyptians surrounding the place which is burning appear to be occupied with no thought but that of preserving their cats." And if a cat died in a home, "every individual cuts off his eyebrows." Felines were so treasured that, according to legend, the Persian king Cambyses was able to conquer Egypt in 525 BC by ordering his soldiers to carry cats into the battlefield; the Egyptians, terrified of harming their sacred pets, dared not shoot their arrows into the invading forces. As other foreigners encroached, the nation created new laws to protect its felines. The Greek historian Diodorus witnessed an incident in 59 BC in which a visiting Roman accidentally killed a cat and was hanged for his crime. Other laws prohibited the export of the animals from the country. But cats eventually dispersed far and wide. And they would conquer Europe long before Europe conquered them.

As ancient Egypt entered its waning centuries, cats began to appear on the other side of the Mediterranean Sea. In a land of giant stone temples and the world's first democracy, felines left their mark on the art of ancient Greece. The animals chased ducks on wall frescoes and played with string on silver coins. But the Greeks would have their most lasting influence via the written word. Egypt may have refined the cat we know today, but Greece gave us its personality.

The cat as character makes its first indelible impression in the Greek fables, some of which Aesop himself may have written. In "The Cat's Birthday Dinner," the animal emerges as a trickster, inviting a group of birds to the party—and then eating them when the door is closed. In another story, a cat is dispatched to kill a cheese-eating rat in his owner's cupboard, but the opportunistic puss eats both rat and cheese. And in "The Eagle, the Cat, and the Wild Sow," the feline outsmarts both bird and pig, convincing each that the other will kill its babies if it leaves its nest; eventually the eagle and sow starve to death, and the cat makes a meal of both of their families. Curiously, despite the vast menagerie of animals that interact in the Greek fables, the cat never quarrels with the dog. That's at least one stereotype that had yet to take hold.

Greek cats were also the objects of scientific inquiry. Aristotle recorded some of the earliest observations of feline mating habits ("Female cats are naturally lecherous and lure the males on to sexual intercourse"). Others noted that cats had rough tongues for grooming and reflective eyes for seeing at night. And in the sixth century AD, medical writer Aetius of Amida, in describing the supposed ailments felines can cause humans, mentions black, white, and pale cats. Though he probably didn't realize it, Aetius had made a stunning observation: the first written evidence that cats had begun to change color.

From what historians can gather from tomb paintings, all cats in ancient Egypt looked the same. Each sported the brown coat and tiger stripes of its ancestor, the Near Eastern wildcat. But at some point, likely between 500 BC and 500 AD, new colors and patterns appeared. Why these changes emerged is unclear. The massive breeding that took place in Egyptian temples may have propagated rare genetic mutations. Or the mere process of selecting for the tamest cats may have altered the animal's entire biology, as happened with the Siberian foxes. As these new varieties showed up, the Greeks would have helped spread them across the Mediterranean, transporting them on ships that traded wine and olive oil. The felines would have proved themselves indispensable crew members, protecting rope and food stores from rats and quashing rodent-born diseases. Few voyages were undertaken without them. (The custom lasted into the modern era; a black cat accompanied explorer R. F. Scott on his expedition to the South Pole in 1912, sunning its days away on a pillowed hammock, and cats were a staple on British naval vessels until 1975.)

It's perhaps not surprising then that many Greeks continued the Egyptian tradition of revering the cat. They even associated their most popular goddess, Artemis, with the Egyptian goddess Bastet, worshipping her in their columned temples. But the cat's exalted status was nearing its end.

The Romans conquered Greece in 146 BC, and though they continued to respect Greek culture, they didn't always respect the cat. Chalk it up to a difference in philosophy: while the Greeks valued liberty and autonomy, the Romans prized loyalty and obligation. The Roman Empire was a place for the dog.

One of the biggest indications of this is the number of breeds that cropped up during the era. Bones unearthed in ancient Roman towns reveal a far greater variety of dog sizes than seen in any other region of the time. The Romans weren't just breeding countless animals, as the Egyptians did; they were selecting for specific traits. They created huge mastiffs for hunting and protection, whippet-sized hounds for chasing down small prey, and, most significantly, very small canines the size of Pekingese that served no practical function. These "lapdogs" did little more than hang out and look pretty. This suggests that the Romans were the first people to stop viewing the dog merely as a working animal—and to begin viewing it as a pet.

Nowhere was this new attitude more evident than in the grief the Romans showed when their dogs died. They didn't bury their pets in separate cemeteries; they were interred in the same prominent locales as people, next to marketplaces and along roadsides. Some of the most renowned poets of the day wrote epitaphs for dogs. Grave markers, frequently etched with a visage of the deceased canine, spoke of the animal's humanlike qualities. Lydia was a faithful hound, "savage in the woods, gentle at home." Sweet Fly was jealous, barking at competitors for her owner's affection. And the loss of at least one small dog in the city of Rome was felt as deeply as the death of a daughter; the pup's tombstone, topped with a statuette of the dog herself (her tail curled, her ears at attention), reads, "To Helena, foster child, soul without comparison, and deserving of praise." Another dog elegy declares, "I am in tears, while carrying you to your last resting place, as much as I rejoiced when bringing you home in my own hands fifteen years ago."

As the Romans expanded their empire throughout Europe, they brought their attitudes—and their dogs—along with them. They also, perhaps grudgingly, brought cats. They must have recognized their utility in keeping taxable farms free of rodents. As these cats spread throughout the continent—sometimes nearly wiping out local populations of felines, including the Scottish wildcat—so too did religions that worshipped them. Cults dedicated to the Greek goddess Artemis and her Roman equivalent, Diana, sprang up in villages and towns. Groups also prayed to the Egyptian goddess Bastet, usually in the form of another Egyptian deity, Isis. And because Isis's sacred color was black, black cats became especially important to these sects, typically dominated by women. Ceremonies took place at night, followers made offerings in temples, and priestesses healed with herbs and potions. The stage was set for the downfall of the cat.

The rise of pagan religions in medieval Europe worried the Catholic Church. It weighed especially heavily on the mind of one man, Pope Gregory IX. Born in central Italy in the mid-twelfth century, Gregory didn't become pope until 1227, when he was already quite old. He was an especially paranoid individual, and he became obsessed with a rise in heresy. Though Christianity had become the dominant religion in Europe, it hadn't solidified its grip. Pagans were a particular eyesore. Cults devoted to ancient goddesses and other deities met in homes with dirt floors and thatched roofs to worship animals and nature. Magic, they believed, was everywhere. Sorcerers healed with potions, fortune-tellers predicted the future, and the old gods of weather and fertility still held sway over daily life.

Gregory vowed to stamp out these so-called evils before it was too late. In 1231, he created the first Papal Inquisition, a group composed largely of Dominican friars who fanned out across the continent, judging heretics and remanding them to the local authorities for torment and execution. One of the most zealous and sadistic of Gregory's crew was an ascetic priest named Konrad von Marburg. Known as "the Inquisitor" by some, he incited panic wherever he went. He traveled from village to village in Germany, hunting down the flimsiest of rumors and threatening often innocent people with the stake until they confessed to the unholiest of sins against the church. Von Marburg cared nothing for class, targeting nobles and peasants alike, and through torture and terror he compelled the accused to falsely denounce their friends and relatives. Scholars believe von Marburg's reconnaissance in a hamlet in southwest Germany led Gregory IX to pen one of his most influential proclamations: a screed that linked black cats to Satan.

In his *Vox in Rama* of 1233, the pope warns German bishops about an evil in their midst. He describes the initiation ceremony of a cult that meets in caverns beneath homes. The followers light candles and chant. Eventually, he claims, "a black cat . . . with an upright tail descends backwards down a statue, which is usually at the meeting. The postulant first kisses the cat's rear, then [so does] the master of the sect, and then the other individuals who are worthy of honor and perfect. . . . Then they face the cat in turn . . . and say, 'We know the master . . . and we obey to you.'" The candles go out, and the cult engages in a bisexual orgy. Finally, a strange creature appears. "His upper body shines with rays brighter than the sun, the lower part is hairy like a cat," Gregory writes. Lucifer has arrived. He accepts a piece of the initiate's clothing and welcomes the person as a new member of the sect. "You have often served me well," says Lucifer to the leader of the cult, "and may you continue to serve me well." Then, the devil vanishes.

Gregory IX authorized the use of any and all force to rid Europe of these witches. "No vengeance against them is too harsh," he wrote. The fate of heretics was sealed. And so too was the fate of the cat. Now seeing these animals as incarnations of Satan, Europeans slaughtered them by the thousands. The ancient pact between human and feline was broken. Once welcomed into prehistoric villages as pest control and companions, cats had become *felis* non grata. People stoned them, drowned them, and burned them at the stake with their witch companions. The more pain the cats suffered, the better, as their dying yowls were believed to scare away the devil.

The hysteria continued for centuries. Cats were thrown from towers, hung from trees, and roasted in a giant bonfire at the coronation of Queen Elizabeth I in 1559. They were even excommunicated from the church. In what may be the most thorough look at felines through the ages, *Classical Cats*, historian Donald Engels estimates that by 1700 tens of millions of the animals had been massacred throughout Europe. In some villages it was impossible to find a cat, and black ones were virtually unheard of. By the mid-1300s alone, enough cats had disappeared to portend disaster. A feline, left to its own devices, can kill hundreds of small animals a year, and without enough cats around, Europe's rodent population exploded. Plague-carrying black rats swarmed the continent and grew to unprecedented size. Europeans didn't do themselves any favors by eschewing bathing and emptying their chamber pots into the streets. But they certainly made matters worse when the Black Death came to town. Instead of blaming the rats, they blamed the cats. And they killed more of them than ever before. By the time Princess Joan sailed into the port of Bordeaux, she was facing almost certain death.

It's unclear why Pope Gregory IX demonized the cat. He wasn't a foe of all creatures; he canonized Francis of Assisi, the inspiration for Blessing of the Animals ceremonies, a mere two years after the saint died. Some say felines' independent nature did them in; not subservient like dogs and livestock, they violated church dogma that man had dominion over all animals. Others blame the cat's nocturnal lifestyle, blood-curdling caterwauling, and spooky, shiny eyes—all easily linked to witchcraft. Cats weren't the only ones vilified. Dogs, far removed from their days as companions in ancient Rome, had become associated with filth and disease. They were killed in large numbers too; there were more dogcatchers than rat catchers in medieval Europe. As the Middle Ages drew to a close, both cats and dogs were among the most reviled animals around. Things would get worse before they got better.

The Unkindest Cut

In the late afternoon of December 10, 1907, a crowd of medical students marched from their campus in central London to the working-class borough of Battersea, intent on destroying the statue of a small dog. As the young men moved south across the River Thames, waving crowbars and hammers, they passed Battersea's slums and factories, the latter belching thick clouds of sulfurous coal smoke into the air. Eventually the mob entered a small park in the middle of a housing development and set its eyes on a seven-foot-tall marble fountain. At the top sat a bronze terrier, its metal eyes staring defiantly over the heads of the students. "Down with the brown dog!" shouted one. And the throng advanced.

The scene had been set in motion nearly five years earlier when two young Swedish women infiltrated a psychology lecture at University College London. The women were ardent antivivisectionists, and they had enrolled as medical students in hopes of exposing barbaric practices at the school. They got what they came for, at least according to their diary. On a February day in 1903, they were seated in a classroom surrounded by young men, all perched behind long wooden desks. At the front of the room stood the professor, a balding, bearded physiologist named William Bayliss, wearing wire-rim glasses and smoking a pipe. A large blackboard loomed behind him, and his hands rested on a laboratory bench. Before him lay a small brown dog that had been tied to a board. The animal, still alive, was on its back, its rear legs stretched flat, its front legs clasped to its sides, and its mouth tightly muzzled. Bayliss moved in with his scalpel.

What happened next is a matter of debate. The women claimed that the dog had not been anesthetized and that it trembled and whimpered as Bayliss cut into its neck to expose its salivary glands, arching its back in an attempt to escape. They also said Bayliss jolted the dog with electricity to get the glands going and that the animal bore fresh incisions on its abdomen, indicating it had been cut open at least once before. The demonstration ended, they wrote, when an assistant plunged a knife into the dog's heart.

A few months later, the women published their account in a book titled *The Shambles of Science*. Bayliss, whose research helped lead to the discovery of hormones, sued for libel. He didn't deny the details of the procedure, but he maintained that the dog had been anesthetized and didn't struggle. He won the case—and the support of local medical students—but the damage had been done. Newspapers heavily covered the story, and the issue of vivisection divided the public. In an unusual alliance, working-class men joined the growing feminist movement in opposing the practice, and nearby Battersea, a hotbed of unionism and radical politics, became the perfect place to erect a memorial to the little brown dog.

As the mob of medical students advanced on the statue in December 1907, factory workers and suffragettes rushed in and forced them back. The students headed down the road and tried to attack Battersea General Hospital, which refused to employ vivisectionists, but they were again pushed away. Finally, the throng retreated back across the Thames and regrouped with supporters in Trafalgar Square. They were now 1,000 strong, shouting and thrusting effigies of the brown dog aloft on skewers. Hundreds of police officers, some on horseback, charged in and fought them for hours, capping the largest of what would later be known as the Brown Dog Riots. Centuries of angst over the souls of cats and dogs had come to a head.

The Middle Ages weren't a bad time for all dogs. Though most were seen as spreaders of filth and disease, a chosen few still held a special place among the aristocracy. The reason traces back to one of their original roles: man's hunting companion.

Medieval hunting wasn't the life-and-death struggle of prehistory. It was a new type of activity: the pursuit of animals not for sustenance or survival but for sport. As early as the seventh century, European nobility began designating large tracts of land for its personal use. In a typical outing, lords would gather on these reserves on a warm summer morning, enjoying food and drink while their servants scouted deer in the forest. (As time went on, the noblemen would leave little to chance, seeding the woods with game from their own stables.) When the prey was spotted, a horn would sound, and the hunting party would take off on horseback, trailing a dozen or more of their hounds at breakneck speeds through brush and stream. Exhausted, the frothing deer would eventually stumble around and face its pursuers, and the leader of the hunting party would run a sword through its neck.

As hunting grew in popularity, it became an important way for noblemen to showcase their skill and courage. It was also a way for the upper crust to distinguish itself from the masses. Peasants were banned from hunting reserves and forbidden to own hunting dogs like greyhounds. "If the greyhound be found within the forest," decreed one eleventh-century Danish law, "the master or owner of the dog shall forfeit the dog and ten shillings to the king." Lapdogs were exempt from such rules, as there was little chance they could be used for sport. To qualify for immunity, they had to be able to walk through a "dog gauge," a metal ring about the size of a Pomeranian.

Hunting dogs ultimately became their own kind of nobility. Lords and kings with the best hounds fared best at the hunt, and thus they began to take special care of their canine companions. Treatises advised owners to speak kindly to their animals and to caress them. Other literature recommended addressing hounds as "sir" and "my friend." And, in a sort of medieval doggy day care, kings housed canines in kennels across their realms, where their paws were soaked, their fur was groomed, and their beds of hay were comfortably prepared, all by servants who were undoubtedly treated less well. King John of England kept a white hunting dog on a manor in Warwickshire, a greyhound on a manor in Hertfordshire, and ten greyhounds in three castles in Monmouthshire.

These noble canines began to transcend their status as animals. The church had erected thick barriers between man and beast; Genesis proclaimed that humans had "dominion over the fish of the sea, and over the fowl of the air, and over every living thing that moveth upon the earth." But the hounds of the aristocracy didn't fit easily into this arrangement. When hunting morphed from sustenance into sport, dogs no longer served man—they stood by him. They gave him his place in the world by helping him subjugate its creatures. This was not an animal; this was a friend, a best friend. By the fifteenth century, the church's barriers had begun to crack. And soon the laws that prohibited the common man from keeping and pampering his own hounds would fade away. But dogs wouldn't come into their own as individuals until the height of the Renaissance.

When dogs first showed up in Renaissance art, they still carried a lot of baggage. Painters saw them not as beings but rather as symbols, and negative ones at that. In the Middle Ages, Christ's tormentors were said to be "evil dogs that stand with their sinful feet in his blood," and in the early Renaissance canines often appeared in paintings about treachery. Snarling curs sit at the feet of Pontius Pilate. Gluttonous hounds fight over discarded bones. Lecherous mutts hang out in scenes of men committing adultery.

But in the sixteenth century, as dogs resumed their classical roles as friends and companions, they began to feature in scenes of domestic life. From the humble homes of the poor to the opulent castles of the aristocracy, they play in yards, beg for table scraps, and sit in the laps of men and women. They also begin to take on human characteristics. In Bartolomeo Passarotti's *Portrait of a Man with a Dog*, a spaniel stares lovingly into the eyes of its owner. In Piero di Cosimo's *A Satyr Mourning over a Nymph*, a dog grieves over the body of a young woman. And in what may be a sort of spiritual redemption, children in Paolo Veronese's *Supper at Emmaus* caress two pups in front of Jesus Christ. Perhaps not coincidentally, the word "pet" entered the vernacular around this time; originally used to describe an indulged child, it began to be applied to animals kept simply for pleasure.

As the skill of painters increased, so did the realism with which they depicted dogs. The animals also became subjects in their own right, emerging from the background in the type of detailed portraits normally reserved for the wealthy. A wolfhound is front and center in Paulus Potter's 1650 painting *A Watchdog Chained to His Kennel*, sporting a ragged coat of short, bristly hairs as he stars longingly into the distance. In Giovanni Francesco Barbieri's *Aldrovani Dog* of 1625, a giant mastiff threatens to overtake the canvas, his family crest displayed prominently on his collar, his gray muzzle marking his long years of service, and his face deeply scarred by the battle wounds of the hunt. The Dutch master Rembrandt may have taken the realism a bit too far: in his 1633 etching *The Good Samaritan*, a dog, squatting in front of a horse, has a bowel movement.

Dogs had reestablished themselves as friends and companions. Cats would have to wait a bit longer. When they do make an appearance in the art of the time, it is usually as objects of curiosity or derision. Leonardo da Vinci painted a series of cats, but he seemed more interested in their anatomy than their company. And in Jan Baptist Weenix's 1650 painting *Hound with a Joint of Meat and a Cat Looking On*, a crudely drawn feline stares antagonistically at a dog guarding a beef bone. If nothing else, the work shows that by the seventeenth century, the cat-versus-dog stereotype had taken firm hold. At least cats were no longer being thrown onto bonfires. The French statesman Cardinal Richelieu kept dozens of the animals at court in the early 1600s, and a century later the wife of Louis XV helped make felines a mainstay of the French aristocracy. But a new threat loomed on the horizon for both cats and dogs.

The Brown Dog Riots may have been sparked by Swedish spies, but their real origin lies in the writings of René Descartes. The seventeenth-century philosopher, perhaps taking a cue from the verisimilitude of contemporary art, was obsessed with the nature of reality. Where do our senses come from? Do we see and feel the world as it actually is? And are we only here because we believe we are? As Descartes famously put it, "I think, therefore I am."

Humans had a mind, Descartes ultimately concluded, but animals did not. His reductionist view of the world saw their bodies as mere machines, devoid of thought or emotion. Their hearts were simply pumps, forcing warm blood through a series of pipes and tubes. Their reactions—hissing, tail wagging—were nothing but mechanical responses, "in the same way a clock, consisting only of wheels and springs, can count the hours and measure the time," he wrote. "Animals don't think, they just behave." Dogs and cats, having finally clawed their way back into the human heart, were now robbed of their souls.

Descartes's attitudes no doubt helped him justify vivisection, which was gaining popularity as doctors strove to understand how the body worked. The philosopher himself was no stranger to the practice. "If you cut off the end of the heart of a living dog," he wrote, "and through the incision put your finger into one of the concavities, you will clearly feel that every time the heart shortens, it presses your finger, and it stops pressing every time it lengthens." If the animal cried out during the procedure, he said, the sound was just the whining of a gear that needed oil. (Ironically, Descartes had a dog of his own, of whom he must have been somewhat fond, having given him the name Monsieur Grat, or "Mr. Scratch.")

Descartes did have his detractors. The English philosopher Robert Hooke, after slicing into the belly of a dog that was kept breathing with a fireplace bellow, wrote in the mid-1600s, "I shall hardly be induced to make any further trials of this kind, because of the torture of the creature." And the French writer Voltaire called vivisection a barbaric betrayal of the trust canines had put in man. If dogs had the same "machinery" that people did—as the dissections had revealed—then certainly they had the same thoughts and emotions. And surely, he said, they also had a soul.

Voltaire gave voice to a new sentimentality toward animals that took hold during the eighteenth century. The movement mirrored a rise in compassion toward people and a concern for what they might become if not properly civilized. The English artist William Hogarth best expressed the feeling in a series of engravings in 1751. Titled *The Four Stages of Cruelty*, the work depicts the life of Tom Nero, who, as a boy in the first scene, stabs a dog with an arrow. (Behind him, cats are strung up from a pole by their tails.) In successive panels, Tom grows into an evil man, beating horses, murdering a servant girl, and eventually being hanged for his crimes and dissected, while a dog eats his heart. The moral: children who abuse animals grow into savage criminals.

A few decades later, British philosopher Jeremy Bentham, an early proponent of animal rights, advocated making cruelty to animals punishable by law. "The question is not, Can they reason? Nor, Can they talk?" he wrote. "But, Can they suffer?" Not until 1822, however, was the first serious animal welfare law passed, thanks to a pugnacious Irishman with a flair for the dramatic named Richard Martin. Revolted by the practices of the notorious French vivisectionist François Magendie—who sliced into the spinal cords of puppies, the cries of which, his colleagues alleged, echoed through the corridors of their medical school in Paris—Martin lobbied successfully for UK legislation outlawing cruelty to horses and cattle and, eventually, to dogs and cats. In 1824, he helped form what would later become the Royal Society for the Prevention of Cruelty to Animals (RSPCA), the world's first animal welfare organization. The RSPCA advocated for tougher anticruelty laws, helping, for example, to ban rickshaws pulled by canines, known as "dog carts."

Eventually, the RSPCA pushed for an antivivisection law, arguing that a civilized society should not tolerate such "physiological butchery." Victorian women, who, as second-class citizens, empathized with the plight of exploited animals, supported the cause. Physicians and scientists, meanwhile, mounted a countercampaign. In 1875, competing bills arrived in the House of Lords and the House of Commons, and Parliament appointed a royal commission to investigate the matter. One of its members, Richard Holt Hutton, argued vehemently that cats and dogs should be kept out of the laboratory. "No class of animals . . . contains so many creatures of high intelligence, and therefore probably of high sensibility, as dogs and cats," he wrote, noting that they had been "civilized" through domestication and were now a part of the human family. "The humble friends of man, which have been taught to obey and trust him, should not be selected as the victims." The eventual bill, the Cruelty to Animals Act of 1876, did not outlaw vivisection, but it did require that practitioners be licensed, use anesthetic, and never cut open an animal more than once.

The two young Swedish women who crashed the physiology lecture at University College London had tried unsuccessfully to convict their professor, William Bayliss, under the act. Instead, his countersuit for libel prevailed. Eventually, the Brown Dog Riots would consume London, and the vivisection debate would help crystallize Victorian attitudes about the special place of cats and dogs in society. The medical students never succeeded in destroying the statue of the brown dog, but in 1910 the Battersea town council grew tired of paying to police the monument. In the middle of the night on March 10, workmen guarded by 120 police officers carried the bronze terrier away and hid it in a bicycle shed. A blacksmith later smashed it to pieces.

In 1985, the National Anti-Vivisection Society and the British Union for the Abolition of Vivisection erected a replacement statue. But this new dog was not the defiant martyr of yore. He was a playful mutt, ears drooped, head cocked, ready to be cuddled. The world of the pet had changed dramatically in seventy-five years.

All Dogs Go to Heaven

The bat mitzvah of Fifi Katz was a gala affair. Its attendees danced to live music on the sand of a California beach in the summer of 1994, ate gourmet Greek food, and sang songs from *Fiddler on the Roof*. The gifts were nearly as grand. One person had planted a tree in Israel. Another brought freshly cut roses. Yet another had purchased a video of birds and butterflies—sure to be appreciated by the guest of honor, a thirteen-month-old cat. As a modified version of "Sunrise, Sunset" filled the air ("Is this the kitty that I carried? Is this the little cat at play?"), Fifi's "father" admitted that the ceremony was mostly for fun. Yet he said there was a serious side as well: though Fifi may not have been a human child, the man and his wife wanted to welcome her into their family traditions. It wasn't quite the lavish festival of Bastet, but cats hadn't been this revered in more than 2,000 years.

The modern era of the pet began shortly after the Brown Dog Riots of the early 1900s; yet it was foreshadowed by the death of a dog named Nero in 1860. Run over by a butcher's cart on a West London Street, the white Maltese mix suffered for months before his owner, the notable Scottish letter writer Jane Welsh Carlyle, could bring herself to have him put to sleep. "I grieve for him as if he had been my little human child," she wrote to a friend. In her note, Carlyle speaks of her "belief in the immortality of animal life" and of her desire to know if she would see Nero again in the hereafter. "What is become of that little beautiful, graceful *Life*?" It's a question a lot of pet owners were beginning to ask.

The rise in sentimentality toward dogs and cats in the nineteenth century didn't just conflict with the barbarism of vivisection; it clashed with traditional notions of heaven itself. Once an ethereal plane where the departed communed with the almighty, heaven had become a tangible paradise, one populated with familiar scenes of garden and home, and family and friends waiting at the welcome. But where were the pets? Orthodox Christianity, for one, was firm on the issue: only man had an eternal soul. That didn't sit well with a culture increasingly enamored of its cats and dogs. Pet epitaphs began to question the will of God openly. "Shall he whose name is love, deny our loving friends a home above?" read a contemporary gravestone belonging to a dog named Tiddy.

Why was it so important that pets be allowed into the heavenly home? Perhaps because they had become such an integral part of the earthly one. In her rich history *Pets in America*, Katherine Grier writes that the middle-class abode became a symbol of late-nineteenth-century America. It was a domestic haven, a refuge from an increasingly industrial world. Father paid the bills, and mother made sure her children grew up civilized. *The Four Stages of Cruelty* had struck a nerve. Women believed that if they didn't teach their sons and daughters kindness from an early age, they would grow into savage human beings. "The private household," writes Grier, "became a laboratory for building better humans."

If home was a laboratory, then pets were the guinea pigs. Children who were kind to their animals would surely grow into respectable adults. But how to teach them? Fortunately for mom, ample advice was cropping up in books, newspapers, and magazines. In an 1865 essay titled "Aunt Esther's Rules," famed abolitionist and author of *Uncle Tom's Cabin* Harriet Beecher Stowe admonished children not to abandon cats and dogs in the woods, where they would "wander homeless, to be starved, beaten, and abused." In other stories, Stowe drew analogies between pets and slaves and even brought religion into the mix. "The care of the defenseless animal creation," she wrote, "is to be an evidence of the complete triumph of Christianity." A few decades later, Margaret Marshall Saunders became the first Canadian to sell more than 1 million copies of a book when she penned *Beautiful Joe*, the story of a horribly abused mutt who finds a loving home. The novel was one of the earliest to be told from a dog's perspective. Mark Twain followed with his own pet "autobiography," 1904's *A Dog's Tale*. "My father was a St. Bernard, my mother was a collie, but I am a Presbyterian," Twain wrote. "I was the same as a member of the family."

Popular paintings reinforced the importance of pets in domestic life. In 1868's *The Season of Strength*, a man coming home from work is greeted by his wife, his children, and the family dog. And in an 1863 lithograph titled *An Increase in Family*, the population of a home is augmented not just by a new baby but by a litter of kittens.

It's no wonder that people began to expect—even demand—that their pets join them in the afterlife. To pave the way, they started giving their cats and dogs proper burials, complete with prayers and small caskets. Some, in a callback to prehistory, even tried to be buried with their pets. An 1888 *New York Times* article reports the story of a Mrs. Mary A. Bell, who asks that her dog be interred in the Bronx's distinguished Woodlawn Cemetery. The befuddled undertaker contacts an "astonished statistician" at the Board of Health, who eventually grants a permit. Mrs. Bell then places the canine (which was being kept on ice) in a casket—"similar to one that would be used in the burial of a child . . . covered with embossed velvet and lined with heavy white satin"—and lays him to rest in a plot she also intended for both her and her husband. A few years later, America's first pet burial grounds would be established when a Manhattan veterinarian allowed a client to bury her dog in his apple orchard. The location became the Hartsdale Pet Cemetery, today the final resting place of nearly 70,000 animals.

The long-standing religious barriers between man and his companion animals had finally crumbled. In her bestselling 1883 novel, *Beyond the Gates*, American author Elizabeth Stuart Phelps Ward imagines a trip to the great beyond. "We stopped before a small and quiet house," she writes. "It was shielded by trees. . . . There were flowers . . . and I noticed a fine dog sunning himself on the steps." Heaven was ready for pets.

Pets had entered the celestial home, but back on earth they still spent most of their lives outdoors. Cats prowled barns and sheds; dogs were chained up in the yard or confined to doghouses. Blame fleas and ticks. Before the advent of medicated soaps in the 1880s, it just wasn't sanitary, or aromatically acceptable, to keep animals indoors. Early shampoos (detergents made with carbolic acid and later DDT) may not have been the safest, but they got the job done. A late-nineteenth-century advertisement for Ricksecker's twenty-five-cent dog soap promised to make your mutt "handsome as a picture—no fleas, no smell."

The products seem to have worked. Photographs from the late 1800s show fewer cats and dogs in the yard and more in the living room. Felines curl up on sofas, and canines slumber next to baby cribs; they also migrate from the floor to arms and laps, positions typically reserved for children. Books and, later, movies featured similar scenes. Pets even moved into the presidential mansion. Abraham Lincoln reportedly fed Tabby, the first White House cat, under the table—with official cutlery. "If the gold fork was good enough for former President James Buchanan," he told his objecting wife, "I think it is good enough for Tabby." Teddy Roosevelt's mutt, Skip, was also a frequent presence in the executive home, often appearing seated on his master's lap. Dogs in particular helped presidents identify with the common man; they also reinforced the ideal of a pet in every home.

Once pets came inside, they were expected to behave like their human counterparts. Early manuals had focused on training dogs to hunt, but when Fido moved indoors, they began offering advice on how to keep him from soiling the rug. One 1878 book spoke of "educating" the dog so that he would become "an agreeable inmate to all members of the household." Cats, meanwhile, needed a toilet. Unfortunately, kitty litter wouldn't be invented until 1947. Until then, owners had to use dirt and torn-up newspaper, which may explain why it took cats longer to become indoor pets.

The move inside turned cats and dogs into vicarious consumers. They didn't just need leashes and litter pans; they required a whole host of new products to keep them fit and entertained. Enter the neighborhood pet shop, a cramped and cluttered store that sold wicker dog beds and rubber chew toys, scratching posts and balls filled with catnip. The "Tug-o-War Exerciser" would keep your dog's teeth in tip-top shape; the windup toy mouse—"Fun for Kitty!"—was sure to satisfy your cat's hunting instinct. Newspaper advertisements reminded owners that pets needed Christmas presents too, which soon came to include luxury products like doggy sweaters and the "V.I.P. Electric Vibrating Pet Brush." Woolworth's and other department stores eventually got into the game, fostering a further explosion in pet merchandise that would ultimately give rise to today's multi-billion-dollar pet-supply industry.

Pets that were members of the household also needed to be fed like members of the household. No more foraging and table scraps. Spratt's Patent was the first big player on the scene, offering fare such as 1881's "Meat Fibrine Dog Cakes," hard-as-a-rock biscuits made of wheat, beetroot, and beef blood; "Such a friend cannot be treated too considerately!" blared one ad. In 1926, livestock companies like Ralston Purina jumped on the bandwagon, being careful to label their pet products "food" to distinguish them from the "feed" intended for less refined domestic animals. In an echo of the modern pet industry's success during the Great Recession, the pet industry of yore proved surprisingly resilient. Sales of dog food alone doubled during the Great Depression; by 1936, Americans were spending more than $100 million per year on pet food, and the industry had become the nation's second-largest consumer of tin cans.

Food and toys weren't enough, however. Every household member deserved good medical care. Until the early twentieth century, veterinarians had focused almost exclusively on economically valuable animals like cows and horses. But as it became clear that owners were willing to shell out for dog beds and premium cat food, vets started to change their tune. Animal hospitals began to resemble human hospitals. New medications and cutting-edge treatments emerged. Prices skyrocketed. And in perhaps the most significant pet medical development of the twentieth century, cats and dogs began to be spayed and neutered in large numbers. The procedure didn't just thwart unwanted litters. By reducing uncivilized behaviors like spraying, fighting, and humping, it completed the process begun thousands of years ago by domestication. Dogs and cats were now nearly as tame and as innocent as children. We had finally taken the animal out of our pets.

And we needed these pets more than ever before. Cats and dogs started to enter our households when our households themselves began to crumble. As America prospered, couples began having fewer children or none at all, and three-generation homes shrunk to nuclear families and empty nests. Meanwhile, thanks to rising divorce rates and longer life spans, more people were living alone than ever before. Society itself was a lonelier place. As a species, we had always been close to nature; from our days as hunter-gatherers to our millennia of living in close quarters with livestock, animals had been ubiquitous in our existence. When they disappeared from our day-to-day experience, we lost part of ourselves.

All of these trends created an emotional void in our lives, one that cats and dogs began to fill. They became the natural world we had lost touch with, the spouses and children who had disappeared from our homes. So we pampered them like never before. We spent billions on them and brought them to church. We transformed our entire society around them. And why not. These once wild animals, these gods and devils, these friends and companions—they had become our family.

FOUR

Canine Einsteins

The Duke Canine Cognition Center is one of the world's most prestigious dog laboratories, but you'd never know it from the looks. Located at Duke University in Durham, North Carolina, it's just three small rooms in the subbasement of the school's Biological Sciences Building, a faded red-brick structure that stands in a clump of similarly nondescript buildings on the west end of campus. My tour of the facility—a modest lounge, a barren rectangular room, and a narrow alcove filled with cabinets—took all of about thirty seconds. It turns out you don't need much to probe the secrets of the dog's mind.

I had come here to witness the final stage in the transformation of our pets from wild animals into family members. Dogs and cats may have entered our homes, but there's still so much we don't know about them. Are they as smart as we think? Do they love us as much as we love them? We can't truly accept these creatures as family until we can glimpse what's going on in their heads.

I actually got my first peek at the canine intellect a day earlier. I had arrived in the middle of a triple-digit heat wave, and the driver of the mercifully air-conditioned shuttle that picked me up from the airport asked why I was in town. In truth, even I wasn't sure. As a deputy news editor at *Science*, I had noticed that we'd been writing a lot more stories about how dogs think, but I didn't know why. I hoped a trip to Duke would answer some questions. "I'm going to visit a scientist who studies dogs," I told the man, a pale gentleman in his early seventies who spoke with a mellow southern accent. Then, guessing a bit, I added, "He's trying to figure out if dogs are smarter than we thought." The driver laughed. "Heck, of course they're smart," he said. "They're smarter than us!"

As the van plowed along a highway that cut through a dense forest of pine trees, the driver told me about Shadow, a four-year-old Siberian husky he'd adopted from a local shelter. The dog, he said, was a regular canine Einstein. "When I go to bed, I look at him and say, 'Shadow, seven o'clock. Shadow, seven o'clock.' And sure enough, at seven in the morning he barks until I wake up. I don't need an alarm clock!" Shadow, the man claimed, could also ring his doorbell and open the sliding glass doors of his boat. He understood more than thirty words and kept track of his owner's schedule. "When I put my suitcase by the front door, he knows I'm going away for a couple of days, and he just sits at the door and sulks." The dog even knew when he'd done something wrong; when he knocked a plant over or whizzed on the carpet, he turned his head and looked away in guilt. "If human beings were as smart as animals," the driver told me, "we'd be a lot better off." After my visit to Duke, I'd realize he was a lot closer to the truth than he knew.

The Dog Lab

When I arrive at the Duke Canine Cognition Center, the man I'm here to see isn't around. Brian Hare, the biological anthropologist who runs the lab, is sprinting across campus with a cooler full of what he later told me was the "world's largest collection of bonobo pee," scrambling to find dry ice so he could ship the samples to a colleague. Fortunately, three of his graduate students are around, and they volunteer to show me some of their work. They lead me to an empty room, a ten-by-sixteen-foot space with a white tile floor that looks like it has been vandalized by a geometry teacher. Multicolored tape decorates the ground in a variety of shapes and patterns: green brackets float near yellow squares; long red lines balance on red triangles. The students tell me the tape designates places where researchers are supposed to sit or where equipment is supposed to stand. The markings ensure that each experiment is replicated precisely.

As the grads begin to move some chairs into the space, something brown whizzes past my ankles. I've just caught a glimpse of Napoleon, a three-year-old, seven-pound Yorkshire terrier whose glossy tan head and legs flash out from a jet-black body. He's chasing a pint-sized tennis ball, tornadoing around the room and jumping onto the legs and crotch of anyone who crosses his path. The dog belongs to one of the students, Evan MacLean, an athletic thirty-year-old who informs me that the tiny dynamo will be our test subject for the day. My eyes widen. I have a hard time believing that Napoleon can sit still, much less participate in a scientific experiment. But when the tests begin, he becomes as serious as a college student during final exams.

The first experiment doesn't seem like an experiment at all. MacLean walks to one side of the room, stands on a stripe of blue tape, and lobs the mini tennis ball toward the opposite wall. Napoleon darts after it, grabs it in his mouth, and scurries back to MacLean, who has turned his back to the dog. Napoleon walks around to MacLean's front side and deposits the ball. "Good job, Polli!" he says.

Napoleon has just passed a test related to having a theory of mind. That's the ability to intuit how others see the world and even, to some extent, know what they're thinking. Humans develop a more complex form of this ability at about four years of age. In a classic test of developmental psychology, a researcher shows a child where a toy is hidden while his mother is out of the room. When the mother returns, the scientist asks the youngster if his mom knows where the toy is. If the child says yes, he hasn't developed a theory of mind, because he assumes his mother knows the same things he does. If he says no, he has the skill; he realizes his mother's knowledge is different from his own.

What Napoleon did wasn't quite that sophisticated. By dropping the ball in front of MacLean, he demonstrated that he knew where his owner's attention was focused, which is not quite the same as knowing what MacLean was thinking. Had he released the ball behind MacLean, however, it would be a pretty safe bet that the dog had zero theory of mind. Chimpanzees pass a similar test. Place two chimps in a room with a plate of grapes, and the chimp lower on the social totem pole won't grab one until the higher-ranking chimp looks away. The animals also clap their hands and make raspberry noises with their lips when they want to get the attention of a researcher who isn't watching them.

In the next experiment, Napoleon does something chimps can't do, however. MacLean stands near a wall with the dog on a slack leash, while a female graduate student sits on a chair in the center of the room.

She sets two opaque red cups upside down on the floor, one on each side of her. Then, as Napoleon watches intently, a third graduate student enters the room. She places the dog's tennis ball under one of the cups and pretends to place it under the other, obscuring her motions with a small black board so the terrier isn't sure which cup contains the ball. If this were a shell game, the dog would have a fifty-fifty shot of picking the right cup. But the seated graduate student gives him a hand, or, more precisely, a finger. She points to the cup on her right, and when MacLean lets go of the leash, Napoleon runs over to it and retrieves his ball. Over several trials, the dog always goes for the cup that is pointed out. Even when the seated student merely gazes at the correct cup, Napoleon gets the message.

This may seem like a simple test, and, indeed, even one-year-old children pass it. But our closest relatives, chimpanzees, fail miserably. They ignore the human helper, pick cups at random, and rarely score above chance. Brian Hare's lab has become famous for spotting this difference. Napoleon has performed more than just a neat cognitive trick. He has displayed a more complex skill related to the development of theory of mind in children. He wasn't just clued into the pointing student's attention; he had shown behavior consistent with understanding her *intention*. He showed that he realized that the student wanted to show him something, that she had a desire.

That's ultimately why theory of mind is so important. It's what allows us to predict and understand the actions of others, to recognize the difference between a hand raised to give you a high five and one raised to slap you, to know to catch a ball tossed by your father instead of running from it. In short, theory of mind enables us to exist as a society. Without it, we can't learn, teach, or communicate at a high level. "The reason we've made such a huge deal about the pointing stuff is because it's really important for little kids," MacLean tells me. "When kids are one to two years old, they engage in a lot of meaningful social interactions where their parents point at something like a picture frame, and the kid learns the word for that object." This seemingly simple skill, he said, is the foundation for understanding the world around us and interacting with other people. "The reason we're so excited about dogs following pointing is that it's really important for our species." Tiny Napoleon had done something more humanlike than a creature that shares 99 percent of our DNA. And that means that, more than any other animal on the planet, dogs could help reveal how our own intelligence evolved.

When Brian Hare finally arrives at the lab about an hour later, he's still adrenalized from his cross-campus quest to cool bonobo pee. But I'd soon learn that Hare is pretty adrenalized at baseline. He's a fast, frenetic talker given to rapid digressions and sudden bursts of laughter, and whenever he gets excited about an idea—which is often—he gesticulates wildly, and his mop of curly brown hair falls onto his half-shaven face. Even when he's sitting, Hare is in constant motion, bouncing his knees up and down, slapping his chair to emphasize a point, and waving at colleagues as they pass by. He wants to be with you, but he also wants to be in fifty other places.

That energy has served him well. Only thirty-five years old, Hare already oversees seven graduate students, twenty-nine undergrads, and more than 1,000 research animals (none of which, he's proud to say, live in a cage). He rarely stays put, dividing his year between dogs and lemurs at Duke, baboons at the North Carolina Zoo, and chimpanzees on an island in Uganda. And, of course, there are the urinating bonobos, which live in a sanctuary in the Democratic Republic of Congo. Since I visited, he's also become the cofounder and chief science officer of Dognition, an online research project and business venture designed to help owners probe their dog's mental abilities.

Hare tells me he got into studying dogs by accident. He was an undergraduate at Emory University in Atlanta in the late 1990s, exploring the cognitive differences between chimps and toddlers. When he conducted a few pointing tests, he and his advisor, Michael Tomasello, were shocked to learn that toddlers had no trouble understanding what a researcher meant when he pointed to a cup, but chimps were totally perplexed. Tomasello concluded that the ability to follow pointing cues was so advanced it must have only evolved in humans. "But I told Mike, 'Um, I think my dog can do that,'" Hare says. "And that's how it all started."

Back then, almost no one was studying dogs. All those thousands of years of domestication, the thinking went, had corrupted them, at least from a scientific standpoint. Because they were no longer wild animals,

researchers considered them artificial and of limited value. If you want
to know how human intelligence evolved, they said, ask a chimp. Maybe
a dolphin or elephant. But never a dog. Ironically, however, the history
of animal cognition research begins with dogs. And perhaps not surprisingly, it also begins with Charles Darwin.

Darwin came along during a time when animals, thanks largely to the writings of French philosopher René Descartes, were viewed as reflex-driven
machines with nary a mind in their heads. Everything an animal did, every
decision it made, was chalked up to instinct. Only humans possessed true
intelligence.

Darwin didn't buy it. Perhaps it was because he had spent so much of
his life with canines. In her revealing book *Darwin's Dogs*, British journalist Emma Townshend writes that the famed naturalist came from a
family of dog lovers, and Darwin himself was no exception. He owned
at least thirteen throughout his life, including a black-and-white mutt
named Spark—a childhood companion he fondly referred to as "little
black nose"—and a white terrier, Polly, who slept in a pillowed basket
near the fireplace as Darwin inked one of his final books, *The Expression
of the Emotions in Man and Animals*, in which Polly appears frequently.
(Darwin, incidentally, was not a cat person, though as his daughter
Henrietta wrote, "He knew and remembered the individualities of my
many cats, and would talk about the habits and characters of the more
remarkable ones years after they had died.")

Darwin appears to have first begun thinking about the mental ca-
pabilities of dogs when he should have had something far more important on his mind. It was early October 1836, and he had just returned
from his five-year voyage on the HMS *Beagle*, a ship that had ferried
him to the Galápagos Islands. The variety of finches and tortoises there
would eventually help inspire his theory of evolution, but upon arriving home to Shrewsbury in western England, Darwin's first scientific
thought turned to dogs. He wondered whether one of his canines, vicious to everyone else, would remember him. "I went near the stable
where he lived, and shouted to him in my old manner," Darwin wrote.
"[He] instantly followed me out walking, and obeyed me, exactly as if I
had parted with him only an hour before." The experience was clear evidence to Darwin that dogs had long memories—and serious intellects.

In later years, Darwin would postulate that dogs were capable of abstract thought, morality, and even language. Dogs, he wrote, understood human words and sentences, and they responded with barks of eagerness, joy, and despair. If this wasn't communication between the species, what was? The observations affirmed his notions that humans were not unique in having complex minds. "There is no fundamental difference between man and the higher animals in their mental faculties," he wrote.

Darwin's close friend and research associate, George Romanes, took that idea and ran with it—some say a bit too far. A Canadian-born biologist forty years Darwin's junior, Romanes wrote the first book on comparative psychology, an 1883 work titled *Animal Intelligence*. It was early days for the science, and he relied heavily on anecdotes, collecting hundreds of stories from naturalists, zookeepers, and pet owners. In one account, a cat that loved to catch and kill brown rabbits one day brings her owner a small black rabbit, unharmed—proof, according to Romanes, that cats were capable of "zoological discrimination." Other cat tales involved felines that sprinkled bread crumbs to catch birds, opened doors and windows with their paws, and rang parlor bells to get attention. "In the understanding of mechanical appliances," Romanes wrote, "cats attain to a higher level of intelligence than any other animals, except monkeys."

Like Darwin before him, Romanes also glorified the minds of dogs. He related stories of how they could sniff out someone's social status, play tricks on people, and even understand the value of money. "My friend was acquainted with a small mongrel dog," Romanes wrote, "who on being presented with a penny or a halfpenny would run with it in his mouth to a baker's. . . . The dog would accept any small biscuit for a halfpenny, but nothing less than a bun would satisfy him for a penny." The wealth of anecdotes convinced Romanes there was practically no difference between the animal brain and the human one.

Stories were one thing. The first real research into the minds of dogs didn't begin until 1884, when an English banker named John Lubbock, who dabbled heavily in the sciences, published the earliest study on language ability in a nonhuman. That nonhuman was a poodle named Van. Lubbock taught the dog to distinguish between blank pieces of cardboard and those with the words "Food," "Tea," "Water," "Bone," and "Out" written on them. Left to his own devices, Van fetched the "Food" and "Tea" cards far more frequently than the other cards, and since tea was one of the canine's favorite treats, the banker concluded that the dog had learned to communicate with him. Van, "the Talking Dog," became an international celebrity, and in a clear rejection of Descartes, Lubbock wrote, "No one, indeed, I think, who has kept and studied pets . . . can bring himself to regard them as mere machines."

The views of Lubbock and Romanes did not sit well with the European intelligentsia, however, who saw the human intellect as sacred and unique. It was what separated man from the animals and from non-European "savages." A pet that could talk was even worse. The 1909 British short story "Tobermory" reflected the sentiment. In it, a scientist teaches the eponymous cat to speak, but the feline becomes so arrogant and condescending to his owners that they decide to poison him, and the scientist himself is later trampled by an elephant. Lubbock himself suffered a similar indignation. As he hobbled into the English parliament one day, an acquaintance shouted, "Got the gout? That comes of teaching dogs to read!"

Scientists themselves pushed back against the ideas of Lubbock and Romanes. One of the harshest critics was a heavily bearded British psychologist named C. Lloyd Morgan, who believed that even seemingly complex behaviors had simple explanations. He used his own dog to prove his point. Morgan's pooch, a fox terrier named Tony, had developed a neat trick for escaping his master's house. Whenever he wanted to venture out, he nudged his muzzle under the latch of an iron gate that separated the yard from the open road, causing the gate to swing open. To a common observer, the act would have looked like brilliant intuition. But Morgan said it was simply trial and error. He'd been paying attention to Tony long before the dog figured out the latch, and he noticed that every time a dog or cat walked by the gate, the terrier frantically stuck his nose between the bars. If he fidgeted enough, he'd eventually strike the latch, and the gate would swing open. Even then, it took Tony weeks to realize he could go straight for the latch. For the longest time, Morgan wrote, "the relation between means and end did not appear to take form in his mind."

The psychologist eventually developed a principle that came to be known as "Morgan's canon." The theory, a sort of biological Occam's razor, stated that scientists should not propose complex explanations for an animal's actions when a simpler answer would do. The canon set the stage for behaviorism, a school of thought that would rule the field of psychology for much of the twentieth century. Behaviorists essentially said that scientists should focus only on what they could observe, not on the intangibles inside a creature's head. Dogs had literally lost their minds.

Not until the 1970s did an American zoologist named Donald Griffin challenge the behaviorist dogma. Griffin had made his name discovering that bats could navigate by bouncing ultrasonic signals off objects, a sonar-like ability he termed "echolocation." But late in his career, he turned his attention to what he felt was a far more extraordinary ability: animals' capacity to think and reason. Lubbock and Romanes were back, but this time they had hard science on their side. In a series of articles and books, Griffin highlighted new techniques and cutting-edge fieldwork that were showing, for example, that monkeys used deception in their alarm calls and that crows could fashion tools out of twigs. His ideas sparked a scientific revolution and a new approach to studying animal minds, which he dubbed "cognitive ethology."

But what about dogs? The old biases—that they were artificial, that they had been corrupted by domestication—still held. Then, two things happened at around the same time. Brian Hare told his advisor that he thought dogs could best chimps at the pointing test, and a Budapest researcher named Ádám Miklósi was told by his advisor to stop studying fish and start studying dogs. Inspired by the antics of his mutt, Flip, the advisor wanted Miklósi (who was later part of the team that tried to tame gray wolves) to figure out why canines were so smart. Unaware of each other's research, Miklósi and Hare both published work showing that dogs could understand human pointing in 1998. Over the next decade, nearly a dozen labs, from Berkeley to Yale, Kentucky to Austria, began studying the canine mind. The canine revolution had begun.

When Brian Hare opened the Duke Canine Cognition Center in 2009, he worried about getting enough dogs for his studies. Instead, he had the opposite problem. "When we run experiments with kids, sometimes the parents come late, or they don't show up at all," he tells me. "Dog owners come thirty minutes early, and there's a line outside the door." They bring their entire families. They volunteer their friends' dogs. Some owners have driven three hours to be at the lab at 9 a.m. on a Saturday. One woman from Brazil wanted to fly her dog over. By the time I visit, more than 1,000 canines have passed through the lab. "The families are just so excited," he says. "We don't have enough parking spaces for all of them."

After all of those experiments, I expect Hare to tell me how smart dogs are; how, more than any other animal, they hold the key to unlocking the secrets of the human mind. But he tells me something far more surprising. "If you want a smart animal," he says, "select for niceness." Intelligence, it turns out, may be nothing more than a good attitude.

Hare had his epiphany while studying silver foxes in Siberia. Yes, *those* silver foxes—the ones researchers have bred for decades to be as docile as golden retrievers. When Hare first noticed that dogs could follow human pointing and chimps couldn't, he initially thought that they must have simply picked the ability up from hanging around people. The idea made sense. Wolves don't pass the pointing test, and because they're nearly identical to dogs, the difference must lie in cohabitation. But when Hare visited the fox farm in 2002, he found that the domesticated foxes were just as good as dogs at understanding human pointing, even though they'd spent almost no time with people. "The control foxes," says Hare—the ones not bred to be docile—"were too freaked out to participate in the study. When you'd walk by a row of cages, they'd all run to the back. It was like parting the sea. And when they did calm down, they weren't interested in interacting with you." The domesticated foxes were a different story. "Their stress response to people was completely gone. And because of that, they could solve all sorts of problems the other foxes couldn't." As Evan MacLean, Hare's graduate student, explained to me, it's as if domestication tunes an animal into the human radio frequency. Chimpanzees and wolves don't understand pointing because they don't get our station. Dogs, on the other hand, are completely tuned in to us. Indeed, we're the only station they listen to.

Now about this time you may be asking yourself what radio station cats listen to. At least I was. Jasper and Jezebel may not like all of my music, but I don't think they've completely tuned me out. Remarkably, one brave scientist tried to find out: Ádám Miklósi. Though the Budapest researcher has been studying dogs for nearly two decades, he's actually a cat person. Don't expect him to solve the secrets of the feline mind anytime soon, however. "We did one study on cats," he laughed over the phone, "and that was enough."

What Miklósi did was essentially repeat the pointing test I saw with Napoleon—with a few small modifications. His team conducted the experiments in the cats' homes, for example, because he thought a laboratory would freak them out. And he used food instead of toys as bait, because he assumed it would be a better motivator. (Even then, not all of the cats were interested in advancing science. According to Miklósi's research paper, seven of the initial twenty-six "dropped out.") Once a cat was comfortable, a researcher picked up two bowls and showed them to the animal. Then she turned her back, placed food in one of the bowls, and set them down on either side of her legs. Finally, she pointed at one of the bowls, and the owner, who had been holding the cat, released it. Over multiple trials, cats followed the gesture, not the smell; they meandered to the bowl that had been pointed at, performing nearly as well as dogs on the same test.

But in another experiment, Miklósi's team spotted an intriguing difference between cats and dogs. This time the researchers created two puzzles: one solvable, the other impossible. In the solvable puzzle, they placed food in a bowl and stuck it under a stool. Dogs and cats had to find the bowl and pull it out to eat. Both aced the test. Then the scientists rigged the exam. They again placed the food bowl under a stool, but this time they tied the bowl to the stool legs so that it could not be pulled out. The dogs pawed at the bowl for a few seconds and then gave up, gazing up at their owners as if asking for help. The cats, on the other hand, rarely looked at their owners; they just kept trying to get the food.

Are cats not smart enough to realize when a task is impossible? Are they just more persistent than dogs? Perhaps they're simply not fully tuned in to our radio frequency. Unlike chimps and wolves, cats can use the information we give them (that is, they understand what we mean when we point), but unlike dogs they don't actively solicit that information. They're surfing other channels on the dial. And that, ultimately, is what makes them so hard to train.

But back to the Russian foxes. Hare's experiments had shown that the ability to understand a human gesture like pointing—something scientists had regarded as an advanced cognitive skill—required nothing more than a friendly disposition. Dogs and domesticated foxes seem sharp because they're calm enough to pay attention to us. Does that mean that doggy smarts are just an illusion? And if so, what does that say about human intelligence? Quite a bit, it turns out. Humans, you see, may also be a domesticated species. That's a controversial statement in the field of anthropology, but when you look at the facts, it's not so far-fetched. Almost all domesticated animals, from cows to pigs to cats, have a few things in common that wild animals don't share: males and females are about the same size, they store more fat than their wild counterparts, they breed multiple times during the year, and they tend to be pretty laid back. Sound familiar?

Most anthropologists don't use the term "domesticated" to describe people because domestication implies a human hand in the process. But the definition still holds if you consider that people, like cats and dogs, may have domesticated themselves. The idea is that, as we began to settle down in large numbers, we ostracized the most aggressive and antisocial members of our groups (a bit like the Russian scientists prevented the most aggressive and antisocial foxes from breeding). Over many generations, the only people left, for the most part, were those who had traits and behaviors that allowed them to get along with the group. Eventually, we began to understand each other's gestures, we developed a complex theory of mind, and we all became fully tuned in to the human radio station.

If you're still not sold, consider the differences between bonobos and chimpanzees. Though the two species are nearly identical in DNA and appearance, they're miles apart in disposition. Chimps are competitive and can be nasty. They rarely work together, even when it's to their benefit. And they often settle their disputes by killing each other. Bonobos, meanwhile, are the hippies of the primate world. They're passive. They're cooperative. And they've found a better way to settle their disputes: they have sex. Bonobos are, in many ways, a self-domesticated species. And not surprisingly, they score much better on theory-of-mind tests than chimps do. "The differences between chimps and bonobos are completely analogous to the differences between wolves and dogs," Hare tells me. And that's one of the main reasons he studies dogs. If we can learn how their intelligence evolved, we can understand how ours evolved too.

Even scientists like Hare would have stopped studying dogs long ago if all they could do was follow a pointed finger, however. Recent studies

have shown they are capable of so much more. They can recognize objects in photos better than any other animal, evidence of Darwin's claims
of abstract thought. Chaser, a South Carolina border collie, knows more
than 1,000 words, the largest vocabulary of a nonhuman, and she learns
them using one of the same techniques children use to learn words. And
dogs can imitate our actions—walking around a traffic cone, for example,
or sticking their heads in a bucket—up to ten minutes after we've done
them, demonstrating a demanding type of memory called "declarative
memory" that's only be seen in people. Canines, in some ways, are even
smarter than we are. We used them as tools for thousands of years—as
hunters, guardians, and herders—but now they use us. When they're
bored, we provide toys. When they poop, we clean it up. And when they
can't figure out a problem, they look to us for information. We've become
the Internet for dogs.

Are our pooches really smarter than other animals because they
can do all of these things? Of course not, says Hare. Every species has
evolved the skills it needs to survive. "You'd be a horrible goat," he says,
"and I'd be a horrible banana slug." The reason dogs seem so smart is
because they've evolved to live in our world, to tackle the same social
and cognitive problems we have. So, in many ways, when we peer into
the mind of a dog, we're really peering into our own.

The Soul of a Pet

Brian Hare had given me a peek inside the mind of the pet. But I also
wanted a glimpse of the soul. Do dogs and cats feel the same emotions
we do? Are they capable of humor, guilt, and even morality? I knew of
one man who could answer these questions. A man who's been living in
the woods for more than three decades. A man who's published countless books and scientific articles on the emotional lives of animals. A
man I'd eventually go to jail with: Marc Bekoff.

I first heard Bekoff speak in 2010 at a conference in Washington,
DC, on the ethics of animal experimentation. When he took the stage,
his attitude was, Animals have feelings—get used to it. "Caring about
animals isn't radical or extreme," he said. "We don't have to be apolo-
gists for caring and feeling." That attitude pervades all of Bekoff's writing. His books are a mix of anecdotes and personal pleas, of hard science

and animal advocacy. One moment he's writing about an extraordinary event he witnessed in the woods, like magpies sitting vigil over a fallen bird, and the next he's discussing the ethics of tossing an elderly man from a lifeboat instead of a young dog. He's a vegan who talks about "whom we eat" and "who's for dinner" and an award-winning researcher renowned for merging the fields of animal consciousness and animal behavior. When I called him to arrange a visit, his voicemail picked up to the sound of yodeling. I knew I had found my guy.

Bekoff's home is just a few miles from downtown Boulder, Colorado, but he might as well live in a different world. To get there, you leave the coffee shops and strip malls behind and snake your way up the foothills of the Rocky Mountains, navigating a pass that eventually splits off into a one-lane dirt road. Follow that for about a quarter of a mile, through a forest of scrub and spruce, and you'll come upon a cabin of cedar planks and green trim nestled into the side of a hill.

I arrive on a warm, sunny morning in late September under a flawless blue sky. Bekoff is outside when I get there. He's everything I expected. Lean and in his mid-sixties, he's tied his wavy, reddish-gray hair back into a long ponytail with a rainbow scrunchie, revealing a thick silver band clipped to his left ear, and he's wearing a T-shirt, shorts, and white socks tucked into bright yellow Crocs. "It doesn't get much more beautiful than today," I say, shaking his hand. "You never know," he smiles. "There's always tomorrow."

After I remove my shoes, Bekoff leads me into his house. It's half library, half museum—all cozy. Hundreds of books pack the shelves of his living room, sometimes spilling onto couches, coffee tables, and small piles on the floor. The walls are a montage of animal photos—parrots, polar bears, elephants—occasionally broken up by a tie-dyed tapestry or Native American quilt. A tall walking stick is propped near the fireplace. Bekoff has everything he needs here, and he often doesn't leave his home for weeks at a time. Even when he was a professor at the nearby University of Colorado (he retired a few years ago but continues his studies), he rarely came to campus. Much of his research involves observing wild animals, and because he's surrounded by mountain lions, coyotes, and porcupines, his backyard is his laboratory. Sometimes he bikes or roller blades into town, but when heavy snow falls, he doesn't despair. "When I get trapped here, it's a blessing," he says. "I live in heaven."

Our first order of business is a two-mile hike around Bekoff's property. As we walk down the path from his house, he points out some landmarks. "This is where Mommy the Bear hangs out with her two cubs," he says, waving to a hillside. Then, gesturing to a tangle of trees, "This is where Henry the Fox lives." We make our way to a trail that hugs a rushing creek, and I begin to pry into the world of animal emotions. Bekoff came into the field early, at about three years of age by his reckoning. Growing up in Brooklyn (his years in Colorado have softened his accent), he would often ask his parents what a particular animal was feeling or thinking. "When I was a few years old, I yelled at a man who was hitting his dog," he says. "And the man came after my father!"

That worldview would eventually derail Bekoff's plan to become a doctor. While getting his MD and PhD at Cornell University in Ithaca, New York, he worked in a lab that was using cats to study vision. Though he knew he had to euthanize the animals at the end of his experiments, he had begun naming them, a big no-no in science. As he wrote in his 2007 book, *The Emotional Lives of Animals*, "When I went to get 'Speedo' . . . for the final exit from his cage . . . he looked at me and asked, 'Why me?' Tears came to my eyes. Though I followed through with what I was supposed to do and killed him, it broke my heart to do so. . . . I never recovered from that experience." Bekoff dropped out of Cornell and vowed never to harm animals again.

But he still wanted to study them. So the day he left Cornell he phoned a scientist at his alma mater, Washington University in St. Louis, named Michael Fox. It was the early 1970s, and Fox was one of the first proponents of studying the evolution of animal behavior, a field zoologist Donald Griffin would soon dub "cognitive ethology." Fox was specifically interested in canids—a group that includes dogs, wolves, and coyotes—and he invited Bekoff to be his graduate student. Bekoff spent the next few years developing a rigorous methodology for documenting canid behavior, filming animals interacting in large enclosures, and playing the movies back frame by frame while he painstakingly jotted down every nip, yip, and lick. "Twenty minutes of film could take a week to analyze," he says.

The data revealed important insights into why the animals became aggressive and how they maintained their tight social bonds. But what changed Bekoff's life was watching them play. The wolves would chase each other, run, jump, and roll over for seemingly no other reason than to have fun. No one had studied play in animals; biologists considered it a waste of time. But Bekoff was intrigued. "Play is a major expenditure of energy, and it can be dangerous," he says. "You can twist a shoulder or break a leg, and it increases your chances of being preyed upon, especially in the wild. So why do they do it? It has to feel good."

Suddenly, Bekoff wasn't just interested in behavior. He was interested in emotions. After he got his PhD in 1972, he took a faculty position at the University of Colorado and began venturing into the wild, spending seven years studying coyotes in Grand Teton National Park in northwestern Wyoming. As a cognitive ethologist, he documented their hunting, scent marking, and reproductive behaviors. But he added something new to the mix: he tried to get inside their heads. He was three years old again, wanting to know what every animal was thinking and feeling. One day, a high-ranking female coyote disappeared from her pack. After she had been gone for nearly a week, her comrades began sniffing around for her and howling. Bekoff was convinced that they were grieving, and he wrote an essay about the sorrow and longing they must have been feeling. Colleagues told him he was ruining his career. But he published study after study about animal emotions until the idea finally began to catch on. It was the beginning of an approach he would later call "deep ethology," and it would pervade his life's work. "When I study penguins, I am a penguin," he likes to say. "When I study coyotes, I am a coyote." But Bekoff didn't have his true emotional breakthrough until he took a closer look at dogs.

Watch a couple of dogs play, and you'll probably see the same things other people do. They bark; they chase; they wrestle. But that's not what Bekoff sees. After decades of documenting canid behavior, he's uncovered an entire hidden language of play—a complex ballet of subtle signals and nuanced conversations, of rapid-fire communication and tense negotiations. Where most of us see frivolous fun, Bekoff sees honesty and deceit, empathy and morality. I didn't quite believe it. So he showed me.

When we return to his cabin, Bekoff leads me around the side to a single-room guesthouse he's converted into a study. Between it and the main house is a large rectangular pen of wood and wire that looks out over the canyon. He built it thirty years ago so that his dogs would have a place to relax outside without being hurt by the wildlife. ("There have been instances of cougars jumping into dog kennels," he tells me.) Its last occupant, a black-and-tan German shepherd–Rottweiler mix named Jethro, was also Bekoff's final dog, a constant companion on his walks and a frequent character in his books. He's owned eight dogs throughout his life, but putting them to sleep just became too emotionally draining. Still, he's rarely without a visitor; neighbors drop their canines off whenever they go away. "I have dog energy here all the time," he says.

The guesthouse resembles the main house, just on a smaller scale. Books lay scattered about the room—the writings of Darwin, tomes on conservation, philosophies of the animal mind—along with a letter from the Dalai Lama and a framed picture of Bekoff with longtime pal Jane Goodall. In one corner sits a small white TV with a slot for a VHS tape. Bekoff pops something in, and we both sit on the floor to watch. Static turns to black, and white tracking lines buzz briefly across the screen as the audio and video synch up. Then, two dogs appear—a large gray-and-white malamute and a smaller black Lab mix—chasing each other around a dirt driveway. Bekoff shot the video outside the guesthouse almost exactly twenty years before. In his early days, he would invite a friend over and then grab a camcorder while both of their dogs played. He never appears onscreen, but he provides occasional breathless narration as he tries to keep up with the frolicking canines: "September 19th. 9 a.m. Cool out. Sasha and Woody are starting to play."

Watching the video, I see what most people would see: two dogs having a good time, leaping, mouthing, teasing, tackling, chasing, panting. But when Bekoff slows the speed down so that the movie crawls from frame to frame, I observe a whole new world. I notice, for example, Sasha—the malamute—crouching on her forepaws and sticking her butt up in the air, a yoga-like pose she seems to be fond of striking, usually right before or after she lunges at Woody. Bekoff calls this the "play bow," and in the language of play, it's one of the most frequently used words. It's a warning and an apology, an instigation and a clarification. Dogs often do it right before they nip ("I'm going to bite you, but I'm just fooling around") or right after some particularly aggressive roughhousing ("Sorry I knocked you over—I didn't mean it").

I also notice Sasha leveling the playing field. Though she's much bigger than Woody, she often rolls on her back to give him the strategic advantage, and she lets him jump on her far more than she jumps on him. This "self-handicapping," Bekoff explains to me, keeps play fair. Sasha could have easily overpowered Woody, but what fun would that be? Other blink-and-you'd-miss-them behaviors, from a sudden shift of the eyes to a particular wag of the tail, are also part of the rich communication of play, ensuring that everyone has a good time and no one gets hurt. "It's amazing how much you miss," says Bekoff, "if you don't know what you're looking at."

For him, these play signals are just the surface of something much deeper. They're a code of conduct, a set of rules that differentiate right from wrong, good from bad. Breaking them elicits surprise, as when Woody bites Sasha too hard and she cocks her head and squints, as if to say, "Hey, that's not fair!" Such infractions can lead to fights, or worse. In the wild, coyotes that don't play by the rules are ostracized from their pack; without the ability to share food and find mates, many die a slow and lonely death. Bekoff calls this rule of law "wild justice," and by adhering to it, dogs show morality, a mind-set once thought to be uniquely human.

Even morality hints at something deeper, however. To enforce moral conduct, dogs must be able to experience a spectrum of emotions, from indignation to anger, guilt to jealousy. They must also be able to read these emotions in others, distinguishing accident from intent, honesty from deceit. And indeed, recent studies by other scientists have found evidence of these abilities. In one experiment, researchers placed two dogs that had been trained to shake hands side by side, but they only rewarded one for performing the trick; the unrewarded dogs stopped participating, a sign that they had a sense of inequity. Other studies have revealed that dogs yawn when we do and that they pay more attention to people they think are crying, both displays of empathy rare in the animal kingdom. Dogs have even been shown to be pessimistic: when a group of canines in a study learned that a bowl placed on one side of the room contained a treat and a bowl on the other side contained nothing, some just sat there when the bowl was placed in the center of the room; they figured it was empty and didn't waste their time. These same dogs were more likely to howl and tear up the house when their owners left for work, possibly because they didn't believe their masters would return.

Today, hundreds of articles have been published on animal emotions. Bekoff isn't surprised at the number, just that it took scientists so long to catch up. After all, if cats, dogs, and other creatures share so many of our other characteristics, shouldn't they share our feelings as well? To deny this, says Bekoff, is just bad evolutionary biology. And speaking of evolution, just as studying canine cognition gives us a window into how our own intellect evolved, the same holds for studying canine emotions. Work like Bekoff's could ultimately help reveal how our emotions became the social glue that helped us build a civilization based on laws and cooperation, empathy and altruism. Play may seem a frivolous behavior, but because it's not simply a survival reflex, it provides the best opportunity to explore who the animal really is, to peer into its soul. "When we study play in dogs," Bekoff says, "we study ourselves."

Bekoff and I chat a bit longer and then hop into his old Subaru Outback and head over to the Boulder County Jail. He's going to let me sit in on a class he teaches on animal behavior. I'm nervous. I've never been inside a jail before. But then, you know how this story ends.

Despite everything Marc Bekoff showed me, it's entirely possible that all of these doggy emotions are just in our minds. A little over a decade ago, a graduate student named Alexandra Horowitz sat with Bekoff as I had, watching dog videos, while he taught her the language of canine play. Eventually, she conducted her own experiments, spending hours in New York's Central Park filming canines frolicking with each other and with their owners. She found that in order for people to enjoy playing with their animals, they had to ascribe certain thoughts and emotions to them. They had to believe that their dog was being sneaky when he tried to steal a ball from behind them, for example, or that he loved nothing more than a good game of tug-of-war. This so-called anthropomorphism, Horowitz found, is critical to our bond with pets. But that doesn't mean it's real.

Take the guilty look. Like the airport shuttle driver who told me his dog Shadow knew when he'd done something wrong, most owners say they can spot guilt in their dogs: the drooping head and tail, the avoid-ing of eye contact, the slinking away. But Horowitz found that it was all a ruse. In a 2009 study, she visited the homes of several owners and asked them to leave the room while their dogs sat in front of a forbid-den biscuit. Sometimes the canines ate the treat; sometimes they didn't. Regardless, if scolded the dogs were far more likely to display behaviors their owners associated with guilt, whether or not they had misbehaved.

Does this mean that dogs don't experience true guilt? No, Horow-itz told me over the phone. But it does show how desperate we are to form that connection, to believe that our pets feel the same things we do. Chalk it up to their wild ancestry. Once dogs and cats became do-mesticated, they couldn't truly enter human society until we believed they were capable of the same thoughts and emotions we were. "We were dealing with formerly wild animals that we suddenly had a lot of contact with," she said. "We could be alarmed by that, or we could imagine that their experience was similar enough to ours that they were going to con-tinue to participate in this relationship rather than suddenly turn on us."

It's a pact that has only grown stronger over time. Today, we anthro-pomorphize because we need to believe that all of the love, attention, and money we pour into our pets is worth it. That the expensive veteri-nary procedures, the doggy day care, and the shared funeral plots make sense. That all of this is somehow reciprocated in their feelings for us. "We've created this imaginary world," Horowitz said, "and whether it's true or not, it's intact as a world."

This is the world we live in today. A world where wolves and wildcats have become our closest companions. A world where soulless automa-tons have become thinking, loving beings. A world where pets have be-come family. But the borders of this world extend far beyond our homes. Cats and dogs are also becoming family in the eyes of the law.

II
PERSON

FIVE

The Eye of the Storm

URGENT—WEATHER MESSAGE . . . DEVASTATING DAMAGE EXPECTED . . . HURRICANE KATRINA . . . A MOST POWERFUL HURRICANE WITH UNPRECEDENTED STRENGTH . . . MOST OF THE AREA WILL BE UNINHABITABLE FOR WEEKS . . . PARTIAL TO COMPLETE WALL AND ROOF FAILURE IS EX-PECTED . . . ALL WINDOWS WILL BLOW OUT . . . AIRBORNE DEBRIS WILL BE WIDESPREAD . . . AND MAY INCLUDE HEAVY ITEMS SUCH AS HOUSEHOLD APPLIANCES AND EVEN LIGHT VEHICLES . . . PERSONS . . . PETS . . . AND LIVESTOCK EXPOSED TO THE WINDS WILL FACE CERTAIN DEATH IF STRUCK . . . POWER OUTAGES WILL LAST FOR WEEKS . . . WATER SHORT-AGES WILL MAKE HUMAN SUFFERING INCREDIBLE BY MOD-ERN STANDARDS . . . THE VAST MAJORITY OF NATIVE TREES WILL BE SNAPPED OR UPROOTED . . . DO NOT VENTURE OUTSIDE!

These were some of the words that greeted Fay Bourg on the morning of Sunday, August 28, 2005. Katrina, once a mere thunderstorm off the coast of Africa, had crossed the Atlantic, growing stronger and angrier as it went. By the time the National Weather Service issued its bulletin, the storm had swelled into one of the most powerful in US history, a Category 5 hurricane 500 miles wide, whipping winds around its eye at 170 miles per hour as it barreled toward the Gulf Coast. At 9:30 a.m., New Orleans mayor Ray Nagin ordered a mandatory evacuation of the city. But Bourg couldn't leave her apartment in nearby St. Bernard Parish. She didn't have a car, and buses weren't taking pets. Short and thin, in her early forties with sunken eyes and ruffled black hair, Bourg refused to abandon her dog, Hunter. The little brown mutt was the closest family she had. So she leashed him up, held him tight, and braced for impact.

Katrina's first rains began to fall on New Orleans that evening. Then came the winds. Trees swayed; houses shook. The hurricane made landfall early the next morning. Though it was now down to a Category 3, it was still a monster. Howling, hundred-mile-an-hour gales stripped shingles off roofs, snapped trees like twigs, and shattered hotel windows, sucking beds and desks into the sky. Lashing rain, falling at an inch per hour, created a deafening din as it pounded roofs and aluminum siding. Lights flickered out, phones went dead, and streets became rivers. Meanwhile, muscled by Katrina's winds, a wall of water charged its way up the Mississippi River–Gulf Outlet Canal, a seventy-six-mile-long shipping channel that led straight into the heart of the city. Levees that were supposed to shield St. Bernard tore open, unleashing billions of gallons of water into the parish. Outside Bourg's second-floor apartment, the deluge was rising fast. She grabbed Hunter and scrambled to the top of her building. By 7:50 a.m. on Monday, 95 percent of St. Bernard was underwater. Bourg's roof was now one of thousands of small brown islands in a rapidly filling lake.

Like many of her neighbors, Bourg anxiously waited for help, still holding Hunter close. Finally, a boat arrived—but it was not the salvation she hoped for. The rescuers reached out to her. She said she would only get in if she could take Hunter. The men agreed, but when both were in the boat, they tossed the dog overboard. Bourg lunged after him, but the rescuers held her down and tied her hands. When Hunter tried to scramble back onboard, the men pushed him back. Then they sped away, Bourg screaming as the dog faded into the distance.

It's unclear where Bourg spent the next few days. The rescuers may have dropped her off in the chaos of the Superdome in downtown New Orleans, where tens of thousands of people sweltered for days with almost no food or water, sleeping among piles of garbage and excrement as they waited for Federal Emergency Management Agency (FEMA) buses to arrive. Or she may have found herself on an unsubmerged strip of Interstate 10, stranded with 4,000 other evacuees as they huddled with their few belongings while bodies rotted close by in near triple-digit heat. But eventually, Bourg, dehydrated and skeletal, was airlifted to a hospital in San Antonio, Texas. That's where she began her search for Hunter.

Bourg told her story to anyone who would listen. Hunter, she said, wasn't just her best friend; he was her ears, barking to alert her to dangers when she had become hearing impaired. He was also easy to spot: a one-year-old beagle-collie mix with a frizzy tail that curved into an upside-down U, and front legs much shorter than his back ones, which caused him to hop like a rabbit. A chaplain at the hospital was so moved by Bourg's account, she began posting it on several Katrina-related websites: "HIGH PRIORITY RE: DEAF KATRINA VICTIM'S HEARING DOG . . . PLEASE TRY to rescue him. . . . She's heartbroken! If you have any information, my home phone is . . . Thanks and God bless you!" The chaplain even hitched a ride to Louisiana to search for Hunter, but she couldn't find him at any of the temporary shelters that had been set up.

A few days later, a post appeared on Petfinder.com, an adoption website that was helping Katrina victims locate their lost animals. Under a picture that resembled Hunter was the following message: "This pet was transferred from Gonzales Lamar-Dixon Shelter on 9-13-05 and is NOW LOCATED AT: Calcasieu Parish Animal Shelter . . . Animal has BROWN collar. . . . Anxiously awaiting owner pickup!! . . . Your pet is in the rescue system and being cared for at this shelter!" Neither Bourg nor the chaplain saw it.

A year passed. Bourg was now living in a cramped FEMA trailer in St. Bernard Parish. One day an organization called Stealth Volunteers contacted her. The online community had been scouring the Internet in an attempt to reunite Gulf Coast residents with their lost pets, and it had matched up the Petfinder entry with the chaplain's posts. What's more, it believed it had tracked Hunter down to a humane society in Marin County, California. The society had flown in more than 1,000 cats and dogs from shelters in Louisiana, Texas, and Mississippi, and Hunter seemed to match the description of an animal in its database. When Bourg contacted the humane society, however, representatives told her that the dog had long since been adopted. Even if the canine was Hunter, there was nothing it could do. Legally, dogs are property, and once ownership is transferred, the adoption is final. Bourg kept searching for Hunter, but she never found him.

In some ways, she was lucky. Nearly half the Gulf Coast residents who didn't evacuate during Katrina stayed because of their pets—and many of them died, killed in storm-shattered homes, drowned in the ensuing floods, or broiled to death in attics as they waited for rescue. Yet Bourg never recovered from the guilt of leaving Hunter behind. "I've been through a lot in my life, and the dog's been there for me, and he's part of my family," she told a Florida television station in 2006. "I just feel like I'm so lost without him." In April 2008, having moved out of her FEMA trailer into an unfurnished apartment just a few miles from her former home, Bourg took a lethal overdose of sleeping pills. A few months later, a final post appeared on Help Bring Hunter Home, a blog created to reunite the woman with her dog. "PEACE TO YOU FAY," it read. "May Hunter bring you many wet loving kisses when you meet at 'The Rainbow Bridge.'"

The Animal Rescuers

Seven years after Hurricane Katrina, St. Bernard Parish is a different world from the one Fay Bourg inhabited. Where houses once stood, now there are just concrete foundations. What once were neighborhoods today are vast fields of grass. The few homes that remain are lonely out-posts in an urban wilderness. Shopping centers are vacant and hollowed out. Strip malls are stripped bare. "This was all populated," says the woman driving me around. "And now there's nothing."

I had planned on being here a week earlier. I wanted to visit New Orleans on the seventh anniversary of Katrina. But the day before I was scheduled to depart, Hurricane Isaac zeroed in on the city, eerily following the path Katrina had taken in 2005. Fortunately, Isaac was a much weaker storm. Still, I had to reschedule my visit. I arrived a few days later, landing in a city that, except for a few lingering power outages and dead streetlights, was no worse for the wear. At least, no worse than the devastation Katrina had already visited upon it. My plan was to fig-ure out why incidents like Fay Bourg's had taken place and what was being done to prevent them from happening again. Almost everyone

I talked to told me to start with an organization called Animal Rescue New Orleans—specifically with its leader, Charlotte Bass Lilly. She was the one showing me around the desolation of St. Bernard. But there was much more to tell.

I had met Bass Lilly a couple of days earlier when I first flew into the city. ARNO is about a fifteen-minute drive from the airport and six miles west of downtown. It's my first destination as I hop into a rental car late on a Tuesday morning. The sun has yet to achieve full blaze, but the air is already hot and sticky, and the car's air conditioner struggles to overcome it. After a few minutes, I begin double checking my map. ARNO is essentially an animal shelter, but it's located in the middle of an industrial area of the city. On the way, I pass warehouses that are home to everything from plastics manufacturers to construction equipment. Even when I hit ARNO's address, I'm not sure I'm in the right place. The shelter is almost indistinguishable from the buildings that surround it. Made of brick and aluminum, it looks like a giant garage from the outside. Two small, weathered school buses bookend the driveway. Propane tanks are lined up next to a large dumpster. I wouldn't have been surprised if someone jumped out to change my oil.

Instead, I'm greeted by dog walkers. Three middle-aged women wearing dark blue T-shirts—a stark yellow "ARNO" in block letters on the front and "Animal Rescue Volunteer New Orleans" on the back—are being dragged by a couple of pit bulls and a chocolate Lab mix over concrete sidewalks and gravel parking pits, the closest they're going to come to a city park. Other volunteers disappear inside the warehouse. Mop buckets roll in; litter boxes fly out. Someone else is refilling water and food bowls in a makeshift kitchen under a white tent. It is by far the most active building on the street.

Bass Lilly is an hour late. She has been up at the nearby Jefferson Parish Animal Shelter collecting donations from a PetSmart Charities truck, which had driven into town to help with Hurricane Isaac relief efforts. Jefferson got first dibs; ARNO could take whatever was left. Unlike other shelters in the area, ARNO is completely run by volunteers. Even Bass Lilly, the executive director, isn't paid for her work. That means the organization has to scrounge for every penny, prescription, and puppy bowl. None of this bothers her. When she returns from Jefferson Parish, she arrives as if she's just come back from the world's greatest scavenger hunt. "It's Hurricane Charlotte!" shouts one of the volunteers as Bass Lilly pulls into the driveway, her blue station wagon packed with supplies. She hops out and begins unloading food bowls and kennel crates. "You won't believe it, Ginnie. It's like a treasure chest," she says, turning to Ginnie Baumann-Robilotta, ARNO's medical and intake coordinator. "Half a football field of stuff. They've got disposable litter boxes made of fiberboard. It's probably $50,000 worth of inventory!"

Charlotte is wearing the same ARNO T-shirt as everyone else. It's a uniform she dons with pride, its lack of adornment a symbol that her organization is here to do one thing and one thing only: save pets. She's built for the job. Sixty-two and stocky, she wears brown shorts and hiking boots; two bushy black ponytails, cascading down from a tightly worn blue baseball cap, drape her face. She notices that my rental car has out-of-state plates. She's always on the lookout for that: people who came to town after Katrina to help rebuild and decided to stay. "Well come on in, baby!" she says, motioning me into the warehouse. "Let's give you the grand tour."

We walk inside, with Ginnie, forty-seven with pale skin and light brown hair clipped back in a bun, in tow. The interior of the shelter is as industrial as the outside. The main section is an expansive garage with a twenty-foot ceiling. Supplies crowd the front: giant bags of puppy chow, cans of cat food, and boxes of leashes, bowls, and bedding are stacked on plywood shelving from floor to roof. Even the recesses near the top of the garage are filled with stuff; cat carriers and cleaning products sit on tall closets under florescent lights. Not an inch of space is wasted.

In the back is row after row of black wire dog kennels, six by five feet and filled with barking mutts of all shapes and sizes, forty-five in all. Charlotte knows each of their stories, and she shouts them to me over the oppressive hum of giant floor fans that keep the garage cool and somewhat stink-free. "This is Magnolia," she says, pointing to a brown German pointer mix. "We found her on the streets of New Orleans East. She's got a neurological problem that makes her wobble when she walks, but we're going to take care of her." Next, we stop at a larger kennel filled with six medium-size white mutts. "These are the Tennessee Six," says Charlotte. They're part of a group of twenty-two feral dogs found on a farm in Jackson. ARNO volunteers drove eight hours each way to get them; the organization is one of only a few in the country that rehabs wild dogs. Other kennels are filled with canines rescued from dog fighting or bad breeders. Some are blind, others weak or elderly. "We take the animals no one else will take," Charlotte says. "The injured, the too old, the too young." And they don't euthanize any of them. The only No Kill operation in the region, ARNO won't even ship its animals to other shelters, a common practice to free up space. "We're too particular about the final destination," she says. "We don't know what will happen to them."

Our last stop in the dog section is Duke, a black-and-brown shepherd with a good dash of Chow Chow. The mutt had belonged to an eighty-four-year-old gentleman Ginnie refers to as "Mr. Leroy" who lived in the low-income Gert Town section of New Orleans. When his home flooded after Katrina, he waded to a highway overpass with his dog swimming behind. The two held out almost four days for help, but when rescuers came, they wouldn't take the canine. Mr. Leroy was finally able to return after several weeks; the dog was still alive, having been fed by ARNO volunteers. A year later, she gave birth to puppies and disappeared. The man kept one, naming him Duke. But like many victims of Katrina, Mr. Leroy, a security guard at a local school, had trouble making ends meet in the aftermath of the storm. He thought he'd have to give Duke away, but ARNO stepped in, adding the man to its Pet Retention Program, a group of about sixty families it's been offering assistance to ever since the hurricane. ARNO drops off pet food, pays for vet care, and even works with landlords to lower rents. "Most of these people will say, 'No way am I taking anything from anybody,'" Charlotte tells me. "But they'll give up their pride for their animals." Mr. Leroy died a few months ago, and ARNO took Duke. Ginnie put him up on the shelter's website and Facebook page, like she does for all the cats and dogs. "Duke adored Mr. Leroy and Mr. Leroy adored Duke," read the posting. "It's up to you to finish the story."

ARNO's cats are housed in a quieter place, a section of the shelter that used to be a reception area back when all of this was a welding shop. A narrow white room is stacked with cages on both sides, leaving little space for navigation. Inside the cages, cats crowd hammocks, which hang above litter boxes to maximize space. At one point, ARNO housed three hundred felines; now it's down to sixty-five. There's Huey P. Long, a gray-and-white kitten thrown out of a speeding car on the eponymous expressway, and Dali Nissan, an Abyssinian mix found on the grounds of a car dealership. "Some of our animals have weird names," laughs Charlotte. "But once you adopt out over 7,000 cats and dogs, you run out of normal ones." A list of five hundred volunteers keeps the shelter running. "Some days, thirty-five to forty people show up," says Ginnie, "others, just five or six."

On the way out, we pass a whiteboard marked with the names of every animal housed at ARNO, noting how many times they've been walked or had their cages cleaned, who gets what medication, who's on a special diet. Next to it is one of the only bare spots of floor I've seen during the entire tour. "That's where four of us camped out last week during Isaac; we took shifts of two hours of sleep to keep the generators running," says Charlotte. "Someone had to watch over these animals."

After the tour, Ginnie and I climb into Charlotte's station wagon, and the three of us head to what Charlotte promises will be an authentic New Orleans lunch. Ginnie immediately gets on her cell phone, and I soon realize she's much more than ARNO's medical and intake coordinator; she's the reason the operation has been able to stretch its limited funds as far as it has. "Sure, we'll take it!" she says, then hangs up. She tells us she's been chatting with a woman who just lost her cat to thyroid cancer. The woman was asking if ARNO wanted the feline's leftover medication. "Whatever people give us, we'll take," says Ginnie. She's set up a wish list on Facebook and Amazon. Some people send money; others drop off food. Cleaning supplies, the giant fans, even building materials—all come from donations. "I hear Home Depot is giving away twenty-five-dollar gift cards to nonprofits," Charlotte says. Ginnie gets back on the phone. "Twenty-five dollars is twenty-five dollars," she smiles.

We pull into Charlie's Seafood, a baby blue shack on the side of the road not far from the shelter. Charlotte doesn't know the waitress, but she chats with her like they are old friends. "Hey, baby, how y'all doin'? How's your house and home? Is your power back on?" We sit down, and Charlotte orders us the shrimp rémoulade and seafood gumbo appetizers. Then, despite my attempts to order a ham sandwich, she convinces me to get the pulled-pork po' boy. "You gotta' have somethin' you can't eat in Baltimore!" she laughs.

As we settle into our meal, guitar and harmonica flowing from overhead speakers, Charlotte tells me how it all began. She grew up as an army brat, moving from place to place until her parents settled in New Orleans when she was in grammar school. She had always loved animals but never thought of making it a career. Instead, she started her own business, running a design and marketing company for banks, concert producers, and other clients. She earned good money, and in the late 1970s she and her husband moved into the Lower Garden District, a nouveau riche area of the city characterized by its grand Victorian homes—and its feral cats. "Within my block, there were over two hundred of them, some sick and dying on the streets," Charlotte says. "I told my husband, 'I can't stand seeing this. We're going to trap them all, spay and neuter them, and fix them up.' He freaked out, but I said, 'Listen, we don't have any children. We can do this.'" There was just one problem: she had no idea how to catch the animals. "I didn't know they sold traps for cats. So I did the Spanky and Our Gang thing, with cardboard boxes propped up on a stick tied to a string." Surprisingly, her primitive methods worked. Within two years, she had gotten every feral on the block fixed.

Charlotte was hooked. "I thought about going back to school, but I liked helping animals too much." So she contacted local rescue groups, spotting them money for vet care and organizing trap-neuter-return efforts throughout the city. "Once I got into rescue work, I realized there were other crazy people like me," she laughs. "I wasn't the only nut." Eventually, the mayor asked her to be part of a task force to deal with the city's stray animal problem. Shortly thereafter, the Louisiana Society for the Prevention of Cruelty to Animals invited her to be on its board, a position she held for nine years. By the time Katrina hit, Charlotte was a well-known figure in the animal rescue community. But the storm would turn her into a superstar.

On the Sunday before Katrina, Charlotte saw the same apocalyptic National Weather Service bulletin Fay Bourg had. She didn't even think about leaving. "The way I looked at it was, my house had been built in 1885. It had been through more hurricanes than had been recorded," she tells me. "Hurricanes here are like backyard barbeques. You get off work, and it's over after the weekend." By the time she realized Katrina was no ordinary barbeque, it was too late to leave. The storm shattered her windows, soaked her floors, and collapsed part of her ceiling. Yet her neighborhood escaped the flooding that devastated so much of the region. She thought she had been spared.

Then the looters came. "Guys were strutting up the street strapped with ammo and holding AK-47s. They were ransacking houses all around us. We were the only ones who had stayed." Charlotte grabbed her two .38 caliber revolvers and her .357 Magnum. "It was like the Wild West," she says. "They were burning houses down, and it was up to you to protect your family and your property." Eventually, her husband convinced her to leave. "He was worried I'd kill somebody—and I was worried I'd run out of ammunition." On Thursday, the two gathered their eight dogs and four cats and hightailed it out of town. By then, the city was in military lockdown, and roadblocks had been set up, but Charlotte was able to bypass them by convincing the police that she was a veterinarian evacuating her clinic. "It didn't hurt that we had so many animals in the car," she smiles.

Charlotte couldn't stay away for long, however. She got word of a temporary shelter that had been set up at the Lamar-Dixon Expo Center in Gonzales, Louisiana, about sixty miles northwest of New Orleans. The facility—a venue for livestock shows, horse exhibitions, and rodeos—would become the epicenter of the largest animal rescue operation in US history, with hundreds of volunteers and veterinarians descending on it from around the country to care for more than 8,000 animals salvaged from the storm. When Charlotte got there, however, she was only the eighth person on the scene, and pets had just begun to filter in. The Louisiana SPCA was running the show. "They said all they could give me was a ratty old animal control vehicle. I said, 'I'll take it.'" The truck wasn't much, but it had police lights, which allowed Charlotte to get in and out of New Orleans without being hassled. She could now begin the grueling work of saving cats and dogs.

In the days after Hurricane Katrina, New Orleans was a poisonous wasteland. Entire neighborhoods were deserted or submerged, and the water itself had turned black, a noxious mix of dirt, sewage, and gasoline the media dubbed "toxic gumbo." Bodies rotted on cars and porches, flies and mosquitoes clouded the sky, and the intense heat and humidity turned the air into sweat soup. "On the first day, fish were jumping out of the water," Charlotte tells me. "After that, nothing was jumping. Even the snakes were dead."

When Charlotte arrived in town in her animal control truck, she hit the neighborhoods she could drive into. Blocks were eerily silent. Almost everyone had left or been evacuated. Power poles and broken trees littered the sidewalks. Houses had fallen like dominoes, spilling their contents onto the streets. "The city looked like it had been bombed," Charlotte says. "Everything had a white, ashen cast to it. Cars were sitting on their nose. Some were twisted, like a giant god had taken them and turned them into a pretzel." She'd drive as far as she could into the wreckage and holler until she heard dogs barking. Then she'd get out and follow the sounds to a house. Some dogs clung to front doors, pressing themselves against mesh screens, begging to be let inside. Others peeked out from behind splits in blinds. She'd break in, climbing through a window or crowbarring plywood off a door, and leash them. Sometimes pets were hiding in the collapsed parts of houses, or they had been locked in bathrooms with food and a tub full of water. Their owners assumed they'd be back in a couple of days. They didn't realize the city would keep them out for a month. Even those who had tried to evacuate with their cats and dogs were turned away by hotels and Red Cross shelters arbitrarily enforcing no-pet policies. All told, about 250,000 animals were left behind.

Rescuers looking for human victims had already searched many homes. They noted their presence with the now infamous spray-painted X's and other markings on outer walls, hurricane hieroglyphics that signaled when they'd come and whom they'd found—dead or alive. "But they weren't going into the attics," Charlotte says, "and I knew that's where the cats were." Sometimes more than cats. In one, she came across an old man, barely alive. "He had been up there so long, he looked like a Shar-Pei, his skin was just hanging off him." She called the army. "When they strapped the guy to a gurney, he asked in a weak voice if they could stop at a Taco Bell. We smiled and told him there weren't any left."

Every night, Charlotte would return to Lamar-Dixon with a fresh load of dogs and cats. The facility had become a miniature city. Crates

full of pets were stacked deep and wide in several open-air barns, veterinarians performed surgeries on foldable exam tables, and volunteers
raced from intake to triage centers, feeding animals, cleaning cages,
and trying to bathe away the toxic gumbo that stuck to skin and fur.
At night, everyone slept in tents or cars. Every morning at 6:00 a.m.,
Charlotte would gather with a group of other rescuers to receive their
assignments for the day. Thousands of owners were calling in, frantically searching for their lost pets or begging volunteers to drive into the
city to save them. Armed with a list of neighborhoods and addresses,
Charlotte and the others would leave in a caravan at dawn and return
after dusk, dropping off hundreds of new animals, sick, emaciated, and
covered in muck. At one point, more than 2,700 pets were living at
Lamar-Dixon. There was no more room in the barns. They sat in cages
in parking lots.

A week after Charlotte returned to New Orleans, she bought a boat
so she could get into the flooded areas. Eighty percent of the city was
submerged, with some places as much as twenty feet below water. She'd
drive onto an expressway and take an exit that descended into the water.
Then she'd stop, unhitch the vessel, and get in. Sometimes bodies had
washed up on these concrete shores, and she'd have to push them out of
the way so she could launch. "It took months for the city to remove the
corpses," she says. "They'd run out of body bags." Once on the water,
she had to steer around traffic lights and power lines. Most of the street
signs were destroyed or submerged, so she navigated by landmark—the
tower of a Buddhist temple here, a grocery store sign there. Dogs stood
on rooftops, whimpering and wagging as she approached. Some cats
were in the water, clinging to pieces of houses or other debris. Bright
green fungi sprouted from the felt of floating pool tables. Oyster-shaped
mushrooms grew on roofs. Military choppers buzzed overhead.

In mid-September, Charlotte boated to the Gentilly neighborhood
on a personal mission. With her was her close friend, Tana Barth, and
a firefighter. The three were on their way to Tana's house, one of hundreds that had flooded in this northeast corner of the city, a diverse,
middle-class area that borders Lake Pontchartrain. Like so many others,
Tana had refused to evacuate because of her pets. On the Sunday night
before Katrina hit, she hunkered down in her attic with her dogs and

cats, writing her Social Security number on her arm in dark, black ink so that rescuers could identify her body. When she woke up the next morning, the water had almost reached her; tables and chairs were floating just a few inches below the attic. She chopped her way onto the roof, using an axe her mother had always told her to keep there. Eventually, a coast guard helicopter came, and a rescuer rappelled down. With the chopper's winds threatening to blow them all off the roof, Tana grabbed two of her cats—Zephie, who trembled from a neurological condition and couldn't survive alone, and Bucky, who had developed a severe overbite from extensive bottle feeding as a kitten—and held tight as the man hoisted her up.

The coast guard dropped Tana off at the University of New Orleans, high ground just a few blocks from her house. About 1,000 people were waiting there with no food or water, so the police smashed their way into a nearby grocery store to get provisions. Tana got a bologna sandwich but fed most of it to her cats. A few days later, the army showed up to evacuate everyone. They wouldn't take pets. So Tana stuck it out for another day until the coast guard came with boats and allowed her to bring Zephie and Bucky. She eventually made it to Baton Rouge and later to Lamar-Dixon, where, as a veterinary technician, her services were in high demand. There, she ran into Charlotte, and the two headed down to New Orleans to save the rest of her pets.

It had taken Charlotte, Tana, and the firefighter five hours to reach Tana's house. A mile-wide ridge ran through the center of Gentilly, and the trio had to lug the boat across it to get back into the water. By the time they reached their destination, it was getting dark. Tana's home was still submerged to ten feet. She scrambled onto the roof and into the attic. Amazingly, the rest of her cats were still alive. But her two dogs had fallen through the ceiling. She never found them. "It was too late to go back that night, so we camped out on the roof," Charlotte tells me. As the three shared a bottle of vodka in the pitch black, Charlotte noticed lights in the distance. Something was happening on the lakefront.

The next morning, the trio headed out to the where Charlotte had seen the lights, their boat full of cats in carriers. It turned out the army had set up a base there, on the grounds of a church. "When we arrived," Charlotte says, "they hosed us down with a bleach solution."

She noticed the church had a large fenced-in area, and she talked the army chaplain into letting her bring dogs there. Every day she'd drop off food and a few canines, which the army guys would walk and play with, and when the grounds got full, she'd drive in with a refrigerated semi (which she'd procured from a produce company) and take the dogs to Lamar-Dixon. "We called it Operation Puppy Chow."

By mid-October, Charlotte had saved more than five hundred pets. But Lamar-Dixon was winding down. Some of its cats and dogs had been reclaimed by their owners, and the rest—possibly including Fay Bourg's dog, Hunter—were shipped or flown to shelters throughout the country, where they would be held for a few months and then adopted out. Meanwhile, New Orleans and the surrounding areas had been drained, and residents were finally being allowed to come back to their homes, and to their dogs and cats. But the pet crisis was far from over. Thousands of animals were wandering the streets, starving and injured, and thousands more were trapped in houses their owners would never return to.

Ginnie witnessed the suffering firsthand. Unlike Charlotte, she had evacuated before Katrina, driving eight hours to Nashville with her husband, two dogs, and three cats. A trilingual tour guide who had run historical tours in nearly twenty states, including Louisiana, she was able to come back to the city soon after the storm on a self-employed business pass. She immediately began putting out food and water for the stray animals she found. Eventually Ginnie hooked up with a California woman named Jane Garrison, who had driven nearly 2,000 miles to save pets and was now leading a team of volunteers out of an abandoned nail shop just south of downtown. Garrison called the group Animal Rescue New Orleans.

Charlotte had also become involved with the organization, and while she was breaking into houses and making friends with the army, Ginnie and the other ARNO volunteers were setting up feeding stations throughout the region. Every other block, they'd put out a tin pan full of dry food and a gallon jug of water with the top scissored off, eventually establishing thousands of stations over more than two hundred square miles. As the weeks passed, however, the animals were becoming more and more feral. Cats were missing eyes and dragging broken limbs; they cowered under porches and fed on garbage. Fluffy white poodles were now soggy and black; dogs traveled in packs and drank from muddy water, bolting when people came too close. Wolves and wildcats had retaken New Orleans.

The rescuers themselves were beginning to look a bit feral. Besides ARNO, hundreds of other animal volunteers were combing the region, wading through the toxic muck and coming down with rashes, chemical burns, and posttraumatic stress disorder. Charlotte dubbed the water "Katrina Nair" after she noticed that all the hair on her legs had fallen off. Ginnie took her own risks, often venturing into some of the most dangerous parts of the city to feed cats and dogs. One day, while she was setting out a station in a neighborhood known for its drugs and violent crime, a dreadlocked, heavily tattooed man came riding up on his bicycle. She grabbed her scissors, the only weapon she had. The man slowed down as he approached. "The good Lord's going to bless you for what you're doing for these animals," he said and pedaled off.

When Ginnie could, she'd trap and rescue the pets she found on the streets. But she realized that wasn't enough. "At one house, people had left food outside, but the dog was trapped inside. He starved to death. I could hear the flies," she tells me. "After that, I broke into every home." As the weeks wore on, pets that had been locked in bathrooms were dead or barely alive. Dogs were living skeletons, too weak to stand, too dehydrated to bark. Sometimes they managed a weak tail wag when Ginnie broke in. Cats had chewed their way into couches and walls. Blocks once full of the sound of woofing were now chillingly silent.

Overflowing with food and pets, ARNO soon outgrew its nail shop. It moved in with Best Friends Animal Society, one of the nation's major animal welfare groups, which would eventually shelter and transport 6,000 animals from the region. The Utah-based organization had set up a Lamar-Dixon-type facility at an abandoned amusement park northwest of New Orleans. "They didn't know the area," says Charlotte, "so they used us as their trappers." Ginnie and the rest of the ARNO volunteers continued to set out feeding stations and rescue pets. Meanwhile, Charlotte rented a warehouse a few miles west of the city to store extra pet food. By early 2006, Best Friends and other organizations had pulled up their stakes. Lamar-Dixon had closed. And Jane Garrison had returned to California, putting Charlotte in charge of ARNO. All told, rescuers would save 15,000 pets. "But when the big groups left, we said, 'What are we going to do with all of these animals on the streets?'" Charlotte tells me. "The vets still weren't open, and we had no place to put the pets. We couldn't just stop rescuing them." So ARNO moved into the warehouse and began filling it with homeless cats and dogs. That's where it's been ever since. "To this day, our shelter is still set up like an emergency triage center," says Charlotte. "That's all we know how to do."

After lunch, Charlotte, Ginnie, and I head to Gentilly. I'm immediately struck by how many of the homes are on stilts. Single-story structures have been hoisted into the air on concrete columns as high as ten feet. After the storm, many residents rebuilt their houses this way—or had contractors jack their surviving dwellings skyward. "When I came through here, there were boats on tops of homes and homes on top of boats," says Charlotte. "After people returned, they weren't taking any more chances."

Ginnie guides us to a neighborhood on the western edge of Gentilly, one that resembles the empty blocks of St. Bernard Parish I'd see a couple of days later. There are more homes here, but those left standing are largely vacant and dilapidated. Windows are shattered, doors are boarded up, and the spray-painted X's of Katrina are everywhere. Faded yellow lines, some above doorways, reveal how high the floodwaters had risen. In the years since the storm, these houses have become refuges for squatters and drug dealers. They've also become a haven for the city's abandoned pets, the closest many of them will get to a real home again.

We pull down a small street that looks like no one has driven through it for years. The asphalt is disintegrating. Front yards have overgrown front porches. A broken water main has created a brook that flows across the middle of the road. Nature is reclaiming this part of New Orleans. Charlotte parks in front of a squat, faded brick house. Bent gutters droop over the walls, and part of the roof has fallen over the side, creating a small triangular porch shaded from the sun. Ginnie has set up a feeding station here, and we've come to check on it. There are only fifty to sixty stations left in the city; feral animals are still a huge problem, but ARNO no longer has the resources to care for all of them. As we approach, something skitters into the bushes. "That must be the feral dog that lives around here," says Ginnie. She ducks under the collapsed roof, weaving around splintered beams, and pours kibble into a shallow cardboard box. Then she sets down a plastic jug of water and cuts off the top. "That should hold him over for a few days," she says.

We visit a few more feeding stations. Some are in the houses themselves: a box of food on a shattered tile floor, a jug of water in a gutted bedroom, candy wrappers and Mardi Gras beads scattered about by trespassers. Toward the end of the day, we stop at Tana's house. Made of light gray wood, it's propped up seven feet on cinder block stilts. Tana welcomes us inside. Short, in her late forties, with curly black hair that had begun to gray, she's just come from work, and her black vet tech scrubs hang loosely over her body. I'm surprised to see that her house is as gutted as the feeding stations we've been visiting. She says she only received $1,200 from FEMA, and she's waiting for funds from a nonprofit called Rebuilding Together New Orleans to finish the home. In the meantime, she's been living with Charlotte. She tells us about the day the coast guard helicopter came. "When I was rescued from here, that was the happiest and saddest moment of my life," she says, tearing up. "I knew I was getting saved, but I had to leave everyone else behind." I notice she's wearing a small glass vial around her neck, filled with gray ash. That's Bucky, she tells me. The cat died of a viral infection just five months after Katrina, and she keeps him close to remind her of the pets she lost in the storm.

In April 2006, Charlotte and Tana drove to Baton Rouge to testify about their experiences in front of the state legislature. Lawmakers led by State Senator Heulette "Clo" Fontenot were considering changes to Louisiana's disaster policies in the wake of Katrina, the costliest natural disaster in US history. More than 1,800 people and 150,000 pets died. "I felt we were derelict in our duties to the citizens of Louisiana," Fontenot told reporters, "because we didn't make arrangements for pets."

Testifying alongside Charlotte and Tana was William Morgan, a veteran in his early seventies who had lost both legs to diabetes. When his home flooded, he was swept from his wheelchair but managed to dive under the water and break through a window to get out, pulling his apricot-colored poodle, Morgan LaFaye, along with him. When they emerged outside, he pushed the dog onto his roof and held onto a nearby tree for fourteen hours, the wind and rain lashing his body as floodwaters threatened to sweep him away. Coast guard rescuers eventually arrived in a boat and threw him a rope, but they would not take "Miss Morgan." "We're not in the dog business," they said. "She was crying, whining, and barking as we sped away," Morgan told the legislators. "Had I known she couldn't come with me, I would have stayed."

On June 27, 2006, Governor Kathleen Blanco signed the Pet Evacuation Bill into law. The act requires the Governor's Office of Homeland Security and Emergency Preparedness, as well as the governments of the state's parishes, to include pets in their disaster planning. State and local governments must now make pets part of their emergency-training exercises, and they must help the public develop their own pet-friendly evacuation procedures. In addition, pets must now be evacuated with people; if evacuation buses cannot accommodate them, officials must provide alternative transportation, such as climate-controlled trucks. And human shelters must now accept pets, or they must set up pet-friendly facilities nearby so that people can keep tabs on their animals. Under one parish's plan, owners and their pets arriving at shelters will be given matching bar-coded wrist bands and collars to make sure no animals are lost. (Only cats and dogs are eligible.)

"Whenever you have something of Katrina's magnitude, there are many phoenixes that come out of the fire," Charlotte tells me. "I knew something good was going to come out of this horror." The Louisiana Pet Evacuation Bill would be only the beginning.

The Pet Bill

The 109th US Congress was hardly a model of bipartisanship. In 2005 alone, Senate Democratic minority leader Harry Reid called President George W. Bush "a loser," Senate Republicans threatened to override Democratic filibusters of judicial nominees by using the so-called nuclear option, and a Republican in the House of Representatives implied that a Democratic colleague and decorated war veteran was a coward, inciting one Democrat to charge across the aisle and jab his finger in the opposition's face. Even by cynical standards, Congress was the most bickering, divided body it had been in at least a half century. Gridlock and obstructionism were the words of the day, as politicians squabbled over everything from illegal immigration to the appointment of US ambassadors. But on May 22, 2006, something remarkable happened. A bill passed the House with near unanimous support. Then, a little over two months later, the same bill passed the Senate, this time without a single dissenting vote. It was one of the only major pieces of legislation to have such overwhelming backing since the 2001 Patriot Act, signed in the wake of the September 11 terrorist attacks. But this bill wasn't about people. It was about pets.

The legislation was born on Thursday, September 1, 2005, three days after Hurricane Katrina struck the Gulf Coast. Most of New Orleans was flooded, bodies rotted in the sun, and the Superdome had become a sweltering hellhole. Its lack of food and water, noxious smell of garbage and excrement, and rumors of rape and murder led USA Today to dub it "the epicenter of human misery." FEMA trucks had finally arrived, and thousands rushed outside, pushing against barricades and each other in hopes of grabbing a seat out of town. But as the crowd jostled in the oppressive heat, a familiar scene played out. Those who had risked everything to bring their dogs and cats to the stadium were told they could not take them on the buses. Some had to abandon the only family they had left. One little boy clung tightly to his small white dog, advancing in line and hoping not to be noticed. The police would have none of it. An officer ripped the dog from the child's arms and carried it away. "Snowball, Snowball!" the boy screamed. He cried until he threw up.

Even for a nation still grappling with the human tragedy of Katrina, the plight of animals struck a nerve. Images of drowned cats, dogs stranded on rooftops, and pets eating garbage off the streets became common in newspaper articles and TV broadcasts. CNN's Anderson Cooper reported from the scene of a massive pet massacre at a middle school in St. Bernard Parish; locals who had been using the location as a shelter were forced to leave the animals behind when they were evacuated, and someone had come in shortly thereafter and shot them. Around the country, people had been looking at the human victims and saying, "That could have been me." Now they were saying, "That could have been my pet." They were heartbroken. Then they got angry. Why weren't emergency responders rescuing cats and dogs? Why had so many people died because they couldn't bring their pets? And what was going to become of these animals?

The questions weren't lost on politicians. Inspired by the Snowball incident, California Democrat Tom Lantos introduced the Pets Evacuation and Transportation Standards (PETS) Act in the House of Representatives on September 22, while rescue operations were still in full swing. The bill would incorporate pets into federal disaster plans, allow federal agencies to create emergency shelters for animals, and permit FEMA to reimburse state and local governments for transporting, housing, and caring for pets during disasters. Emergency responders would now evacuate pets as well as people. Red Cross shelters and hotels would not turn away cats and dogs. And pets could ride on buses or would be provided their own transportation out of town. "Without a corrected protocol, pet owners are unnecessarily forced to choose between their own safety and the safety of their pets," Lantos proclaimed on the floor of the House. "I cannot help but wonder how many people could have been spared the wrath of Hurricane Katrina if only they could have taken the family pet." President Bush himself said that if he had to evacuate, the first thing he would grab would be his Scottish Terrier, Barney.

The PETS Act had powerful backers in the animal welfare community. The Humane Society of the United States, the American Society for the Prevention of Cruelty to Animals, and Best Friends Animal Society—all of which had played major roles in sheltering and saving Katrina's pets—pushed strongly for the bill. They also met with Lantos and his Republican cosponsor, Christopher Shays, to suggest provisions. Other prominent groups chimed in too. In the years leading up to Katrina, the Animal Legal Defense Fund, once a small, fringe collection of lawyers interested in representing animals in the courtroom, had grown into a legal powerhouse, eventually establishing an animal law committee in the prestigious American Bar Association (ABA). When the committee got word that the Senate was considering its own version of the PETS Act, cosponsored by Republican Ted Stevens and Democrat Frank Lautenberg, it drafted a letter of support endorsed by every section of the ABA. The weight of the country's largest society of lawyers was now behind the bill. The public also made its voice heard, flooding Congress with letters, e-mails, and phone calls. "Never before in my long congressional career have I received so much support and encouragement for a piece of legislation," Lantos remarked. "On behalf of the tens of millions of families across our nation who have pets, I urge all of my colleagues to vote for this important legislation."

Lantos got his wish. The PETS Act became law on October 6, 2006. In terms of federal disaster planning, cats and dogs would now be treated like people.

The federal and Louisiana pet evacuation bills were just the beginning of a new political awareness of the importance of rescuing cats and dogs in natural disasters. To date, more than thirty states and the District of Columbia have passed their own versions of the acts or have created plans to deal with pets in emergencies. Several have formed animal response teams, which work directly with state and local governments to draft evacuation plans for animal shelters, maintain lists of veterinarians who can perform triage during disasters, and build Internet databases to facilitate reunions of lost pets with their owners. The plans have been implemented in everything from tornadoes to wildfires.

Perhaps nothing exemplifies the impact of the PETS Act better, however, than the Louisiana SPCA. The state's oldest and largest animal welfare organization was a big supporter of the bill—with good reason. Katrina destroyed its fifty-year-old headquarters in the Ninth Ward, ripping off its roof and flooding the building into oblivion. Fortunately, the society had a history of being prepared for natural disasters. Implementing its "trigger point plan," it evacuated its 263 cats and dogs a full two days before the hurricane struck, transporting them to a shelter in Houston. Days later, it began a massive rescue operation out of the Lamar-Dixon Expo Center. When Lamar-Dixon closed, it returned to New Orleans, setting up shop in an abandoned coffee warehouse east of downtown. Hundreds of makeshift kennels and cages sat in a tattered and torn building, with no plumbing or drainage. It must have resembled ARNO's current digs.

Today's Louisiana SPCA looks nothing like ARNO, however. I visit it on my last day in New Orleans. Opened in 2007, it's a stunning $8 million facility that lies on ten grassy acres less than a mile from the coffee warehouse. The centerpiece is a 21,000-square-foot rectangular building, two stories high and deep blue in color. Next to that sits a community clinic, offering low-cost vaccinations and high-volume spay/ neuter programs. When I enter the lobby of the main structure, I'm greeted by four receptionists behind a large curved desk. One is talking a family through its adoption procedures; another is on the phone about a missing pet, promising to scan the city's lost-and-found postings to track it down. To the right is a gift shop full of brightly colored dog collars and bags of treats. To the left is a waiting area with giant paintings of cats and dogs on the walls.

A couple of staffers greet me and show me the rest of the facility. There's an intake room, where animals have their photos snapped when they first arrive, a behavior-evaluation area to determine how much training a pet needs before it's adopted out, a room for grooming, an office for health checkups, and a community outreach and education center that sponsors everything from "Camp Love a Pet" for elementary schools to pet first aid and CPR classes. The SPCA's cats live in a baby blue adoption wing, spending their days in spacious glass enclosures, complete with plush beds and shelves to jump on. Drawings of the animals line the wall, crayoned by visiting children. Dogs hang out in large runs filled with toys and have use of a gravel-and-grass exercise yard in the back. Next year, the SPCA plans to break ground on an additional building that will house larger play areas and so-called real-life rooms: generous living quarters for cats and dogs lined with carpeting and filled with furniture. "We want to create spaces people can envision in their homes," the shelter's CEO, Ana Zorrilla, tells me. "We want people to see pets as part of the family." FEMA is footing the bill.

The government's fingerprints are here in other ways as well. A white, climate-controlled semi sits in the parking lot, ready to evacuate up to one hundred animals at a moment's notice. Behind the shelter is a giant aluminum warehouse, filled with extra food, crates, and emergency supplies. And unseen are detailed documents that make the Louisiana SPCA a critical part of federal and state emergency procedures. In response to the PETS Act and its state equivalent, the society is tasked with taking the lead in ensuring that animals, their owners, and even other shelters and veterinary clinics are properly evacuated in a disaster. When Hurricane Gustav struck in 2008, the Louisiana SPCA spearheaded the first mandatory evacuation of a US city and its pets, helping to transport more than four hundred cats and dogs whose owners had no vehicles of their own, setting up a temporary shelter in Baton Rouge to care for pets whose owners had been evacuated elsewhere, and launching a website to help owners locate pets displaced by the storm. The society's disaster plans have proven so effective that emergency responders around the country have asked for a copy.

The new procedures were put to the test exactly seven years to the day after Katrina struck the Gulf Coast, when Isaac pummeled the region, unleashing seventy-mile-per-hour winds and twenty inches of rain. More than 60,000 people were told to evacuate, and nearly 1 million homes and businesses lost power. The storm largely spared New Orleans, but just southeast of the city in Plaquemines Parish, a levee failed, flooding some areas with up to fourteen feet of water. Sitting at home, seventy-year-old Fred Leslie had ignored the evacuation order. When water began pouring through his windows and rising fast inside, he sloshed into the attic with his four medium-size mutts. National Guard troops arrived the next day, navigating the floodwaters in their boat and axing their way through Leslie's roof. The man sent his dogs out first. Battered by wind and rain, the rescuers grabbed each one and put it in the boat. Then Leslie came out, inching his heavy frame down the side of the roof. As he entered the vessel, one of his dogs fell out. A rescuer reached into the water and pulled it back onboard. Then the boat sped away, Leslie cradling one of his mutts in his arms.

Before I leave New Orleans, I pay one last visit to Charlotte and Ginnie. I meet them in front of Charlotte's house, a light purple two-story Victorian, which still exhibited Katrina damage until it was repaired about a year ago. Charlotte is out front, wearing her blue ARNO T-shirt and shouldering a twenty-pound bag of dry food into her station wagon. "How was the Louisiana SPCA?" she asks. "Very nice," I respond. "One day . . . " she says, her thoughts trailing off. The three of us hop into the car and head to St. Bernard Parish and the Lower Ninth Ward, northeast of downtown. Ginnie gets on her cell phone with a woman from

California who's interested in donating to ARNO. Charlotte reminds Ginnie to call Best Friends afterward to see if they offer any grants for spay/neuter programs.

St. Bernard is a wasteland, and the Lower Ninth is worse. Only 3,000 people have returned to the latter, a mere 15 percent of its pre-Katrina population. Among the empty lots and abandoned houses, a few white FEMA trailers remain. In some grassy areas, concrete steps lead up into thin air. Yet there are signs of recovery. A police station is being rebuilt, bigger and more modern than before. Schools that were once among the worst in the country are now prestigious charter programs. And strange new structures have begun to crop up in the middle of devastated neighborhoods: pastel-painted homes with sharply angled walls and glossy black solar panels on their roofs tower on concrete stilts, hovering over modest shotgun houses like monuments from the future. Designed by internationally recognized architects for actor Brad Pitt's Make It Right Foundation, eighty-six have already been built, and another sixty-four are on the way. They're made of recycled materials, sport hurricane-proof glass, and contain escape hatches to the roofs. "Some of them were even built to float," Charlotte says.

We park in front of one of them. A more subdued example, it's painted beige and looks a bit like a floating rectangle from a distance. Inside lives Robert Green, a Katrina survivor Ginnie met four months after the storm. She was running devastation tours in the neighborhood at the time when she noticed police cars around his house. He waved her down and said he had just found his mother's body. Then he told her what happened.

Green had tried to evacuate his family before Katrina, but he turned around when he hit heavy traffic on the interstate and long lines at the Superdome. Back at home, he and his brother, mother, and three granddaughters fled to the attic when floodwaters poured through their windows. As his granddaughters screamed, the house began to move, torn from its foundation when the homes on either side crashed into it. Green's brother punched a hole in the roof, and the family scrambled on top. But their ordeal was far from over. The house continued to drift, splintering apart as the flood carried it for two blocks until it slammed into another home. Green's three-year-old granddaughter,

Shanai, slipped off the roof and was swept away. His seventy-three-year-old mother died shortly thereafter, expiring from the stress and heat as they waited for rescue. Green found her skeleton when he returned to the Lower Ninth, still wrapped in the shawl she had worn on the night of the storm.

Green walks out to his front yard to greet us, and the four of us take refuge in the shade beneath his house. A couple of cars are parked there; a white pit bull sits in a dog pen. After a few minutes, Green—in his late fifties, looking like a slightly younger Danny Glover—invites us inside. On the walls are blown-up photos of him taken by newspaper and magazine photographers: he sits on the steps of his former home, a white FEMA trailer behind him; he looks upward at an ominous sky, draped in an American flag. Green pulls out a signed letter from President Barack Obama and postcards from people he met while living in his trailer for three years. He says he's happy in his space-age home and is hopeful that, one day, people will return to his neighborhood. Every year he hosts a party on the anniversary of Katrina. He sets up giant pots over propane flames in his front yard, cooking shrimp, crabs, oysters, and crawfish. Family and friends drop by to enjoy the food and dance to live jazz. "You've got to shake your groove thing," Green says. "That's how we live life to the fullest. That's how we move on."

Green didn't have any pets before Katrina, but he has three dogs now, including the pit bull we met under his house. When Isaac struck, he grabbed them and had no trouble finding a hotel where they all could stay. "Nobody's going to leave their pets anymore," Charlotte tells me as we drive away. It was a watershed moment in history, she says. "There was before Katrina, and after Katrina. It's a permanent mark in time that will probably exist here forever." She's referring to the city, but she's also talking about how society views cats and dogs. "I don't think the world realized what pets meant to people before Katrina," she says. "Now they know there's a human-animal bond that can't be broken."

As we drive back to Charlotte's house, Ginnie gets on her cell with a young man who has just left ARNO with his first dog, a black Lab–border collie mix named Salvador Dali. She's teaching him how to house-train. "You really want to give her praise when she pees outside, like she's just won the Olympics. She'll listen to you; she's very smart." Meanwhile,

Charlotte is calling someone who wants to create a pet pinup calendar for the shelter as a way to raise money. A short while later, she pulls up to her house, and I get out. The sun has begun to set, and the air has cooled a bit. Ginnie waves and smiles, then dials someone else up. "Do you have a window after five when you could come and volunteer?" I hear her say. Charlotte jumps out, gives me a hug, then jumps back in. "Gotta' go, baby," she says. "I've got 50,000 messages on my phone!"

Charlotte was right. There is an unbreakable bond between people and their pets. Owners recognized this a long time ago. Now, thanks in part to Hurricane Katrina, the law is finally catching up. But the PETS Act was hardly the first step. The gears have been turning for decades, as new legislation and court decisions gradually recognize that cats and dogs aren't just objects, and they aren't just property. They're family members. And one day they could be something even more: legal persons.

SIX

The Protected Pet

A 1 a.m. phone call jolted Hector Sanchez from his sleep. The detective, an eighteen-year veteran of the Los Angeles Police Department, who had spent much of his career investigating human trafficking and sex crimes, was accustomed to such late-night disturbances. They usually brought bad news. A pimp had kidnapped a prostitute's baby and was threatening to kill it. A rapist was loose in a downtown neighborhood. But this call was especially troubling. As Sanchez squeezed his hand over his eyes and cradled the phone to his ear, an officer at the LAPD's Real-Time Analysis and Critical Response Division—a new, high-tech, twenty-four-hour command post that monitors crime throughout the city—told him that a transient digging through a dumpster had come across the severed heads of two large dogs. Patrol officers were already on the scene, but they had no idea how to handle the case. Sanchez told the command center to patch him through. After talking to the cops for a few minutes, he eased himself out of bed, made a cup of coffee, and headed out the door. His wife and kids were still sound asleep.

Eight months earlier, Sanchez—in his early forties, sporting a fit frame, hazel eyes, and short, black hair slightly graying on the sides— had assumed command of the LAPD's Animal Cruelty Task Force. It wasn't a position he'd wanted. He had spent his childhood in the ghetto, where gang members bullied and beat his friends and neighbors. He decided that when he grew up, he would do something about it. Sanchez studied his way into UCLA, majoring in political science, but he told everyone he was going to be a cop after he graduated. His roommates laughed it off; his girlfriend told him he was nuts. But he followed through with his plan. He finished police academy training in 1994 and spent his early years in the vice division, working undercover to root out prostitution rings and organized crime. Hanging out in smoky bars, he posed as a john looking for a good time or a bookmaker working for a local drug lord. His investigations earned him accolades, and in 2000 he made detective, spending the next decade supervising units that busted rapists, pedophiles, and even other cops. When his boss told him to take charge of the Animal Cruelty Task Force—a specialized unit created in 2005 to investigate crimes against cats, dogs, and other creatures—he felt like he'd been demoted. Oh great, he thought, the puppy police. But by the time he got the 1 a.m. call, he'd long since realized he was now doing some of the most important work of his life.

It was still pitch-black when Sanchez arrived at the crime scene: a dark alley in South Central Los Angeles wedged between the bare back-end of a CVS pharmacy and a slatted iron gate capped with spikes. This was a commercial area, filled with low-end shops and parking lots. Just across the street, behind a single strip of train track and a low cinder block wall scribbled with graffiti, sat row after row of small, tattered houses, most with bars on the windows. About a mile from here, truck driver Reginald Denny was nearly beaten to death during the 1992 Los Angeles Riots. When Sanchez pulled into the alley, it was vacant, save for a black-and-white police cruiser. Next to it stood two cops. And next to them, beside a green dumpster, lay a clear plastic garbage bag stretched flat on the asphalt. The dog heads were on top.

Sanchez got out of his car. In the lights of the cruiser, he saw that the dogs had clearly been large animals: one a chocolate Lab mix, the other a tan shepherd mix. The cops had propped the heads upright, as if the bodies of the animals might be standing just below the street. When Sanchez got closer, he noticed the precision of the decapitations. The cuts, about three vertebrae down, were clean, almost surgical. That ruled out a wild animal. And surprisingly, there was very little blood. The dogs must have been killed in another location, Sanchez reasoned, and then someone had dumped the heads here, a place no one would be watching. But why? Had the dogs been victims of some sort of satanic ritual? Sanchez had investigated such crimes before—a dead cat found in an abandoned city park, in one case, its body limp on a makeshift shrine, surrounded by candles, beads, and pentagrams. But he saw none of that here. Had the canines been used for dog fighting? Unlikely; the heads were free of scars. A teenage prank? A serial animal killer? He scanned about for a murder weapon, perhaps a Samurai sword from the look of things, but saw nothing. Just the two heads.

Sanchez got out his flashlight and donned a pair of latex gloves. He lay the heads flat and stuck his fingers in the necks, probing for a micro-chip the size of a grain of rice. Perhaps he could use it to trace the dogs to an owner. But again he came up empty. As a detective, he treated each investigation like a scientific experiment. You develop hypotheses and then rule them out one by one, until you're left with the solution. But nothing made sense here. He wasn't even sure where to start. He told the cops to file a report and to check the local shelters for anyone looking for missing pets. Then he got in his car and drove to LAPD headquarters, weak sunlight starting to filter through the smoggy air. When he sat at his desk, he began to pore over a pile of other animal abuse cases. But the heads were on his mind all day.

I arrive in Los Angeles a week later. A deputy district attorney named Deborah Knaan, who supervises the prosecution of all animal crimes in LA County, has invited me out to spend some time with the Animal Cruelty Task Force and go on a few ride-alongs with Detective Sanchez. I meet both of them on a busy street corner downtown. It's a warm morning, and the bright sun reflects strongly off the surrounding build-ings, none more so than the unusual structure Knaan and Sanchez are standing in front of, a cube of glass and sharply angled limestone that, from some vantage points, resembles a Borg ship from *Star Trek*. This, I would soon learn, is the new headquarters of the Los Angeles Police Department. Knaan smiles as I approach. She's fifty, with olive skin, and stands no more than five feet tall. Oversized sunglasses cover much of her face, and she lugs a large yellow purse. Yet she looks tough as nails, hardened by her years of prosecuting rapists and child molesters, not to mention her time as a platoon sergeant in the Israeli army, commanding a division of soldiers with criminal backgrounds. She has the rugged in-terior of a New Yorker with an LA makeover.

I had assumed we would go out on patrol right away, so I'm surprised to see Sanchez in a suit and tie. "There's been a change of plans," Knaan tells me. Sanchez has been summoned to appear at a press conference at city hall, and we need to head over there immediately. It's about the dog heads.

City hall is just a block from where we are, and I had been using it as a landmark ever since I got to LA. It's that tall white building with tiny square windows you might remember from old TV shows like *Dragnet* and *Adventures of Superman*. As we walk over, traffic racing by, Knaan and Sanchez banter about the dog head case. Perhaps it was a botched veterinary procedure, and someone was covering his tracks. Maybe the dogs were killed for food. Knaan is a fast talker who speaks with a mild Long Island accent and frequently checks her BlackBerry for new messages. Sanchez is quiet and introspective. He talks slowly and calmly, and he answers Knaan's rapid-fire questions with short, thoughtful answers. His eyes are kind, but they mask an intensity. Deep down, he's still the child who bristled at injustice. I have no intention of getting on his bad side.

Los Angeles City Hall is filled with marble columns, arched passageways, and intricate, multicolored designs tiled into the floor. Unfortunately, the press conference takes place in a much blander locale, a small, featureless room with gray carpet and a sun-bleached photo of the city's skyline plastered to the back wall. But what the room lacks in panache, it makes up for in hustle and bustle. Three television cameras have been set up on one end, and reporters mill about with voice recorders, as dressed-up men and women—some wearing suits, others police uniforms—buzz about. Within minutes of our arrival, twenty-five people have crowded into the space, and a few of them—clearly the heavy hitters—have lined up behind a podium facing the cameras, a navy blue curtain draped behind them.

LA City Councilman Paul Koretz speaks first. A short, round politician behind some of the city's most progressive animal legislation, including a ban on cat declawing, he opens with a quote from Mahatma Gandhi. "The greatness of a nation can be judged by the way its animals are treated," he says. "The same is true of our city." Calling the dog beheadings a "heinous crime" and a "gruesome act of animal cruelty," he announces a $20,000 reward for information leading to the perpetrator's capture and conviction. "We hope at some point, someone will turn in a friend or relative."

A few minutes later, City Attorney Carmen Trutanich, a commanding presence who dwarfs the podium and speaks in a booming voice,
takes the stage. He vows that his office will "expend whatever resources
necessary" to bring the offender to justice. "We're gathered here today
to send a very clear message," he says. "This conduct cannot be tolerated in a civilized society. . . . I can assure you that when apprehended,
these persons or person will be punished to the full extent of the law."

The LAPD commander speaks next, and then Detective Sanchez
walks up to the microphone. He calls the crime "despicable" and urges
the public to phone in with any information that might be useful. The
reporters, antsy in the back row, can't hold their questions any longer:
Have you seen anything like this before? What can you tell us about the
murder weapon? Has anyone phoned in about missing pets? Sanchez
says he won't comment on an ongoing investigation and leaves it at that.
Then he steps back and tries to blend into the background. A woman
next to me whispers that she's never seen a press conference like this
for an animal crime. The big shots, the TV cameras, the huge reward.
This is the type of attention a serial rapist would get, she says. Standing
there, I realize I'm seeing the future of animal justice in America—one
that wasn't even fathomable 150 years ago.

"The Great Meddler"

In 1863, while the Civil War raged in America, a fifty-year-old New
Yorker named Henry Bergh fought a much smaller battle on the streets
of Russia. Bergh, a thin, towering man with a long, narrow face and a
woolly moustache, had inherited a large fortune from his shipbuilding
father, and his silk top hat and fur-lined frock coat reflected a life of
status and luxury. His political connections had landed him a posh diplomatic position in the city of Saint Petersburg, appointed by none other
than President Abraham Lincoln. Bergh and his wife were world travel-
ers, and he looked forward to future diplomatic assignments around the
globe. But one evening, as the couple was ferried to yet another lavish
social engagement in a cushioned carriage, Bergh saw something that
would change his life forever.

From his window, he noticed a modest, uncovered carriage stuck on
the side of the road. The horse strapped to it was clearly injured, holding

its right front leg off the ground. The driver had dismounted and was shouting at the animal. As Bergh watched, the man raised a heavy stick and began viciously beating the creature on the head and neck. Panicking, the horse tried to pull away, but it was held in place by the cart, and the blows continued to fall. Bergh was an avid meat eater and no particular fan of animals. He had never even owned a pet. But something inside him snapped. He yelled at his driver to tell the man to stop, and amazingly the man did. The horse was spared further cruelty. "Encouraged by my success," Bergh later told a newspaper, "I made up my mind that when I came home I would prosecute those who persecuted poor dumb brutes." The pampered diplomat had found his true calling. The American animal welfare movement had begun.

Bergh had his work cut out for him. New York City—crowded, dirty, and corrupt—was no friend to animals. It wasn't much of a friend to people either. Stroll down the tidy blocks of today's Manhattan, and you'll have a hard time believing that in the mid-nineteenth century, many residents couldn't cross the street without paying a broom-wielding kid to sweep a path for them. Rotting vegetables, broken furniture, and thousands of pounds of horse, pig, and even human feces formed a knee-deep sludge the locals called "corporation pudding," after a government too crooked and disorganized to clean it. Overcrowded slums roiled with gangs, prostitution, murder, and disease, feeding a mortality rate equal to that of medieval London. As Charles Dickens wrote of a particularly nasty district he visited, "What place is this, to which the squalid street conducts us? A kind of square of leprous houses . . . narrow ways diverging to the right and left, reeking everywhere with dirt and filth." Sailors claimed they could smell the city six miles out to sea.

And then there were the horse carcasses. Before the age of the automobile, New York ran on equines. Hundreds of thousands of the animals towed railroad cars and fire wagons, barges and slaughter carts. They also transported people, sometimes far too many people: as few as two horses pulled streetcars overflowing with more than one hundred passengers. "Never full, pack 'em in. Move up, fat man! Squeeze in thin!" went a popular song. "Forty seated, forty standing. Forty more on either landing!" Horses were so plentiful that it was cheaper to work them to death and buy new ones than to care for them properly. And so they were starved, whipped bloody, and left to die on the side of the road when they collapsed. Too heavy to move, their bodies were allowed to rot until they had decomposed enough for wagons (drawn by horses) to pick them up and dump them in the river or transport them to a factory on Barren Island in Jamaica Bay that turned them into glue, grease, and fertilizer. Horses can live for more than thirty years; in New York, they were lucky to make it through two.

When Bergh returned to the city in 1864, the horrors that had once escaped his attention came into sharp focus. He had resigned his diplomatic post in Saint Petersburg, and on his way back to America he stopped in England to visit the leaders of that country's largest animal welfare organization, the Royal Society for the Prevention of Cruelty to Animals. The work of Richard Martin and his successors convinced Bergh that he could create an analogous society in New York. But he wanted more than a charity. He wanted a police force.

On a stormy night in early February 1866, Bergh gathered his high-society friends at the Mercantile Library, a venue that had previously hosted such luminaries as Frederick Douglass and Mark Twain. In front of a large gathering of philanthropists, real estate tycoons, and past, present, and future mayors, senators, and governors, Bergh railed against the evils of bullfighting, vivisection, and foie gras. He had drafted a "Declaration of the Rights of Animals," a document modeled after the Declaration of Independence that promised freedom from abuse, and he asked all present to sign it. "This is purely a matter of conscience," Bergh proclaimed. "It has no perplexing side issues." By April, the state legislature in Albany had approved a charter for Bergh's new organization: the American Society for the Prevention of Cruelty to Animals. And, as Bergh had pushed for, the legislature granted ASPCA officials the ability to enter homes and make arrests, haul abusers to court, and collect fines for their offenses—extraordinary powers for a private organization. Bergh had his anticruelty army. He was ready to take his fight to the streets.

Police power was one thing. But Henry Bergh knew that to truly protect animals, he had to get an effective animal welfare law on the books. Others had tried; yet early statutes lacked teeth. An 1846 Vermont act, for example, made it a crime to kill an animal, but the creature had to belong to someone else, and it had to be economically valuable, like a horse or a sheep. There was no mention of cruelty. Plus, the fact that you could abuse your own animal without repercussion meant that all the law was really concerned with was protecting the property of others. Beating a horse to death was fine, as long as it was yours.

Bergh aimed to change that. Less than two weeks after the New York state legislature sanctioned the ASPCA, he lobbied it to pass America's toughest animal welfare law. Ownership no longer mattered, meaning the animal itself was being protected, and new abuses like neglect, abandonment, and cockfighting were added to the list of misdemeanors. In 1867, Bergh got the law strengthened to include "any living creature," not just those judged economically valuable. Even supposedly useless animals like dogs and cats now had the right to be protected. "The blood-red hand of cruelty," he declared, "shall no longer torture dumb beasts with impunity."

Bergh didn't waste any time enforcing the new law. He patrolled the streets of New York City with a copy of it in his pocket and, pinned to his coat, the ASPCA's shiny silver badge (its design: an angel swooping down to save a beaten horse). At first he found that his words didn't carry as much weight as they had on the streets of Saint Petersburg. On the day he returned from Albany, he ordered a truckman to stop whipping his horse; the man laughed and fought him off. But the next day, Bergh ran down a butcher's cart that was carrying live calves tied at the feet and stacked like cordwood. He dragged the driver to court and secured a $10 fine, the first recorded conviction for animal cruelty in the United States. Bergh was emboldened. He dogged abusers across the state, often spending entire days in court, bringing perpetrator after perpetrator through the doors. By the end of the ASPCA's first year, he and his "Berghsmen" had prosecuted 119 cases and secured sixty-six convictions. Judges who had once laughed such crimes out of their courtrooms were slowly finding an appreciation for the severity of animal abuse.

That's not to say that Bergh was loved by his fellow citizens. He became infamous for pulling drivers off their wagons when they would not give their horses rest, and he created daylong traffic jams when he ordered passengers to disembark from overloaded streetcars. He also broke up lucrative dog-fighting rings, pushed for the humane slaughter of farm animals, and assailed P. T. Barnum for his cruel treatment of circus creatures. Bergh received death threats, and newspapers branded him "The Great Meddler," accusing him of valuing animals over people. "The officers of the SPCA live like parasites on the public," wrote one. "They belong to the same party whose humanitarian tenderness stirred up a Civil War."

Over the next decade, however, Bergh gained the public's respect. Perhaps because his efforts coincided with people's increasing affection for animals, especially cats and dogs. Pets were about to enter heaven in popular literature, and early flea-control products were bringing them indoors. "Almost every fourth person knows him by sight, and the whisper, 'That's Henry Bergh,' follows him, like a tardy herald, wherever he goes," read an 1879 article in *Scribner's Monthly*. "Parents stop and point out to their children 'the man who is kind to the dumb animals.'" Even P. T. Barnum became a convert, joining the ASPCA and erecting a statue in Bergh's honor.

By the time Bergh died in 1888, his society had prosecuted 120,000 cruelty cases, and thirty-seven of the thirty-eight states had enacted animal welfare legislation based on the New York law. The organization's modest headquarters in two attic rooms in Lower Manhattan had moved to a large building in the heart of the city. And dozens of local SPCAs had cropped up across the country, inspired by Bergh's vision. *Scribner's* called the ASPCA "one of the greatest moral agencies of the time."

Yet times were changing. Henry Bergh had been galvanized by the suffering of the horse. But as the nineteenth century drew to a close, humane organizations were turning their attention to a new concern: the plight of cats and dogs.

On September 13, 1899, a dour-looking Manhattan real estate salesman named Henry Bliss stepped off a streetcar near Central Park. As he turned back to the trolley to help his female companion disembark, an electric taxicab struck him. The carriage-like vehicle knocked Bliss to the pavement and ran over his head and body, crushing both. When he died the next morning, he became America's first pedestrian killed by an automobile.

Bliss's untimely demise signaled a new era for New York. On city streets, the once reverberating clip-clop of the horse gave way to the buzz of the automobile. Henry Bergh may have saved horses from cruelty, but Henry Ford would soon make their suffering obsolete. That could have caused an identity crisis for a humane movement built around the equine. But by the time Bliss became a traffic fatality, the ASPCA had already moved on to cats and dogs.

The reason would have been clear to anyone reading the *New York Times* on June 2, 1881. An article published that day described the standard method of euthanasia for dogs at the city's overflowing pounds. Dozens of canines were herded into an iron cage and driven to the East River. Things got grimmer from there:

> Over the edge of the river hangs a derrick, from the crossbeam of which dangles a big iron hook. The hook is fastened in an iron ring in the top of the cage, which is then hoisted with a rope and pulley till it is clear of the car, when it is then swung over the river and lowered. In six minutes the dogs delight to bark and bite no longer, and the cage is hoisted up again. Their dead bodies are taken to Barren Island where they are "manufactured" into various articles. Just what those articles are, perhaps it is better for the public not to conjecture.

The citizens of New York had tolerated such cruelties for decades. Cats and dogs, though fine as pets, were a nuisance on the streets. Tens of thousands roamed uncontrolled, pooping, biting, and spreading disease. Their reputation wasn't much better than that of their counterparts in the Middle Ages. And so dogcatchers rounded up homeless cats and dogs by the truckload and killed them, often in the most inhumane manner. If they weren't drowned, they were strangled with nooses or clubbed to death with wooden mallets. (Shooting was too costly.)

As time went on and people became increasingly enamored of their feline and canine companions, however, they could no longer stomach such cruelties. The dogcatchers weren't helping matters. This curious breed of practitioner had evolved from the "pound master" of the American colonies, an individual who used to round up escaped farm animals. Pigs, cows, and chickens were kept in deplorable conditions until their owners came and paid a "redemption fee." If the owners didn't show—or refused to pay—the pound master simply sold the animal for meat. That wasn't an option for cats and dogs, but holding pets for ransom was. And this seems to have turned the average dogcatcher into a frightful human being.

Rounding up strays wasn't profitable; no one would claim them. So dogcatchers turned to pets, often brazenly snatching them from yards. Newspapers told stories of shady men following people as they walked their dogs, then nabbing the mutts and thrusting them into their coats when the owners' backs were turned. Victims chased the offenders down the street, sometimes pulled by a leash they were still holding. Other dogcatchers extorted "protection money" from owners to ensure that their pets would not be kidnapped. And some, as this 1877 *New York Times* article relates, graduated to physical assault:

> On Friday evening, while [Mrs. Fredericka Fleming] was seated on the stoop of her residence, a poodle reposing peacefully in her lap and another dog of uncertain breed sleeping behind her, [dogcatcher Thomas] Birmerhorn appeared on the scene in a dilapidated wagon, accompanied by a juvenile assistant. Alighting in front of Mrs. Fleming's door, the dog-catcher unceremoniously appropriated the poodle, while the assistant took charge of the unoffending nondescript canine slumbering behind his mistress. Recovering from her surprise, Mrs. Fleming sought to regain possession of her pets, and was, as she alleges, struck violently on the breast by Birmerhorn and knocked down. He then threw the dogs into the wagon and drove away.

It's no wonder we used to insult politicians by saying they couldn't be elected dogcatcher.

Bowing to public pressure, New York asked the ASPCA to step in. By this time, the organization had become a paragon of the community, and in 1894 it agreed to take over the city's animal control duties. A bill drafted by the state legislature authorized the society to collect stray pets, create shelters for their safekeeping, and humanely euthanize the animals if necessary. The ASPCA was to pay for all of this with fees collected from dog licenses. In the first eight months, the organization removed more than 22,000 animals from the streets. Only about six hundred of these were retrieved by their owners. That meant the society spent much of its time killing the very animals it was trying to protect. Still, it strove to make the process as quick and painless as possible, experimenting with everything from sealed chambers filled with chloroform-soaked sponges to asphyxiation with the gas used to light homes. By 1908, the ASPCA had sheltered or euthanized 800,000 cats and 400,000 dogs.

Newspapers praised the society for cleaning up the streets, ridding the city of rabies, and ending the reign of the notorious dogcatchers. They were also grateful for its humane treatment of New York's favorite pets, be they owned or stray. "The business [of animal control] is now conducted on kind and merciful principles," wrote Brooklyn's *Sunday Advertiser*, "and even the 'Wandering Willie' of dodgem will be treated with consideration." At the same time, the humane movement itself was maturing. As far back as 1877, Henry Bergh had recognized the need to combine the efforts of the various animal welfare societies that were cropping up around the country, and he and several others created an umbrella organization called the American Humane Association. By the early twentieth century, the AHA had grown powerful enough to sponsor several national initiatives. It launched an annual "Be Kind to Animals Week," with brochures, contests, and radio addresses geared largely to children. It created the American Red Star to care for animals wounded in battle. And in 1939, when filmmakers on the set of *Jesse James* killed a horse on camera by blindfolding it and driving it off a forty-foot cliff, the AHA became the official watchdog for animals in the movie industry. Though you may not have heard of the American Humane Association, you've likely seen its stamp of approval: "No animals were harmed in the making of this film."

Still, despite the AHA's efforts to bring animal welfare issues to the public's attention, the humane movement was increasingly bogged down in the day-to-day work of animal control. Dog-licensing fees weren't bringing in nearly enough money to cover the cost of collecting and sheltering thousands of animals, and the resources needed to run these activities sapped the movement of the energy it needed to truly make a difference on a national scale. All the while, the population of America's pets continued to explode, causing the ASPCA and its sister organizations to spend more and more of their time euthanizing animals. Shelters had become little more than slaughterhouses.

If a Russian horse sparked the American humane movement, a Pennsylvania dog brought it into the modern era. In the summer of 1965, a Dalmatian named Pepper disappeared from her family's eighty-two-acre farm seventy miles north of Philadelphia. The Lackavage family—mom, dad, and their four daughters—searched frantically for the animal, putting up flyers, scouring the hillsides around their home, and driving back and forth to all of the local shelters. Nothing. Eventually, they tracked Pepper down to a research hospital in New York City. But by the time they arrived, the dog had died in a pacemaker experiment gone wrong. Her body had been incinerated.

Pepper hadn't arrived at the hospital by accident. New York's infamous dogcatcher had morphed into a new breed of animal collector known as a buncher, who rounded up dogs and cats for scientific studies. Like their predecessors, bunchers were often accused of stealing family pets, though instead of holding them for ransom, they sold them to a booming research industry hungry for experimental subjects. The scientific enterprise exploded in the United States after World War II, and long before companies began mass-breeding mice, rats, and other creatures for the nation's laboratories, cats and dogs were the guinea pigs of choice.

The public didn't bat an eye. Though the Brown Dog Riots and related battles had raised the specter of vivisection in the United States and abroad, people had fallen in love with medical research. Every year ushered in new miracles, from vitamins to insulin to novel classes of antibiotics. Science was the great savior; attempts to impede its progress were frowned upon. The humane movement, still distracted by its shelter work, could do little to influence public opinion. And when it did try to pass bills limiting animal experimentation, a new and powerful research lobby crushed it at every turn. Doctors and researchers branded their opponents communists and antiscience extremists; they even coined a new medical term: "zoophilpsychosis," the psychotic love of animals. Eventually, the research lobby became so powerful that it accomplished something the humane movement never thought possible: beginning in 1948, it pushed through laws in several states that required shelters to surrender their unclaimed cats and dogs to hospitals, universities, and pharmaceutical companies. The ASPCA and its allies, the supposed protectors of America's pets, were now forced to hand them over for medical research.

Rather than continue to fight the research lobby, the American Humane Association, the ASPCA, and several other animal welfare groups looked for a compromise. They promised not to oppose so-called pound seizure if they could at least inspect the laboratories that were using dogs and cats. Disgusted with such capitulation, several high-ranking members of the AHA resigned and formed their own humane association. They called it the National Humane Society. But it would soon change its name to the Humane Society of the United States.

Unlike the ASPCA, the HSUS structured itself as a national organization. Cats and dogs would remain its central focus, but it would not devote its time to municipal animal control. Instead, it established a headquarters in Washington, DC, began a massive fund-raising campaign, and set about combating the powerful research lobby. The society struggled at first. Then Pepper's story made national headlines. The following year, *Life* magazine published a photo exposé about an especially notorious Maryland animal dealer who kept emaciated dogs and cats (some suspected to be former pets) chained up in the cold and crammed into chicken crates, destined for medical research. The piece was titled "Concentration Camps for Dogs." Tens of thousands of letters flooded into Congress, eclipsing the number received on Vietnam and civil rights issues combined. The HSUS had the ammunition it needed. In 1966, it helped pass the Laboratory Animal Welfare Act, a federal law that placed strict regulations on bunchers and other animal dealers and mandated the humane treatment of laboratory animals. It was the most comprehensive animal welfare legislation in US history.

Pets slowly began to disappear from research laboratories. And state after state banned pound seizure. Yet cats and dogs were still being euthanized by the millions.

In 1973, the National League of Cities ranked pet overpopulation as one of the most serious problems facing the modern metropolis, calling it "a threat to health as well as an assault on urban aesthetics, a pollutant, and a safety hazard." The following year, a survey of US mayors found that animal-related issues were the top complaint received by their offices. Stray dogs and cats were everywhere, canines in roving packs, felines in feral colonies. The increasing popularity of pet keeping, exacerbated by uncontrolled breeding and a proliferation of puppy mills, had overflowed shelters and flooded into the streets. Animal control organizations were rounding up millions of cats and dogs annually and spending half a billion dollars to put them to sleep.

Free of such responsibilities, the HSUS was able to formulate a national strategy to combat pet overpopulation. It launched ad campaigns ("Don't be responsible for more suffering and needless death," read one poster featuring a skinny black cat with a litter of kittens), subsidized low-cost spay/neuter clinics, and pressured shelters to make sterilization a condition of adoption. The veterinary profession was surprisingly hostile to the effort, calling it "socialized medicine" and a threat to its bottom line. It even opposed federal legislation that would have funded low-cost clinics. But eventually veterinarians came around, and by the late 1970s pet sterilization was becoming widespread, reducing the number of dogs and cats killed in US shelters from a peak of about 20 million per year to just over 3 million today.

The aggressive spay/neuter campaign didn't just save lives. It helped turn dogs and cats into true family members, desexualized and without their wild urges. It also had a broad impact beyond pets. The HSUS could now focus its attention on other animal welfare issues, from improving conditions at factory farms to protecting wildlife. By the 1990s, it had grown into one of the world's largest animal welfare organizations. A mission that started with cats and dogs now impacted hundreds of species around the globe. But pets still remained the HSUS's core concern, and in the mid-1980s it began exploring new ways to protect them.

Henry Bergh may have started an animal welfare revolution, but the laws he pushed through had not kept pace with society's evolving attitudes toward pets. When dogs and cats were tortured, beaten, or set on fire, courts could only charge perpetrators with a misdemeanor—if they bothered to charge them at all. Police and prosecutors had little incentive to go after such lightly punished crimes when they had felonies to worry about. The HSUS aimed to change that. Beginning in the mid-1980s, it started collating a growing body of scientific literature that pointed to a strong link between animal abuse and human abuse. Study after study showed that people who hurt animals were far more likely to beat their wives and children and even murder other human beings.

An analysis by the Massachusetts SPCA and Northeastern University, for example, found that individuals who abused animals were five times more likely than nonabusers to commit violent crimes against people. And almost every serial killer, from Ted Bundy to Jeffrey Dahmer, started out torturing animals.

The HSUS took its information to the people. It ran heartrending ads, raised money, and lobbied law enforcement and legislators. The effort paid off. Before 1986, only four states had felony anticruelty laws. In 1992, one state a year began passing such laws. Then two states a year. Then more. Today, forty-nine states have felony anticruelty legislation on their books. Many of these laws contain snippets of Bergh's original language, but the penalties are much harsher, calling for fines of up to $125,000 and ten years in prison. They also cover new crimes, from animal hoarding to selling videos of animal abuse. And several place new mandates on owners, requiring them to provide exercise, wholesome food, and access to veterinary care. Many people had already begun treating their pets like children; now the law made sure everyone did.

Though most of this legislation covers a variety of animals, politicians have singled out cats and dogs for special protections. So-called aggravated cruelty laws, which cover particularly heinous abuse, only apply to dogs and cats. Punishments for dog fighting far exceed those for cockfighting. And the federal Dog and Cat Protection Act, passed in 2000, bans the manufacture and sale of any product made from cat and dog fur. By the beginning of the twenty-first century, cats and dogs had become the most legally protected animals in the country.

In the meantime, the ASPCA had finally freed itself of New York's animal control duties, voting in 1994 to sever its one-hundred-year contract with the city. It now joined the HSUS in making sure police and prosecutors took animal cruelty seriously. That was an easier sell now that so many states had felony laws on the books. Still, as Henry Bergh had learned, having the law is one thing, enforcing it another. So since the turn of the twenty-first century, the ASPCA and HSUS have helped train police officers, funded forensics investigations, and worked with prosecutors to make sure crimes against animals aren't discarded on the courtroom floor. Without these organizations, Los Angeles's Animal Cruelty Task Force wouldn't exist. Detective Hector Sanchez would never have received that 1 a.m. phone call. And when he spoke at the city hall press conference, representatives from the ASPCA and HSUS wouldn't have been standing right behind him, backing him up every step of the way.

Animal Cops: Los Angeles

After the press conference, I walk back to LAPD headquarters with Detective Sanchez and Deputy District Attorney Knaan. The Animal Cruelty Task Force lives in the middle of a sea of cubicles in a large, windowed room that houses units dedicated to everything from piracy to prostitution. Only the photos of cats, dogs, and the occasional horse framed on desks and flashing by on computer screens set it apart. Sanchez's workspace is the exception. Save for a mouse pad sporting the image of a pug, it's stack after stack of files containing cases in progress. "I'm not really an animal person," he admits. "But the more time I spend here, the more attached I get."

Besides Sanchez, there are two other detectives on the task force, plus three lower-ranking cops and two officers with the city's Department of Animal Services, Yvette Smith and Tami Shepphird. DAS runs the city's shelters and handles day-to-day animal control issues, from collecting strays to licensing dogs. Like the Berghsmen of yore, DAS officers have some police powers, but they don't carry guns and aren't authorized to use force. Still, Sanchez tells me, the task force wouldn't work without them. DAS has been around since 1947, and its agents know more about animals than almost anyone in the city. When the cops are unsure if an animal has been abused, DAS officers talk to veterinarians and get autopsy reports. When cats and dogs are removed from violent homes, DAS puts them in shelters for their safety. And when Sanchez reaches the limit of his expertise, he only has to look over his cubicle wall. "If I don't know something about dog anatomy or how long it takes maggots to appear on a wound, I just ask Yvette and Tami," he says. "They're like encyclopedias."

When we arrive, the unit is in full swing. LAPD officer Kim Lormans is scanning recent cases on her computer, DAS officer Smith is on the phone with a shelter about a recent impound, and Sanchez's partner for the day, LAPD officer James Cherrette—short and muscular, with pale skin and a crew cut—is leaning over his cubicle, chatting with both of them. "Hey, do you remember what we booked that guy for last time?" he says. Then later, "Can you really break a dog's leg with a rolled-up magazine?" Sanchez escorts me into a side room to brief me for the ride-along. He has changed out of his suit and is now wearing jeans and a tucked-in flannel shirt. He has holsters on each hip, one for a cell phone, the other for a gun, right next to his silver, blue, and gold LAPD badge. A projector is set up, and I take out a PayDay candy bar and begin eating it. I soon regret that. Over the next half hour, I see things no one should see. And if you don't want to hear about them, I advise skipping the next paragraph.

"This is a trimmed-down version of the presentation we give to officers in our vice school," Sanchez says. "They're the ones who might stumble across these crimes, and we want them to know how serious they are." A litany of horrors flashes on the projector screen: a cocker spaniel that has been kicked so hard in the head, its lower jaw is at a right angle to its nose; a kitten whose throat has been slashed in front of a small child; a dog tied up in a backyard and forgotten about, so skeletal it could be a medical exhibit; a German shepherd chained behind a truck and dragged for miles—burnt black holes where its fur should be, its face missing. Thousands of years as friends and companions, and this is how we've repaid them.

Before the Animal Cruelty Task Force was set up, cops often didn't report these crimes, Sanchez says. And many still don't. "If you have a body on the street, officers are so good at it. They'll put up crime scene tape, set up a spot for the media, send out all the notifications. They're like on autopilot. But when it comes to animal crimes, they don't know that they're supposed to treat it like any other crime." Often, when Sanchez hears about animal abuse, he'll discover that police already visited the scene, but they never filed a report. Or they've just issued a citation and didn't collect any evidence. Knaan had told me about a case where a man tried to drown a cat in a toilet, gouged its eyes out, and eventually strangled it to death. Officers showed up and threw the cat's body in the garbage. In another case, a guy shot a man's puppy, and the police wrote it up as vandalism. That's why when Sanchez got the call about the dog heads, he headed to the scene himself.

Getting other cops to take animal crimes seriously is part of the task force's job. It can be a tough sell. "Sometimes it's a macho thing," Sanchez says. "They don't care because it's not a murder." So he tells them about the link between violence against animals and violence against humans. He also tells them that, where there's dog fighting, there are often guns, drugs, and organized crime. He gives them another incentive too: if officers can't book thugs for anything else, they may be able to take them away on animal abuse. "Sometimes you can't get the gangster for the gang crime, but you can get them for animal cruelty. There's more than one way to skin a . . . gang member," he says. "I used to say 'cat,' but people looked at me funny," he smiles. If all else fails, the presentation I just saw usually does the trick. "Some officers walk out, they're so upset," Sanchez says. "Others come up to me afterwards and say, 'I want to join your unit. I want to catch the guys who are doing this.' You see the lightbulb go off. They realize we're not just the puppy police."

An hour later, we're out on patrol, headed to a house in a neighborhood just a few miles south of where the dog heads were found. Sanchez drives, sharing the front of his unmarked gray Ford 500 with Officer Cherrette. Deputy DA Knaan and I sit in back. About eight months ago, a neighbor left an anonymous message on a dog-fighting tip line that Knaan created in 2009 with funding from the HSUS. She told Sanchez about the tip, and he set up what he asks me to refer to only as "unorthodox surveillance," given the cutting-edge nature of the investigation. That's something he's brought to the task force since taking command in 2011. He wants to make sure his unit is employing the same state-of-the art techniques others are using to bust gangsters and drug dealers. In the coming months, he's planning on introducing everything from undercover investigations to CSI-style forensics. "We had a guy going around a neighborhood putting rat poison in ground beef and throwing it into people's yards," he says, raising his voice so he can be heard over the crackle of the police radio. "If we could trace the source of the poison, we might be able to nab someone."

Sanchez's high-tech surveillance hadn't produced the expected results. Thanks to the presentation he gave me earlier, I knew the signs of dog fighting: shredded faces, missing ears, and a smorgasbord of paraphernalia, from weighted collars to build neck muscles to wooden break sticks used to pry the jaws of one dog from the body of another so that they can continue tearing each other apart. Sanchez hadn't seen any of that in this location. Instead, he'd observed three pit bulls and a bulldog being kept in squalid conditions, wasting away their days in small, make-shift pens, paw-deep in feces and without adequate food and water. Now we're heading over to inspect things firsthand.

We pull up to the house, a squat, off-white dwelling that can't pos-sibly contain more than a single bedroom, sunk under a tattered gray roof that bleeds blue insulation over windows and walls. In the front yard lays the bleached shell of an ice cream truck, and a small girl, per-haps around six years old, sits on a crumbling porch surrounded by a few teenagers and a middle-aged woman wearing blue sweats and a stained white T-shirt. A couple of large guys emerge from nearby homes. San-chez puts his car in park and turns to face me and Knaan. "There's a lot of gang activity in this area—and a lot of contempt for law enforce-ment," he says. "I want you to keep a clear line of sight to the car. If things get crazy, run back here. This place can go from zero to sixty in a second." Cherrette gets on the radio to dispatch: "Is there any way you can have a patrol unit in the area in case things go sideways on us?" We exit the car.

Sanchez hands me and Knaan a pair of white booties to slip over our shoes, and we walk up to the house. DAS officers Smith and Shepphird have arrived a couple of minutes before us. They're already talking to the people on the porch. The middle-aged woman, who refers to herself as "Auntie," is getting nervous. "Why it take so many of y'all just to check on a few dogs?" she shouts. Sanchez holds us back. He figures a couple of animal control officers will arouse less animosity than a pair of gun-toting detectives with a reporter and a county prosecutor in tow. He's right. Within a few minutes, Auntie has calmed down, and she al-lows us behind the house where the dogs are being kept. The backyard is worse than the front, littered with broken TVs, car tires, a discarded toilet, shards of glass, and a crushed baby crib. The smell of dog feces is overpowering. Flies are everywhere.

The first dog we see is a brown-and-white pit bull sitting in a four-by-four chain-link cage. He has an open wound on his chest about the size of a silver dollar, and red bumps and bald patches on his face that look like mange. He wags his tail as we approach. Sanchez pulls a bacon treat from his back pocket and pushes it through the cage. The other dogs are in small runs separated by plywood barriers, their enclosures barren save for empty aluminum bowls and chewed chunks of mattress lining. One of the home's teenagers—wearing a bright yellow shirt, gleaming white shoes, and tight blue jeans with the tags still attached—approaches us. "This your dog?" says Sanchez, pointing at the wounded pit bull. "Naw," the teenager says. "Any of these dogs belong to any of you?" Sanchez asks, turning to the others who, along with a few neighbors, have now gathered around us. Same response. "Well this dog needs medical care," he says sternly. "If you don't take him to the vet by Friday, Animal Services is going to come and impound him." Then we make our way through the crowd and leave.

I'm surprised Sanchez didn't do more. When we're back in the car he tells me there's a limit to what the LAPD can do without a warrant. We were mainly there for the DAS officers' protection. If the wounded dog was in immediate danger, Smith and Shepphird could have taken him. And on Friday they probably would. Still, Sanchez says he has seen enough that he could likely come back and make arrests. "These guys probably aren't engaged in dog fighting, but it looks like they're trying to breed dogs for fighting. At the very least, they're violating a penal code section that requires you to provide animals with a sanitary place to live. Not to mention giving them adequate food and water. We could charge them with neglect. And if that one dog's injuries are life-threatening, and we can get a vet to back that up, we might be able to get them on a felony."

The four of us stop for lunch at a deli not far from LAPD headquarters. As we sit at a table waiting for our order, Sanchez tells me that one of the most impressive things about the case we just saw is that a neighbor had reported it. "This is a neighborhood where you have gangsters that essentially shut down entire streets and have parties. If you call the police, they'll beat you up or kill you. Someone really stuck their neck out here." Still, he isn't surprised, given his experiences during his short time with the task force. "I have eighteen years in law enforcement, and I've seen a lot," he says, chewing on garlic bread and sipping coffee. "But animal cruelty takes things to whole new level." And it doesn't just get to him—it gets to the public. "I think we've become desensitized as a nation to crimes against humans. Shootings and police chases are on the news every day. But how many times do you hear about someone decapitating a dog? Animal abuse smacks people in the face front and center. Society has drawn a line in the sand: if you do this to an animal, there's a special place in hell for you."

That's what keeps Sanchez motivated. When he worked human trafficking, he'd spend hundreds of hours on an investigation, only to have the case fall apart because judges or juries didn't find the victims credible or because prosecutors didn't want to deal with pimps and prostitutes. And he got no support from the public. "I was spending a lot of time away from my family and getting nothing in return," he says. But animal abuse is a different story. A few months ago, the chief of police was going to disband the task force. Budgets were tight, and he wanted to move the officers to "more important" units. But when the public got wind of it, Sanchez says, "thousands of e-mails came into our command staff. They were inundated. They had to shut down because they couldn't work. Finally, they said, 'OK, we get it!'" And unlike with human trafficking, when Sanchez's animal abuse cases go to court, judges and prosecutors are receptive, and it doesn't take much to get a conviction. "The animal is the most powerful evidence," he says. "You show a picture like one of the ones I showed you, and you're done. How can someone defend that?" A year ago, Sanchez was burnt out on police work. Today he's thinking about a permanent position as head of the task force. "This unit has completely recharged my batteries," he says. "For the first time in a long time, I go home feeling a sense of satisfaction."

A lot of the credit goes to the woman sitting across from him: Deborah Knaan. Like Sanchez, she wasn't an animal person. "I never had pets. I didn't give a rat's behind about them," she tells me. Then, thirteen years ago, her husband brought home a Jack Russell terrier puppy named Ziggy. "I guess," she pauses, "it's a feeling that most women have when they have a child. It totally changed me." Knaan soon adopted another dog. She went vegetarian. And she started learning about animal cruelty and pet overpopulation. She became obsessed. She began visiting her local shelters and looking for the hardest-luck cases she could find:

fourteen-year-olds with heart conditions, mutts missing most of their teeth, blind dogs with arthritis that were about to be euthanized. Then she took them back to her place, cared for them for a few months, and found them homes. But it wasn't enough. "There were tens of thousands of dogs I wasn't helping," she says. "I was essentially sticking my finger in a dyke."

By then, Knaan had been a deputy DA for a few years, hauling rapists and child molesters into court for the LA County District Attorney's Office, the largest prosecuting agency in the country. Now she wanted to go after animal abusers too. But there weren't enough cases coming in. The Animal Cruelty Task Force didn't exist, and cops weren't taking the trouble to investigate these crimes. So Knaan volunteered to serve on a city commission that oversees the Department of Animal Services. There, she helped set up a program to license dogs online, which increased spay/neuter rates, and she got animal control officers to start asking questions whenever someone tried to drop off an injured pet at a shelter. "They used to just accept the animal, no questions asked," she says. "Now they take people aside and talk to them. 'If it's clear that the person harmed the animal,' I tell them, 'you can't let them walk out the door without filing charges.'"

In 2005, Knaan returned to the idea of prosecuting animal crimes full-time. The Animal Cruelty Task Force had now been set up, and she wanted a similarly specialized unit within the DA's office, one that would take animal abuse as seriously as human crimes. "I wanted to make sure cruelty cases didn't slip through the cracks," she says. She pestered her boss, the head DA, for two years. Finally, she got her way. In 2007, the DA's office created the Animal Cruelty Prosecution Program, the only one of its kind in the country. It put Knaan in charge. "It was a dream," she says. "It combined the best of everything I cared about."

Today, Knaan oversees twenty-eight prosecutors in offices around LA County. She trains them in the complexities of animal law and makes sure each follows the entire case, from filing to verdict. Knaan calls this "vertical prosecution," and she said the only other programs that do it are those dedicated to sex crimes and domestic violence. "In other crimes, a typical case can go though four to six prosecutors. Someone handles the filing, someone else handles the preliminary hearing, another person handles the pretrial, and still others handle the trial itself." With animal cruelty, cops have a direct bridge from arrest to conviction. "It makes you feel like whoever gets the case, there's ownership," Sanchez tells me. "We build a working relationship with these people, and it makes our unit better." All the while, Knaan tracks every case that comes in, making sure the correct—and toughest—charges are being filed. Her program has prosecuted hundreds of cases of animal cruelty. The majority of these have culminated in convictions, putting animal abusers behind bars for years.

Knaan has also become an unofficial member of the Animal Cruelty Task Force, sitting in on briefings, tagging along on investigations, and brainstorming cases with Sanchez and his colleagues. In one recent incident, a man brought a dead dog into the vet. Officers suspected abuse, but they didn't have enough evidence. So Knaan told them to get a polygraph and to have the vet take X-rays. Someone, it turns out, had shoved a toothbrush down the animal's throat. She's going to prosecute this one herself.

In the meantime, Knaan has continued to fight for animals outside the courtroom. She crafted a state law that prohibits anyone convicted of mistreating an animal from owning pets for up to ten years. She frequently speaks to the public about how to spot and report animal cruelty. And she's planning on creating a program that will train grocery store employees to look for cats and dogs trapped in hot cars as they collect shopping carts. She also travels the state, trying to get other DA offices to create their own animal cruelty prosecution units. "Once you have a program like mine, it ups the ante for everybody," she says. "Whatever I've done here, I want to make sure it keeps going after I leave."

The following day, I say good-bye to Detective Sanchez. We're at a large city shelter, and he and a couple of members of his task force have just given a presentation to a group of elementary school children in a classroom here on how to spot and report animal cruelty. After the talk, Sanchez and I walk out into a courtyard, the afternoon sun scattering in the branches above our heads. The shelter is full of pets—cage after cage of cats and dogs rescued from the street, from hoarders, from dog fighters, from neglect and abuse—and I can hear the barking and meowing as we sit down. Sanchez tells me that when he was just a beat cop, his supervisor made him issue a citation to a street vendor who was selling corn. The man would slather it with mayonnaise, and kids would line up around the block, as if he were the ice cream truck. The man didn't have a license to sell food, but Sanchez didn't want to bother him. What harm was he doing? Dutifully, he walked up to the cart and just happened to glance into the jar of mayonnaise. It was full of mold.

"Some people don't understand why we spend time on these crimes," he tells me. But take the pit bull we saw yesterday, he says. He'll probably be brought here, and if he's lucky, he'll find a new home. "The worst thing that can happen is for us not to do anything," he says, looking back at the classroom. "What kind of message would that send to these kids?"

Sanchez's phone buzzes on his side. It's his partner, James Cherrette. He gets up and tells me he has to go back out on patrol. A call has come in, and he might have a lead on the beheading case. Afterward, he'll head home and feed his new dog—the first pet he's ever had.

SEVEN

My Cat Is Not a Toaster

On a drizzly Sunday in mid-December 1894, Minnie McCleary spotted her Maltese cat in the backyard of James H. Friedel, a local restaurant owner. Both lived in the Canton neighborhood of East Baltimore, a couple of blocks from the harbor. When she demanded the animal back, Friedel refused, claiming it was his. The feline, he asserted, had been a gift from his daughter-in-law, who had obtained it from a British ship. But McCleary knew better. She had owned the cat for a year, ever since her brother-in-law brought it to Baltimore in a grape basket. And there was one thing Friedel had overlooked.

McCleary summoned the constable, who arrested Friedel, charged him with larceny, and brought him before Justice George A. Cook. What followed was a most unusual trial. Cook's first order of business was determining who really owned the cat. He seized upon a key difference in the testimony: McCleary said the Maltese was a female; Friedel claimed it was a tomcat. Apparently not wanting to investigate for himself, the judge convened a committee of six local citizens—three men and three women—to inspect the feline, currently being held at the Canton police station. Each visited the cat, and each came back with the same verdict: female. That was good enough for Justice Cook. He ordered the animal returned to McCleary and focused his attention on punishing Friedel. There was just one problem: Maryland law did not consider a cat property. So had Friedel actually committed a crime?

Justice Cook wasn't sure. Neither were prominent legal experts. "If they are domestic animals, I see no reason why they should not be called property as any other tame animal is," opined Major R. M. Venable, a law professor at the University of Maryland. A fellow professor at the university disagreed. "Cats are wild animals," said Edgar H. Gans, "and as such they cannot be called property in the state of Maryland." It wasn't a trivial debate. "The question is a very important one," said Skipwith Wilmer, a cofounder of the Bar Association of Baltimore City. "It is of great interest to all the citizens of Baltimore whose slumbers are disturbed by the nightly concerts of feline prowlers." Could one throw a shoe at them? Or shoot them? Not, said Wilmer, if they were someone's property.

With no resolution in sight, Maryland Attorney General John P. Poe stepped into the fray. Unlike his second cousin, Edgar Allan, the state's chief legal advisor was apparently no fan of felines. "A cat," he said, "is not legal property. . . . It is of no utility. It is as much a wild animal, in a legal sense, as are its relatives—the tiger and the wild-cat. I should not consider that the taking of a cat without the consent of its owner was an indictable offense." Poe's opinion swayed Justice Cook. He released Friedel without sentence. In the eyes of the law, a man who had stolen a cat had stolen nothing at all.

The Road to Property

One of the great ironies of the anticruelty laws created by Henry Bergh and his followers was that they turned cats and dogs into some of the most legally protected animals in the country long before the law recognized them as things of value. You could be thrown in jail for kicking a dog but go scot-free for snatching it. Livestock didn't have this problem. Chickens, pigs, and horses had a clear market value. Their meat and their services were worth something to society. They were, in the eyes of the law, valuable property. Peer far enough back, however, and nothing was property.

Once upon a time, all of nature was owned by everyone and by no one. Our early human ancestors—the small, roving bands of individuals who trekked through cold, dry Europe 30,000 years ago, perhaps domesticating the dog in the process—had little need for more than the basic material goods: a bow, a hide, and maybe a few carved figurines. But as we began to settle down about 12,000 years ago, building the first permanent villages and burying our dead (and sometimes our pets) under our homes, we started to trade jewelry and other goods. Items that once belonged to the earth now belonged to us. Soon, we turned nature itself into property, cultivating crops, domesticating livestock, and passing our accumulated wealth down through the generations. We occupied; we owned; we coveted. And we needed laws to protect all of it.

Early laws were oral, recited by tribal elders around campfires and taught by fathers to children in small, round huts. Then, as villages grew larger and coalesced into cities and civilizations, we began writing our laws down. Some of the earliest examples are found on clay tablets unearthed in Mesopotamia. Carved around 2100 BC, just as cats were beginning to make their mark on Egyptian society, they concern penalties for murder, robbery, and sorcery. "If a man, in the course of a scuffle, smashed the limb of another man with a club, he shall pay one mina of silver," reads the Code of Ur-Nammu, discovered in modern-day Iraq. Later laws speak of animals as property and lay out the penalties for harming or taking them. "If anyone steals a bull . . . he shall give 15 [head of] cattle," reads one of the Hittite laws, written in cuneiform around 1600 BC in what is today Turkey. "If anyone blinds the eye of an ox or horse, he shall give six shekels of silver and pledge his estate as security," commands another.

More than 1,000 years later, Rome created its Law of the Twelve Tables, a code that guided the republic for centuries and became the blueprint for Western jurisprudence. Under Roman law, you were either a person or a thing. At various points, women, children, and slaves were all things. A father could even sell his kids to another family. But domesticated animals were always things—and always property. "If anyone kills . . . a four-footed beast of the class of cattle," read one Roman law, "let him be condemned to pay the owner the highest value that the property had attained during the preceding year."

Roman law eventually gave way to the laws of the church, which dominated well into the Middle Ages. Here, the status of animals as property was even clearer. Man, according to Genesis, had "dominion over the fish of the sea, and over the fowl of the air, and over every living thing that moveth upon the earth." Stealing animals was such a big deal that the crime made its way into the Tenth Commandment: "Thou shalt not covet thy neighbor's house, thou shalt not covet thy neighbor's wife, nor his manservant, nor his maidservant, nor his ox, nor his ass, nor any thing that is thy neighbor's." Being property had its advantages for animals. It meant they were valued. It meant they were protected. At least, if they were farm animals. Dogs and cats weren't mentioned much.

One notable exception appears in the writings of Hywel the Good, a tenth-century Welsh king who crafted a set of laws widely considered among the most just and compassionate of their time. Recognizing the utility of cats in protecting human food stores, Hywel's codes placed a high value on them as property. "The worth of a kitten from the night it is kittened until it shall open its eyes is a legal penny [the same as a lamb]; and from that time until it shall kill mice, two legal pence; and after it shall kill mice, four legal pence." If a cat was killed or stolen, Hywel wrote, "its head is to be put downwards upon a clean, even floor, with its tail lifted upwards, and thus suspended, whilst wheat is poured about it, until the tip of its tail be covered, and that is to be its worth." Hywel's laws also valued dogs—based mostly on their breeding and status. The king's greyhound was worth 120 pence; the lapdog of a foreigner, 4 pence.

But when the Black Death swept Europe, dogs and cats lost their value once again. For centuries, legal scholars argued that, among animals, only livestock could be considered property. The biggest proponent of this view was also one of the most influential jurists of all time, an eighteenth-century Englishman named William Blackstone. Blackstone came along during a period when the common law of England, derived from centuries of court decisions, had grown into a morass of legalese so complex and esoteric that even experts had a hard time penetrating it. He brought clarity and structure. In his *Commentaries on the Laws of England*, published in four volumes in the mid- to late 1760s, Blackstone broke the law down into concise, accessible, and sometimes poetic language, creating a legal bible that even nonlawyers could understand. And "bible" was the appropriate word, as many of his arguments drew heavily on the holy book. Animals, for one, held a familiar status:

> They are distinguished into such as are *domitæ* and such as are *feræ naturæ*: some being of a *tame* and others of a *wild* disposition. In such as are of a nature tame and domestic, (as horses, kine, sheep, poultry,

and the like) a man may have as absolute a property as in any inanimate being. . . . The stealing, or forcible abduction, of such property as this, is also felony; for these are things of intrinsic value, serving for the food of man, or else for the uses of husbandry . . . but not so, if they are only kept for pleasure, curiosity, or whim, as dogs, bears, cats, apes, parrots and singing birds; because their value is not intrinsic, but depending only on the caprice of the owner.

Blackstone's book became required reading in England's law schools, and it sold out repeatedly, turning generations of university students into lawyers. Its influence in America was even more profound. The young country had little case law to go on, especially as it expanded into new and wild territories. In some places, *Commentaries on the Laws of England* literally became the law of the land; it was often the only book horseback-riding judges could afford to carry. One story has Abraham Lincoln purchasing all four volumes from a man in a covered wagon heading west. John Adams was also a fan, as were other drafters of the Declaration of Independence and the US Constitution.

Blackstone's words echoed through the halls of American courts for more than a century. In 1897, the US Supreme Court quoted him almost verbatim in the case of a dog struck and killed by a train in New Orleans. The canine, a pregnant Newfoundland named Countess Lona, had wandered onto the tracks, and her owner sued the railroad company for negligence. The man didn't have a case, the court ruled, in part because his dog was not property in the eyes of the law. Dogs, wrote Justice Henry Billings Brown, "are not considered as being upon the same plane with horses, cattle, sheep, and other domesticated animals, but rather in the category of cats, monkeys, parrots, singing birds, and similar animals, kept for pleasure, curiosity, or caprice. They have no intrinsic value." Still, the court left the door open for the law to evolve. "It is purely within the discretion of the legislature to say how far dogs shall be recognized as property," wrote Brown. That time was almost at hand.

On May 16, 1917, a four-and-a-half-pound Pomeranian pranced down the streets of San Francisco, his owner's two maids in tow. He was a blue blood among dogs, bestowed with the kennel name "Encliffe-Masterpiece" and having taken first place at every dog show in which he'd competed. None of this mattered to the Airedale terrier quickly approaching from behind. The terrier had a vicious reputation—and it was out alone. Before the maids could react, it pounced on the Pomeranian's back and broke his neck, killing him instantly.

The Pomeranian's owner sued the owner of the Airedale, and the case wound its way to a California court of appeals. Like the US Supreme Court twenty years earlier, the appellate court invoked the words of William Blackstone—but this time to repudiate them. "As Blackstone puts it, dogs . . . had no intrinsic value," the court said. "But that day has passed, and dogs now have a well-established status before the law." In a surprisingly sentimental opinion, the court spoke of the Pomeranian's having "crossed to that shore from which none, not even a good dog, ever returns" and of the important role canines had played in human civilization: "From the building of the pyramids to the present day, from the frozen poles to the torrid zone, wherever man has wandered there has been his dog." Canines, ruled the court, "have a pecuniary value, and constitute property of their owners, as much so as horses and cattle or other domestic animals." It awarded the Pomeranian's owner $500 in damages, about the price of a Model-T.

By the early 1900s, as dogs entered our homes (and the homes of judges and politicians), they were finally beginning to enjoy a legal status as valuable animals. Several states had passed laws declaring them property and imposing punishment for their theft. Cats, meanwhile, perhaps because they still spent most of their time outside, hadn't progressed very far from their ignominious days in Baltimore. A law article from the time reflects the state of affairs:

> It is an interesting but ambiguous commentary on the character of the cat that in all the literature of judicial opinion, English or American, hardly more than a dozen cases can be found in a which a cat has played a principal role, as aggressor, as sufferer, or as object of proprietary value. This may be a tribute to the harmlessness of her nature; it may be due to her silent elusiveness and diabolic stealth; or it may bear the simple, prosaic interpretation that litigation has passed her by because *de minimis non curat lex* ["the law does not concern itself with trifles"]. Her

hereditary canine rival . . . has barked, bit, and egg-sucked his way into numberless pages of the books until a monumental system of tort and property law has been erected on his head. . . . But *Felis domestica* is almost conspicuous in her absence from the records of the forum.

It took a literal fight with a dog for cats to finally get noticed. A 1914 Maine Supreme Court case concerned a foxhound named Tray that chased a cat onto the property of Alonzo Carter. Carter, the cat's owner, shot and killed the dog. In his defense, he cited a state statute saying that "any person may lawfully kill a dog which is found worrying, wounding, or killing any domestic animal." The dog's owner sued Carter for $50, claiming that cats did not qualify as domestic. To settle the case, the judges cracked open several dictionaries, all of which supported Carter. The court went on to opine,

> The time of its first domestication is lost in the mists of the dawn of history, but it is apparent that the cat was a domestic animal among the early Egyptians, by whom it came to be regarded as sacred, as evidenced by the device of Cambyses during his invasion of Egypt B. C. 525 or 527, which could scarcely have been feasible if the animal was then wild. From that day to this it has been a dweller in the homes of men. In no other animal has affection for home been more strongly developed. . . . It is clear, therefore, from the popular meaning of the word "domestic" and from our knowledge of its habits gained from fact and experience that the cat is a domestic animal.

The decision wasn't a total victory for cats, however. Though the court sided with Carter, it also stated that "the cat is not the subject of larceny." Poor puss could still be stolen without repercussion.

Things finally began to change in the early 1930s. In one notable case, police in Topeka, Kansas, threatened to throw a man named William Smith in jail for keeping eight cats in his house. A city ordinance forbade owning more than five. Smith sued all the way to the Kansas Supreme Court, which ruled that the police had violated his property rights. Referencing everything from the cat's darkest days as the supposed incarnation of Satan to the contemporary craze of feline photography, the court wrote that "the worth of the cat as a contributor to the felicity of the home is alone sufficient to require that it be regarded as property of the owner in the full sense of the term property." It cleared Smith of the charges and declared the city ordinance void—a violation of life, liberty, and the pursuit of happiness.

As the decades ticked by, courts and legislators imposed stiffer and stiffer penalties for the stealing of cats and dogs. Arkansas made dog theft a felony in 1951. Other states levied fines of up to $2,000. A rash of pet thefts to supply a growing biomedical industry probably helped spur some of these statutes. Snatching a dog or a cat had become a big deal.

That didn't stop a man named Robert Sadowski. On the evening of February 12, 1982, he parked his Honda in front of the Los Angeles home of Veronica Meleson. As she watched from inside, Sadowski walked onto her driveway and grabbed her lynx-point Balinese cat, Truffle. Meleson ran out the door yelling, and Sadowski dropped the cat. Four days later, he returned and sped away with the feline before Meleson could stop him. When Sadowski was arrested and tried, he claimed he had committed no crime because it wasn't illegal to steal a cat under California law. The court disagreed. It charged him with grand theft and sentenced him to three years in prison.

Fighting for Cats and Dogs

The marriage of Stanley and Linda Perkins began on an ominous note. Mere days before their wedding in 1994, Stanley's dog attacked and killed Linda's cat. The childless San Diego couple gave the dog away and began looking for a pet they could own together. Two years later, they adopted Gigi, a pointer-greyhound mix. Two years after that, they divorced.

That was hardly the end of the story. Over the next two years, the Perkinses waged war in one of the most bitter and expensive pet custody battles in US history. Arguments began in superior court in 1998, with Linda, a thirty-six-year-old small-business owner, claiming she was Gigi's "mommy." As evidence, she showed the judge a birthday card: To "a special 'Mom,'" it read. "Love, Gigi." Stanley, a forty-two-year-old anesthesiologist, charged that if Linda was Gigi's mom, she was an unfit one, who couldn't provide the home life and emotional support he could. To make matters worse, Linda owned a cat named Muffin. "Gigi and Muffin do not play together and they never have," he asserted in court. The two, he said, were "natural enemies." Exasperated, the judge granted temporary custody of Gigi to Stanley, with Linda allowed weekend visitations.

The arrangement didn't take. Four months later, with the ownership dispute still unresolved, the judge told Stanley and Linda to consult a specialist. So they hired an animal behavior expert. Acting like a social worker in a child custody case, the behaviorist visited both Stanley's and Linda's homes and ran through a checklist of doggy well-being: Who walked Gigi more? Who fed her better-quality food? Who lived in a safer neighborhood? Ultimately, the behaviorist decided that it was in Gigi's best interest to live with Linda. The judge reversed his original decision. He granted Linda custody of the dog, with weekend visitation for Stanley.

Like many children of divorce, however, Gigi didn't take well to split custody. She was stressed out. She became skittish. "She wasn't," said Stanley, "her normal happy self." In 2000, he and Linda returned to the judge and asked him to award one of them full custody. This time, Linda's lawyer had a trick up her sleeve. An experienced family law attorney, she employed a tactic that had worked well in child custody cases: she shot a "day in the life" video. In it, Gigi naps under Linda's desk, walks in the park, and frolics on the beach. Two years after her divorce, and $146,000 in legal fees later, Linda got full custody of the dog.

By the mid-twentieth century, dogs and cats had earned their place as legal property. Yet, once again, public opinion was far ahead of judicial rulings. People had begun to see their companion animals as family members, a burgeoning pet industry was supplying them with everything from premium dog food to kitty condos, and pet hospitals had started to resemble human ones. So when courts began to refer to cats and dogs as mere property—no different from a couch or a car—it didn't sit well with owners.

It wasn't just the sentimental attachment people had for their pets. Dogs and cats don't exactly fit well into the property mold. First, the obvious: they're alive. They're also unique; clones and twins aside, no two dogs have ever been the same. And their value is almost impossible to calculate. Horses and cows have an established market price, based on their age and utility. But my cat Jasper—who's been the closest thing

I've had to a child for eight years; on whom my wife and I have now spent more than $10,000 to keep alive through cat fights and kidney failure; and who, as I type this sentence, sits on my lap purring—how much is he worth? About fifty bucks. That's what it would cost me to get another cat from the shelter. Jasper may be my fur baby, but in the eyes of the law, he's a toaster.

That's a real problem when it comes to tort law, the branch of jurisprudence concerned with people's responsibilities to one another. When someone harms you, and you decide to sue, you're hoping the judge will award you enough money to "make you whole." If a neighbor breaks your window, $100 might do it. If he kills your son, it could take millions. Tort law is the foundation of civil society. It ensures that we go to court to hash out our differences rather than shooting each other in the streets. But tort law doesn't work if we feel that courts are being unfair. If Jasper means $50,000 to my heart, and a judge gives me $50 if someone kills him, I'm still going to be $49,950 worth of pissed off.

By the 1960s, judges were starting to get the message. In a landmark 1964 case before the Florida Supreme Court, a garbage collector had come to pick up the trash of Phyllis La Porte one morning while she was making breakfast. She had her miniature dachshund, Heidi, tied up in the yard. As La Porte watched from her window, the man picked up an empty trash can and hurled it at Heidi, killing her. He then laughed and left. La Porte was so upset, she sought medical treatment; her physician described her as incoherent and hysterical. The court awarded La Porte $3,000 in damages, including compensation for "mental suffering"—one of the first times such a claim had been allowed in a case involving a pet. Though La Porte had purchased the dog for only $75, the court felt that simply compensating this amount would not make her whole. "The restriction of the loss of a pet to its intrinsic value in circumstances such as the ones before us is a principle we cannot accept," it ruled. "We feel that the affection of a master for his dog is a very real thing and that the malicious destruction of the pet provides an element of damage for which the owner should recover, irrespective of the value of the animal."

Cats and dogs were making progress, but they were still essentially being treated like pieces of property in the courtroom. Awards in the thousands of dollars were certainly a big deal—especially for animals that, until recently, hadn't even merited larceny charges—but people could seek similar "noneconomic damages" for the loss of a number of inanimate objects. If someone came into my house and, hoping to traumatize me, set my great grandmother's wedding dress or my family photo album on fire while I watched, I could sue for the same type of damages Phyllis La Porte got for her dog Heidi. Today, the claim would be called "intentional infliction of emotional distress." I couldn't sue, however, if someone had caused the damage negligently. Most states put severe restrictions on so-called negligent infliction of emotional distress claims, limiting them to harm done to immediate family members. Not even fiancées and best friends qualify.

That's what made the 1979 New York court decision *Corso v. Crawford Dog and Cat Hospital, Inc.* so remarkable. The case involved not the death of a pet but rather what happened to it after it died. In late January 1978, Kay Corso brought her fifteen-year-old poodle to the veterinarian to be euthanized. She told the vet she wanted an elaborate funeral, and he agreed to make the necessary arrangements. But on the day of the service, with a headstone, epitaph, and mourners already in place, Corso opened the casket to discover the body of a dead cat inside. She sued for mental suffering. Despite the fact that negligence was involved, the judge allowed the claim, and in his decision he made it clear that pets had moved beyond the realm of mere property:

> This court now overrules prior precedent and holds that a pet is not just a thing but occupies a special place somewhere between a person and a piece of personal property. . . . This decision is not to be construed to include an award for the loss of a family heirloom which would also cause great mental anguish. An heirloom while it might be the source of good feelings is merely an inanimate object and is not capable of returning love and affection. It does not respond to human stimulation; it has no brain capable of displaying emotion which in turn causes a human response. Losing the right to memorialize a pet rock, or a pet tree or losing a family picture album is not actionable. But a dog, that is something else. To say it is a piece of personal property and no more is a repudiation of our humaneness. This I cannot accept.

A year later, another New York court went even further. When an elderly woman's German shepherd mix died at a kennel under unclear circumstances, the judge allowed her to recover damages for loss of companionship, a legal claim even more restricted than negligent infliction of emotional distress. Some states don't allow it at all, and those that do typically limit it to husband-wife or parent-child relationships. What's more, the relevant laws always refer to the death of "a person." The court found that the German shepherd essentially fit these criteria. The woman, it noted, had acquired the animal shortly after she lost her husband, and it had become "her sole and constant companion." It slept with her, guarded her house, and accompanied her on her nightly walks. The dog, the judge reasoned, had taken the place of her former spouse. "It would be wrong," she ruled, "not to acknowledge the companionship and protection that Mrs. Brousseau lost with the death of her canine companion of eight years."

For the next two decades, judges showed an increasing openness to treating cats and dogs like people. But the decisions were sporadic, and they almost never set precedent that future courts could rely on. Then, one night in August 1999, Tennessee state senator Steve Cohen let his twelve-year-old Shih Tzu, T-Bo, out to do his business. Roaming the Nashville neighborhood was a larger dog, and when it saw the Shih Tzu, it attacked and nearly killed him. Cohen rushed his pet to the emergency clinic, but the dog died three days later. When he sued the larger dog's owner, the judge limited his compensation to vet bills and the cost of replacing T-Bo with a similar dog. "It was then I realized that the law didn't deal with loss of affection and companionship," Cohen remarked at the time. "Dogs, cats, pets were treated as any inanimate, personal property—like losing a shirt or damaging a lamp." He aimed to change that. In 2000, Cohen introduced the T-Bo Act, a law that would allow owners of cats and dogs in Tennessee to recover up to $5,000 in noneconomic damages for the loss of a pet, even if it was the result of a negligent act. It was the first of its kind in the country, and it passed with overwhelming support. Since then, Illinois and Connecticut have enacted similar laws, and fourteen other states have proposed them, some with caps of up to $100,000.

By the turn of the twenty-first century, the law was beginning to recognize dogs and cats as family members. And yet it was always the *owner's* loss, the *owner's* anguish on trial. What about the feelings and interests of the animals themselves? Remarkably, judges would begin to consider those too.

Stanley and Linda Perkins' war for Gigi may have been one of the most extreme custody battles over a pet, but it wasn't the first. That honor belongs to a 1944 Indiana case. When John Akers and Stella Sellers divorced, a trial court divided up their property but made no mention of their Boston bull terrier. Sellers got the house, and since the terrier was living there, she took the dog too. Akers sued to recover the animal, and an appellate court heard the case. Acknowledging that such matters might be considered "a trespass on the court's time and an imposition on our patience," it nevertheless stated that "no man can be censured for the prosecution of his rights to the full limit of the law when such rights involve the comfort derived from the companionship of man's best friend." In the end, however, the court decided to treat the dog like any other piece of property. Though it admitted that the terrier might be better off with the husband (the wife had shown little interest in the animal during the proceedings), the court allowed Sellers to keep the canine, noting that Akers had gifted it to her during their marriage. "Whether the interests and desires of the dog, in such a situation, should be the polar star pointing the way to a just and wise decision, or whether the matter should be determined on the brutal and unfeeling basis of legal title, is a problem concerning which we express no opinion," it ruled.

Forty years later, an Iowa court finally waded into those waters. Like the Indiana case, the Iowa trial involved a husband gifting a dog to his wife before they divorced. Jay Stewart had given the animal, Georgetta, to his spouse for Christmas. But even though this gave legal title to the wife, the court awarded custody to the husband. "The dog accompanies Jay to the office and spends a substantial portion of the day with Jay," it noted. The judges still regarded Georgetta as property, but they said that, when deciding custody, "courts should not put a family pet in a position of being abused or uncared for"—the first sign that courts were willing to consider the best interests of a pet.

Best interests are a staple of child custody cases. Judges are required to place children in the most appropriate home. They must ask themselves questions like, Which parent do the kids have a closer relationship with?

Where are they most likely to thrive, socially and educationally? Where will they be the safest? But pets are property, and property shouldn't have interests.

That's what made the years following the Stewart case so extraordinary. With increasing regularity, courts were willing to consider cats and dogs as beings whose interests mattered. Societal trends didn't hurt. In the post–World War II era, pet ownership exploded—and so did divorce rates. This resulted in more and more court cases centered on the custody of pets. And the custody of pets was at issue in the first place because dogs and cats were more a part of the American family than ever. Spouses were fighting over cats and dogs like children because these pets had *become* children.

This relationship has only grown stronger in recent years. Though no one seems to keep figures on these things, a 2005 *Los Angeles Times* article, quoting a legal scholar, estimates there has been a hundredfold increase in pet custody cases since 1990. And unlike traditional custody battles, you don't have to be married to feud over the ownership of a pet: unmarried couples and even roommates are bringing custody suits.

One of the most cited pet custody cases is a 1997 battle between two men who shared an apartment in Arlington, Virginia. When they decided to go their separate ways, they fought over a gray, long-haired cat named Grady that they had lived with for about a year. Under a strict property analysis, Grady clearly belonged to one of the men, a twenty-one-year-old named Kovar Gregory. A friend had given him the cat and granted him sole ownership. But the other man, thirty-year-old Andrew Zovko, claimed he had been a better parent to the feline, feeding and cleaning up after him while Gregory did almost nothing. Zovko slept with Grady, shared his vet bills, and even taught him tricks. When he moved out, he took the cat with him. Gregory charged him with larceny. A detective seized the cat and placed him in a shelter for three months while the former roommates battled each other in court. Zovko visited the cat sixty-four times, Gregory only twice, according to a shelter worker. This appears to have swayed the judge. On the day of his ruling, he ordered the cat brought to court. After removing Grady from his cardboard carrier, putting him in his lap, and giving him a treat, he said he would decide "what is in the best interest of Grady the cat." Turning to the two men, he said, "From what I have seen, Grady would be better off with Mr. Zovko. . . . Go, with my blessing, with Grady the cat."

Best interests aside, pet custody cases have begun to mirror child custody cases in other ways. In 1994, an Arkansas judge ordered a divorcing husband to pay $150 per month in dog support. (The arrangement has become so common, it now has a name: petimony.) In 2000, a Minnesota court granted joint custody for a dog named Rudy and sicced the county sheriff on the husband when he refused to return the animal after his scheduled visitation. And in perhaps one of the most colorful pet custody cases, a Tennessee judged ruled in 1987 that a Doberman-Labrador mix dividing his time between ex-spouses must "not be allowed to associate with any ill-bred animals" or "to drink any alcoholic beverages" while in either's company.

Battles over the family cat or dog have become such an issue that in 2007 lawmakers in Wisconsin proposed an act to govern pet custody cases. Inspired by the divorce of a state representative that included a bitter fight over the family Labrador, the legislation, which would have been the first of its kind in the nation, would have required splitting couples to include their pets in divorce proceedings and state whether they had made arrangements for their custody. It would also have given courts the ability to determine the best placement for the animals, including granting visitation. In 2008, lawmakers in Michigan proposed a similar law.

All of this still leaves the problem of how a judge is supposed to decide a pet's best interests when the animal can't speak for itself. One option, which has largely fallen out of favor, is a calling contest. Warring spouses meet in a neutral location like a park, stand at equal distances from their dog, and call for it to see which person the animal comes to. (Some sneaky owners have been known to rub their hands with sausages beforehand.) Other judges, as in the Gigi case, employ animal behaviorists to conduct in-home evaluations. And still others simply tally who has invested the most time and money in the animal, or they go by the so-called Toto Principle, placing the pet with whichever parent gets the kids.

There may be a better way. In a 2010 law review article, law student Tabby McLain says judges should harness the power of science. If a couple is fighting over custody of their cat, for example, the court could order that the feline spend a month with each owner. At the end of that time, a veterinarian would visit both homes, take a blood sample from the animal, and observe its behavior. Excessive grooming, a sign of stress, would be a clue that the cat is not happy in its current environment. High levels of oxytocin and prolactin in the animal's blood would indicate the opposite, as both hormones have been linked to trust and maternal bonding.

When Stanley and Linda Perkins fought over their dog Gigi back in 1998, the battle made the front page of the *San Diego Union-Tribune*. But such cases have now become so common that they hardly warrant mention. In the meantime, something far more fundamental has begun to alter the legal status of pets.

What's in a Name?

Elliot Katz slumped over the exam table, cradling his eleven-year-old Doberman–German shepherd mix. As his young daughters stood sobbing in the background, he drew his head close to the dog's ear and told him not to be scared. A veterinarian himself, Katz—thin, in his early sixties, with a salt-and-pepper beard and short, white hair—had administered the final injection countless times. Now an aggressive form of bone cancer had put him on the other side of the table. As the vet approached, needle in hand, Katz held out the dog's leg so the doctor could find a vein. "It's OK, Manco," he cooed, nuzzling into the dog's neck. "I love you."

A few months later, Katz penned the following message:

To the veterinarians who had treated him, to the humane societies that "licensed" him, to the court and state agencies that had "protected" him, Manco was my "property." I was his "owner." But Manco was not my property, and I was not his owner. . . . I was his foster parent, his friend, his companion, his guardian, his protector, his advocate. . . . The kind of mindset, the kind of legality that treats a being like Manco as property to be bought or sold must end. It is time for our society, and our courts, to see animals as the individuals they are, with their own needs,

wants and rights. It is time we demanded an end to the misguided and
abusive concept of animal ownership.

The words appeared in the spring 1994 newsletter of In Defense of Animals, an organization Katz had founded eleven years earlier. They would
launch one of the most important campaigns in its history. Katz had
established the Northern California–based group in response to complaints that researchers at the University of California, Berkeley, were
not treating their lab animals humanely. He rallied the local community
and was arrested, but he got the school to improve its conditions. Today,
IDA has 80,000 members worldwide and has launched crusades ranging
from organizing boycotts of the fur industry to the 1990 March for the
Animals on Washington, DC, considered the animal rights movement's
first major show of strength in the United States.

Still, despite his group's best efforts, Katz felt that he was only addressing the symptoms of the problem. If he could get people to think
about animals as more than property, perhaps they'd treat them better. If he could get them to use the word "guardian" instead of "owner,"
perhaps they'd reevaluate their relationship with the creatures around
them. And if he could focus his efforts on dogs and cats, perhaps the
public would actually pay attention. In 1997, Katz visited the Marin
Humane Society and the San Francisco SPCA to rally support for his
idea. Two years later, he approached the San Francisco Commission of
Animal Control & Welfare about inserting the word "guardian" into all
of the city's animal-related statutes and literature: everything from leash
laws to the forms at animal shelters (where you're already "adopting"
a pet, not "buying" one). The commission approved the idea, but its
board of supervisors shot it down.

Katz wasn't deterred. He has a reputation as a pit bull; once he
chomps down on an issue, he doesn't let go. He spent the next few years
writing about the "Guardian Campaign" in IDA newsletters, encouraging his supporters to contact their local humane societies and to cross
out the word "owner" on any pet-related forms they had to sign. He also
enlisted high-profile endorsements from prominent politicians, veterinarians, and celebrities like Peter Falk and Jane Goodall. At one point,
he was on a radio show with Carl Friedman, San Francisco's director of

animal care and control. Every time Friedman used the word "owner," Katz interrupted him and asked him to say "guardian" instead. "In the elevator on the way down from the show," Katz told me, "Friedman said, 'Elliot, I give up. You win.'" In 2003, the city added the term "guardian" to its municipal codes.

By then, six other cities had done the same. Though Katz's initial meeting with San Francisco's animal control commission hadn't produced results, it received national media coverage. A thousand miles away, a friend told Boulder, Colorado, resident Rita Anderson about the "guardian" idea. She approached the city council. Local newspapers voiced support, as did fellow resident Marc Bekoff, taking a break from his studies of dog play. In 2000, the city council voted overwhelmingly not just to add "guardian" to all of its ordinances but to strike all instances of "owner" when it referred to companion animals. "In order to purchase a city dog license, a guardian must provide proof of a current rabies vaccination," reads one law.

As of this writing, nineteen cities—from San Jose to St. Louis—two counties, and the state of Rhode Island have added "guardian" language to their animal laws. Some have placed it alongside the word "owner"; others have eliminated "owner" entirely. Katz concedes that the changes don't legally alter the status of pets. But he hopes they will inspire judges and politicians to do so. "The law should recognize that dogs and cats aren't just commodities," he told me. "They aren't just things."

Perhaps Katz is being uncharacteristically modest about the impact of his campaign. The biomedical research community was so unnerved by the effort that in 2004 it lobbied the Council of State Governments to adopt a resolution that forbids any future "guardian" language at the state level. (The language can still be adopted at the city level.) In a fact sheet, the California Biomedical Research Association highlighted the significance of the issue:

> A change in terminology is more than mere semantics. The concept embodied in the word "guardian" is radically different from that in the word "owner." If one concept replaces the other, eventually the legal impact of guardianship will be felt by those with custody of animals, and animals will be afforded rights now reserved for humans. . . . This could

very simply change the status of animals, all animals, from property to persons, legally.

But this change was already underway.

The year 2000 was proving a banner one for dogs and cats. The Gigi case and T-Bo Act showed that judges and politicians were finally recognizing pets as true members of the family. In Defense of Animals scored a huge victory in Boulder, Colorado, legally turning pet owners into pet guardians. And Congress, recognizing the value of companion animals in the home, passed the Pet Ownership in Public Housing law, which allowed residents of federally funded housing to own cats, dogs, and other animals after decades of heavy restrictions. Yet pets were still property. Not a single law or court decision had changed this. Then, as 2000 drew to a close, a small group of lawyers drafted a piece of legislation that, somewhat inadvertently, finally began to crack the legal barrier between pets and people.

What was most surprising about the breakthrough was that it occurred in one of the most conservative areas of law: trust law, a body of rules that relies on ancient and stubborn doctrines. Trust law stretches all the way back to the Middle Ages. Franciscan friars, adhering to St. Francis of Assisi's vow of poverty, were not allowed to own property. But if someone else held the property in trust for them, they could use it. Over the centuries, trusts evolved into a mechanism whereby a man could continue to provide support for his wife and children after he died or became incapacitated. But even in the early years, people also tried to provide for their animals. In the thirteenth century, the Egyptian sultan Baybars bequeathed a garden near his mosque in the north of Cairo to feral and abandoned cats. (Various owners of the garden continued to put food out for local felines well into the twentieth century.) Six hundred years later, a British man left £750 for the care of his horses and hounds, specifying that if the horses needed to be killed, they "shall be shot with a double-barreled gun, both barrels loaded at the same time, with clean barrels and a full charge."

Early courts paid little attention to such gifts. If relatives didn't challenge them, the judges usually let them slide. One exception was the first

US case that dealt with a trust for a specific animal. In 1923, a Kentucky woman left $1,000 for the care of her dog, Dick, stipulating that he be "kept in comfort, that is being well fed, have a bed in the house by a fire and treated well every day." When the woman's relatives objected, a lower court voided the trust. But the state's highest court allowed the gift on a technicality, noting that Kentucky law permitted trusts for a "humane purpose" and that Dick's well-being constituted just such a cause.

Most courts were far less permissive, however. Typical of judicial attitudes was a 1968 California Supreme Court case that involved the estate of a woman named Thelma Russell. Russell had died three years earlier, writing the entirety of her last wishes on a small card: "I leave everything I own Real & Personal to Chester H. Quinn & Roxy Russell." Quinn was a close friend; Roxy was an Airedale terrier. Russell's niece contested the will, arguing that dogs, as property, could not legally inherit money. The court agreed. "As a dog cannot be the beneficiary under a will," it ruled, "the attempted gift to Roxy Russell is void." The niece got the dog's half.

Decades of similar decisions followed, with animals usually coming out on the losing end. No matter how much money owners left their pets in trusts or wills or how many pages they dedicated to the care of their companion animals, courts ruled the gifts void or severely curtailed the amounts. And with relatives squabbling over the remainders, cats and dogs got lost in the shuffle. Some were euthanized. Others lived out the rest of their lives not in a bed in a house by a fire but rotting away in a small cage in a shelter. And yet, by the turn of the century, up to a quarter of pet owners were including animals in their estate planning, and more than 1 million cats and dogs had been named the beneficiary of a trust or will. Something had to be done.

As it happened, a group of lawyers with a government advisory agency known as the Uniform Law Commission had begun meeting in 1994 to revise the law of trusts. Like William Blackstone two centuries before them, they wanted to bring clarity to an area of the law that had become inaccessible, inconsistent, and convoluted—the first time such a thing had been attempted for trust law. When she got wind of the effort, Barbara Newell, a lawyer with an organization called the Animal Legal Defense Fund, contacted the chief drafter of the new legislation,

David English, who was a friend from law school. She told him about all of the pets being euthanized and abandoned, despite the wishes of their owners. English inserted a section into the document, which eventually became known as the Uniform Trust Code, that for the first time made trusts for animals as valid and enforceable as any other type of trust. Formally approved in 2000, it allows owners to leave money to a trustee—a bank, for example—which then doles the funds out to a caretaker appointed by the pet's owner.

Thanks to the UTC, owners can now safely leave thousands—or, in the case of hotel magnate Leona Helmsley, millions—of dollars to their pets after they die. But the true implications are far more profound. As property themselves, animals shouldn't legally be able to inherit property, and the departed shouldn't be able to leave a provision to care for them in their wills. What's more, the UTC and similar guidelines, which have now been adopted in nearly every state, permit courts to enforce these trusts. That means if a trustee is not doing his job, a judge can appoint someone to advocate for the animal's right to inherit its money; or an outside party, like a humane society, can come into court and fight for the animal itself. The arrangement effectively allows animals legal representation for the first time in US history. In the eyes of trust law, pets have finally begun to be seen as people.

EIGHT

Civil Rights for Pets

Nearly a century before Henry Bergh witnessed a horse being beaten on the streets of Saint Petersburg, John Quincy Adams had his own transformational experience in the Russian city. Traveling in 1781 as part of a diplomatic delegation seeking recognition of the newly formed United States, the fourteen-year-old future American president wrote his father in shock about the treatment of Russian slaves. "They are bought and sold like so many beasts, and are sometimes even chang'd for dogs and horses," he said. "Their masters have even the right of life and death over them, and if they kill one of them they are only obliged to pay a trifling fine."

A half century later, Adams was confronting slavery again, this time on his home turf. By 1836, he had lost a bitter presidential reelection campaign to Andrew Jackson and was five years into a remarkable seventeen-year run in the US House of Representatives. Slavery was everywhere he looked. Before the Civil War, Washington, DC, was home to the most active slave trade in the country. The gateway to the Deep South, it provided the roads, rivers, and rails to convey thousands of blacks to a lifetime of backbreaking labor on cotton, rice, and sugar plantations. As they awaited transport, slaves were kept in dark, cramped pens just blocks from the nation's Capitol Building, eventually emerging shackled at the hands and feet, roped to each other, and whipped to keep pace as they shuffled down the cobblestone streets. Everywhere Adams looked, human beings were sold: men and women stood dejected on auction blocks as bidders in coats and top hats grumbled over their market value, probed their biceps and teeth, and ripped wives from husbands and children from parents, tearing families asunder forever.

Washington's robust slave trade provided abolitionists with endless fodder for their cause. In pamphlets and newspaper articles, they pointed out the cruel irony of manacled men being traded and sold in the heart of the supposed land of the free. They flooded Congress with tens of thousands of petitions, decrying slavery as evil, un-Christian, and an anathema to democracy. So many petitions came in that legislators had a hard time conducting their other business. In an effort to stop the deluge, South Carolina representative Henry Laurens Pinckney drafted a resolution declaring that Congress had no authority to interfere with the institution of slavery and mandating that all abolitionist petitions be tabled without being read. But the abolitionists had a powerful ally in Adams. The ex-president's hatred of slavery had only grown stronger since his days in Russia, and he vowed to fight what he called "the great and foul stain upon the North American Union." He had presented many of the petitions, and when Pinckney tried to block them, Adams took to the House floor, blasting the resolution as a violation of free speech. It passed anyway.

For the next several months, Adams fought what became known as the "gag rule." Despite his nearly seventy years of age, he was a firebrand—combative, unapologetic, and fiercely independent. Though some called him "Old Man Eloquent," his confrontational approach had earned him the moniker "the Massachusetts Madman." Adams ignored Pinckney's order and repeatedly tried to introduce abolitionist petitions. Each time, his colleagues shouted him down. In February 1837, the former president tried a different tack. He asked the Speaker of the House if he could introduce a petition not from abolitionists but from twenty-two Virginia slaves. The chamber exploded. "It is an outrage!" cried one congressman. "He ought to be expelled!" shot another. "Slaves have no right to petition," said South Carolina's Waddy Thompson Jr. "They are property, not persons; they have no political rights." Pinckney also chimed in, snarkily wondering whether Adams was next planning to introduce a petition from dogs or horses. "Sir," Adams fired back, "if a horse or a dog had the power of speech and of writing . . . I would present it to the House."

When the chamber regained its composure, it decided not to censure Adams. Instead, it passed a new resolution stating that slaves did not have the right to petition. But the clever ex-president wasn't as defeated as he appeared. He had achieved his goal of forcing the House once again to discuss the issue of slavery—a dialogue the gag rule had tried to silence. (The slave petition was a forgery, by the way, and Adams knew it.) In a letter to his constituents the following month, Adams wrote that his only offense had been to treat slaves like human beings: "The very essence of the crime consists in an alleged *undue* regard for [slaves'] rights; in not denying them the rights of human nature; in not classing them with horses, and dogs, and cats."

Over the next several years, Adams continued to introduce abolitionist petitions—and his colleagues continued to shout him down. Finally, in 1844, he was able to convince a majority of them to repeal the gag rule. Congress could debate slavery once again. In his remaining years, the Massachusetts Madman carried on his lifelong fight against the great evil. But it would take another two decades and a civil war for his dream to become reality.

A New Breed of Lawyer

By the turn of the twenty-first century, cats and dogs had achieved a legal status unheard of for a nonhuman. In the eyes of the law, they were closer to being people than any animal had ever been. To truly become legal persons, however, they would need more than a handful of court cases and legislative victories. They would need a revolution. A new movement would have to arise. Thousands would have to join. And they would need to desire nothing less than to change the world.

That movement is already here.

On a drizzly gray day in mid-October, I arrive in Portland, Oregon, to meet an animal revolution in the making. I immediately feel out of place. This is a city of hipsters and indy rockers, of grungy coffee shops serving locally sourced soy lattes and fast-food restaurants offering gluten-free menus. Portland is home to one of America's first openly gay mayors and the world's first vegan strip club. The city's aesthetic has become such a stereotype that an entire TV series is based around it. "Portland," a main character proclaims in the first episode of *Portlandia*, "is a place where young people go to retire."

It's also where they go to rebel. There are the minor protests: a Mc-Donald's billboard advertising the Egg McMuffin sandwich has been defaced. "Every egg's dream" is now, thanks to some black paint, "Every egg's nightmare." Downtown, a more substantial demonstration is going on. Hundreds of people have camped out in a small park near city hall, living in a makeshift village of multicolored tents that features every-thing from a community kitchen to a first aid center—and, of course, a recycling area stocked with composting bins. This is Portland's chapter of the Occupy movement, a global revolt against financial inequality, ostensibly pitting 99 percent of society against the wealthiest 1 percent. A week earlier, 10,000 people had marched through nearby streets, shouting through megaphones and holding signs that read, "Delete the Elite" and "Make Jobs, Not War." But the revolution I'm interested in is taking place five miles away, in a handful of buildings nestled among a forest of Douglas firs: the site of Lewis & Clark Law School.

I'm here to attend the Animal Law Conference, an annual gathering of students, lawyers, and teachers dedicated to the burgeoning field of an-imal law. Some of these folks have played critical roles in the dramatic le-gal rise of dogs and cats, arguing before judges and influencing politicians. None is more important than the woman who stands before us on the Fri-day night before the conference begins, looking out from her podium onto a crowd of hundreds who have gathered in a chandeliered oak ballroom of downtown's historic Benson Hotel, noshing on vegan hors d'oeuvres. Her name is Joyce Tischler. Short, in her late fifties, with dark brown hair tied back in a bushy ponytail, she has been introduced as "the mother of animal law." It's an apt moniker. Tischler almost single-handedly created the animal law movement, and she continues to view its converts as her children. Her tone is kind and reassuring, but when she talks about the challenges facing animals, her face hardens, and her soft New York voice turns stern.

As Tischler begins to speak to the crowd, pictures of animals illumi-nate a projector screen behind her: cows munching peacefully in a grassy field, dogs curled up at their owners' feet. "This is who your client is," she says. "This is who you're working for, and what you're working for." She tells the audience about a Jewish concept known as *tikkun olam*, Hebrew for "mending the world." In her case, that means ending animal cruelty.

She speaks of monkeys being vivisected in research laboratories, of hens packed together so tightly on factory farms they can't spread their wings. But tonight she has one animal in particular on her mind.

Six years ago, the organization Tischler founded, the Animal Legal Defense Fund, scored one of its biggest courtroom victories when it filed a lawsuit that freed three hundred dogs from hellish conditions on the property of a North Carolina animal hoarder. Tischler flew out to help care for the canines in a makeshift shelter while they waited for new homes. As she walked among cages filled with yapping, jumping boxers, Pomeranians, and miniature pinchers, one dog caught her eye: an old black Boston terrier with a white muzzle and eyes clouded by cataracts that just sat there, glumly watching the world go by. Tischler felt an immediate connection; she had lost her husband to lung cancer a few years earlier, and she too had shut herself off from those around her. She named the dog Edgar and began spending more and more time with him, lifting him gingerly out of his cage and petting him on her lap during her breaks, trying to stroke away years of neglect. When she returned to California, she couldn't stop thinking about the dog. Four months passed. No one adopted him. So she flew back out to North Carolina and brought him home. Edgar found his place in a house filled with two other dogs, five cats, and Tischler's teenage daughter. Slowly, his spirit returned. He learned the joy of being a dog. Tischler too returned to the land of the living, rediscovering her laugh when the little terrier engaged her in staring contests and made slobbering sounds when he ate. She healed him, and he healed her.

Now, a few months after Edgar passed away, Tischler is hoping to heal the world. As a woman, she changed the life of one animal. As a lawyer, she saved the lives of hundreds more. Tonight, she is here to show what can happen when one lawyer becomes thousands. "We know that the world is a very unjust place for animals," she tells the crowd. "They suffer enormously. In the spirit of *tikkun olam* we're going to do something about it. I want you to stand beside those who are wounded and defenseless. To reach out to those who are ignored and abused. To wrap your arms around those who suffer." The road ahead, she says, won't be easy. The lawyers and future lawyers who stand before her will fail more than they will succeed. The work will be difficult and draining. "But I hope you will hang in there," she says. "I hope you will continue what we started. Together, we will mend this world and make it a better place for all animals. Now roll up your sleeves and get in there."

Looking around the room, I see that this next generation of lawyers plans to do exactly that. Over the next couple of days they'll gain the knowledge and contacts they need to power a revolution decades in the making. From here, more than 100,000 strong, they'll bring a once fringe field of law into the mainstream, penetrating the country's top law schools and the highest branches of government. And they'll score unprecedented victories, perhaps eventually abolishing the long-standing legal barrier between animal and man. Not bad for a movement that got its start with a disgruntled attorney and a chance find in the phone book.

Four days before Christmas in 1979, an elderly woman named Mary Murphy overdosed on sleeping pills in her San Francisco apartment. When police found her body, they also discovered Sido, a ten-year-old collie-sheltie mix with a white chest, brown eyes, and a long, thin snout. She was overjoyed to see them. The cops brought the dog to the San Francisco SPCA, whose president, Richard Avanzino (later a key supporter of the Guardian Campaign), brought her home to live with him. Or so he thought. Murphy's will stipulated that Sido be "immediately put to death." She probably feared that the dog would rot away in a shelter—not an unreasonable concern in an era before the Uniform Trust Code. The executrix of the will, Rebecca Smith, demanded that Sido be turned over to her so that she could carry out her friend's wishes. Avanzino refused, saying he would rather go to jail than give up the dog. So Smith sued him.

The case made international news. "Dead Woman's Will Says Kill My Pet," blared one headline. "SPCA Battles to Save Collie Condemned to Execution in Will," read another. On a June day in 1980, Avanzino and Smith faced off in front of a packed superior court. Next to the SPCA president sat boxes overflowing with 3,000 letters from around the country—some pleading for Sido's life, others offering to adopt her. An animal law group known as Attorneys for Animal Rights had also lent its support, sending member Laurence Kessenick, who submitted expert advice in the form of an amicus brief. The document argued that killing

Sido was "inhumane," a violation of the state's anticruelty laws, and "contrary to public policy." In the middle of the proceedings, a light began flashing. The judge hustled to his chambers to take an urgent phone call from the governor's office. The California Assembly and Senate had rushed through a bill to save Sido, and the governor had just signed it.

Though the trial was now moot, the judge proceeded with the case so that his decision would be on record. Echoing the language of the Attorneys for Animal Rights brief, he ruled the will's order invalid and against public policy. When Avanzino emerged from the courtroom, a throng of reporters and photographers greeted him on the steps of city hall. And racing toward him, tail wagging, was Sido. The dog lived with Avanzino for six years, never leaving his side until she died from heart failure in 1985. He credits her with sparking the No Kill shelter movement.

The Sido case was an important victory for Attorneys for Animal Rights, a group founded just a year earlier by Joyce Tischler. Born in 1953 in New York City, Tischler had always wanted to be a veterinarian, but "I was miserable at math," she tells me, as we sit in an office at Lewis & Clark the day after her speech. So she did the next best thing, patrolling her neighborhood as a child and rescuing "lost" cats. "I was probably stealing them," she laughs. At age fifteen, Tischler became politically active, organizing high school protests against the Vietnam War and spending a summer at the local Democratic Party office, where she stuffed envelopes for Eugene McCarthy's campaign against Lyndon Johnson. There, she ran into lawyers using their skills to further the cause. "From that point on," she says, "I decided I was going to go to law school and change society."

But animal issues kept intruding. In college at the City University of New York, Tischler got sidetracked by feral cats wandering the school grounds. She joined what she calls "the campus cat people," who were feeding the felines, taking them to the vet to get them spayed and neutered, and trying to find homes for them. They handled about a hundred cats a year and sold T-shirts to cover the costs. "That's how I spent four years of college," she chuckles. "Going to school, trying to get the best grades possible, trying to get a boyfriend, and taking care of the cats." Not until Tischler entered law school, however, did she find her true calling.

The moment that changed her life was picking up a copy of Peter Singer's *Animal Liberation*. Published in 1975, the book is considered the bible of the animal rights movement. In it, Singer, later appointed professor of bioethics at Princeton University, argues that people are guilty of "speciesism," an attitude of human superiority over all other animals that has justified everything from vivisection to factory farming. "The core of this book," he writes, "is the claim that to discriminate against beings solely on account of their species is a form of prejudice, immoral and indefensible in the same way that discrimination on the basis of race is immoral and indefensible." Singer's graphic descriptions of cosmetic testing on rabbits and military experiments on chimpanzees have birthed countless animal rights activists, and his harrowing depictions of assembly-line slaughterhouses and hormone-treated cows have turned generations of readers into vegetarians.

The book gave Tischler the vocabulary she needed to finally put her thoughts about animals down on paper. "All of a sudden," she says, "I went from being an animal lover to, 'Oh wait, there's a philosophy here. I can argue rationally about this now.'" But where Singer focused largely on primates and farm animals, Tischler turned her attention to pets. In 1977, while still in law school, she published a law review article, "Rights for Nonhuman Animals: A Guardianship Model for Dogs and Cats." It argued that politicians and judges could transform companion animals from property to persons in the same way they had for women and slaves. "I chose cats and dogs because those were the only animals I could relate to at the time," she tells me. "And I thought those would be the animals that judges and readers would most relate to."

In the article, Tischler advocated for the type of felony anticruelty laws that would be passed two decades later, and presaging the Uniform Trust Code, she talked about a day when pets could own property of their own. But she went even further, envisioning a world where dogs and cats—through a human guardian—could sue people in court for injuring them or for failing to take proper care of them and collect any monetary awards for themselves. "The guardianship model would have the psychological impact of making humans understand that dogs and cats are members of society who deserve and will receive real protection under the law," she wrote. "It is time for a drastic reevaluation of their present status in our legal system."

The article was ahead of its time—perhaps too far ahead. "People found me somewhat odd," Tischler says. "They couldn't wrap their heads around what I was saying. I felt a bit out in the wilderness." Entering the job market didn't help. Though she had started thinking about fighting for animals in court, there was no such thing as animal law. So she took a job at a small firm in Oakland, California, that handled real estate cases. "I was there for three and a half years," she says, "and I was quite miserable."

Desperate to do something for animals, even if it meant volunteering at a local shelter, Tischler scanned the yellow pages for the word "animal." She came across something called the Animal Switchboard and gave it a ring. A woman answered, telling Tischler she was just there to give advice on animal issues, like how to find a good veterinarian or what to do if your landlord doesn't allow pets. But the two got to talking, and the woman offered to introduce Tischler to her daughter, who worked for the San Francisco branch of an animal advocacy group called The Fund for Animals. The daughter, in turn, introduced Tischler to a San Francisco lawyer named Laurence Kessenick, who was also interested in animal legal issues. "If there are two of us," Tischler recalls thinking at the time, "maybe there are more." In 1979, she and Kessenick placed an ad in the local legal newspaper announcing a meeting for like-minded lawyers at The Fund for Animals office. To their surprise, six people showed up. The group began gathering once a month. It called itself Attorneys for Animal Rights.

AFAR moved gingerly in those early months. Everyone had a full-time job, and they had no idea how to make animal law work in the courtroom. There were no classes, no teachers, no textbooks. So they taught themselves. They gave each other assignments: write a report on a state or federal law that pertains to animals; discuss a recent court case that involved a cat or a dog. "We had to build a field from scratch," Tischler says. All the while, they were searching for legal strategies that worked, for a way to argue intelligently about animals before a judge. It was tough going, but Tischler was invigorated. "I was most alive when I was at those meetings," she says. "I didn't feel lost in the wilderness anymore. I felt found."

One by one, more lawyers joined the group. Still, AFAR kept a low profile. "We had jobs to protect," Tischler tells me, "and we were terrified that people would start contacting us, thinking we could litigate." By 1980, however, AFAR had gained enough confidence that it planted its flag in the Sido case. The positive outcome was a boost for the fledgling group. But it would turn out to be a rare victory.

By 1984, Attorneys for Animal Rights had grown into a modest-sized organization. It counted a few hundred members from around the country, including two individuals, Detroit College of Law professor David Favre and Boston attorney Steven Wise, who would later be instrumental in shaping its philosophy. The two had met Joyce Tischler in 1981 at the world's first animal law conference, held in New York City. One session at the meeting drew parallels between rights for animals and rights for slaves; another addressed how to best fight for noneconomic damages when pets were injured. Two years later, Favre wrote the field's first textbook. Animal law was beginning to take shape.

AFAR had even begun litigating its own cases. It stepped into the fray in March 1981 when a handful of animal protection organizations began calling Tischler and one of her Los Angeles colleagues, telling them that in less than two days the US Navy planned to kill hundreds of feral burros at a weapons base in California's Mojave Desert. Naval forces had already shot more than six hundred of the animals, claiming that they posed a safety hazard on the airfield and roads. Tischler stayed up all night and, with only hours to spare, flew to Fresno to obtain a temporary restraining order. After a series of meetings with AFAR, the navy agreed to allow a team of cowboys to ride onto the base, lasso the burros, and relocate them. Stunned officers captured the whole thing on videotape.

The burro case was a major victory for AFAR. It put the young organization on the map, and the publicity led to its first income: a $6,000 grant from an animal advocacy group. AFAR used the money to hire Tischler as its executive director, its first full-time staff position. She quit her job at the real estate law firm and began focusing on turning her group into an animal law powerhouse, creating a membership directory and communicating with various local chapters that had cropped up across the country. But the money was running out. "Five months in, there was only $1,000 left in the bank account," she tells me. "We were living hand to mouth, and so was I. I'd wake up in the middle of the night in a cold sweat. And this is long before I had hot flashes."

Desperate for funding, AFAR reached out to the country's largest animal organizations, including the American Society for the Prevention of Cruelty to Animals and the Humane Society of the United States, offering to help them fight for animals in the courtroom. Those that actually responded turned them down. "They didn't see the benefit of litigation," Tischler says. "We were trying to sell them something they had no desire to buy." The HSUS, for one, was lobbying for felony anticruelty laws at the state level. So AFAR turned to direct mail campaigns. "The first company we hired to do this for us said, 'You've got to change your name,'" says Tischler. "No one wants to give money to attorneys, and 'Animal Rights' is just too radical.'" So in 1984, AFAR rechristened itself the Animal Legal Defense Fund. The strategy worked. By the end of the year, it had raised about $30,000. Tischler was still working out of her house, but at least she wasn't living on the street.

Money would turn out to be the least of ALDF's problems, however. Emboldened by the burro victory, it began litigating nearly every case that came through the door. The results weren't pretty. In 1984, ALDF sued Stanford University and a nearby veteran's hospital on behalf of three local humane societies for the mistreatment and death of a dog in a research laboratory. The judge threw the case out, ruling that the humane societies were not sufficiently impacted by the incident—a lack of so-called legal standing that continues to haunt ALDF to this day. The following year, the organization sued New York's Department of Environmental Conservation to prevent hunters from using leghold traps in the state. It lost, and lost again on appeal. And in one of its most devastating defeats, ALDF's Boston chapter, led by Steven Wise, spent a year researching state and federal laws so that it could sue a major veal producer in the district court of Massachusetts, arguing that the practice of raising veal calves violated state anticruelty laws. In a 1986 opinion, the court called ALDF's efforts "misdirected" and ruled against it. Demoralized, the Boston chapter disbanded.

While ALDF was losing in the courts, it was also suffering in the court of public opinion. Despite its name change, it had become closely affiliated with the animal rights movement. Peter Singer's *Animal Liberation* had helped birth People for the Ethical Treatment of Animals (PETA), as well as countless protests and demonstrations across the country. When animal rights activists were arrested for assaulting fur wearers or break- ing into research laboratories, they turned to ALDF for legal representa- tion. In the early years, Tischler and her colleagues were happy to oblige. Tischler herself became involved in a high-profile 1989 incident in which seven animal rights activists had camped out on top of a 160-foot-high crane at the University of California, Berkeley, in an attempt to halt the construction of a new biomedical research facility. She drove out to the campus, and, in a suit and high heels, climbed a metal ladder to the roof of a nearby building so that she could shout to the protestors. Her orga- nization was beginning to look ridiculous—and fringe.

The struggles took their toll on ALDF. Its knee-jerk litigation strat- egy was draining its funding, and it had failed to gain the respect of fel- low attorneys. "When Steve Wise and I would go into court, we'd get laughed at," Tischler says. Lawyers would bark and catcall. "We weren't talking a language they could understand." Meanwhile, the organization itself was suffering from an identity crisis. Some members wanted it to become the legal arm of the animal rights movement, using its know- how to help end animal testing and factory farming. Others pushed for a more measured approach, arguing that it should abandon animal rights and focus instead on improving animal welfare. Push too hard for the former, and ALDF risked alienating judges and the public. Don't push hard enough, and how could it justify its existence? What was it really fighting for? It was quickly becoming apparent that Tischler's organiza- tion had no long-term strategy and that it had spread itself too thin. By the end of the 1980s, it was in danger of imploding.

On the verge of going broke and fracturing, ALDF took a long, hard look at the organization that had inspired its name: the NAACP Legal Defense Fund. The fund was the legal arm of the National Associa- tion for the Advancement of Colored People, which formed in 1909 to battle segregation and racial violence. John Quincy Adams's dream of abolition had come true; yet blacks were still second-class citizens. Jim Crow laws prevented them from associating with whites in restaurants and schools, and roving mobs, especially in the South, terrorized black men, lynching them and burning them alive for offenses as trivial as looking at a white woman. Blacks found no sanctuary in the halls of government. The 1896 US Supreme Court decision *Plessy v. Ferguson* declared that separating the races did not violate the Constitution as long as both had access to equivalent facilities, a doctrine known as "separate but equal" that sanctioned segregation throughout the country. If blacks were ever going to become full citizens, they'd need to fight fire with fire. Enter the NAACP.

In its early years, the NAACP took on a variety of cases, challenging everything from residential segregation to death penalty verdicts handed down by all-white juries. But the battles drained its limited resources and had no impact on a national level. So in the early 1930s, the organization began thinking big: it had to strike at the heart of racial segregation—it had to overturn *Plessy*. The NAACP's first order of business was building an army of black lawyers. It recruited prominent attorneys in the field and transformed Howard Law School, a little-known and little-respected night school, into a legal-education powerhouse. The school taught students, including future Supreme Court justice Thurgood Marshall, that they could change the world and gave them the skills to do so. In 1940, the NAACP created the Legal Defense Fund to better coordinate its courtroom efforts. Over the next decade, the fund conducted a concentrated attack against school segregation, launching class action lawsuits against discriminatory school boards across the country. The effort paid off. In 1954, the Supreme Court bundled a number of NAACP-litigated cases into *Brown v. Board of Education*, which struck down *Plessy v. Ferguson* and outlawed segregation. Legal rights, the NAACP showed, could be won through litigation.

Joyce Tischler was no stranger to the story of the NAACP. She kept a book about its history nearby at all times—dog-eared, highlighted, and underlined. "It felt like a roadmap," she tells me. And that roadmap was showing that ALDF had to completely rethink its strategy. It couldn't continue to take every case that walked in the door. It had to coordinate its efforts. It had to strike down its own *Plessy v. Ferguson*.

As a first step, ALDF refused to take any case that didn't have a shot at chipping away at the property status of animals. No more representing animal rights activists; no more capricious battles with the federal government or multi-million-dollar corporations. It was time to build a national movement. In the early 1990s, the organization consolidated its various member chapters and established a central office in Northern California. It also began seeking legitimacy from the country's largest society of lawyers, the American Bar Association. In 1992, it was able to convince the ABA to include a session on animal law at its annual meeting. Tischler spoke at the session, as did William Kunstler, one of the nation's foremost civil rights attorneys. The room was packed with lawyers, most of whom had never heard of animal law.

Meanwhile, Steven Wise, the former head of ALDF's Boston chapter, was beginning to think about how to introduce animal law to the wider public. He found the lessons of slavery particularly instructive, especially the case of a Missouri slave named Dred Scott. Scott had petitioned the US Supreme Court for his freedom in 1856, arguing that by traveling with his master to slavery-free zones of the country, he had become emancipated. But the court, in what is widely regarded as the worst decision in its history, declared that blacks were a "subordinate and inferior class of beings" and that, as a nonperson, Scott had no right to citizenship. For Wise, animals—especially cognitively advanced animals like chimpanzees, elephants, and dolphins—were modern-day Dred Scotts, imprisoned in zoos and laboratories and denied their basic freedoms. In his 2000 book *Rattling the Cage*, he wrote about the steps it would take to turn these creatures into legal persons. "The entitlement of chimpanzees and bonobos to fundamental legal rights will mark a huge step toward stopping our unfettered abuse of them," he wrote, "just as human rights marked a milepost in stopping our abuse of each other."

The book was a success. It attracted the attention of some of the world's most prominent legal scholars, including Laurence Tribe, a leading authority on constitutional law; Cass Sunstein, who would later become President Barack Obama's "regulations czar"; and überlitigator Alan Dershowitz. All subsequently wrote their own articles supporting legal rights for animals. Jane Goodall called the book "the animal's Magna Carta, Declaration of Independence, and Universal Declaration of Rights all in one." Harvard invited Wise to teach a course on animal law at its law school.

The public was also getting wind of the animal law movement. "Legal Pioneers Seek to Raise Lowly Status of Animals," announced a 1999

New York Times headline. "These lawyers are more than brief-writing counterparts of animal activists who throw paint on fur wearers," the article stated. "They are filing novel lawsuits and producing new legal scholarship to try to chip away at a fundamental principle of American law that animals are property and have no rights." A year later, the *Los Angeles Times* declared that "2000 is shaping up to be a watershed year for the fledgling legal movement." And indeed it was.

By 2000, ALDF had extended its reach into various areas of law. It offered legal assistance to prosecutors of anticruelty cases, fostering the expansion of felony anticruelty laws across the nation. It helped pass a Florida act that required more humane treatment of farm animals. And when ALDF's Barbara Newell heard that a group of lawyers was meeting to revamp trust law, she got the Uniform Trust Code to include a section that enabled animals to inherit money for the first time, fundamentally transforming the status of pets in the courtroom.

ALDF scored one of its biggest legal victories in 2005. A year earlier, the organization had begun receiving disturbing e-mails about a dog hoarder in the rural North Carolina town of Sanford. Barbara Woodley, a retired factory worker in her late sixties, had been breeding and selling canines for more than twenty years, but buyers who had recently visited her property reported being horrified by what they saw: hundreds of terriers, boxers, and other breeds trembling in cramped wooden crates, some stacked high in a closed garage with the dogs on top defecating on those below them. Malnutrition had rotted jaws, tiny cages had disfigured limbs, and the collective fumes of years of urine baking in the southern heat had created an ammonia fog that burned skin and blinded eyes.

Normally, ALDF would be able to do little, as both it and local humane societies lacked the legal standing to take Woodley to court. But thanks to some clever sleuthing, the organization discovered an obscure North Carolina statute that allows private citizens to sue suspected animal abusers. The only one of its kind in the country, the law had never been employed successfully before. ALDF lawyers spent the next several months gathering witnesses and building a case. In a verdict that made headlines across the country, a judge convicted Woodley of animal cruelty and transferred all of the dogs to ALDF's custody. The canines had been emancipated. While caring for the rescued animals, Tischler fell in love with Edgar, the sad-sack Boston terrier, and ultimately brought him home. "It's probably my favorite single case we've ever worked on," she says.

The Woodley case brought the issue of animal hording into the national spotlight. It also imparted to ALDF two important lessons. One was that by concentrating its resources, it could achieve dramatic victories for animals in the courtroom. The other was that its best chances of success lay not with chimpanzees or farm animals but with pets. Steven Wise's arguments may have stimulated the minds of legal scholars, but judges ruled with their hearts. If ALDF really wanted to transform the legal status of animals, it would need to start with dogs and cats.

But first, it was going to have to build an army.

Tischler knew that churning out generation after generation of highly trained lawyers had been critical to the NAACP's success. Yet, before 2000, ALDF hadn't put much thought into legal education. A few schools offered courses in animal law, but they came and went, depending on the schedules of the local attorneys who taught them. And in terms of teaching materials, things hadn't changed much since she began meeting with a small group of lawyers in 1979; instructors were pretty much making up the classes as they went along. Tischler realized that if ALDF was going to change the world, it would need to pass its lessons on to the next generation. It would need to create a movement to fight for the cause.

In 2000, the organization began dedicating a third of its budget to education and outreach. It contacted law school administrators, sending them teaching materials and a new textbook, and it offered seed grants for first-time courses. Tischler herself visited several schools to talk about the growing field of animal law and the need to offer classes in it. ALDF's efforts got a huge boost from Bob Barker. In 2001, the *Price Is Right* host and longtime animal advocate (Barker closed every show with a reminder to spay and neuter, and he eventually banned prizes made from animals) started giving $1 million endowments to a number of universities, including Harvard, Stanford, and Duke, stipulating that the money be used to create animal law courses, conferences, and internships at law firms. Just nine schools offered animal law classes in 2000. Today, the field is taught on nearly 150 campuses, representing almost every ABA-accredited law school in the country.

Some of the impetus for these classes has come from the students themselves. Inspired by the work of Tischler and her colleagues, law students began establishing campus chapters of ALDF as early as 1993. These student ALDFs, or SALDFs, campaign for courses in animal law, raise funds for local animal welfare organizations, and push for animal-related legislation. By the turn of the century, ALDF was communicating heavily with these chapters. It provided grant money, helped them shape their bylaws, and nurtured the development of new SALDFs throughout the country. Most major law schools now have an SALDF, and international chapters have sprung up in Canada and New Zealand.

ALDF's involvement doesn't stop at graduation. It helps new animal lawyers find jobs. Some go into private practice, litigating emotional distress, custody, and trust cases that continue to blur the line between pet and person. Others work for government agencies or animal welfare organizations like the Humane Society of the United States, which is now—in a far cry from the days when it rejected ALDF's offer of legal assistance—the world's largest nonprofit employer of animal lawyers. Still others enter more traditional areas of law but have joined ALDF's massive network of pro bono attorneys, ready to take on boundary-pushing cases at a moment's notice. Many of these lawyers will become judges and legislators themselves some day—or they will be in a strong position to influence them. Meanwhile, Tischler is working on a textbook that will expose students in non–animal law classes to the field. "The goal is to get animal law into the mainstream. To give it a life of its own," she tells me. "To get it to a point where it won't need us anymore."

Today, thanks to the efforts of ALDF, animal law is one of the fastest-growing areas of law, pumping hundreds of new lawyers into the field every year. And with a budget of over $6 million and more than 100,000 members across the country, Tischler's once tiny organization finally has the resources it needs to change the world. It also has a powerful ally in Lewis & Clark Law School.

Lewis & Clark has been in the animal law education game even longer than ALDF. It created the country's first SALDF in 1993, followed shortly by the first animal law legal journal and the first annual animal law conference. In 1998, responding to a growing interest in the subject, the law school asked the head of ALDF's criminal justice department,

Pamela Frasch, to teach a weekly seminar. Frasch soon helped write the field's first casebook, which has become the primary text for teaching animal law throughout the country. In 2008, she became head of the school's newly minted Center for Animal Law Studies, a national think tank and the world's largest animal law program, with twenty courses and more than a dozen full-time and visiting faculty. The center also offers the world's only advanced degree in animal law. If there's a West Point of animal law, it's Lewis & Clark. I had come to Portland to meet the cadets.

A Meeting of the Minds

The day after Joyce Tischler's pep talk at the Benson Hotel, the Animal Law Conference begins in earnest. Lewis & Clark has been the host every year since first launching it in 1993, and the meeting has been sold out for months. Hundreds of students and lawyers from around the country have gathered for two days of presentations and workshops at the school's wooded campus, a collection of modern glass and steel buildings connected via narrow paths that cut through a canopy of plants and trees. It's a legal powerhouse in a national forest.

Things kick off on Saturday morning with a breakfast for the SALDF chapters. Over vegan donuts, forty students representing various law schools share ideas on how to fund-raise and spread the word about animal law. Some have organized charity races or Bob Barker Beer Pong Tournaments. Others have taken photos of pets on campus and turned them into calendars. A lot of them entered law school never having heard of animal law, but they got hooked once they joined an SALDF. "I came here to learn, to network, to get ideas, to find out what's hot right now," one of the students tells me. Her contempt for dog fighting and animal neglect makes her want to go into animal criminal law. "But in this job market, you've got to be willing to work anywhere," she says. "Everyone in this room wants to be an animal lawyer."

Later that morning, ALDF senior attorney Matthew Liebman and the ASPCA's senior vice president of government relations, Nancy Perry, tell a packed room about the field's recent successes. Last year alone, more than one hundred animal protection laws were passed, Perry says, including new felony anticruelty legislation and crackdowns on puppy mills. The duo offers advice on crafting ballot initiatives and rallying public support around court cases. Los Angeles Deputy District Attorney Deborah Knaan hosts a subsequent session on how to litigate animal cruelty cases. She shares her struggles to create the country's only animal cruelty prosecution program and speaks about her work with Detective Hector Sanchez and the Animal Cruelty Task Force. "I am living proof of the fact that you can create your own job," she says. "Never, never, never give up. See a need, and go for it." Another session advises attendees that even traditional areas of law can be applied to animals: contract law can be used to forge agreements between divorcing spouses in pet custody cases, for example. "You can incorporate your love of animals into any practice area," says Valparaiso University Law School professor Rebecca Huss, who was appointed the legal guardian of the pit bulls rescued from football player Michael Vick's dog-fighting operation. "You just have to be creative about it."

The following day, ALDF's director of litigation, Carter Dillard, broaches two questions that have haunted his organization since its inception: Should animals have rights? If so, what would these rights look like? Critics have argued that animals can't have rights because they can't comprehend them. "You have the right to remain silent" implies that you know you could incriminate yourself by talking. Your right to free speech does not include yelling "fire" in a crowded theater. But Dillard argues that plenty of human beings—children, the mentally disabled—have the same rights as the rest of us, even though they don't necessarily understand them. What's more, due to the work of ALDF and other organizations, animals already do have some rights: the right to be free from cruelty, the right to inherit money from a trust. And as the struggle of blacks in America has shown, rights are not set in stone. The signature of the president or the decision of a Supreme Court can give rights to an entire group of people. Society decides what it means to be a "person."

Still, Dillard acknowledges that rights for animals are in their infancy. ALDF's future, he says, will be marked by pushing for more sophisticated freedoms. Current anticruelty laws punish abuse, for example, but they don't prevent it. His organization began thinking about how to change this in the 1990s when legislators passed a series of "Megan's Laws"—named for a seven-year-old girl raped and murdered by a neighbor who had prior convictions for sexual assault—that require sex offenders to register their address and convictions on a publicly accessible database. ALDF wants the same thing for animal abusers. In 2009, it launched a public awareness campaign, and the following year Suffolk County, New York, created the nation's first animal abuser registry. Two other New York counties followed suit. To date, half of all states have considered such a registry, some with names like "Dexter's Law" and "Heidi's Law" after the pets whose deaths inspired them. Meanwhile, ALDF has pushed to expand the number of professions legally mandated to report animal abuse, including social work and firefighting. It's also lobbied judges to include pets in domestic violence restraining orders; many women don't leave their abusive partners because they fear for the safety of their cats and dogs, and many battered women's shelters don't allow pets.

On the federal level, ALDF has drafted an Animal Bill of Rights. The petition to Congress would guarantee, among other liberties, "the Right of companion animals to a healthy diet, protective shelter, and adequate medical care." It has already gathered nearly 300,000 signatures. The organization would also like to see a day when animals are entitled to the same type of legal representation people are in court, whether it's fighting for emancipation from an abusive home or suing for their own damages in a veterinary malpractice case—just the type of thing Joyce Tischler wrote about in law school.

Not everything is about cats and dogs. ALDF is also fighting to improve conditions on factory farms and in animal research laboratories. And early member Steven Wise hasn't given up on personhood for dolphins and great apes. In 2007, he launched the Nonhuman Rights Project, a group of lawyers and academics who have spent thousands of hours building a legal strategy to turn his writings into reality. Even Wise, however, admits that personhood could start with pets. "That there are so many dogs and that such a large percentage of people embrace them as family, even as children, may make it easier for judges to place them where they belong," he writes in *Drawing the Line*, his follow-up to *Rattling the Cage*. Tellingly, the ALDF seal depicts two animals reaching for the scales of justice: a chimpanzee and a cat.

One of the last sessions of the conference brings together animal law's two major powerhouses: ALDF, represented by recently minted attorney Matthew Liebman, and Lewis & Clark, represented by veteran professor Kathy Hessler, the first person in the country hired to teach animal law full-time. Echoing Joyce Tischler's speech from a couple of nights before, the duo caution that the road ahead will be challenging. "We're in the midst of a legal system that denies animal interests at almost every turn," says Liebman. "But we've got to continue to bring litigation that fundamentally changes speciesism and anthropocentrism." Hessler speaks about her days in law school, where she learned about the legal challenges of slavery and about women being denied the right to vote. "It was always couched in terms of, 'Well, people just didn't know any better. Now we know better,'" she says. "That's incorrect. People knew better back then. There were always people opposed to these practices as long as they have occurred. And that makes me exceedingly hopeful for the future." Owners already treat their pets like family, she notes. Judges and legislators are finally respecting the animal law movement. And every year, more animal lawyers enter the fray. "If you look at any social justice movement, nothing happens overnight," she says. "But every step in the right direction is a good step."

Two centuries ago, John Quincy Adams dreamed of a day when slaves would be recognized as fellow people. He didn't want them classed with dogs and cats. Now a new generation dreams of turning those beings into legal persons as well. The struggle will bring unique challenges. At the end of the day, slaves were always people. And the animal law movement has yet to find its *Plessy v. Ferguson* to overturn. Yet it's hard to believe that, with the forces these revolutionaries have on the ground and the recent enthusiasm with which science, the law, and society have embraced pets as fellow members of our family, they won't one day succeed. If they do, cats and dogs could someday join us as fellow persons. Beyond personhood, however, lies an even greater status, one filled with as much promise as peril. Pets may be on the road to citizenship.

III

CITIZEN

NINE

The Perils of Personhood

The rats had returned to France. Nearly two centuries after their brethren invaded Bordeaux, spreading the Black Death that would kill millions of Europeans, rodents descended on a medieval town 350 miles to the northeast. Autun, as it was known, had been built on the ruins of a Roman city; its surrounding wall and churches held the stones of the ancient empire, and the sharp spire of its cathedral cut high into the sky, towering for miles over rolling countryside. Unlike their predecessors, the rats hadn't come to spread disease—they'd come to ravage crops. As they multiplied in the barley fields, the townsfolk became increasingly anxious. The vermin were on the verge of causing a famine. All attempts to exterminate them failed. So in 1522, Autun's residents turned to the only option they had left: they put the rats on trial. Hoping to have the creatures excommunicated, they took their case to the town magistrate, who relayed it to the bishop's vicar, who ordered the rodents to appear in court. The vicar also appointed one of France's rising legal stars to defend them, a Burgundy-born jurist named Bartholomew Chassenée.

Chassenée was no fool. He knew he was fighting an uphill battle. The power of the church was supreme, and the voracious rodents didn't exactly make sympathetic defendants. So he did his best to delay and derail the proceedings. He argued that the rats were too spread out to have heard the summons. In response, the vicar asked every church in every parish harboring the animals to publicize the trial. When the rodents still didn't show, Chassenée contended that their journey to Autun was too hazardous; not only would they have to travel vast distances to reach the town, but they'd need to avoid the watchful eyes and sharp claws of their mortal enemy, the cat. Surely the judges were aware, he said, that defendants could refuse to appear at trial if they feared for their own safety. When *that* didn't work, Chassenée appealed to the court's humanity: It wasn't fair to punish *all* rats for the crimes of a few. "What can be more unjust than these general proscriptions," he asked, "which destroy indiscriminately those whom tender years or infirmity render equally incapable of offending?" The judge, whether moved by Chassenée's words or simply exhausted by his tactics, adjourned the proceedings indefinitely.

Autun's trial of the rats was not a one-off historical curiosity. Europeans had been taking animals to court for centuries. In 824, an ecclesiastical judge excommunicated a group of moles in Italy's Aosta Valley. In 1314, a French court sentenced a bull to hang for goring a man. And in 1575, the Parisian parliament sent a donkey to the stake for having sexual relations with a human being. But of all the animals prosecuted, the most frequent defendant was the pig. In his exhaustive 1906 book on medieval animal trials, culled over four decades spent in the archives of Munich's Royal Library, the American historian Edward Payson Evans records nearly thirty swine cases stretching over six centuries. The most notorious example concerns a sow that tore the face and arm off a child in his cradle in the French city of Falaise in 1386. After a trial, the judge ordered the animal mutilated in the same way—a common punishment for human criminals—and then hung. The pig was dressed in a man's vest, leggings, and gloves. Then her snout was cut off, her legs mangled, and the mask of a person placed over her face. A professional hangman, wearing new gloves provided for the occasion, strung her up in a crowded town square while the judge watched on horseback.

In all of these trials, the animals were treated just like human defendants. The court appointed them lawyers, heard testimony from witnesses, and considered the possibility of prison and parole. Even the punishments were surprisingly human—though, as in the case of the Falaise sow, that usually wasn't a good thing. Some creatures were drawn and quartered. Others were stoned to death. And still others were tied to the rack, their cries a form of confession. Due process was so highly valued that when a German hangman took matters into his own hands before the trial of a pig had commenced in 1576, he was permanently banished from his village.

The purpose of these trials remains mysterious. Some say they were simply a way to dispatch troublesome animals. But then why all the pomp and circumstance? Why not just run a sword through them and be done with it? A more popular theory is that the proceedings were a way to impose order on an increasingly chaotic world. In the Middle Ages, people were living in closer proximity to often unpredictable animals than at any time in our history. Pigs were especially ubiquitous, roaming streets, filling backyards, and breaking into houses. Many towns tried to ban them, but swine were too economically important. And so, bad things were bound to happen, especially to small children. An animal, particularly a domestic animal, that attacked a human wasn't just a danger to society—it violated man's God-given dominion over the fish of the sea, the fowl of the air, and every living thing that moveth upon the earth. The trials, in all their elaborateness, were an attempt to restore the cosmic hierarchy.

One of the last cases Evans records is an 1864 prosecution of a Slovenian pig for biting the ears off a one-year-old girl. The animal was executed, cut to pieces, and thrown to the local mutts. In retrospect, the gesture seems like a symbolic passing of the torch. For 150 years later, when people began taking animals to court once again, it would no longer be the pig on trial. It would be the dog.

Creating a Monster

Kno sits alone in a beige cinder block cell. A dog bed is on the floor. A metal bowl of water lies in the corner. The seventy-pound, copper-colored pit bull, with a body like a tank, ears cropped to stubby triangles, and a jaw that dwarfs his face, has been here for more than five months. His only window is a chain-link door, covered in Plexiglas; clipped to it is a green sign scribbled with black marker: "!Caution! DO NOT Let 'Kno' Out. Keep Other Dogs Away." Those other dogs bark around him, locked in their own kennels in the quarantine room of Effingham County Animal Control, a modest Georgia shelter about twenty-five miles northwest of Savannah. Some were picked up off the street. Some had been tied to posts. And some were rescued from hoarders and abusers. Kno is the only one awaiting trial.

The incident that brought Kno here took place on a Tuesday morning in late July 2012. Five-year-old Wesley Frye had spent the night at his friend's house, a red-brick bungalow on a grassy cul-de-sac in the small, largely middle-class town of Rincon. When the boys woke up the next morning, they went into the living room to watch TV, while the friend's mother cooked breakfast. After a while, the kids began wrestling and roughhousing. Suddenly, the mom heard Frye scream. She ran into the living room and saw Kno on top of him, biting his face, neck, and legs. She grabbed the dog and dragged him outside. By the time a police officer arrived, paramedics had already rushed Frye to the local hospital. Doctors there judged his condition so severe that he was airlifted to a medical center in Savannah. Frye underwent two surgeries to save his life. The right side of his face was paralyzed. Meanwhile, the officer transported Kno to the Effingham shelter, where he was declared dangerous and has been held ever since.

It wasn't easy for me to see him. When I called the shelter's director, Romie Currier, she told me she couldn't answer any questions about the dog. "Everything has to go through his attorney." Attorney? "Yes," she said. "The dog has a lawyer." Eventually, I obtained permission to come out, arriving on a cool but humid afternoon in early January.

The Effingham County shelter is at capacity. A red sign on the door tells anyone thinking about dropping off an animal to turn back. Inside, Currier—slight, in her fifties, with long, rumpled black hair—is accommodating but harried. She's juggling phone calls, telling employees which kennels to clean, and drawing up vaccinations, all at the same time. I take a seat in the lounge, where a black cat named Tennessee is sprawled out on a chair at the reception desk, exposing his white belly as he curls on his back. When Currier catches her breath, she walks me into the main kennel, where dogs of various shapes and sizes bark from their runs. In the back is a door marked "Employees Only," barred by a thick yellow chain. It leads to the quarantine room.

Currier seems bemused by her role as Kno's warden. When the dog was brought in, she wasn't sure whether to treat him like a rescue or a prisoner. She debated keeping him locked up full-time, for the safety of her employees and the other canines. But she couldn't stomach the thought of Kno spending his last days confined to a kennel. If he was going to be executed—the typical punishment for dogs in his situation— she'd be the one administering the lethal injection, and she wanted him to continue to live life as a dog before he died. So he gets two walks a day in the shelter's fenced-in yard, ironically by inmates who volunteer from a prison across the street.

Kno is getting an extra walk today because I'm here. Currier opens his kennel, clips a raggedy leash to his collar, and leads us outside. Then she lets him loose. Testes intact, the pit bull immediately begins making his rounds, peeing on the fence, a tire, and his favorite patch of dirt. "He knows his daily routine," Currier smiles. Kno strikes me as more purposeful than friendly. He doesn't pant. He doesn't trot over to us seeking affection. He just goes about his business, a dog on a somber mission to mark his territory. When Kno finally allows me to pet him, he doesn't lean into me, and he doesn't seem to be enjoying himself. He may have been a family pet, but there is something feral about him— something I don't quite trust. I feel like I'm back at Wolf Park.

Kno's attack divided the community. When police brought him in, three TV stations descended on the shelter, and local residents crowded the gates near where we are standing, hoping to catch a glimpse of the suspect. Some wanted to rescue him. Others wanted his head. "People were shouting, 'Kill him!'" says Currier. "It was a circus." Things became so volatile that Effingham County Superior Court chief judge William E. Woodrum Jr. appointed the dog a lawyer. "He wanted to make sure the county thought things through before it decided Kno's fate," Currier says. Local attorney Claude "Mickey" Kicklighter took the case pro bono. In a series of moves that would have made Bartholomew Chassenée proud, Kicklighter has been delaying the trial ever since, in hopes of finding Kno another home before the county decides to execute him.

Currier herself is on the fence about the dog. She understands those who want him destroyed. "I like Kno," she tells me. "But I wouldn't want to have him as my next door neighbor, you get my drift?" At the same time, she thinks people need to see things from his point of view. Kno, she says, was raised to catch hogs. His original owners trained him to attack wild boar that had invaded people's property and were destroying their crops. "They probably cut his ears off when he was a puppy so the hogs wouldn't rip them off," Currier says; he was never meant to be a family pet. "Now you've got these two little kids running around the house, fighting and squealing, and the dog thinks his own boy is being hurt. You do the math."

Ultimately, neither Currier nor the community will decide Kno's fate; it's in the hands of the legal system. The dog will stand trial, just like a human defendant. Call it the perks—and the price—of citizenship. As cats and dogs have gained rights, they've also gained responsibilities. In some cases, that means being held accountable for their own actions. In others, it means enduring discrimination. And in still others, it means being forced to fight to be seen as equal members of society. For Kno, it's all three.

The road that would eventually lead to the trial of Kno the dog begins just a few years after the last European pig was dragged before a judge. The scene is Ming's Opera House in early August 1882. The ornate, three-story theater, erected just two years earlier on a bustling street in downtown Helena, Montana, has already become a national sensation. Singers, actors, and magicians travel via steamboat and wagon from as far away as San Francisco to entertain the city's elite, bathing in the glow of dozens of gaslights before packed, nine-hundred-seat crowds. Tonight's performance is especially thrilling. A slave named Eliza is running across the stage, cradling a small child in her arms. A pack of dogs barks ferociously in the background. Then, bam! They burst onto the stage, four large bloodhounds, snapping and snarling in close pursuit, as Eliza runs for her life. "As far as the brutes are concerned, there is no acting," a breathless reviewer writes the next day in the *Daily Helena Independent*. "For true to their own ferocious instincts, their thirst for blood is evidenced by their savage baying and eagerness to get at the prey." The audience gasps, then erupts in applause. "The entertainment is of the very best class," gushes the reviewer, "and is well worthy of being seen several times."

The play was based on *Uncle Tom's Cabin*, Harriet Beecher Stowe's bestselling antislavery novel. One doubts she approved of the bloodhound scene. Stowe was an influential champion of kindness to animals, and her writings helped usher in an era in which pets would become family members. Like many adaptations, the *Uncle Tom's* of the stage bore little resemblance the book. Producers amped up the drama and gore, especially when it came to Eliza's flight across the frozen Ohio River. The bloodhounds, in all their ferocity, were pure invention. Audiences ate it up. The more vicious the dogs, the higher the ticket sales. By the 1890s, more than four hundred "Tom Shows" were touring the country. Bloodhounds had become the movie monsters of their day.

The breed didn't always have such a vicious reputation. It was just a victim of bad timing. In the mid-nineteenth century, as man was trusting his dog like never before, he was trusting his fellow man less. The rise of crowded cities and the crime they brought required an aggressive defender of shop and home. Dogs had always been guardians, ever since wolves began defending our campsites tens of thousands of years ago, ripping invaders to shreds. But millennia of domestication had softened our canine companions. To build a guard dog for the modern world, one that would attack intruders without mercy, we had to break the human-animal bond. We had to reintroduce the beast.

Early methods were as brutal as the dogs we hoped to create. And they haven't become gentler over time. The first step was to start with a large and powerful breed like the mastiff, Newfoundland, or bloodhound. (Not to be confused with the droopy-faced breed of today, nineteenth-century bloodhounds were more streamlined and muscular.) Then, owners had to make it clear to these animals that they were not family members: they chained them up all day, confined them to dark cellars, and banished them to backyard sheds. Finally, to break the bond of domestication and turn humans into enemies once more, owners abused the hell out of their guard dogs, kicking them, starving them, and spraying them with scalding water until they were snarling, salivating beasts. The monster had returned.

Bloodhounds were especially prized as guard dogs, not only because of their size and strength but because their noses made them excellent trackers. An escaped prisoner or slave didn't just have Fido on his tail— he had a land shark. The dogs became so vicious that when Confederate captain Henry Wirz employed them to maim and kill Union prisoners at Camp Sumter during the Civil War, the government used the evidence to charge Wirz with war crimes and hang him.

But the monster could not be controlled. No longer able to distinguish friend from foe, bloodhounds killed intruders, neighbors, and small children alike. Newspapers reported thirty-eight severe or fatal maulings from 1855 to 1910. Bloodhounds had become the country's most dangerous dog, killing more people than all other breeds combined. In 1864, a bloodhound tore the ears and scalp off a ten-year-old New Jersey boy. In 1873, a bloodhound mauled a New York woman washing clothes in her yard. And in 1891, a bloodhound killed a Pennsylvania schoolgirl by biting her forty times. It's no wonder that when producers of the Tom Shows went casting about for a villain, they seized upon the breed.

All of this negative press had a curious effect. Bloodhounds became *more* popular than ever, especially among a certain segment of society. It was a vicious cycle that would repeat itself with other breeds over the next century. As Karen Delise writes in *The Pit Bull Placebo*, her expansive analysis of dog attacks from 1850 to modern times, a type of dog valued for its loyalty and companionship would be corrupted by brutal owners and demonized in the press, then become ever-more sought-after by those seeking to exploit its viciousness, leaving a growing trail of human victims in its wake. By the turn of the twentieth century, Newfoundlands and Saint Bernards would take the bloodhound's place. Great Danes and German shepherds followed. Then Dobermans and Rottweilers. Even the collie had its dark days. In newspapers around the country, it ripped the flesh of children, killed small girls for their dolls, and ran down farm boys in large packs. The bad press continued until a collie named Lassie made her debut in 1938. In the books, movies, and TV shows that followed, the noble canine didn't just rescue Timmy— she saved an entire breed.

Brutal owners went looking for a new dog to corrupt. They found their ultimate monster in the pit bull.

> Fire burst from its open mouth, its eyes glowed with a smouldering glare, its muzzle and hackles and dewlap were outlined in flickering flame. Never in the delirious dream of a disordered brain could anything more savage, more appalling, more hellish be conceived than that dark form and savage face which broke upon us out of the wall of fog.

So began a 1987 *Time* magazine article on the pit bull. Titled "Time Bombs on Legs," its language was only slightly less hyperbolic than this passage from the Sherlock Holmes mystery *The Hound of the Baskervilles*. The article claimed that pit bulls "seized small children like rag dolls and mauled them to death in a frenzy of bloodletting" and that the dog's "steel-trap jaws . . . which can exert as much force as 1,800 lbs. per sq. in." classified it as a "lethal weapon." None of this was true. But like the Tom Shows a hundred years earlier, it made for great entertainment. This time, however, such portrayals would help justify the banishment of an entire breed.

At first, pit bulls followed a similar trajectory as the bloodhounds, Newfoundlands, and collies that had come before them. The canines were prized for their courage, tenacity, and muscular build. That made them excellent guard dogs, farm dogs, and even police dogs. Newspaper articles in the early 1900s extolled the virtues of the breed, though the media conflated "pit bull," "bulldog," "bull terrier," and related types, often calling them all "bulldogs." A 1903 article reported the heroic deeds of Bum, a police bull terrier, who led his partner to a blind man drowning in New York's East River. Two years later, the *New York Times* recounted the tale of a Greenwich, Connecticut, bull terrier who saved his female owner from a vicious setter, tackling the dog when it pulled the woman to the floor. Other stories spoke of "hero" bulldogs rescuing their masters from fires, burglars, and oncoming trains. Theodore Roosevelt had a bulldog in the White House. A pit bull named Stubby delivered messages between battalions in World War I and assisted in the capture of a German spy; the breed even represented America in a propaganda poster from the time. And Petey, an American Staffordshire terrier, was nearly as famous as the Little Rascals he hung around with in the *Our Gang* films of the 1920s and beyond.

But the breed's shady beginnings eventually caught up with it. Pit bulls trace their origins to dogs used to take down large game in the blood sports of sixteenth-century England. In a common spectacle, owners would stand on the periphery of a small arena in which a bull had been tied to a stake. Then, one by one, they'd release their hounds. If these "bull dogs" were good, they'd avoid being tossed or gored by the horns of the panicked animal and clamp onto its nose or face, holding on for dear life until the bull collapsed from exhaustion or loss of blood. The rise of English animal welfare laws in the early 1800s made such bullbaiting illegal, so owners turned to a new sport—and a new dog. They bred their bulldogs with more agile game terriers, creating a nimbler, more streamlined breed that retained the sturdiness and strong jaw of its predecessor. Then they set the dogs on each other, forcing them to fight in pits while spectators cheered and placed bets. When these "pit bull" fights came to America, Henry Bergh and his ASPCA did their best to stomp them out, breaking up dog-fighting operations and passing a law that made the practice illegal. But dog fighting didn't disappear. It just went underground. And its clientele became more and more disreputable. If the dogs weren't aggressive enough, owners abused them until they were.

In a now familiar chain of events, the more vicious the pit bulls got, the more likely they were to attack innocent people. And the more the media covered these attacks, the more popular the breed became among the basest members of society. From 1983 to 1984 alone, the United Kennel Club reported a 30 percent increase in registrations of American pit bull terriers. The dog was turning up regularly in narcotics raids and busts of inner-city dog-fighting operations. Where there was gambling, violence, and guns, there were pit bulls. The breed had become a symbol of the underworld. It was society's new demon dog. Yet something was different this time around.

The first deviations cropped up in the popular press. Before, when newspapers covered dog attacks, they rarely focused on breed, instead devoting most of their ink to the temperament, function, and size of the dog. "Guard dogs" were "large" and "savage"; they were rarely "bloodhounds" or "mastiffs." The media was also as likely to blame the human as the canine for the attack. When an Ohio Newfoundland mangled a little girl's face and neck in 1891, a local paper made it clear that incident was instigated when a boy ripped a bone from the dog's mouth and threw it in the girl's direction. Similarly, a collie that tore into the chest and arms of a ten-year-old Massachusetts boy in 1910 was reportedly harassed by a group of children poking it with sticks. The press also attributed attacks to canines being kept in excessive heat, starved, and abused. "There are two sides to the vicious dog stories," the *Fort Wayne Daily News* stated in 1905.

By the 1980s, however, the *breed* was the story. And pit bulls didn't need a reason to attack—they attacked because they were pit bulls. "PIT BULL HORROR," blared one headline. "GNAWED BY JAWS," another. And putting the Tom Shows to shame, "Killer Pit Bulls Rip Granny to Shreds." The breed also began to acquire outlandish characteristics. Chief among its supposed demonic attributes was a locking jaw, bred into a veritable steel trap over generations. "Because a bulldog's lower jaw is longer than the upper jaw, it is physically impossible for the dog to let go while there is any tension on whatever it is gripping," read a story about an attack on a five-year-old in Texas's *Big Spring Herald Sun*. The pit bull's choppers were so strong, the mythology went, it could bite down with a force of more than 2,000 pounds per square inch. Other outlets reported that the breed mauled without provocation and felt no pain. The public couldn't get enough. In 1986, newspapers and magazines ran 350 articles on pit bulls. Just a year later, that number had more than doubled.

The year 1987 saw not just a spike in pit bull coverage but a whole new level of demonization that crescendoed with three sensational articles in some of the country's top magazines—all in the same month. *People Weekly* (now just *People*) led the pack with a July 6 story titled "An Instinct for the Kill." The item began with the account of a two-year-old San Jose boy mauled so severely by a pit bull that a paramedic said he was "unrecognizable as a human being." The breed was the "Rambo of the dog world" and a "shark," according to experts. A few weeks later, *Time* followed with its "Time Bombs on Legs." Then, on the same day, *Sports Illustrated* ran a demon-eyed pit bull on its cover, its mouth agape and teeth bared as if ready to eviscerate the reader. Over its head in bold white lettering: "BEWARE OF THIS DOG."

The pit bull wasn't just the latest demon dog. It had become a new breed of monster, wild and terrible like nothing that had come before. Isolated attacks were reported as epidemics. Maulings by other breeds were virtually ignored. And even minor incidents warranted major headlines. "Elderly Man Narrowly Escapes Pit Bull Attack" topped a story about a Californian who said a couple of dogs chased him as he was taking out his garbage. "Pit Bull Angers Resident," ran an article about a canine stealing food from a bird feeder.

The pit bull also received something no other breed had: supposed scientific confirmation of its evil tendencies. In 1989, the Centers for Disease Control reported that pit bulls were involved in 41.6 percent of dog-related human fatalities from 1979 to 1988, three times more than the next breed, German shepherds. A subsequent CDC report, published in 2000, came to similar conclusions, finding that pit bulls caused nearly twice as many deaths as any other breed of dog. Though both studies conceded that they were based in part on media coverage, which tended to overreport pit bull attacks and made it hard to verify the actual breed responsible, the media ran with the figures. The press could now back up its hyperbole with science, even though science had based its own figures on the press. By 2006, more than 2,800 newspaper articles had "pit bull" in the headline.

The public was whipped into a panic. Pit bulls seemingly lurked around every corner, ready to rip you apart with their steel-trap jaws and sharklike feeding frenzies. Never mind that your chances of being killed by a canine, let alone a pit bull, were nearly three times less than being struck by lightning. People became so hysterical that owners, convinced that their docile dogs would turn on them without warning, began having them euthanized at record rates. The same month that *People*, *Time*, and *Sports Illustrated* ran their articles, more than three hundred pit bulls were turned into the Los Angeles County Animal Care and Control Department. Containing the demon wasn't enough, however. Society demanded excommunication.

Banishing the Breed

On a cold, gray morning in mid-December, I drive across town to the northeast corner of Baltimore. Past boarded up brownstones. Past liquor stores with bars on the windows. Past faded murals on brick walls, their African American heroes urging residents to "BELIEVE"—believe in God, believe in the city, believe in a life free from drugs, violence, and poverty. Eventually, I reach my destination, an enclave of 1,500 brick and cinder block row homes known as Armistead Gardens. I pull into a large asphalt lot and park my car.

Wedged between two highways in an industrial part of the city pockmarked with cemeteries, packing plants, and budget motels, Armistead was built as public housing in the World War II era, which explains why many of the homes look like barracks. Whites from West Virginia to

Tennessee came to work in shipyards and steel mills, and the demographics haven't changed much since then; up until 1988, only one black family had been allowed to reside here. The crime, meanwhile, got steadily worse for decades. Newspaper articles from the 1990s describe the neighborhood as a den of prostitutes and drug dealers, where "a body gets carried out of one of the establishments every so often." Things are safer today, though drugs are still a problem and nearly half of the families live below the poverty line. But this is a close-knit community, where people have grown up for generations, everyone knows each other, and dogs are family. Recently, however, the management has said that some of that family must go.

I get out of my car and approach one of the dwellings, a small white row home packed in the middle of five others. It faces a similar clot of houses across a narrow alley, the two connected by low, crisscrossing power lines. The front door is decorated like a giant present, covered in green foil with the image of a red ribbon running down its length. "BEWARE OF DOG" signs hang in the two front windows. Jenine Gangi comes outside to greet me. Short, in her mid-twenties, with dyed red hair that has begun to grow out, exposing deep brown roots, she sports holey jeans, a tongue piercing, and a gray T-shirt that reads, "Don't Bully My Breed." She leads me inside to a combination kitchen/living room. A mini fridge sits in the corner. A dog bed lies on the floor. Two pit bulls rush us as we enter: a fifty-pound black dog with a white chest, gremlin ears, and a furiously whipping tail, and a larger, mellower brown dog. "These are my girls," Gangi smiles.

Gangi was born and raised in Baltimore, or "Bawl'mer" as her accent attests. She's always had pit bulls, and they've always been family. Tank Girl—the brown dog, now curled up on the couch while Gangi and I sit in the kitchen—has been with her the longest. She calls her "my planned baby" because she's the only pet Gangi set out to own; the others fell into her lap. Gangi got Tank from an acquaintance six years ago when the puppy was just six weeks old, and the two have been inseparable ever since. When Gangi left home at age nineteen, she took the dog with her. When her boyfriend kicked her out a few years later, she moved from friend's house to friend's house, sleeping on couches and in basements—even in her car for a few nights—always with the pit bull by her side. And when Gangi's sister died in a car crash, the dog was there for her, smothering her with her furry weight and licking away her pain. "My family disintegrated after my sister passed away," she tells me. "If I didn't have Tank, I probably would have killed myself."

Gangi paid it forward by saving Baby Girl, her black dog, who now sits wriggling in her lap, lashing Gangi's chin with her tongue. About a year ago, someone left the puppy in front of the PetCo store where Gangi works, dropped off at night in a tiny crate, covered in urine and feces. She was thin and lethargic, and none of the other employees wanted anything to do with her. So Gangi took her to the Baltimore Animal Rescue and Care Shelter in hopes she would be adopted. But like many animal shelters, BARCS was overflowing with unwanted pit bulls, and it called Gangi a few days later saying it was going to euthanize the dog. "I was on vacation with my mom in Ocean City," she says, "but I rushed home to save her." Gangi didn't have the $40 to adopt Baby Girl, so she offered to foster her until BARCS could find a home. She's had her ever since.

The three share the small home with Chuck Norris, a slightly tubby orange tabby. "He was destroying stuff in my house," Gangi smirks. "That's why I named him that." She found him wandering her parking lot a few months ago and brought him to the animal hospital where she works as a veterinary assistant—her second job—to have him neutered. She also had his ear clipped (a sign that a cat has been fixed), assuming she'd release him back outside. But as with Baby Girl, she couldn't let him go. "He's my son," she says. True to his namesake, Chuck Norris holds his own against the pit bulls. When Tank Girl jumps off the couch and heads toward him, he sends her packing with a glare and a swat. It's clear Gangi sees a bit of herself in the cat; "I can be a firecracker," she tells me, and I'd soon learn that she too doesn't back down from a fight.

It hasn't been easy for Gangi to keep her family together. Even with her two jobs, she can barely afford the rent. And moving somewhere else isn't an option; none of the other places she looked at allowed pit bulls. "I'm embarrassed about living here," she says, "but it's the only place I could have my dogs. I wasn't going to go anywhere without them." Soon, however, Gangi may not have a choice. Four months ago, Armistead sent her a letter saying she had to get rid of Tank and Baby or be evicted. And she's not the only one.

Gangi's troubles began on a sunny Saturday afternoon in April 2007. A ten-year-old named Dominic Solesky was playing Nerf tag with three other boys in their Towson neighborhood, about eight miles north of Baltimore City. Dominic and his friend, Scotty Mason, were on one team, defending their home base by shooting a barrage of orange foam darts from their plastic guns. At some point, Scotty wandered away in pursuit of the enemy, disappearing into a nearby alley. He didn't return. A while later, the two other boys came running, shouting, "Time out!" and saying Scotty had been bitten by a dog. Dominic, suspecting a trick, followed them warily into the alley. Scotty's toy gun lay on the ground, next to a spatter of blood. Then Dominic heard a fence rattling. He looked up and met the eyes of Clifford, a large, light brown pit bull with a white chest staring him down from within a four-foot-high, chain-link pen in a nearby yard. The dog shared the small enclosure with a female pit bull, and as Dominic watched in horror, Clifford jumped on the female's back and vaulted over the fence. The boy ran, but he wasn't fast enough. Clifford tackled him from behind and tore into him. He ripped off part of Dominic's cheek, gashed open his left thigh to the bone, and severed his femoral artery. The boy's mother, who arrived on the scene shortly after the mauling, would later testify that "it looked like a shark attack."

Two weeks after the incident, Baltimore County councilman Vince Gardina called for the creation of a task force to determine if pit bulls posed a unique threat to county residents. He hoped the panel would recommend special restrictions on the dogs, including keeping them enclosed in kennels behind higher fences than for other breeds. The task force recommended community education instead, encouraging *all* dog owners to be more responsible with their pets. So Gardina proposed his own law singling out pit bulls and pit bull mixes. The dogs would have to be locked up in covered enclosures while in their yards and muzzled when out in public. Violators would be fined $1,000 a day.

Several months later, the Solesky family pursued civil action against the pit bull's owner, Thomas O'Halloran. Dominic had spent seventeen days in intensive care, requiring multiple surgeries and blood transfusions and racking up thousands of dollars in medical bills. O'Halloran, the Soleskys argued, was a negligent owner: not only had he kept Clifford in a cramped, easily escapable pen, but he knew the animal was vicious.

Indeed, just minutes before their son was mauled, the dog had bitten his friend, Scotty. O'Halloran had witnessed the incident, according to court documents, and taken the boy into his house to clean him up. Scotty also said O'Halloran warned him not to tell anyone about the attack.

O'Halloran declared bankruptcy, so the Soleskys continued their case against his landlord, eighty-nine-year-old Dorothy Tracey. Under Maryland law, landlords were not liable for the actions of their tenant's dogs if they didn't know the animals were dangerous. But the Solesky case changed everything. Though a trial court ruled against the family, Maryland's highest court took a far different stance. Relying on the 2000 CDC study, which had been based partly on media stories, as well as claims that pit bulls "bite to kill without signal," have "high insensitivity to pain," and sport "massive canine jaws [that] can crush a victim with up to two thousand pounds of pressure per square inch," it ruled that pit bulls and pit bull mixes were "inherently dangerous." Anyone harboring them was liable for their actions, even if the dog had never been aggressive before. The 2012 ruling, *Tracey v. Solesky*, overturned more than a century of common law. Owning a pit bull, or renting to someone who did, was effectively the same as having a land mine on your property.

The actions of Councilman Gardina and the Maryland Court of Appeals weren't unusual. Throughout the United States and Canada, lawmakers had been trying to place restrictions on pit bulls, and courts had been singling them out for condemnation. A politician in Ontario called the dogs a "menace" and a "loaded weapon"; the District of Columbia Court of Appeals compared them to corrosive liquids and hand grenades. Those were the tamer responses. Beginning in 1980, municipalities across both countries—no longer content to simply denigrate pit bulls—began to ban the breed. Denver outlawed the dogs in 1989, allowing police to go so far as to enter people's homes to confiscate them. That same year, Ohio branded the canines "vicious," imposing severe restrictions on the breed statewide. And in 2006, Maquoketa, Iowa, equated pit bulls with wild animals, placing them on its list of forbidden species, right between piranhas and pumas. Some communities based their prohibitions on single incidents. Others, perhaps believing they were heading off a pit bull apocalypse, outlawed the dogs proactively. By the end of the twentieth century, more than two hundred municipalities had banned or severely restricted the canines or any breed that resembled them. Pit bulls weren't just the new demon dog. They were a cancer that had to be eradicated from society.

This intense vilification of a single type of dog helps explain why pit bulls like Kno are starting to be put on trial. Prior to the 1980s, if a dog attacked and severely injured someone, its owner was charged with a crime. But over the last few decades, as pets have been seen less like property, judges and animal control boards have increasingly turned their attention to punishing the dog itself, with more and more elaborate trials and proceedings. The canines sit in shelter "jails" while evidence is presented, expert witnesses take the stand, and a new generation of animal lawyers defends them. The only difference between these trials and those against animals in the Middle Ages is that the excommunication is physical, not spiritual; guilty dogs are banished from the county or state. And executions aren't carried out by hanging in the town square; they're performed via lethal injection behind the closed doors of an animal control facility.

Yet the same questions confront today's animal trials as confronted those trials hundreds of years ago. Why drag a dog before a judge in the first place? Why not just euthanize the canine and be done with it? The answers may be the same as they were back then. Pit bulls became the demon dog du jour just as pets were turning into full-fledged family members. We put rats and pigs on trial in medieval Europe because they had violated the cosmic order: they destroyed our crops and killed our children even though they were supposed to be subservient to man. Today, dogs *are* our children. When they kill our babies, they don't just violate God's plan; they violate the new reality we have constructed—a world where cats and dogs are family. So we denigrate pit bulls in the press. We ban them across the country. And we stage elaborate trials to restore the cosmic order. The proceedings effectively treat Kno, Clifford, and other dogs like leprous appendages, hacking them off lest they infect everything we have created.

Back in Armistead Gardens, Jenine Gangi is feeling the effects of this new world order. She didn't hear about the *Tracey v. Solesky* decision until she got a letter from the neighborhood's management. Sent a few

months after the high court's verdict, it referenced the ruling that pit
bulls are "inherently dangerous" and that landlords are liable for pit bull
attacks: "The board of directors has decided that it is in the best interests
of Armistead Homes Corporation and the residents to ban pit bulls and
cross-bred pit bull mixes. **Therefore, no pit bulls or cross-bred pit bull
mixes are permitted on Armistead property**. If you have a pit bull or
cross-bred pit bull mix, you must get rid of the animal immediately. . . .
The board may take legal action, including termination, against lease-
holders that fail to comply with the ban" (emphasis in original).

Gangi panicked. "I called up my mom and dad," she says. "I was
screaming. I was crying. I didn't know what I was supposed to do or
where I was supposed to go." Terrified that Armistead would take Tank
and Baby while she was at work, she began bringing them with her, using up her limited savings to board them during the day. "I would have
lived in my car before I got rid of my kids," she tells me. Other neighbors, worried about being evicted, didn't take any chances. They turned
their dogs into local shelters, where they faced almost certain euthanasia. The ruling affected an estimated 84,000 pit bulls and pit bull mixes
in the state. Owners left them tied to posts. Hundreds were abandoned
at BARCS alone.

Meanwhile, Gangi wasn't getting much support from those around
her. Neighbors who had been friendly before the court ruling suddenly
started avoiding her. PetCo customers would remark that the state
should just "kill 'em all." And when she walked her dogs down the
street, people crossed to the other side. "One woman pulled her dog
away, screaming that she didn't want her to get pregnant," Gangi tells
me. "She thought Tank Girl was a boy." Others refused to make eye
contact. "I felt discriminated against just for having them," she says. "It
was like dogism."

But true to her personality, Gangi didn't back away from the fight.
She joined a lawsuit filed by a neighbor to get Armistead's board of directors to reverse its decision. And a few weeks after the housing development's management sent her the letter, Gangi helped organize a
demonstration at one of its board meetings at a local church. Her house
became the headquarters of the insurrection. Fellow pit bull owners
came by to commiserate and make signs: "My Dog Is Family," "The Cost

of Freedom Is Always High, but Pit Bulls Have Always Paid It." Then they descended on the church, crowding it inside and out. Local papers and a TV crew showed up. Gangi unloaded on anyone who would listen. "We wanted to put pressure on Armistead Gardens," she tells me. "We wanted to show them that we weren't just going to lie down and allow them to take our kids. We were going to fight."

On the street, Gangi became a one-woman PR campaign. If people gave her grief when she walked her dogs, she'd grit her teeth. Then she'd start telling them about all of the great things her pit bulls do: how both donate blood, how she uses Baby to socialize other animals she fosters from BARCS, which helps them get adopted, and how even the "BEWARE OF DOG" signs in her front windows are a bluff; she's just trying to scare off criminals. As if to prove her point to me, Gangi makes a gun with her fingers and pretends to shoot Tank Girl. The dog falls to the floor, but she can't stop her tail from thumping the ground. "You're useless," Gangi smiles.

Gangi hopes her efforts will convince her friends and neighbors—as well as Maryland lawmakers—that pit bulls are not demons. "I'm fighting for my children and other people's children," she says. "These animals that live with you, they love you. You're their hero. You can't give up on them. You have to keep fighting." But she and those like her have a long road ahead.

All Dogs Are Created Equal

Not long after I visit Jenine Gangi, I find myself in downtown Baltimore's Westminster Hall, a 150-year-old former Gothic church and the final resting place of Edgar Allan Poe. I'm here for the Mid-Atlantic Regional Animal Law Symposium, a local version of the Animal Law Conference I attended in Portland. About eighty lawyers sit around circular tables where pews used to be, as the bright morning sun shines red and blue through arched stained glass windows. On stage, her back to the undulating shape of a pipe organ, is Ledy VanKavage. In a nation with its share of pit bull haters, she's the breed's best friend and staunchest ally, a senior attorney with Best Friends Animal Society who has helped push through more than thirty animal welfare bills across the country and who has lobbied tirelessly on behalf of America's demon dog. She's a fast, animated speaker in her mid-fifties with feathered blonde hair, and she's almost always smiling—even now, as she rips into the *Tracey v. Solesky* decision, calling it a modern-day version of the Dred Scott case. If society is going to turn pets into people, VanKavage is here to make sure they all have equal protection under the law.

VanKavage sees many parallels between the plight of pit bulls and the experience of blacks in America. It's not just her allusions to Dred Scott. She tells the crowd that the hysteria around the breed has led to Jim Crow–like segregation, with the dogs being banished from cities and counties. She also says that law enforcement is engaging in a canine version of racial profiling, singling out dogs not for who they are but for what they are, not for what they've done but for what they might do. In some cases a passing resemblance to the breed is enough to condemn them. She recounts a 2009 incident in Salina, Kansas, in which animal control officers spotted a black-and-white puppy with a stocky build and boxy head in her owner's yard. The city had a ban on pit bulls, and the officers grabbed the dog, named Lucey, threatening to expel her or take her to a municipal shelter where she might be destroyed. Desperate to get her back, Lucey's owner had a DNA test done. The "pit bull" was only 12.5 percent Staffordshire bull terrier; twice as many genes pegged her as a Bernese mountain dog. The city dropped the charges and released her.

Cases like Lucey's make VanKavage cringe every time she hears about a city that has passed laws singling out pit bulls, commonly known as breed-specific legislation. "There's nothing *specific* about these laws," she says. "You can't tell what a dog is just by looking at it." To drive her point home, she puts up a slide she's fond of showing police officers and lawmakers: two dozen headshots of canines that all resemble pit bulls. Only one is, and every time she shows it, almost everyone gets it wrong. Even the experts have trouble; a recent study found that 87.5 percent of dogs adopted out by shelters were mislabeled, and that more than twenty-five types of canines are commonly mistaken for pit bulls. The American Kennel Club itself doesn't recognize "pit bull" as a true breed.

VanKavage—who owns two pits, including one rescued from a dog-fighting bust—is also battling to restore the breed's original reputation as a hero and friend. She's had some help from recent studies, which have started to debunk the myth that pit bulls are inherently dangerous. A 2005 analysis found that all dogs bite down with forces ranging from 200 to 450 pounds per square inch, not the 2,000 attributed to pit bulls, and that the American pit bull terrier's snap is softer than that of German shepherds and Rottweilers. What's more, two research papers published in 2008, one that surveyed owners and one that subjected dogs to a variety of stressful situations, concluded that pit bulls are as docile as Golden retrievers; the Chihuahuas, dachshunds, and Jack Russell terriers were most likely to bite. (Though, to be fair, when pit bulls do clamp down, they inflict a lot more damage.)

All of this shows, says VanKavage, that laws targeting pit bulls aren't just flawed; they're prejudiced. That's why she's taken to calling them breed *discriminatory* legislation. It's also why, she says, they fail to work. Studies have found that dog bites have actually increased in the United States since breed-specific laws were first enacted and that many municipalities with such laws have simply seen attacks by other dogs go up. Such legislation, she tells the crowd, does nothing but score easy points for politicians while giving citizens a false sense of security. It's also expensive, costing cities thousands or even millions of dollars a year to enforce. Even the Centers for Disease Control, author of two of the reports that pegged pit bulls as the country's most dangerous dog, has come out against the laws.

Instead, VanKavage and others have pushed for legislation that targets all dangerous dogs, not just dangerous types of dogs. "Ban the deed, not the breed" has become the rallying cry. She also wants to shift the responsibility for bad behavior back onto the owner. A quarter of pit bulls that attack people are chained up all day, and a quarter are used for dog fighting. The vast majority are not family pets. And like Kno and Clifford, nearly all are unsterilized. Some municipalities have begun to take notice. Washington, DC, makes owners of canines that have attacked without provocation neuter and register their pets. In Illinois, dangerous dogs must be microchipped. And other communities have begun to ban the bans. Ohio overturned its statewide restrictions in 2012. That same year, Massachusetts made it illegal for any of its municipalities to outlaw specific breeds, becoming the thirteenth state to do so. Due to the efforts of VanKavage and others, breed-specific legislation has begun to disappear. Breed-neutral legislation is taking its place. "The trend is in our favor," she declares. "This is America. Every American should be allowed to own whichever breed of dog they choose."

The reputation of pit bulls may be finally starting to recover. Perhaps nothing illustrates this better than the fate of the fifty-odd canines rescued from football player Michael Vick's Virginia dog-fighting operation in 2007. Despite the breed's bad rap, the public rallied around the dogs, outraged by allegations that they had been brutally trained and that others had been killed by hanging, drowning, and electrocution. Normally animals taken from such places are euthanized. This time they got a lawyer. The judge in charge of the case appointed Valparaiso University law professor Rebecca Huss to look after their welfare. Despite everything they had been through, the vast majority passed aggression tests, and Huss was able to place them with rescue organizations throughout the country. "At the end of the day, the breed of these animals didn't matter," VanKavage tells me after the conference. "Dogs, like people, are individuals."

Things may be beginning to change in Baltimore too. Pauline Houliaras, president and cofounder of B-More Dog, a local pit bull advocacy group, deserves much of the credit. If Ledy VanKavage is leading the symbolic civil rights march for dogs, Houliaras is heading the literal one. I rendezvous with her on an unseasonably warm Sunday morning in mid-January, the day before Martin Luther King Jr. Day. We meet on a narrow field of grass overlooking Baltimore's Inner Harbor, a promenade of tourist shops, museums, and pricey restaurants that curves around a thumb-shaped inlet of the Chesapeake Bay. A few joggers are out, and in the distance I hear the approaching din of a marching band, the trombones and tap-tap-tap of snare drums growing ever louder.

I've come to observe Pit Bulls on Parade, a monthly procession of local dog owners organized by Houliaras. She's in her mid-forties, wearing a purple knit cap, and sports the charcoal hair and olive skin of her Greek ancestry. She holds a leash attached to Ruby, a five-year-old yellow pit bull with white splotches on her feet and a purple Baltimore Ravens bandana around her neck. (Purple will turn out to be the color of the day; Baltimore's home team is about to challenge the New England Patriots for a spot in the Super Bowl.) Houliaras's group formed in the wake of the Dominic Solesky attack. When she heard that Councilman Vince Gardina was going to propose severe restrictions on the breed at a county council meeting, she spread the word to the contacts she had made through her work as a dog trainer and BARCS volunteer. "They had more people there than at any meeting in the council's history," she tells me, as we sit on the grass. In the end, Gardina was outvoted six to one. Houliaras and a few others formed B-More Dog to commemorate the victory. They thought they had won the battle against breed-specific legislation. Then *Tracey v. Solesky* happened.

"We were completely blindsided by that ruling," Houliaras says, as more pit bulls and their owners begin to gather in the field. Like Jenine Gangi, she immediately felt the impact of the decision. "It created an atmosphere of fear. We were afraid to take our dogs outside." But Houliaras knew that Ruby wasn't "inherently dangerous," and she set out to show the public the same thing. Pit Bulls on Parade was born out of that sentiment. "We wanted to improve the image of pit bulls and show people what the average dog owner looks like," she says. "What you see on TV is not reality."

It's 11:15 now, and twenty-odd owners and their pit bulls have gathered around Houliaras. Ruby is whining and whipping her tail, anxious to join the others. "I know, it's very exciting," Houliaras coos to her. "Just relax. This isn't a play date." If anyone could convince the public that pit bulls aren't demons, it's Ruby. With her soft, golden eyes and gentle demeanor, she's a giant pillow of love, and I have trouble taking notes because she keeps licking my face. She has no reason to be so friendly. Houliaras got her from a friend, who found her wandering the streets. Ruby's face is pitted with small, furless patches that Houliaras says are likely scars from dog fighting. Some say Ruby was a "bait dog"—too docile to attack others, her former owners sicced other pit bulls on her to train them to fight. They also may have forced her to breed, strapping her down to "rape stands" common to the blood sport. When she ceased to be useful, they threw her away. "She was malnourished. She wasn't housebroken. She didn't know any commands," says Houliaras. "But she was a sweetheart." Now, in addition to leading the parade, Ruby accompanies Houliaras to inner-city schools, where she sits patiently as children with autism and educational disabilities read books to her.

"They won't read to anybody else, but they'll read for Ruby," Houliaras says. "She doesn't judge them. She just looks at them adoringly."

Houliaras gets up and addresses the small crowd. "How many people are here for the first time?" "Who has dogs up for adoption?" Then she lays out the ground rules: If anyone approaches you, feel free to stop and tell them about your dog; you can catch up to the rest of us later. There are ducks in the water; if your dog gets excited by wildlife, be vigilant. If your dog gets stressed out, take a break. "It's supposed to be fun for them too." Then we're off, walking along the harbor toward the crowds on the promenade. We pass the marching band I heard earlier, huddled by the side of the path for a photo op. About thirty strong, its members are dressed in purple and white, and they've unfurled a banner that reads, "Lesbian and Gay Band Association." They cheer and tap their drumsticks as we pass.

I separate from Houliaras and approach a young couple walking Lilly, a brown pit bull in a red sweater. When I enquire about the dog, the woman, Erin, smiles. "We're accidental pit bull owners," she says. "We'd been looking for a dog for two years. We kept going back to shelters, but I kept saying, 'I don't want a pit. I don't want a pit.' We didn't know anything about them except for what was in the news. Then we saw Lilly at BARCS. They found her in an abandoned house with a bunch of dogs who were in bad shape. She was adorable; we just had a good feeling about her. And I was like, 'OK, I want her.'" This is their second time at the parade. "Lilly's super sweet," says the man, Amir. "She's a great ambassador."

Next, I pass Liz and John, a couple in their mid-twenties with a tan pit bull named Sunny in tow. She's wearing a purple harness, but it's just a coincidence. "You're talking to two of the least football fans in the world," laughs Liz. Sunny is tugging on her leash, eager to catch up with the other dogs. "She's excited," says John. "She's being a pain in the butt today." A five-year-old boy clings to his mother as they pass. "Is he going to bite me?" he asks her. A few minutes later, a girl of similar age walks by with her mom. "Awww . . . a doggy," she says, reaching to pet the pit.

We've hit the halfway point, the main part of the promenade, where locals and tourists have gathered to window-shop and gape at the historic ships in the harbor. I notice that a small crowd has congregated around two parade walkers, Lauren and Keith, who look to be in their late teens, and their two pit bulls. (A magician nearby making balloon animals is virtually ignored.) They own one, Colby, a brown dog with a white face and paws, wearing a Ravens jersey. The other, Bumble, is brindle on her top and white on her front and has an "Adopt Me" sign on her back. Lauren and Keith have been participating in the parade for five months now, partly to help a local shelter adopt out dogs like Bumble, partly to overcome the pit bull stigma. "When I'm out walking Colby, people will actually run away from me," says Lauren. "One woman was petting him, and when I told her he was a pit bull, she jerked her hand back like she had just touched a hot stove." Today's crowd is decidedly more open-minded. Some want to pet the dogs, others say they have pit bulls of their own at home, and still others express a genuine interest in adopting Bumble. Keith tries to seal the deal by picking up the sixty-pound canine and cradling him in his arms like a teddy bear. "Please, mom, please can we have him?" says an eight-year-old boy to his mother. A tall ship nearby fires its cannon. The people all jump out of their skin, but the dogs just keep wagging their tails.

I hang out with Lauren and Keith for so long that I eventually see Houliaras approaching. She and a few others have already reached the end of the route, and now they're headed back. When we meet up, she tells me about B-More Dog's recent campaigns. In addition to the parade, the group brings pit bulls into elementary school classrooms and uses them to teach the students to be kind to animals. "The theme is dogs and cats have feelings too," she tells me. "Sometimes the kids will say it's the first time they touched a dog." The group also stages Community Pit Bull Days, traveling to poor areas of the city and offering free vaccines and spay/neuter services. It held one at Armistead Gardens, shortly after management sent out the letter threatening to evict pit bull owners. Houliaras passed out flyers to residents telling them that, legally, they didn't have to give up their animals. B-More Dog has also been lobbying the Maryland legislature to effectively overturn *Tracey v. Solesky*, rallying outside the statehouse and testifying in front of a task force on breed-specific legislation. "They've got to fix this thing," Houliaras says.

She, VanKavage, and others are fighting for more than pit bulls. They're fighting for all pets. As cats and dogs take on new rights, new roles, and new responsibilities, they're not just becoming more like people—they're becoming more like citizens. Yet the path to citizenship isn't a smooth one, and pets may not complete the journey. Their evolving status will face new obstacles and new enemies. Their fate—and the future of society—will hang in the balance. Dogs and cats are entering uncharted territory. They're going to need all the help they can get.

The parade ends on a grassy hill, just a few yards from where it began. The group is a bit thinner now; only about eight pit bulls remain. The rest have gone home or are still entertaining strangers on the promenade. Owners lounge on the ground, while the dogs catch their breath and chew twigs. I ask Houliaras what it will take for society to fully embrace pit bulls again. "Sometimes I think it's impossible," she sighs. "It's like when I talk to my vegan friends; are they really going to get Americans to give up their hamburgers? But who knows? We've definitely seen a shift in how people care about their dogs. They're definitely much more a part of the family." Then she glances over at Ruby, sprawled out on the grass, gazing back into her eyes. "As soon as people meet one or two pit bulls," she says, "they usually fall in love."

A jogger runs by in a purple-and-white jersey. "Go Ravens!" Houliaras shouts. "Go pit bulls!" he shouts back.

TEN

Citizen Canine

A funny thing happened on the way to Lackland Air Force Base. I was at my gate at the Baltimore/Washington International Airport, waiting for a flight to San Antonio. My plan was to check out Lackland's Military Working Dog Program, the largest operation in the world dedicated to turning canines into soldiers. As cats and dogs become family members and quasi-persons, they're also taking on new roles critical to the survival of our increasingly dangerous and isolating society. These jobs will earn them a sort-of citizenship no animal has ever achieved. And nowhere are pets closer to earning this status than at Lackland. Before I even boarded the plane, however, I met my first canine military hero: Rambo, a scrawny five-year-old German shepherd missing his left front leg.

Standing at attention near the gate entrance, Rambo cut quite the figure. He wore a green camouflage vest festooned with military patches, including a POW insignia, two American flags, and a dog skull and paw prints that represented a canine unit serving in Afghanistan. Across his chest hung a gold Marine Corps badge flanked by three stripes that designated him a sergeant. His owner—Lisa Phillips, thirty years old with translucent blue eyes—sat nearby, holding him on leash. I walked over and introduced myself.

Phillips told me that Rambo had trained at Lackland. He spent four months learning how to sniff out explosives and take down bad guys. After that, he was shipped off to the Marine Corps air station in Cherry Point, North Carolina. There, while taking part in a routine exercise where he lunged at volunteers wearing protective body suits, he injured his left shoulder and never recovered. The military invests an average of

$16,000 per canine, and it was loathe to take him out of service. But after a year, Rambo developed degenerative joint disease, and the Marine Corps medically discharged him. For the first time in its history, Cherry Point held a retirement ceremony for a dog. Phillips, whose own military career was cut short by a knee injury during army training, adopted Rambo in 2012. She had studied as a veterinary technician and soon assisted in the amputation of his leg.

That was just the beginning of their story. As Rambo's medical bills piled up, Phillips began to wonder why the military had taken such good care of her—covering 70 percent of the expenses from her five knee surgeries—and yet did nothing for Rambo. The problem, she soon discovered, was that the Department of Defense doesn't classify its canines as soldiers; it considers them equipment, no different from a gun or a pair of boots. Phillips vowed to change that. She started to tell me about it when the intercom cut in, informing us it was time to board the plane. I took my place in line, but it wouldn't be the last time I'd hear about the dog. Shortly before we landed, the head flight attendant's voice crackled over the cabin speakers. "We have a special guest aboard," she said. "He never made it overseas, but he did a lot of work here in the States. Let's give Rambo a big round of applause. We support all of our military heroes, the two-legged kind and the four-legged kind."

To Serve and Protect

I arrive at Lackland at 8 a.m. sharp on a Monday in mid-February. The weather is cool, with a slight wind, and dark gray clouds fill the Texas sky, threatening rain. My contact, Public Affairs Officer Dona Fair, meets me in a black Mercedes sedan at the main gate. I get inside, and we drive up to the guard station, where a serviceman in desert camouflage waves us through. When I tell Fair what my book is about, she laughs. "When I grew up, we chained the dog in the backyard," she says. "Now our dog goes to the spa more than I do."

Beyond the main gate Lackland sprawls into a self-contained city. Across a vast, flat landscape, hotels, chapels, and shopping centers sit interspersed among hundreds of barracks. There's a dental clinic, a playhouse, even a TV studio. More than 52,000 people call the base home;

over half are military, though thousands of families also live here. Despite its civilian amenities, it's not hard to remember you're in a military installation. Vintage World War II aircraft dot the grounds. All the buildings are painted beige. And almost everyone walks in lockstep, whether marching behind a commanding officer or just out for a stroll.

Our first stop is a large, aluminum-sided auditorium. We're met outside by Jason Silvis, an imposing navy chief petty officer in dark blue camo, and Grant Fyall, a slighter air force captain in muted green fatigues. Inside, a group of canines is learning how to detect bombs. "Safety is the main rule," Silvis warns before we enter. "All these dogs are trained to bite. Try to stay ten to fifteen feet away. Do not pet them."

The auditorium is filled with about three hundred seats. Along the back wall is a large white shield depicting the silhouette of a canine bisected by a lightning bolt. "Military Working Dog," it reads. "Guardians of the Night." Another wall features pictures of dogs posing with handlers who have been killed in action. Above the frames is a banner: "In Canis Confiderus"—In Dog We Trust. From the stage a few service members look on as a burly man in a hunting cap and brown overalls snakes a dog around the chairs row by row. The canine, a two-year-old brown Belgian Malinois with a black muzzle and black-tipped ears, is named Basco. He looks a bit like a German shepherd on steroids. When he sits—a signal that he has detected something—his handler begins whooping and hollering. Then he rubs Basco on the head and tosses him a bright red chew toy.

The auditorium is one of the main training areas for Lackland's military working dogs. Here they learn to distinguish the various chemicals that make up the improvised explosive devices (IEDs) and other bombs that have maimed and killed more US troops than anything else in Iraq and Afghanistan. Today Basco is sniffing for potassium chlorate, one of the ingredients of these explosives. It's hidden in metal boxes underneath some of the seats. He's near the end of his second month of training and can already distinguish nine bomb-making materials, including C4, TNT, and smokeless powder. Canines that detect these odors in combat not only protect troops from a particular bomb but can disrupt entire supply chains. "These dogs can find the most minute amount of explosives," says Basco's brawny handler, Master Trainer Jeff Justice, in a deep southern accent. "If someone's just touched an explosive and then a door handle on a vehicle, the dog can pick it up. These dogs pick up on so much stuff that you and I cannot even begin to fathom. It's like if you go into McDonald's and order a Big Mac, you see the whole sandwich. Well this dog, he breaks it down by component. He smells the cheese, the beef, the hands that touched it, and what those hands touched before that. He picks up on odors that we have no idea are there."

Those abilities aren't just an academic curiosity for Justice. He served in the US Air Force in northern Iraq with a German shepherd named Akki. Though the military forbids him from discussing his experiences in detail, he says Akki spotted numerous IEDs and random munitions caches. "I know my dog saved my life on more than one occasion," he says. "When mental fatigue starts to wear on you, you start missing stuff. But the dog, his synapses are always firing. His change in behavior alerts me to what's going on. He'll stop me in my tracks." Justice has a deep scar below his left bicep, incurred while trying to save his comrade's life. Akki was severely wounded in action, and as he lay dying, covered in blood, Justice reached in to try to save him. "When I touched the injury, he lashed out," Justice says. "He was my buddy for over two years. Now I have a German shepherd at home that has his name."

Remembering Lisa Phillips's remark about the government's classification of Rambo, I ask Justice if he views military working dogs as equipment. He shakes his head. "Me and my dog have a personal connection," he says assertively. "I don't have that with my body armor or rifle. You sleep in the same area. You share your meals. You do everything together. If my rifle breaks down, it's like, whatever, get me another rifle. If my partner goes down, it's a whole other story. He's not a piece of equipment. He's my friend."

The military is slowly coming around to Justice's point of view. It's been a complicated journey.

Dogs are a relatively recent addition to the US Armed Forces. Benjamin Franklin suggested using the animals in skirmishes against Native Americans in the mid-eighteenth century, and Stubby the pit bull delivered messages between battalions and helped capture a German spy during World War I. But it wasn't until World War II that the United States fully realized the utility of canines in battle.

Even then, the impetus didn't come from the military. A group of dog fanciers calling itself Dogs for Defense began training canines for war in 1942, schooling them mostly in sentry work. The armed forces weren't interested. But as concerns about spies and sabotage mounted, they began accepting DFD's dogs to guard forts and munitions factories. The Department of Defense soon set up training centers across the country, teaching dogs additional duties, including search and rescue, patrol, and messaging. Most of the animals came from members of the general public, eager to do all they could for the war effort—even if it meant sacrificing the family pet. "Sure I feel pretty bad about Teddy going into the Army," a boy told the *Washington Post* as he loaded his seventy-pound German shepherd mix into a DFD truck. "But I bet the Germans will be even sorrier!"

In its first two years, DFD accepted some 40,000 dogs, about 10,000 of which served in the military. Some stayed on the home front, working with the coast guard to patrol shores for German and Japanese subs. Others were shipped overseas, where their night vision proved useful on evening patrols; a few even parachuted from airplanes with their handlers. And still others entered army training to become "demolition wolves." The macho title belied a darker truth: the dogs were to enter enemy bunkers strapped with explosives. Though shut down before it was implemented, the top-secret program was an early sign that the military regarded its canine soldiers as little more than equipment.

The public clearly didn't share that attitude. It flooded the Army Quartermaster Corps with Christmas cards and letters asking how its canine heroes were doing. Perhaps put off by the experience, the military stopped accepting pets from ordinary citizens after the war. Instead, it began purchasing dogs directly from breeders. That's when Lackland entered the picture.

The air force base, founded in 1942 to meet the high demand for aircrews following the Japanese attack on Pearl Harbor, played a major role in supplying dogs for the Vietnam War. It dedicated more than seven hundred acres to training canines and their handlers, and in 1965 it began sending hundreds of dogs (mostly German shepherds) to Southeast Asia. These canine soldiers took on even more dangerous jobs than their predecessors. They walked ahead of their handlers in the dense jungle, scanning for snakes and trip wires. They charged after fleeing enemies as bullets whizzed by. And they sniffed along roads and railways for buried mines and hideouts. Over the course of the war, the dogs carried out 84,000 missions, killing and capturing thousands of enemy soldiers and exposing more than 2,000 tunnels and bunkers. They saved an estimated 10,000 lives. When Sergeant Robert Himrod was on patrol with his dog, Miss Cracker, six miles south of Saigon, the duo was hit by a booby trap bomb. Miss Cracker took most of the blast. Despite Himrod's attempts at CPR, she died a short time later. "It may sound funny to someone else, but she was more than a dog," he later stated. "She was also a close friend and the only reason I survived that day."

Hundreds of similar stories came out of the war. Yet, when it was time for the United States to pull out of Vietnam, it left its dogs behind, abandoning them along with scores of other excess equipment. It was just easier and cheaper than bringing them home. "Officially, no one really knows what happened to them," writes Michael G. Lemish in *War Dogs*, his fascinating history of canine soldiers. "The only questions that really remain are how many were killed, eaten, or just simply starved to death."

Master Trainer Justice doesn't reflect back fondly on those days. Though he was born after Vietnam ended, he's spoken to plenty of servicemen from the war. "You talk to any handler from that era and they hated that," he tells me in the auditorium. "It was like leaving a fellow soldier behind. We don't do that anymore."

After the auditorium, Dona Fair drives me to a two-story barracks with a white sign out front. "DANGER," it reads. "EXPLOSIVE DOG TRAINING IN PROGRESS. KEEP OUT." We enter the first floor, a long, narrow hallway lined with open doors. The rooms look like a tornado ripped through them. Furniture is toppled, mattresses hang over desks, and closets have spilled their contents onto the hardwood floor. "Dog comin' in!" someone shouts, and I lurch out of the way just in time to avoid being trampled by a massive Belgian Malinois yanking his handler down the hall. The duo bursts into one room, then another, spending only a few seconds in each. In the third, the dog sits in front of a closed cabinet. His handler begins whooping. "Way to go, Big Earn!" he says and throws him a chew toy.

The barracks are where Lackland separates the men from the boys—or, more accurately, the dogs from the pups. Big Earn and his fellow canines, who tear through the building every ten minutes, are only about a month into their training. They're just learning to respond to odors. A handler starts by showing a dog a cloth bag filled with a scent. As soon as the dog puts his nose in it, he gets a toy. The handler does this about fifty times, until the dog starts freezing up when he smells the odor, in anticipation of getting the toy. Then the handler trains the dog to sit after he freezes. That takes about a hundred more trials. "Once they've got the first odor down, they pick up the others pretty quick," one of the servicemen, a young marine corporal named Eduardo Bonilla, tells me. The handlers too are early in their training. They're just learning to interpret their dog's body language—to pick up on subtle cues that could save their lives in a war zone. Though the hierarchy isn't official, the military ranks its dogs one level above their trainers. "That teaches the junior handlers that you've got to respect your partner," says Bonilla.

Just as not all humans are cut out for the military, not all dogs are cut out to be soldiers. Lackland gets most of its canines—typically Belgian Malinois, German shepherds, and Labrador retrievers—from Europe, though it has begun breeding Malinois on base. In their first few months, the animals are treated like any other pet; they live with foster families and get a normal upbringing. At about seven to twelve months, they come back to Lackland, where the military begins developing their "drive"—their desire to play, to act boldly, to compete. At one year, they learn to become soldiers. They spend 120 days at Lackland, training in detection and patrol work. Then, like Rambo, they're shipped to bases around the world, where they can specialize in advanced explosive detection and enemy takedown. They hear gunfire and search mock villages; some learn how to climb ladders and jump out of helicopters. Those that don't develop a good drive or that become freaked out by messy rooms or hardwood floors drop out and become pets or police dogs. There are about nine hundred canines on base at the moment; 14 percent will wash out.

The rest go to war. Hundreds of military working dogs served in Iraq, choppering into villages wearing earmuffs and goggles (or "doggles," as some call them). They searched three-story buildings in as little as four minutes, minimizing the amount of time troops had to spend under hostile fire. Meanwhile, hundreds of other dogs were deployed to Afghanistan, and one, a Belgian Malinois named Cairo, accompanied SEAL Team Six in its takedown of Osama Bin Laden in Pakistan. Though details are scarce, experts say the dog likely rappelled from a helicopter into the al Qaeda leader's compound wearing a Kevlar vest and infrared camera, $20,000 worth of gear in all. Once inside, Cairo may have sniffed out booby traps and even Bin Laden himself.

The US military currently has about 2,500 dogs, making it the largest canine force in the world. It's also the most valuable. The Pentagon spent $19 billion trying to develop a machine that could do as much, as effectively, as the dog can. It failed. "The capability they bring to the fight cannot be replicated by man or machine," General David Petraeus, former commander of US forces in Afghanistan, has said. "By all measures of performance, their yield outperforms any asset we have in our industry." As these animals gain ever-more-specialized training and take on ever-more-dangerous duties, their value will only increase. The arms race of the future won't just be about who has the best weapons; it will be about who has the best dogs.

In the late morning, I arrive at one of Lackland's most unique buildings, the Holland Military Working Dog Hospital. With its large glass windows and open lobby featuring wood paneling and cushy couches, it's certainly more welcoming than the stark, blocky barracks. The base opened the $15 million, 38,000-square-foot facility in 2008. It's been called the "Walter Reed for dogs," and with good reason. Twelve veterinarians and a staff of over forty tend to up to four hundred canines a year, offering everything from regular physicals to shock trauma. The hospital's underwater treadmills, digital radiography, and long-term rehabilitative care also treat dogs returning from war zones, some with gunshot wounds and broken bones, others near retirement, with blistered paws, arthritis, and poor eyesight. "They get better medical than we do," Corporal Bonilla joked to me at the barracks.

Holland handles far more than physical injuries, however. For years, the military has been noticing troubling symptoms in its combat dogs, some of which serve up to twelve years. When they return from war zones, a few of the animals are skittish around loud noises. Others are overly clingy or aggressive with their handlers. In 2010, a blue-ribbon panel concluded that about 5 to 10 percent of deployed military working dogs suffer from posttraumatic stress disorder (PTSD). Like their human counterparts, canines with the longest deployments and those on the front lines are the most susceptible. "It's a major cause of dogs not working well in the field," Holland's chief of behavioral medicine, Walter Burghardt, tells me. And the problem is only likely to get worse as the military pushes the limits of these animals. "It all depends on how far we stretch them and what we ask them to do," Burghardt says. In the meantime, the military tries to keep its PTSD dogs in service by prescribing them the same antianxiety and antidepressant medication it gives to its human soldiers.

Not all dogs can return to combat, however, and that's where Air Force Tech Sergeant Joseph Null comes in. My last stop of the day is Lackland's Military Working Dog Adoption Program, housed in a small building just a few steps from the veterinary hospital. Null, young and bespectacled in forest-colored fatigues, has been running the program for more than two years. Before it was instituted, most dogs that could no longer serve were euthanized; the military worried about placing animals trained to attack in people's homes. But in 2000, after an eight-year-old Belgian Malinois suffering hip dysplasia was put to sleep despite the desperate efforts of his handler to save him, Congress overwhelmingly passed the Robby Law. Named after the dog, it permits the Department of Defense to retire its canine soldiers. Today, most military working dogs are adopted by their handlers, though the process isn't quick. Null himself had to wait ten months to adopt a German shepherd named Luca that he served with in Iraq and on two Secret Service missions. "She wanted to keep working," he laughs. Luca died in 2011, but Null says he's thankful she got to spend her retirement days with him. "She was my couch potato for a year."

Meanwhile, Lisa Phillips has been pushing for a much more profound legal change. I spoke to her on the phone a couple of weeks after we met at the airport. A few months after she adopted Rambo, she contacted North Carolina representative Walter Jones. She wanted to know if he would sponsor a bill that would provide medical care for retired military working dogs, create a way to honor their service, and—most importantly—reclassify them as "canine members of the armed forces." It would be the ultimate promotion. Jones agreed. He was soon joined by Connecticut senator Richard Blumenthal, who called the dogs "comrades in arms." The bill passed Congress with wide bipartisan support. At the last minute, however, someone stripped out the reclassification clause. President Barack Obama signed the legislation in 2013.

Phillips hasn't given up on the "equipment" classification issue. In 2011, she founded the Retired Military Working Dog Assistance Organization in Universal City, Texas, about twenty miles northeast of Lackland. The group hopes to help handlers transport their adopted dogs back from overseas (an expense the military doesn't cover), create a special cemetery just for military working dogs, and continue to push for legislation to have canine soldiers recognized as fellow troops. Rambo is the organization's mascot. "He's a great conversation starter for our mission," Phillips said.

Thanks to the 2013 bill, all retired military working dogs receive a certificate stating that they served their country honorably. But actual medals may be in the works. In 2012, a two-year-old Belgian Malinois named Layka was shot several times in an ambush in Afghanistan. Despite her injuries, she subdued the assailant, saving the lives of several members of her unit. She lost a leg and was later flown to the Holland Military Working Dog Hospital for rehab. "Once we got wind of it, we set up a military working dog medal of heroism medallion," says Null, "which is comparable to the medal of honor for humans." Though the medal was not official, word came down from the Department of Defense that Lackland should look into creating real medals for its canine heroes. "It was probably one of the best moments of my military career to be involved with that," Null says.

A few months after I visited Lackland, the base unveiled the US Military Working Dog Teams National Monument. Cast in bronze, it depicts a serviceman on patrol with the canine heroes of every major conflict since World War II. A Doberman, German shepherd, Labrador retriever, and Belgian Malinois stand at attention, each about five feet tall. The statue sits in a grassy area of the base, not far from a black B-26 bomber. It's the first of its kind dedicated to military working dogs, and as a designated national monument, it's in rarefied company: others include Fort Sumter, where the Civil War began, and the Statue of Liberty.

The Path to Citizenship

If military working dogs are ever reclassified as canine soldiers, it will be the most dramatic acknowledgment yet that pets truly are becoming people in the eyes of the law. But legal personhood is only the first step. In order for cats and dogs to become genuine members of society, they'll need to be embraced as fellow citizens.

That's a lesson blacks learned when they were still fighting for their own personhood. The infamous 1857 *Dred Scott* Supreme Court decision didn't just deny slaves the right to be seen as people; it denied their membership in society. "The only matter in issue before the court [is whether blacks] are citizens of a State," the justices ruled. "We think they are not, and that they are not included, and were not meant to be included, under the word 'citizens' in the Constitution." Curiously, however, the Constitution never defined citizenship. That's perhaps not a surprise given that the word has had a slippery meaning for millennia. The ancient Greeks, credited with developing the concept, used it to denote a way of belonging to a larger group that included not relatives or tribesman but society as a whole. The Romans extended citizenship to conquered people who paid taxes and fought for the empire. And in early America, white landowners and then most white males could lay claim to the status. But it took *Dred Scott* to force the United States to confront what "citizenship" really meant.

The high court's verdict helped ignite the Civil War. As hostilities commenced, blacks enlisted in droves; 200,000 eventually served. By fighting—and dying—for their country, they began to become a part of it. President Abraham Lincoln, initially skeptical of a fully integrated society, pushed through the Thirteenth Amendment, which outlawed slavery and turned blacks into legal persons, in 1865. But personhood wasn't enough. Blacks wanted citizenship. Just what was a citizen, however? The Fourteenth Amendment, adopted three years later, finally answered that question. A citizen was someone born or naturalized in the United States. A citizen was subject to the country's laws but also defended by them. And, most importantly, a citizen was entitled to the same rights and privileges as any other citizen, thanks to the Equal Protection Clause, which finally struck down *Dred Scott*. The Fifteenth Amendment, ratified in 1870, added the right to vote, regardless of race or color. Blacks had earned their citizenship on the battlefield.

But citizenship could be won in another way too, as women showed in the early 1900s. Women had long been excluded from true citizenship, even in America, which denied them the right to vote and, well into the nineteenth century, prohibited wives from owning property and earning salaries. War proved the solution this time too, but women didn't become citizens in combat—they became citizens by joining the workforce. World War I sucked so many men into the military that desperate employers began hiring women for a variety of jobs once reserved for their male counterparts. They became mechanics, bank clerks, and streetcar conductors. In World War II, "Rosie the Riveters" unloaded freight and built ships, packed artillery shells and flew cargo planes, and gathered intelligence and broke codes. They earned their right to vote, and they earned their citizenship. Like blacks, they became true members of society by performing jobs critical to its survival.

The concept of citizenship continues to evolve. As does the variety of people it includes. But one thing has remained constant for the last century and a half: the best way for a marginalized group to attain the status is to fight for it or to work for it. The same may hold true for dogs and cats. By showing their valor on the battlefield, military working dogs have come closer than any other animal to being legally recognized as members of society. Their fellow companion animals may achieve the same by entering the workforce.

With her eyes sewn shut, her white muzzle, and her short, gray fur beginning to thin after fourteen years, Angelina hardly seems like she can take care of herself, much less someone else. But when the cat enters a room full of Alzheimer's patients, something magical happens. Fourteen women and one man, ranging from about seventy to ninety, sit on floral-patterned chairs and couches around a TV blaring *I Love Lucy*. Some are slumped over, their mouths agape. Others stare off silently into space. Almost no one is watching the program. By the time

Angelina leaves, people are smiling, talking, even laughing. The room has come alive.

I'm in "the Gathering Place," a ward of lost souls at the Genesis Eldercare nursing home in Westfield, New Jersey. Most of the patients here are essentially waiting to die. Their bodies are failing them. Relatives are strangers. Even the television provides no distraction. Into this environment, Bill and Margaret Edwards bring their cats for weekly visits. The diminutive couple—Bill, soft-spoken and nearly bald, and Margaret, slightly more animated with a bell of graying brown hair—are in their early seventies. They've been coming to the nursing home for more than a decade, ever since they certified their first cat to do therapy work. That feline, a full-bodied orange tabby named Madison, had been abandoned by his owners when Margaret spotted him at a local shelter. He put his arms around her. She took him home. "One day, he was standing at the door to my apartment," she says. "I opened the door, and he walked to the elevator and turned around to face me. It was like he knew he had work to do."

Bill and Margaret drove Madison and another cat named Mitzie to the American Society for the Prevention of Cruelty to Animals headquarters in New York City. Joining with an organization called the Delta Society (now Pet Partners), the ASPCA was hosting a class on how to turn your pet into a therapy animal. "It was *all* dog people," Bill says. "They had had a couple of cats in the past, but they had flunked the evaluations." Bill and Margaret persisted. The instructors put the felines through a gauntlet of stressors: large crowds, dogs barking, actors banging walkers and shouting, "You took my mashed potatoes!" Madison and Mitzie remained calm. "We got our certificates and were encouraged to find a facility," says Bill. The two started with Genesis Eldercare but soon branched out to other nursing homes, hospice centers, psych wards, and eventually the local veteran's hospital, making up to three visits per week. Today, they own twelve cats, half certified as therapy animals, the other half in training.

When we enter the TV room at the Gathering Place, it takes a couple of minutes for the residents to notice we're there. Bill walks toward a woman in her mid-eighties sitting near the television. She looks up from the floor and seems wary as he approaches. "Would you like a visit?" he says. "I'm scared of cats," she replies faintly. "Now just try," Bill says. He picks Angelina up out of a black fabric carrier and whispers in her ear, "It's time to go to work." He holds the feline, wearing a pink harness and leash, close to the woman's chest. Hesitatingly, she reaches out and touches Angelina on the head. The cat starts to purr. The woman smiles.

On the other side of the room, Margaret has placed another cat—a thirteen-year-old British shorthair mix named Gray Bear—in the lap of a woman wearing a knitted blue sweater. She's beaming. "You're a pretty boy," she says to the feline as he purrs. "That's something that cats do that dogs don't," Margaret tells me later. "The purr is instant gratification. It injects itself into people's souls." Cats, she says, are an "abiding presence." "They don't need to be petted; they don't need to be given a treat. They just attend to people. If there's just a pinhole of light left in a person, the cat will find it." Cheryl, the nurse who oversees the enclave, agrees. "We have a dog that comes in, but he's so clumsy," she laughs. "The residents can't put their arms around him. They can't embrace him." The cats bring out something in the patients that no one else can. "People that don't respond to TV or games suddenly engage," Cheryl says. "I see a recognition, an emotion come to their face. Residents who haven't spoken for days will begin to talk about the pets they used to have. The cats really awaken something in them. I've been here for seventeen years, and this is the most beneficial thing I've seen."

Bill has moved on to a woman in her late eighties sporting shaggy red hair and a lavender tracksuit. She sits on a couch between two other residents. He places a mat over her knees and sets Angelina on top. Guiding herself by smell and touch, the cat gingerly settles in. She lost her eyes to infection as a kitten, and she needs all four paws on someone in order to feel comfortable. That makes her an excellent lap cat. "What's the dog's name?" the woman asks. "Well," Bill says patiently, "this is a cat." "Yes, right, cat," the woman says, embarrassed. Bill cheers her up, telling stories about Angelina climbing ladders and jumping onto counters. "She still gets in trouble," he says. "You'd never know she was blind!" The woman smiles. The feline's disability seems to strike a chord. For the elderly resident, it's the first time in a long time someone is dependent on her. "Oh, you poor thing," she says, stroking the cat.

"You poor baby." It's a moving scene that almost turns devastating when Bill picks up Angelina to leave. "Do you have to take her home?" the woman says, as the feline nuzzles into Bill's neck. Then, turning to the elderly man on her left, she says, "How did I just get attached to a cat? How can I miss her already?"

After a half hour, Bill and Margaret have hit almost every lap, and the room is buzzing. "Did you get a visit?" "Did you hear him purr?" Bill turns to me and says the visits help him as much as the residents. A few years ago, he was diagnosed with PTSD. He served in Vietnam as a night duty officer in the air force. He'd drive around in the pitch black and stop at all the bunkers and security posts. "Every night, they were unloading body bags off C-130s," he says. "Hundreds of them." His outpost came under twenty-nine rocket attacks in six months. He began sleeping under his bunk. "You realize how vulnerable you are in a war zone," he says. "We were sitting ducks." When Bill returned to the United States, he'd dive to the ground when a car backfired and hurl objects across the room for no reason. "The cats help me forget my troubles," he says. "They get me out of myself and into others. They're better than any medication." Doctors seem to agree. Some have begun to "prescribe" cats to veterans with PTSD.

Angelina gets something out of the visits too. In 2012, both she and Madison (who passed away at age seventeen) were inducted into the New Jersey Veterinary Medical Association's Hall of Fame for their therapy work. Though the felines could care less about the award, Bill says it acknowledges the important role they play in society. "These cats seem to know why they're here," he says. "They know they have a purpose. And that purpose is to be more than a companion animal."

We leave the TV room and walk into an adjoining kitchen where a few elderly women sit alone at small tables draped in pink cloth. As we prepare to go, a gaunt resident in her mid-nineties lifts herself up and taps Bill on the shoulder. "Can I see a cat?" she says sheepishly. Bill sits her down and tells her to put her knees together. Then he places a mat across her lap and sets Gray Bear down on it. "Any way you want to pet him is fine," Margaret says. The woman clasps her hands around the cat's arms, taps his head, strokes his fur against the grain—all things that would make Jasper and Jezebel give me a dirty look before they hightailed it out of the room. Gray Bear just sits there, staring into her eyes. "Can you hear him purring?" asks Margaret. The woman nods: "I wish people would act this way," she says, her eyes moistening. "This is God's work."

Angelina and Gray Bear are part of a new generation of assistance animals. More than 100,000 dogs and cats (dogs are the vast majority) in the United States work for people, doing everything from guiding the blind to treating autism. They're performing important jobs in society— jobs that, in some cases, human beings used to do. They've been training for these roles since domestication.

The very first cats and dogs were assistance animals. Dogs dragged firewood and guarded campsites. Cats killed rodents and protected crops. Though they've largely given up lives of hard labor today, they still retain the skill set. Dogs in particular, having coevolved with humans for perhaps tens of thousands of years, can follow a pointed finger, intuit what we're thinking, and produce a variety of barks that signal everything from danger to joy. That's probably why, when the disabled first looked to animals for help, they turned to canines. Paintings and frescoes suggest that the earliest so-called service animals were guide dogs, leading the blind through crowded Roman cities and medieval European villages. The job wasn't officially documented until after World War I, when Dorothy Harrison Eustis, an American breeder living in Europe, described a school in Germany that was training German shepherds to lead war veterans who had been blinded by mustard gas. "It is a little short of marvelous how a raw dog can be taken into the school and in four months be turned out a blind leader," she wrote in the *Saturday Evening Post* in 1927. "From the very small beginnings of becoming absolutely house-broken, he is taken step by step upward to his life work of leading a blind man, of being that man's eyes and his sword and his buckler." When Eustis returned to America, she founded The Seeing Eye, the country's first guide dog school.

Guide dogs were just the beginning. In 1974, hearing dogs joined the ranks of service animals, listening for doorbells and honking cars. Soon, canines were pulling wheelchairs, picking up dropped canes and glasses, and providing physical support to owners who otherwise couldn't get around their homes. Today, in the United States, 35,000 service dogs

assist people with a wide variety of physical and mental disabilities. Seizure and hypoglycemia alert dogs detect unusual body odors and behavior changes, nuzzling their owners or staring at them intently until they
take their medication or contact help; some even fetch pills or injec-
tions. Psychiatric service dogs interrupt compulsive behaviors, like excessive washing or hair pulling; they can also anticipate manic episodes
and combat hallucinations (for example, by failing to detect "intruders"
in the room). Other service dogs treat depression and predict asthma
attacks. "We don't just study dogs to figure out how smart they are,"
biological anthropologist Brian Hare told me when I visited the Canine
Cognition Center at Duke University. "We also want to know how far
we can push them. Because dogs do a lot of important jobs in our econ-
omy. And they're getting more."

As they get more jobs, they also get more rights. At first, service
animals had few legal protections. Many public places banned them,
as they did all cats and dogs. But in 1931, airlines and trains began allowing them onboard. A decade later, post offices granted them entry.
Today, they are allowed pretty much anywhere a cane is—and in most
places that otherwise prohibit pets. The Americans with Disabilities Act
(ADA) of 1990 requires hotels, restaurants, and other businesses to admit service animals, even if customers have allergies or a fear of dogs.
An amendment to the Civil Rights Act of 1968, also known as the Fair
Housing Act, mandates that landlords must allow tenants to keep service
animals, regardless of whether the building has a no-pets policy. And the
Department of Education dictates that service animals must be allowed
to accompany their owners to school. "Service animals are working animals, not pets," according to the ADA, meaning they are not subject to
the same laws that cover normal cats and dogs. They live on a higher legal plane. They are more integrated into society. They are, for all intents
and purposes, closer to citizenship. But additional animals may soon be
joining their ranks.

The gunman had been hiding out for hours in an abandoned bar in
Upstate New York. He was suspected of killing four people. Officers
tried to send a robot in, but debris blocked its path. So in went Ape,
a two-year-old Czech German shepherd and FBI tactical dog, wearing

a camera and bulletproof vest. State police and federal agents followed close behind. When the gunman saw the shepherd appear in the doorway, he opened fire. Officers shot back and killed the man. But it was too late for Ape. The team performed CPR and rushed him to a nearby veterinary hospital; however, the dog—only two weeks on the job—died shortly after arrival. A few days later, the FBI held a memorial service for the canine at its academy in Quantico, Virginia. Bagpipers played as a small white coffin draped in an American flag was carried past a line of police officers and federal agents, their hands over their hearts, their dogs at their sides. Ape's name was inscribed on an FBI memorial wall and added to the Officer Down Memorial Page, a website that compiles law enforcement fatalities dating back to 1790. He was listed along with four other animals that had died in the line of duty by mid-March 2013—including a Homeland Security dog, a California Department of Corrections dog, and two police dogs—and thirty-one human officers.

Dogs first joined law enforcement in the early 1900s. South Orange, New Jersey, added the animals to its police force in 1907, and New York City followed a few months later. Training was minimal, as was the role the canines performed. They tripped subjects, searched homes for burglars, and guarded prisoners. That's not to say the animals weren't effective. A 1911 newspaper article reported that after the introduction of canines to the New York police force, "crime was reduced more than fifty percent, and . . . burglaries are now of such rare occurrence that it may almost be said they never occur." By the 1960s and 1970s, dogs—typically German shepherds—had become auxiliary policemen in forces around the country. They also joined new government agencies like the National Park Service and the Secret Service, as their training became more rigorous and specialized. They learned to sniff out bombs, comb building wreckage for survivors, and control crowds. (In this latter role, police dogs became infamous for a time when officers in the South used them to attack civil rights demonstrators.) Today, due in part to the Oklahoma City bombing, the Columbine massacre, and the 9/11 terrorist attacks, more than 15,000 canines walk the beat of American cities, patrolling airports and subways and leading FBI agents into dangerous hideouts. In New York City alone, the canine police force nearly doubled between 2001 and 2012, while the number of human officers dropped by 17 percent.

Police dogs have become such an important part of society that in 2012 the US Supreme Court heard not one but two cases involving the animals. In the first, the court assessed the veracity of a drug-sniffing dog's nose. Aldo, a German shepherd, alerted his handler to the presence of methamphetamines during a routine traffic stop, but the defendant argued that dogs make mistakes just like humans do. The judges ruled that, as long as a dog has been well trained, its nose should be trusted, but defendants have the right to challenge the canine's qualifications in court, just as they can with a human officer. The second case, decided a month later, concerned whether a police dog sniffing for drugs outside a house violated the homeowner's right to privacy. If a human officer can't detect the scent of marijuana but his dog can, is the canine's alert sufficient for a warrant? That is, should the dog be treated like high-tech equipment or just another officer? The majority of justices ruled that a police dog is essentially no different from "super-high-powered binoculars"; thus the dog in this particular case had violated the homeowner's rights. The dissenting justices, however, argued that "a dog . . . is not a new form of 'technology' or a 'device'" but rather an integral part of the human police force. A dog's nose, they said, is no different from the refined nose of a wine taster.

Like service dogs, law enforcement dogs have gained rights not afforded to pets. In 1978, Massachusetts became the first of several states to impose higher fines and prison terms for hurting police dogs as opposed to companion animals. Congress followed suit in 2000 with the Federal Law Enforcement Animal Protection Act, which imposes up to ten-year prison sentences for anyone who harms or kills an animal working for the government. "Animals that serve in law enforcement shouldn't be treated as mere property," proclaimed one senator who supported the bill. And in the aftermath of the FBI bar shootout, New York passed Ape's Law, which increases the penalty for killing a police dog from a misdemeanor to a felony. Just as injuring a member of law enforcement is a more serious offense than injuring a civilian, the same holds for canine cops. An officer is an officer.

Angelina and Gray Bear don't dodge bullets. And legally, they're not service animals. The Department of Justice limits that designation to dogs, and only those specially trained to assist a single individual with a physical or mental disability. But other cats and dogs are taking health-related jobs that are just as important, and they've been doing so for decades.

In 1961, a New York psychologist named Boris Levinson noticed something unusual about his dog Jingles. Levinson had been having little success treating a severely disturbed and uncommunicative child at his home. One day, he left the room, and Jingles wandered in. When Levinson returned, the child was talking to the animal. The doctor soon observed similar effects with other psychologically impaired children. He published his findings and coined the term "pet therapy." In the ensuing decades, researchers would show that cats and dogs with no special training could relieve anxiety, lower blood pressure, reduce the incidence of cardiovascular disease, and curb the symptoms of autism and a variety of other disorders. Meanwhile, Pet Partners and similar organizations began certifying people like Bill and Margaret Edwards to bring these "therapy animals" into nursing homes, hospitals, and other settings. Today, the animal-assisted therapy movement is booming.

There are currently about 50,000 therapy animals in the United States. Chances are you've seen dogs in red vests visiting people in hospitals, comforting cancer patients, or motivating stroke or accident victims to get out of bed. Or perhaps you noticed gaggles of Golden retrievers on the news, dispatched to the children who survived the mass elementary school shooting in Newtown, Connecticut, or to the victims of the Boston Marathon bombings. And maybe you've even met a therapy dog, as I met Ruby, the Baltimore pit bull who visits inner-city schools, helping children with learning disabilities read in front of their classmates.

In the coming years, therapy animals won't just treat our various maladies; they may help prevent them. Recent studies have shown that dogs can detect incipient tumors and distinguish the types and grades of numerous cancers, sometimes simply by smelling their owner's breath. Dogs can also sniff out dangerous bacteria like E. coli in public water supplies and "superbugs" in hospital wards. And anecdotal evidence suggests that cat purring may boost bone density and prevent muscle wasting—a serious problem for astronauts, though as yet no one has advocated for cats in space. The alternative medicine of the future won't just be about herbs and acupuncture; it will be about furry bodies and wet noses.

Despite this caseload, therapy animals don't have the same legal rights as service or law enforcement animals. They're excluded from most places that ban pets, and they don't enjoy more protections than normal cats and dogs. But that may be changing. States like Kansas have begun permitting therapy dogs on public transportation, as well as in hotels and restaurants. The Air Carrier Access Act allows animals that provide emotional support into airplane cabins. And the Pet Ownership in Public Housing rule, enacted by the Housing and Urban Development Department in 1999, states that residents in federally assisted public housing, regardless of whether they're disabled, can have pets, subject to some restrictions. Among the rationales for these changes is lawmakers' increasing recognition that cats and dogs play an important role in human health and well-being.

Today, a therapy animal is one that helps comfort and heal us. Tomorrow, it may simply be an animal we keep for companionship. That is, therapy animals could soon be indistinguishable from any other pet. If that happens, and if therapy animals continue to earn advanced rights, *all* pets could inch closer to citizenship. The role they play as family members could be enough to make them bona fide members of society. Yet their most important role may still lie ahead: saving society itself.

Pete, forty-six, is trapped in an unhappy marriage. He doesn't communicate with his spouse. He feels disconnected from his children. As he pushes one on a swing in a park outside Boston, he types on his iPhone, talking to his "virtual wife," Jade. The two married a year earlier in the online simulation Second Life, surrounded by virtual friends. Pete has never met Jade in person, but the two chat every day about their loves and anxieties. They even have virtual sex. "Second Life gives me a better relationship than I have in real life," he says. "This is where I feel most myself." All around him, other parents are similarly engaged in their mobile devices. Are they living second lives as well?

Pete's story is recounted in Sherry Turkle's 2011 book *Alone Together*, an exploration of how technology is eroding our social fabric. His experiences may be an extreme example of how we have begun to disconnect from the real world, but there's a bit of Pete in all of us. Every year we separate further from our friends and family. We talk less and text more.

We like people on Facebook instead of in person. We gather in homes and cafes but spend more time staring at our phones than engaging with each other. "We live in a culture of simulation," writes Turkle. "Tethered to technology, we are shaken when that world 'unplugged' does not signify, does not satisfy."

Our disconnection from reality didn't start with the Internet. We've been ceding our social interactions to technology for more than a century. The telephone allowed us to talk to friends and family without being in the same room. The radio and television gave us something to gather around instead of gathering together. But the reach and scope of the Internet and the devices it has spawned are unprecedented in human history. More than 80 percent of US adults over eighteen are at least occasional users of the Internet, up from 53 percent in 2000. Two-thirds of American adults are on Facebook. We spend more than four hours a day online, and for those under thirty it's even more. We say goodnight to our laptops and good morning to our smartphones. Like Pete, we have begun to exchange real life for a virtual one.

This is all pretty striking, especially in view of the fact that technology isn't making us happier. Absent human contact, we feel more isolated than ever before. Scholars call this the "Internet paradox": we're more connected than we've ever been, yet also more alone. Between 2000 and 2010, the percentage of US adults over forty-five identified as chronically lonely rose from 20 to 35 percent. Those numbers have been bad for our health. Socially isolated individuals are at higher risk of cardiovascular disease, high blood pressure, and mental deterioration. Obesity is on the rise, as is depression. Loneliness is killing us.

We can't blame everything on our iPhones. Our families have shrunk, we've cut ourselves off from the natural world, and if we do make it to old age, we're more likely to live alone than at any point in modern civilization. In 1950, a mere 1 percent of Americans aged eighteen to twenty-nine lived by themselves; today it's 7 percent. During the same period, the number of Americans over sixty living alone rose from one in ten to one in three. Less than 10 percent of homes contained only one person in 1950; now more than a quarter do. Half as many women are having children. Divorce rates are through the roof. And the number of people we consider close personal confidants has plummeted. We are entering an age of isolation like never before. Loneliness has become an epidemic. The bonds that unite us are breaking. And it's only getting worse. As society fractures, can anything hold us together?

Cats and dogs just might. Companion animals keep us anchored to the real world. You can't play with your dog on Facebook. You can't cuddle your cat with a Tweet. Their love and warmth are the antidote to an increasingly cold and indifferent society. Their presence in our lives fills a void left by disappearing friends and family. The cat is the child who doesn't move away. The dog is the buddy who doesn't tune us out for a glowing screen. Nearly a third of all Americans and half of all singles say they rely more on their pets than on other people for companionship. Cats and dogs also stave off the ill effects of loneliness: a 2011 study found that pet owners weren't just healthier than nonowners; they also had higher self-esteem and felt less alone and depressed. Perhaps that's why more homes have dogs and cats than have children. Or why pet ownership has ballooned as our social networks have shriveled.

Critics have argued that pets can never fully cure our loneliness because they aren't the real thing. A cat is not a child. A dog is not a human friend. Perhaps that's why we've tried so hard to turn them into people. We need human contact more than ever before, and when humans don't satisfy—or technology and modern living robs us of their presence—we humanize our pets. We call them our kids; we spend thousands on vet care; we take them to doggy day care. When we turn to companion animals in today's world, we are trying to reestablish our connection to humanity. As pets become people, they become the saviors of society. And they truly earn their citizenship.

ELEVEN

The Meowist Revolution

Marc Bluestone upended his life for his dog Shane. A former All City high school athlete then in his early fifties, he had adopted the sandy-brown Labrador mix as a puppy in 1996. By the time the dog was three, she was suffering from regular seizures. Bluestone built an office in his Los Angeles home so he could care for her during the day, and he refused to travel anywhere he couldn't take Shane with him. Eventually, his veterinarian recommended the dog see a neurologist. So Bluestone drove an hour and a half to a specialty vet hospital renowned for its cutting-edge procedures. What he thought would be a single day of treatment dragged on for months—and resulted in the largest veterinary malpractice award in US history.

Shane was seen by a vet whom Bluestone later alleged represented himself as a neurologist, despite the fact that he was not board certified as such. From January through March 1999, the dog received radiation, blood transfusions, and, according to Bluestone, thirty different drugs. Bluestone drove to see Shane every day, sometimes curling up with her in her cage. In all, he spent $24,000 on her care. By the time the clinic released her, Shane had suffered liver disease, internal bleeding, and a failed immune system. She died a few days later.

Bluestone sued for $500,000, quitting his job running a textile company to pursue the case full-time. He alleged that the veterinary hospital had misdiagnosed Shane, lied about her condition, failed to disclose the risks of treatment, and given unnecessary and improper medical care. He also consulted an outside expert who concluded that malpractice had taken place. The case made its way to a California superior court, where Bluestone was represented by a lawyer who served on the board of In

Defense of Animals, the animal rights group whose Guardian Campaign had convinced a number of cities to use the word "guardian" in addition to or instead of "owner" in their pet-related ordinances. The trial lasted seven weeks. In February 2004, after a day and a half of deliberations, the jury found the vet liable for Shane's death and awarded Bluestone $9,000 for medical bills and an additional $30,000 for the "special and unique" value of Shane. Bluestone had paid $100 for the dog. "I can't get my baby back," he said at the time, "but I did get justice."

He also gave the veterinary community an ulcer. A few months after the verdict was handed down, the American Veterinary Medical Association created a task force to explore the impact of the changing status of dogs and cats on the profession. The AVMA's annual meeting, held that same month, featured three panels on veterinary malpractice in a single day. The following year, the organization took a hard line on any attempts to treat pets as more than property in the courts, arguing that damages awarded beyond an animal's market value would drive vets out of business, flood the legal system with litigation, and ultimately harm pets by making veterinary services prohibitively expensive. Gerald Eichinger, a veterinarian with a law degree, summed up the prevailing anxiety in a law review article he penned in 2006. "Veterinary medicine does not realize the danger that the animal law movement poses to the profession," he wrote. "Unless veterinarians are so myopic that they choose to ignore the effect that 'jackpot' noneconomic damage awards have brought to the human medical field, they would be wise to call their members to battle stations instead of assuming the role of passive bystander."

Veterinarians aren't the only ones who have heeded the call to arms. As pets have inched toward legal personhood, a wide range of industries—from agriculture to biomedical research—have ramped up their attacks, fighting everything from "guardian" language to animal welfare laws. Meanwhile, one psychologist's studies have questioned the notion that dogs and cats deserve citizenship, finding that, far from helping society, they may actually be destroying it. And a former animal lawyer has turned against the animal law movement, blasting its mission and advocating for the elimination of all pets, full stop.

The next step in the evolution of cats and dogs won't be a peaceful one.

Breaking the Bond

No other field has a more intimate relationship with dogs and cats than veterinary medicine. And no other profession is being as dramatically impacted by the changing status of pets. In the war over the future of our companion animals, vets are on the front lines. They're not just fighting the animal law movement; they're fighting owners, society, and even themselves. To get a sense of how things are shaping up on the ground, I paid a visit to the man in charge of these forces: the president of the American Veterinary Medical Association.

I had expected the meeting to take place in a tall office building in Washington, DC. Instead, I find myself standing in front of a two-story house about a mile outside the center of White Plains, New York. Actually, it isn't really a house—or at least it hasn't been for some time. In the early 1900s a family probably lived here, but today the yellow structure with a gabled roof and aluminum-sided walls is one of a number of former homes converted to businesses on what was once a tree-lined residential avenue, now taken over by car dealerships and convenience stores. A sign on the front lawn reads "Bond Animal Hospital." The name is both appropriate and ironic: veterinarians owe their livelihood to the human-animal bond; yet critics charge that vets have exploited this relationship for their own financial gain.

Inside, Bond is one of the smaller vet clinics I've been in. The owners have tried to cram as much as they can into the confines of the structure; that means low ceilings, a narrow waiting area, and three cramped exam rooms. Dog treats sit in glass jars on the front desk. Posters of cats, dogs, ferrets, and hamsters line the walls. Business cards read, "We treat every patient like a member of the family."

It's a chilly gray morning in late March, and the clinic has just opened. A man sits in the waiting room with a cat in a carrier as a few flakes of snow fall outside. A couple of minutes later, a woman is dragged in by a border collie. As the clinic begins to bustle, a door opens behind the reception desk, and out walks Douglas Aspros, the head of the AVMA. Unlike the other vets I'd see that day, dressed in white coats with stethoscopes dangling from their necks, Aspros is wearing khakis and a tie. He's sixty years old, sporting straight salt-and-pepper hair parted down the middle, and he reaches out his hand, greeting me with a warm smile. Then he leads me to the interior of the clinic, into an office the size of a walk-in closet he shares with another vet, Geoffrey McKenzie. There's barely enough room for the three of us to sit down. Veterinary technicians in dark blue scrubs hustle by outside, cradling cats or walking dogs on leashes. Occasionally, one pops in to hand McKenzie a chart.

Aspros and I chat for three hours. He's a soft and precise speaker who never rushes his words. Each sentence comes out carefully constructed, and he rarely backtracks or corrects himself. He tells me he didn't become a vet for the typical reasons. Growing up in a small apartment in Queens, he didn't have a pet until he was in fifth grade. He had no contact with cats and dogs, much less a desire to heal them. Instead, his only relationship with animals was with dead ones. He spent Saturdays at his father and grandfather's fur shop, hanging out in a back room where they kept pelts of minks, foxes, and other creatures. "I loved the softness of the fur," he says. He found himself comparing their eyes and faces to his own. "For a kid who grew up with very little exposure to animals," he says, "the experience left a mark."

By the time Aspros was in high school, he knew he wanted to be a vet. But he still wasn't drawn to cats and dogs, and his interests were mainly scientific. After graduating, he interned at a dairy farm, where he milked cows and baled hay. In college he worked part-time at the US Department of Agriculture, studying the effects of malnutrition on cow reproduction. "I had never even been in an animal hospital until I started looking for jobs in my final year of vet school," he says. In 1975, he joined his first practice, a cozy small-animal clinic (also in a former house) in Westchester County, about thirty miles north of New York City. One vet lived across the street, the other two upstairs. "We spent a lot of time together, drinking beer and discussing cases," Aspros says. "It was a bit like *All Creatures Great and Small*."

Even in his early days as a veterinarian, Aspros was thinking beyond the clinic. He wanted to improve vet education and work with legislatures on animal health issues. "When you're in the office, you have a hermetically sealed view of the profession," he says. "I wanted to get out into the world." When the senior vet at the clinic, who was active in a regional veterinary society, asked Aspros if he was interested in writing the group's newsletter, he jumped at the chance. Aspros became the society's president a few years later. Then president of the Westchester County Board of Health. Then president of the New York State Veterinary Medical Society. By early 2000, he had begun to move up the ranks of the AVMA itself, serving on the association's political action committee and its council on education. He still devoted time to his clinical duties—until one day he found he could no longer perform them.

"It was April of 2004, and I had been down in Philadelphia working on the national veterinary licensing exam," he tells me. "When I came home, I had a pain in my jaw. The next day, I was on the treadmill, and suddenly it was like someone just shot me through the brain. It was the most intense little pain." Aspros took a shower and started reading the newspaper, but the words didn't make any sense. His wife took him to the hospital, where he underwent four brain scans. "The next morning I woke up with no speech and no movement on the right side of my body. They told me I had a stroke." What I initially thought was a careful speaking style is actually Aspros concentrating to form words. Even today he struggles with tough ones. "I still have no feeling in the fingers of my right hand," he says. "I just taught myself how to use chopsticks again."

The stroke took Aspros out of the exam room, but it allowed him to turn his full attention to policy work. He began consulting on veterinary education across the globe, served on bioterrorism advisory committees, and in 2012 became president of the AVMA. He's younger than typical presidents, who tend to be past retirement and who have already sold their practices. That explains why he's still at Bond Animal Hospital, which he joined in 1981 and now manages. Despite its size, Bond (named after the founding vet, who used to live upstairs) is typical of modern veterinary practices. It sees thousands of clients, has a staff of fifteen, and offers cutting-edge services, from chemotherapy to digital radiology.

As president of the AVMA, Aspros has to manage more than just this small clinic. He has to oversee the entire future of veterinary medicine. That means figuring out how to deal with a world where pets are moving closer to legally being seen as people. So far, the AVMA has chosen to fight this movement, using every tool at its disposal to quash rulings and legislation that would give dogs and cats more rights. The association fears that pet personhood could destroy the profession. Ironically, the current situation is one vets helped create.

The veterinarian of 150 years ago would have been flabbergasted by Bond Animal Hospital. Dogs and cats hadn't moved indoors. They didn't even warrant the meager legal status of property. Instead, livestock ruled the day. The most important animals were the ones people ate and relied upon for economic survival. Horses pulled streetcars. Cows fed families. When they got sick or injured, it made sense to fix them. Treating a cat or dog would have made about as much sense as bandaging up a pet rock.

That's not to say livestock practitioners were respected for their work. American veterinarians in the mid-nineteenth century didn't need a degree. Most came into the practice via apprenticeships, farm animal breeding, or farriery—that is, shoeing horses. They were viewed as drunks, quacks, and imbeciles. The profession was held in such ill repute that when vet schools began to crop up in the late 1800s, they struggled to attract quality applicants. "Nobody was laughed at more than the horse doctor," wrote a practitioner from the time.

By the turn of the century, livestock had become critical to urban living, and vets found themselves held in higher esteem. You couldn't walk down the streets of most major US cities without taking in the thick smell of manure and the din of clucking chickens. Cows inhabited backyards—one for every forty-three people in New Orleans. Pigs rummaged dusty streets and crammed stockyards at the edge of town; Chicago alone was home to more than 50,000. New York ran on 150,000 horses, and it ran them into the ground. Meanwhile, one in eleven US factory workers and tradespeople worked in an animal-related business, from wool milling to meatpacking. Entire neighborhoods were nicknamed after local industries: "Pigtown" in Baltimore, "Butchertown" in San Francisco. Society lived on livestock. And veterinarians were needed to keep that livestock healthy.

Vet schools began filling their classes. Now, only licensed practitioners could enter the profession; the era of the ignorant horse doctor was over. And yet, the veterinarians of the early twentieth century were still vastly different from the vets of today. Though they had earned respect, they were still seen as little more than mechanics, fixing a malfunctioning machine so that it could continue to produce milk or pull freight. Common veterinary procedures included administering strong laxatives, cauterizing open wounds with a red-hot iron, and roping bulls

down for castration without anesthesia. There was little time for sentimentality. Indeed, there was hostility to it. Though women had begun to
make gains in the workforce, their "delicacy of feeling" had no place in
veterinary medicine, stated an 1897 editorial in *American Veterinary Review*. "If the practice of veterinary surgery consisted in making a round
of visits among lap-dogs," it continued mockingly, "then and only then,
the profession might be a suitable one for women." Veterinary medicine,
however, was about to confront a crisis that threatened to destroy it.
And those lapdogs would save the day.

A couple of decades into the twentieth century, livestock had begun
to disappear from cities. Concerns about sanitation and public health,
not to mention the expansion of railroads and the advent of refrigeration,
pushed farm animals farther and farther out of sight, until urban residents
had little connection to—or conception of—the industries that put meat
on their plates. The advent of the automobile, meanwhile, nearly drove
the urban horse to extinction. City vets were rapidly running out of clients. Even those in rural areas found themselves out of work, as farmers
and giant livestock operations began administering their own antibiotics and vaccines. Applications to vet schools plummeted. From 1914 to
1924, enrollment dropped 75 percent. In 1926, only 130 new veterinarians entered the field, roughly the number graduated by a single school
three decades earlier. Vets began to panic. "I do not know," fretted one
practitioner in 1925, "whether [the profession] will live or die."

On the brink of obsolescence, veterinarians found salvation in cats
and dogs. Urban dwellers, living far from livestock for the first time, were
embracing pets like never before. Dogs and cats—our last connection to
nature in a society increasingly dominated by machines—filled a void.
They became more than just animal companions, however. Flea products and litter boxes were bringing them indoors, and the ideals of the
Victorian era had made it socially acceptable to love them like members
of the family. Pets needed their own food, their own toys, and, yes, their
own doctors. Vets were quick on the uptake. Schools began teaching
companion animal medicine, and practitioners transformed their clinics
into small-animal hospitals. Dank horse stables became comfy waiting
rooms and bright surgical suites. Grungy aprons were shed for white coats
and stethoscopes. And red-hot irons gave way to cutting-edge therapies.

"If you were an ailing dog," stated a 1951 article in *Science News Letter*, "you'd probably be treated with essentially the same techniques that medical doctors use on human patients." By mid-century, the number of vets in the United States had quintupled, and pets had become their most reliable source of income. The profession had literally gone to the dogs.

A more fundamental change had taken place, however. Veterinary medicine was no longer focused on the economic value of animals; instead, it relied on the sentimental bond between owner and pet. For the first time, writes Susan Jones in *Valuing Animals*, her engaging history of veterinary medicine, clients were spending more than their animal was worth, sometimes in a single visit. Far more than toys or specialty food, the vet clinic provided an outlet for owners to express their true devotion to their pets; they were no longer just spoiling them—they could now save their lives. Meanwhile, by providing humanlike medicine, vets signaled to society that pets were worthy of such care, elevating their status above that of any other animal. The behavior of owners, combined with the services offered by veterinarians, helped turn pets into true family members. Owners became parents. And vets, far from their days as the mechanics of livestock, became the pediatricians of fur babies.

By 2000, veterinary medicine had become one of the most respected professions in the country, ranking just behind doctoring and nursing. Spending on veterinary services had tripled from the previous decade, topping $18 billion annually. Yet all of this success came at a price: vets viewed like human doctors soon found themselves sued like them.

Veterinarians make some of the same mistakes physicians do. They leave sponges in bodies during surgery. They operate on the wrong appendage. But with euthanasia on the table, the chance of committing a deadly error is even greater. When I worked at a vet clinic in high school, one of the doctors told me the infamous story of three black cats named Smith: One had come in for grooming, one for boarding, and one to be put down. There was a mix-up, and the outcome wasn't pretty. Despite this sort of negligence, it has traditionally made little sense to sue for malpractice. Bringing such litigation can cost tens of thousands of dollars, and because cats and dogs are property, the award has usually been limited to the market value of the animal (plus, perhaps, a refund of payment for services rendered). Even wealthy individuals had a hard time finding lawyers who would take such cases. But as pets have become more like people in the courts and legislatures, judges have increasingly allowed awards far beyond the market value of the animal—so-called noneconomic damages that include claims like emotional distress and loss of companionship, which are typically limited to suits involving the death of a spouse or child. And with a proliferation of animal lawyers, thanks in part to the efforts of the Animal Legal Defense Fund, owners now have little trouble finding a willing attorney.

Today, veterinary medicine is, in many ways, a victim of its own success. In an age of kidney transplants and stem cell therapy for pets, owners are less likely than ever to euthanize a dog or cat whose health starts failing. Clients will shell out hundreds or even thousands of dollars to extend the lives of their furry children by just a few months. No price is too great to save them—and no amount is too much to sue for when things go wrong. The Bluestone verdict was just the tip of the iceberg. In 1997, a Kentucky jury awarded $15,000 to the owner of a German shepherd that bled to death after surgery. In 2000, a California woman successfully sued her vet for $28,000 for a botched dental procedure on her Rottweiler. And since Bluestone, owners have sued—though not won—for damages in excess of $600,000. From 2000 to 2005, veterinary malpractice claims tripled, with settlements regularly reaching more than $10,000. Such cases, critics say, could put thousands of vets out of business. Cats and dogs may have saved veterinary medicine, but some fear they are now on the brink of destroying it.

Douglas Aspros takes veterinary malpractice seriously—perhaps because he himself has been on the receiving end of a couple of suits. As we chat in his office at Bond Animal Hospital, he tells me about both cases. In one, a client thought Aspros made an improper diagnosis and sued for $600 in small-claims court. The other involved a nearby emergency clinic that Aspros helps manage. A family's dog died at the hospital, and the children saw the body before the staff could make it presentable. The parents claimed their kids suffered emotional distress and sued for $1 million. The clinic's insurance company settled for $15,000.

Aspros worries about the impact such lawsuits could have on the profession as a whole. Human doctors have seen malpractice cases rise precipitously in the last two decades, with a spike in average awards; today, some verdicts are in the millions or tens of millions of dollars. As veterinarians are increasingly seen as human doctors, Aspros worries the same could happen to them. Vets have malpractice insurance, but the rates are low, and they don't make the same salaries physicians do. Any awards, he contends, should be limited to the market value of the animal and the cost of services rendered. Adding noneconomic damages could be disastrous. "From a small-business perspective, it puts us in a lot of jeopardy," he says. "It doesn't take much to ruin a career."

It's not just the financial impact. Aspros says a rise in malpractice suits could irrevocably damage the vet-client relationship. Today's vet is more than a doctor; he's a translator, a counselor, and a priest. He doesn't just deal with the pet; he deals with every member of the family. And he often sees them at some of the most vulnerable, emotional moments of their lives. In an ironic historical twist, the veterinarian has become the holistic practitioner, while the physician has become the mechanic. This special relationship could disappear, says Aspros, if malpractice cases continue to rise. Suddenly, the vet is no longer a healer; he's a mistake waiting to happen. And the owner is no longer a client; she's a potential litigant. "Malpractice changes the entire landscape of healing," says Aspros. Even if the dollar amounts aren't large, "it's a tremendous psychological burden. It casts a pall over your life and practice."

Critics say the AVMA is being hypocritical. Veterinarians, they note, have spent decades treating cats and dogs like people. They send sympathy cards after euthanasia. They refer to pets as patients and members of the family (recall Bond's business cards). And they owe their entire livelihoods to the fact that they're able to bill for amounts far in excess of what companion animals are worth. "You can't charge your client thousands of dollars to fix a cat, and then turn around and say that cat is only worth fifty bucks," Chris Green, director of legislative affairs at the Animal Legal Defense Fund, told me. "You can either have the professional benefits of pediatricians or the legal liability of garage mechanics. You can't have both."

Aspros says it's not that simple. He pulls out his iPhone and shows me pictures of his Norfolk terrier and a "wonderful cat" named Oz. He may have grown up without pets, but he now has two fur babies of his own.

"I know cats and dogs aren't toasters," he says. "But this life is the world we've allowed lawyers to make for us." The law, he says, is black-and-white. If pets aren't property, they're people. And if owners really want their pets treated like people, they better be ready for the consequences.

The headaches begin in the courtroom. If cats and dogs aren't property, they don't have owners. So who gets to sue if something happens to them? "If the dog is owned by the family, do the mother and father and the kids get to sue, requesting different amounts of money based on how much they loved the dog?" says Aspros. "Does the grandmother who used to babysit the dog get to sue? How about the dog walker?" And what's to stop the pet from suing on its own behalf? Kno the pit bull had a lawyer. So did Alex the dog. Neither animal was suing anybody, but now that pets can have attorneys, it may only be a matter of time before a cat drags its owner to court for the emotional distress of being locked up in the house all day. Perhaps pets could sue each other, taking cat-and-dog fights to the next level. And pets that sue can also be sued: think about that next time your dog poops on someone's lawn. "Now that you have real money on the line and plenty of lawyers to take these cases," says Aspros, "it wouldn't be hard to flood the courts."

Outside the courtroom, things get even more complicated. Animals without owners will get to make their own decisions. But since they can't talk, who will make choices for them? "If you have a seventeen-year-old cat peeing on the floor, who's to decide whether he gets euthanized or gets $5,000 worth of chemotherapy?" says Aspros. "What if you decide to let the cat die at home? Is that criminal negligence?" Could your neighbor or your local humane society petition for guardianship, forcing you to go through with the chemo even if you can't afford it? As an owner, you control what you do with your property. As a parent, society also has a say. And it's not just in life-and-death decisions. Children need exercise. They need to go to school. Should you be fined for not playing with your cat? Should you go to jail for not taking your dog to obedience classes? "Do you want pet social services coming by to see if Fluffy is housebroken?" says Aspros.

Such scenarios are not outside the realm of possibility. In 2012, New Jersey considered a law that would have mandated that pets wear seat belts in cars. And just a couple of weeks after the Bluestone verdict was handed down, the American Society for the Prevention of Cruelty to Animals participated in the prosecution of a man for failing to treat his dog's tumor. The ASPCA argued that the definition of cruelty has evolved since Henry Bergh's time and now includes an obligation to provide a basic level of veterinary care. Several states, including Michigan and Oregon, already mandate such care in their anticruelty laws. What might the statutes of tomorrow require?

"We have to be very careful about upwardly defining the status of cats and dogs," says Aspros. "If we get to the point where we have to treat them like children, not a lot of people are going to have pets." That's why, he says, the AVMA has fought so hard to stop personhood.

The first battles played out in state legislatures. As the Guardian Campaign picked up steam in the early 2000s, the AVMA lobbied the Council of State Governments—an advisory group to various state legislatures and executive branches—to oppose any further "guardian" language at the state level. Rhode Island had been the only state to adopt such language, and none have endorsed it since (though many cities have). Meanwhile, the AVMA has fought tooth and claw against a number of bills that would have permitted the recovery of noneconomic damages when a cat or dog was killed. Tennessee's landmark T-Bo Act, the first in the country to allow such damages, almost didn't pass due to veterinary opposition; the senator who sponsored it said he only got it through by exempting veterinarians. Since then, related bills in other states have died without even coming to a vote.

The veterinary community has been so successful at the legislative level that it has now turned its attention to the courts. Here it's come face-to-face with the animal law movement. In a series of high-profile cases, the two groups have fired salvos of amicus briefs at each other, hoping to sway the opinions of judges. The battle has taken its toll on animal lawyers; the movement to grant more rights to cats and dogs has begun to suffer serious setbacks. In a 2009 Vermont case, in which the owners of two cats said that a vet clinic had negligently prescribed lethal doses of hypertension medication, a judge shot down their claims for emotional distress and loss of companionship, stating that such awards would place pets above humans. And in 2013, the AVMA and the Animal Legal Defense Fund squared off in a Texas Supreme Court case involving the accidental euthanasia of a dog at an animal control facility. Here the owners weren't asking for anything close to personhood; they just wanted to recover damages for the sentimental value of their dog, the same as if someone had destroyed a wedding dress or photo album. But even that was a bridge too far for the AVMA, whose amicus heavily influenced the judges to deny the claim. As the law now stands in Texas, you can recover more money if someone destroys a picture of your dog than if they destroy the dog itself.

Going forward, the AVMA is working to stop anything with even a whiff of personhood for pets. That could include legislation that would make it easier for divorcing couples to fight over the custody of their cats and dogs. Anytime a judge or politician considers granting more rights to companion animals, the veterinary community will be there to oppose it. Yet this war is being fought on many fronts. Veterinary medicine isn't the only profession with something to lose.

In November 2010, 26,000 scientists descended on the San Diego Convention Center to attend the annual meeting of the Society for Neuroscience. They weren't alone. On the first day of the conference, thirty protestors gathered outside to denounce the use of animals in research laboratories. Some were spattered with fake blood; others held pictures of kittens and monkeys with their brains exposed. The meeting's organizers had already prepared a counterattack. Two days after the demonstration, the conference held a symposium—not-so-subtly titled "Conferring Legal Rights to Animals: Research in the Crosshairs"—on the threat of the personhood movement. The session's panelists—two scientists, a professor of veterinary medicine, and a law professor—warned attendees about the growing field of animal law and urged them to do a better job fighting back. The rise of cats and dogs, they said, could doom biomedical research.

The scientific community has always had an uneasy relationship with dogs and cats. Ever since René Descartes first sliced into the heart of a living dog in the mid-1600s, animal researchers and animal welfare advocates have sparred over the ethical use of pets. The Brown Dog Riots of 1907 only added fuel to the fire. For the better part of the twentieth century, a rapidly expanding research enterprise relied heavily on cats and dogs—seized from shelters and snatched by bunchers—to test new drugs and surgical procedures. Controversy over the provenance of these animals helped spawn the Humane Society of the United States, which successfully lobbied for the tightest controls on animal research in US history. Science fought back with its own lobbying group, the National Association for Biomedical Research (NABR), which since 1985 has pushed for the continued use of lab animals. Today, dogs and cats have largely disappeared from the laboratory, thanks to changing social attitudes and the rise of cheaper animal models, like mice and fruit flies, but their specter still looms large over scientific research.

The San Diego symposium was the culmination of years of anxiety over the evolving status of pets. Like the veterinary community, research organizations had been keeping a wary eye on the proliferation of noneconomic damages cases and the success of the Guardian Campaign. As early as 2004, shortly after the Bluestone verdict was handed down, NABR created an "Animal Law Section" on its website to track everything from anticruelty legislation to pet custody cases. Though the organization's primary concern is direct attacks against the use of mice and nonhuman primates, like chimpanzees, it frets that rights for cats and dogs could spill over to all lab animals. "We're worried about the slippery slope," NABR's president, Frankie Trull, told me. "Once you assign rights to animals, you can't do animal research without it being challenged on every level. There's not a single disease that's studied that is not studied first in animals." Important work on Alzheimer's, birth defects, cancers—"all of it," she said, "would come to a screeching halt."

Trull's concerns are well founded. As Americans have embraced pets as children, they've also soured on animal research. In 2000, 70 percent supported such studies; by 2009, only 52 percent did, and just 39 percent of those under thirty. Meanwhile, organizations born out of a concern for the welfare of cats and dogs are now looking for ways to protect lab animals. Both the Humane Society of the United States and the Animal Legal Defense Fund have pushed hard to end animal testing. The HSUS has carried out undercover investigations of research labs and lobbied to end invasive research on chimpanzees. ALDF has filed a landmark lawsuit against a California biotechnology company for failing to properly care for its animals, and it's petitioning Congress for an Animal Bill of Rights, which includes "the right of laboratory animals not to be used in cruel or unnecessary experiments."

The HSUS and ALDF have also targeted Big Agriculture. Here, too, the HSUS has carried out undercover work—infiltrating meatpacking plants, for example—and it has successfully campaigned for statewide bans on veal crates, sow gestation crates, and cramped wire cages for hens. ALDF, meanwhile, has fought foie gras and pork producers in court, and it filed a lawsuit against the Food and Drug Administration for failing to enforce the veracity of humane labels on eggs. Critics say both organizations have amassed members and money on the backs of cats and dogs and are now using these resources on efforts that could destroy the livestock industry.

Researchers and factory farmers haven't taken such assaults lying down. Thanks to heavy lobbying, most state anticruelty laws exempt lab and farm animals. And in 2006, NABR joined forces with the National Cattleman's Beef Association, the American Veal Association, and other farm industry groups to help pass the Animal Enterprise Terrorism Act. The law, which imposes penalties of up to decades in prison and hundreds of thousands of dollars in fines for individuals who interfere with biomedical research, is mainly aimed at animal rights protestors who destroy property and threaten lives. But opponents say it demonizes anyone who questions the use of animals in research. The livestock industry has also helped pass so-called ag-gag bills in several states, which effectively make it a crime to conduct undercover investigations at factory farms.

Breeders have joined the battle against personhood too. Cats and dogs that are legal persons can't be mated against their will. They also can't be bought and sold—that would make them slaves. The Cat Fanciers' Association and the American Kennel Club have fought vehemently against any attempt to grant pets more rights. Both, for example, filed amicus briefs in the Texas Supreme Court case that denied sentimental damages for the death of a dog. The AKC also helped defeat the 2003 Puppy Protection Act in Congress, which would have limited the number of dogs an individual could breed and required that the animals be socialized, and it has successfully lobbied against bans on tail docking and ear cropping. But overall, breeders have suffered far more losses than their counterparts in other animal-related industries. In 2012, for example, Los Angeles banned the sale of commercially bred dogs and cats; today, there are almost no pet breeders left in the city. Dozens of other cities nationwide have passed similar bans. What's more, by supporting the mass production of tailored pets for the open market, breeders have increasingly found themselves out of touch with a public that views its companion animals as family, not products. The AKC faced especially withering criticism in 2012 when the Westminster Dog Show (which it governs) terminated its relationship with Pedigree, a pet food company that was promoting shelter and mixed-breed dogs in its ads. The club's registrations have plummeted since the 1990s.

Still, the push to grant cats and dogs additional rights has been taking some pretty serious blows. Perhaps no criticism is more damning than that coming from Richard Cupp, vice dean of Pepperdine University School of Law. Cupp, a panelist on the "Research in the Crosshairs" session who has advised both the AVMA and NABR, is a hugely influential force in the antipersonhood movement. Though he is a pet lover, he has written that equating animals with people devalues humanity. "When we allow animals into our inner circle, we erode the notion that humans are unique," he told me. "When animals are on the same plane as humans, we no longer have the moral responsibility to care for them. And when humans are on par with animals, what's to stop us from euthanizing humans?" Legal rights, he said, are a serious business. They don't just give us the ability to live our lives relatively unencumbered. They enter us into a contract with every other member of society, a world built on the give-and-take between *human* rights and *human* responsibilities. As he wrote in a 2007 law review article, "A powerful argument may be made that granting rights to animals that do not possess moral responsibility represents a rejection of the foundation of human civilization."

NABR's Trull laments the current state of affairs. "It's much more combative than it used to be," she told me. And things are only likely to get worse. She sees where the other side is coming from, especially when it comes to pets. "I'm a crazy cat person," she laughed. "I adore my animals." But personhood is off the table. Any attempts to assign more rights to animals, even dogs and cats, will meet with fierce opposition. "We're going to fight this with every bit of resource we have."

With so many battles being waged over pets, it's hard to know who will end up winning. The outcome may depend on the next generation.

Toward the end of our conversation in his office at Bond Animal Hospital, I ask Douglas Aspros if there's any room for compromise in the fight over the evolving status of cats and dogs. He says he doesn't think the AVMA is going to support more rights for pets anytime soon. But he does acknowledge that the veterinary profession is changing. It's more focused on companion animals than ever. It's increasingly urban and suburban. And, perhaps most importantly, it's now dominated by women. An occupation that once scorned the fairer sex's "delicacy of feeling" is currently churning out graduating classes that are 80 percent female. It may be a stereotype, but many people I spoke to say women are bringing an unprecedented level of sensitivity to the field and, with it, a new openness to concepts like personhood. Yet gender isn't the only issue. The generation entering the profession today grew up with cats and dogs not just as pets but as family—in some cases, they practically viewed their pets as siblings. The same is true in other fields like biomedical research. "We have to be more reflective of the society around us," says Aspros. "And to some extent the pet parent thing reflects society. We live in this world too. We have animals ourselves. We understand."

Aspros and I get up, and he gives me a tour of the rest of the clinic. We navigate a tight hallway that leads to the surgical suite. Inside are a couple of metal exam tables, an X-ray machine, and a brightly lit operating room. Two veterinary technicians are holding an orange tabby down on a table while one injects a sedative. The feline is about to have a mass removed from its ear for analysis. The injector is Rachel Brady, thin, in her late twenties, with dark brown hair tied back in a ponytail. She's part of the next generation of vets Aspros was telling me about: in a few months, she'll be heading to one of the country's top veterinary schools, the University of California, Davis.

After the procedure, Brady and I walk down to the basement, where the employee lounge is located. There's a couch, a kitchenette, and a charming black-and-white cat named Zorro, named for the masklike markings on his face. Brady tells me that his owner wanted to euthanize him because he has hypothyroidism, but the clinic persuaded her to sign the cat over to it instead. "We've been trying to adopt him out ever since," she says. "He's a really sweet boy."

Unlike Aspros, Brady has wanted to be a vet her entire life. "It's all I've ever talked about since I was a little girl," she says. But she differs from her boss in a deeper way. "I definitely think dogs and cats should have a different legal status," she says. "It seems absurd they're considered property." Brady acknowledges that there are some advantages to the property status; Zorro's owner wouldn't have just been able to sign him over if he were a child, for example, and she worries about the impact of veterinary malpractice lawsuits on the profession. But ultimately, she says, none of this outweighs giving cats and dogs their deserved place in society. Personhood, she says, is just the latest campaign in a quest for social justice that began with race and gender equality. "Just because you're scared of what's going to happen doesn't mean it's not worth doing."

The Social Parasite

It was a damp, overcast Saturday morning in late November 2012 when the Kuljian family—a couple, their teenage son and daughter, and their gray-and-black shepherd mix, Fran—headed down to Big Lagoon County Park, a V-shaped inlet of the Pacific Ocean about fifty miles south of the California-Oregon border. The beach there had a dangerous reputation. It angled sharply into the surf, and so-called sneaker waves broke right on shore, emerging from nowhere to suck unsuspecting visitors into the riptide. Yellow signs warned guests not to turn their back on the ocean. The words were lost on Fran, who was playing with a stick near the water's edge. Suddenly, she was gone; the remnants of a ten-foot wave receding into the surf. The boy jumped in after her, battling the roiling water, and his father and mother followed. Held back by a bystander from diving in herself, the daughter watched helplessly as, one by one, her family disappeared. The coast guard sent in lifeboats and a helicopter, but it was unable to find anyone. A few hours later, the bodies of both parents washed up onshore. The son was never found. Fran, meanwhile, had pulled herself out unscathed.

I had this story in mind when I phoned John Archer at his home in Preston, England, about an hour's drive north of Liverpool. The evolving status of cats and dogs isn't just facing opposition from veterinarians and biomedical researchers; it also has a few sociologists concerned. Archer is among them. A sixty-eight-year-old semiretired psychologist, he's one of the few researchers who have argued that our relationship with dogs and cats is not as mutually beneficial as it seems. The money we spend, the sacrifices we make—they all hurt us in the end. We are the Kuljians, jumping in after Fran and losing everything in return.

Archer first had the idea in the early 1990s when he was teaching a class on grief and loss at his local university. "We touched on the anguish people feel when their pet dies, and it got me thinking about our attachment to these animals," he told me. "I wanted to view the relationship like a zoologist would. You have these two species, humans and pets, living together. Are they benefiting each other, or is one taking advantage?" Put starkly, are pets pals or parasites?

Pets were certainly pals at the beginning of domestication. Human beings, living hand to mouth, couldn't afford to waste time or resources on a potential competitor. Dogs and cats had to work for their keep; they helped us hunt and guarded our crops, and in return they got scraps and shelter. Today, the scales have tipped significantly in pets' favor. In an age of Frisbee catching and lap sitting, Archer said cats and dogs are doing relatively little to justify our massive expenditures on food, veterinary services, and doggy day care—not to mention the vast amounts of time we sink into them. Yes, pets provide love and companionship, and a few work as assistance animals; yet, he said, "on the whole, the negatives outweigh the positives."

None of this would matter in a world of unlimited resources. But given that we only have so much time and money and must spend some of them on ourselves and our own children, Archer fears we are compromising our ability to survive and reproduce—our "evolutionary fitness"—for our pets. Take the couple who decides not to have kids because they are too preoccupied with their dogs. Or the woman who mortgages her house so she can afford her cat's kidney transplant. Or the Kuljians. The whole thing reminds Archer of cuckoos, which lay their eggs in the nests of other birds; when the eggs hatch, the chicks kick out the native offspring and trick their adoptive parents into caring for them instead. Except we do cuckoos one better: we put the parasites in our nests ourselves.

It's not all our fault. The whole reason we were attracted to puppies and kittens in the first place is because they shared many of the same

features as our own babies. Their large eyes, snub noses, and round foreheads hijacked the "cute response" we evolved to take care of each other's children. Over the millennia, we've consciously and unconsciously
selected for traits that have only strengthened this response. Now, even
adult pets resemble human infants (compare cocker spaniels to wolves),
dogs have acquired a "theory of mind" that has convinced us that they
think just like we do, and cats have evolved a high-pitched purr that
contains a frequency similar to that of a baby's cry. It's no wonder we
talk to our pets the same way we talk to our infants. It's also no surprise
that recent scientific studies have shown that people rank the faces of
pets as equally attractive as those of human babies and that, when we
interact with cats and dogs, our levels of oxytocin—a hormone linked to
maternal bonding—surge. Like the cuckoo's victim, we're having a hard
time telling someone else's children from our own.

The impact goes beyond our individual nests. In an age of ubiquitous technology and disintegrating human relationships, pets have become the glue holding society together. But they're also ripping us apart,
Archer told me. "It's fine to rely on a pet as a companion, but for some
people the pet takes the place of the human." The more addicted we
become to our animals, he said, and the more we treat them like people,
the less likely we are to seek out real human contact. Far from staving
off loneliness, cats and dogs may isolate us like never before.

So what does Archer think we should do about it? Not much, it
turns out. As we chatted, he let on that he has a cat of his own, Daisy,
and that he and his wife dote on her as much as anyone. "We behave
in all of the ways I talk about," he laughed. Sometimes, he said, when
he's petting Daisy, he wonders if he's the host and she's the parasite.
Then he decides he doesn't care. Even if we're all the victims of some
vast evolutionary conspiracy, "I don't necessarily want to change human
behavior," he said. "Not even my own."

Archer may not think we need to get rid of cats and dogs to save
society. But there is one man who does.

The Abolitionist

About a year after I traveled to Portland for the Animal Law Conference, I attended another animal law meeting, this one via the Web. Held

at DePaul University College of Law in Chicago, it focused on the use of animals in entertainment. Are racehorses being properly cared for? Do circuses violate the Animal Welfare Act? Cats and dogs were hardly on the agenda. That didn't matter to me. I had tuned in for the keynote speaker, a Rutgers University law professor named Gary Francione. Francione, I knew, was considered a radical, even within the animal law movement. But it wasn't until the conference that I realized how radical he really was.

Stepping up to a gray podium in an auditorium filled with about a hundred attendees, Francione began a fiery sermon. He was fifty-eight and twiggy, with a mop of dark brown hair graying at the sides, and he blasted the current status of animals in society. As long as animals are property, he said, they are slaves. And if we don't act, we are culpable in their suffering. "We think in a delusionally confused way about animal issues," he said, pounding his fist on the podium. "We're not taking animals seriously."

So far, this was shaping up to be a boilerplate animal law talk. But Francione wasn't there to extol the virtues of custody cases, veterinary malpractice lawsuits, or even personhood. He was there to rip animal law a new one. "For those of you who think animal welfare reform is doing something, you're dreaming," he said. "The notion that the law is ever going to deal with animal issues in an effective way is on the level of believing that a weight-challenged man slides down your chimney at Christmastime and puts things in your stockings. The idea that we as lawyers are going to change the world is a fantasy." Toto, we weren't in Portland anymore.

Francione was just getting started. He denounced the animal rights movement, mocked the topic of the conference, and chastised the audience for not becoming vegan. Then came the kicker. "We'll never find our moral compass as long as animals are sitting on our plates, they're in glasses on our tables, they're at our feet, they're in our beds." Wait, what? *They're at our feet, they're in our beds?* Was he talking about getting rid of cats and dogs? Indeed, he was.

I had to meet this guy.

Francione is as spirited in person as he was at DePaul. I wait for him in late January in his office on the fourth floor of Rutgers's modern Center for Law and Justice Building in downtown Newark, New Jersey. Outside, an icy wind howls. Sitting next to me is his partner of thirty-five years, Anna Charlton; fifty-six, with long, dark hair and a British accent, she's an adjunct professor at the school. Vegan bumper stickers plaster the door. A picture of former US Supreme Court justice Sandra Day O'Connor hangs on the wall, not far from a newspaper clipping headlined "Animal Research Data Ordered Released."

Francione bursts in, breathless. He drove in to work earlier than usual to meet me, and the garage denied his parking pass. "They tell me I have a part-time pass that's only good past three o'clock," he says to Charlton. "I said, 'I've been doing it this way for ten *fucking* years.'" Then he grabs the phone and gets an administrator on the line. "You're telling my wife she can't teach before three?" he fumes. "That's discrimination. There must be some sort of civil rights action I can bring." He winks at Charlton. "But I can get out of the fucking lot tonight, right? I'll sue for false imprisonment if I can't get out." He slaps down the receiver, turns to me, and smiles. "Hi, David, how are you?"

Francione's journey to work today isn't the only thing that's fraught. His entire career has been filled with battles. When I ask him what set him on his current path, he laughs and says, "I was raised by wolves." In truth, animals didn't play a large role in Francione's early life. "I always liked cats and dogs," he tells me, "but I never really related to them in a significant way." Like Douglas Aspros, he grew up in a small New York apartment without pets. It wasn't until he entered law school in the late 1970s that he began thinking seriously about animal issues. "A friend convinced me to visit a slaughter house," he says. "I was a big meat eater; my father was in the restaurant industry. But the slaughterhouse changed my perceptions on everything. I became a vegetarian."

He was living with Charlton at the time. The two had met while Francione was at the University of York in England studying philosophy. "I was young and foolish," she smiles. When they returned to the United States, she convinced him to adopt a dog from a local shelter. That was the beginning of their pack; they have five dogs now and have had as many as seven at one time. After law school, Francione clerked for Justice O'Connor. One day, a pit bull mix was hit by a car in front of the Supreme Court building. "I brought the dog into the court, much to the consternation of

Justice Rehnquist," he says. "I got a lot of blood on the carpet." He called the Washington Humane Society, which sent over an animal control officer. The dog had died by then, but the officer started talking to Francione about animal rights. "She said her name was Ingrid Newkirk, and she and her boyfriend, Alex Pacheco, had just started a group called People for the Ethical Treatment of Animals. I remember thinking that was an incredibly boring name," he laughs. Francione invited them over for dinner. When Newkirk found milk and eggs in the refrigerator, she dumped them down the sink. Then she schooled Francione and Charlton on the evils of the livestock industry. "I had never heard the word 'vegan' before," he says. "We haven't eaten animal products since."

Francione worked on many of PETA's early animal rights cases, helping to both promote and legitimize the group. In 1984, shortly after he became an assistant professor at the University of Pennsylvania Law School, animal rights activists broke into a research lab on campus and stole video tapes showing baboons being subjected to gruesome head injury experiments. PETA publicized the videos and led a sit-in at the National Institutes of Health; Francione represented the activists and pushed for congressional hearings into the research. The school eventually shut the lab down. Francione went after his own university again a few years later, suing the veterinary school for expelling two students who refused to perform surgery on healthy dogs—the first litigation of its kind in the country. "The associate dean of the law school was married to the dean of the vet school," Francione says. "He was not happy."

Around this time, Francione also became involved in one of the most famous animal rights cases in US history. In 1981, PETA's Pacheco had gone undercover, volunteering in the Silver Spring, Maryland, laboratory of a neuroscientist named Edward Taub. There he photographed seventeen monkeys being kept in filthy conditions, some with open sores and missing fingers. Police raided the lab later that year, and Taub was found guilty of animal cruelty, the first such conviction ever for a US researcher (though it was later overturned). The case dragged on for years. In the later stages, Francione worked to free the monkeys and to help PETA prepare briefs for the US Supreme Court. PETA lost both battles, but the Taub case turned it into a national organization and helped give rise to the modern animal rights movement.

In the late 1980s, Francione moved to Rutgers, where he's been ever since. There, he began teaching animal law and started the world's first animal law clinic. Run with Charlton, the clinic allowed students to work on real-world animal rights cases, including representing prisoners who wanted to eat vegan food and fighting wild-horse roundups. It even got New Jersey's governor to effectively pardon an Akita sentenced to death under the state's dangerous-dog law. Later, Francione became chair of the American Bar Association's Animal Law Committee and briefly served on the board of the Animal Legal Defense Fund.

Despite his bona fides, Francione was becoming disillusioned with the animal protection movement. It started in 1991 when he got word that PETA had euthanized thirty-two animals—eighteen rabbits and fourteen roosters—at its Aspen Hill sanctuary in Maryland. The group claimed it didn't have room for them. "I couldn't defend it," he tells me. "If you're an animal rights organization, you just don't kill healthy animals." He also objected to PETA's "I'd Rather Go Naked Than Wear Fur" campaign, launched that same year, which featured photos of nude women. "I thought it was sexist and trivialized the issue," he says. "Would Martin Luther King say, 'I'd rather go naked than sit in the back of the bus'?" He confronted Newkirk. It didn't go well. "The writing was on the wall," he says. "I thought it was time for me to go off on my own." Francione had broken with the animal rights movement. He was about to break with the animal law movement as well.

It may seem like a stretch to keep comparing the journey of cats and dogs to that of African Americans. But if we're talking about a group of beings once considered wild animals, then declared property, and finally granted personhood, blacks are the only precedent pets have. Like the natives of Africa, cats and dogs were removed from their original environments and transplanted into "civilized" society, where they worked for and among people without being considered one of them. Philosophers denied them souls and called them machines. Over time, social attitudes began to change, as science broke down the barriers between man and "beast." A group of reformers rose to push for personhood: the abolitionists for blacks, the animal law movement for cats and dogs.

But for Francione, that's where the analogy ends. Whereas the abolitionists sought to turn blacks into people with a single sweeping piece of legislation, the animal law movement has pushed for more incremental reforms: a noneconomic damages case here, a felony abuse law there. That struck Francione as the wrong way to go about things. "You cannot take incremental steps toward personhood," he says. "We didn't make slavery more and more humane until it went away. Abolitionists weren't supporting softer whips or fewer beatings."

Francione went public with his frustrations. In 1996, he published *Rain Without Thunder*, an excoriation of the movement he'd long been a part of. "Despite an ostensible acceptance of the animal rights position, the modern animal protection movement has failed to translate the theory of animal rights into a practical and theoretically consistent strategy for social change," he wrote. The campaign, he said, was so resistant to criticism it had effectively become a cult. "In a nutshell, things are worse for animals than they were one hundred years ago; the present strategy is simply not working."

The book didn't earn him many friends. "After I wrote *Rain Without Thunder*, everyone stopped talking to me," he says. "I went from speaking at fifteen to twenty animal rights conferences a year to not getting invited anywhere. It was like I didn't exist." Francione himself had become a nonperson.

He found his new status liberating. Though he had never censored himself before, he now attacked with new zeal. He also began to focus on social change rather than legal change. Famed civil rights lawyer William Kunstler once told him, "Don't ever kid yourself. Lawyers are never going to change the system. What we can do is keep the good people out of jail while they change the world." For Francione, that meant defending the animal activist rather than the animal. It also meant promoting veganism: trying to save billions of animals on factory farms rather than the occasional one in the courtroom. In typical Francione fashion, he penned a 2007 *Philadelphia Daily News* op-ed titled "We're All Michael Vick." Written shortly after the football player pleaded guilty to federal dog-fighting charges, it didn't mince words. "There is something bizarre about condemning Michael Vick for using dogs in a hideous form of entertainment when 99 percent of us also use animals that are every bit as sentient as dogs in another form of entertainment," he wrote. "How removed from the screaming crowd around the dog pit is the laughing group around the summer steak barbeque?"

Francione spreads his gospel wherever he goes, even at DePaul, one of the rare animal law events he's spoken at in the last fifteen years. He only went on the condition that the conference not serve animal products and that it allow him to talk about veganism. "They want to use me because I'm colorful," he tells me. "Well, fuck you, then I'm going to say what I want to say." Still, Francione's dietary advice sometimes conflicts with his animal rights philosophy. What about cats, I ask him, knowing they're the only domestic animal that needs to eat meat. Should cats starve so cows can live? Should cows die for the family pet? It's one of the few questions he doesn't have a ready answer for. Finally, he draws a semantic line, saying it's not *justifiable* to feed cats meat, but it is *excusable*. "Look, it's not a perfect solution," he says, seeming flustered for the first time. Then he laughs. "I wish the only problem I had in this world is what to do about nonvegan cats!"

The conversation reminds me of why I'm here in the first place. I ask Francione about his line at DePaul, the one about getting rid of pets. What does *that* have to do with animal rights? Francione's animal law class is about to begin. He invites me to attend for the answer.

Francione, Charlton, and I head down a couple of flights of stairs to a classroom of long desks facing a wooden podium. Francione takes his place up front, and Charlton sits next to him at a small table. She's always at his side, it seems. In a world turned against him, she remains his best friend and most fervent supporter. She also helps keep him focused. The class covers typical animal law topics, but Francione treats it more like a philosophy lecture, latching onto an idea and seeing where it takes him, sometimes appearing to invent new doctrines as he speaks. He moves from one tangent to another, seemingly at random, until all of it, when viewed from a great height, coalesces into a singular argument. The class is driven as much by student questions as by Francione's personality, and he allows single queries to hijack the discussion for large chunks of its running time. When he leads his students too far into the wilderness, Charlton throws him a lifeline, and he pulls them back out.

About forty law students filter in, taking seats and hinging open their laptops. Today's topic has been chosen to suit my presence. Francione starts by telling the room about another recent, yet rare, appearance at an animal conference. He spoke at a meeting of the New York State Bar Association's Animal Law Committee in Manhattan. Attendees talked about drafting contracts to buy and sell horses and how to make sure their clients had the right insurance to transport cows. When it was Francione's turn to speak, he, as usual, ripped the field a new one. "A woman came up to me afterwards and asked me if I thought we should have pets," he tells his class. "'I love dogs,' I told her. 'But if there were two dogs left in the world and it were up to me to decide whether to let them breed, the answer would be no. We shouldn't bring any more cats and dogs into existence.' The woman was horrified." She wasn't the only one. The students look at Francione in disbelief. The questions start flying. They demand he explain himself.

For Francione, the reasoning all comes back to slavery. We may think we've given cats and dogs all sorts of rights, he says, but we can still buy, sell, and declaw them. And we kill millions in shelters every year. As long as they are not legal persons, our interests will always trump theirs in a court of law. They will always be Dred Scott. They will always be slaves.

So why not just fight for personhood, like the abolitionists did for blacks? That's where traditional abolitionism ends and Francione's abolitionism begins. "Slaves were human beings that had a particular status," he says. "We just removed that status. Domestication is a biological condition. You can't say to a dog, 'You were once a domesticated animal. You are now no longer a domesticated animal.' It makes no sense." Pets, he says, are trapped in a state from which there is no escape. "Domestication has essentially created a mentally disabled child bred to be dependent on us. My dogs will never get to the point where they'll become wolves and live the way they're supposed to live." We wonder why our pets are neurotic, he says, why dogs chew themselves raw and cats shred the drapes. "It's because they're not supposed to be living with us. They exist in this netherworld between humans and animals. They're in this really bad space; I think it's scary for them. I love my dogs, but they don't belong here. They're refugees from a life they can't get back to anymore." When it doesn't make sense to turn animals into legal persons, and it's morally wrong to keep them as pets, Francione's answer is to prevent them from breeding until none are left. For him, "abolition" isn't the abolition of slavery—it's the abolition of the animals themselves.

It may be a drastic solution, he acknowledges, but it solves all sorts of problems. Without pets, there is no more cruelty, no more suffering. There's no more hand-wringing about nonvegan cats or whether it makes sense to spend $20,000 on chemotherapy for your dog. And what's true for cats and dogs holds for cows, chickens, and all other domestic animals. "In my ideal world," says Francione, "we have wild animals, which we leave alone, and us."

The students are not swayed. "Charles, you look very upset. Why are you upset?" Francione says to a young man in the back row wearing a red Rutgers hoodie. "Dogs and us have a symbiotic relationship," the student protests. "We provide shelter, they provide affection." Yes, says Francione, but our needs do not justify their slavery. "You're playing God," another student exclaims. "Would you have eliminated slavery by neutering the slaves?" And then another: "Cats and dogs have been with us for thousands of years. We don't exterminate humans with mental disabilities." Things threaten to get heated. And then, the class ends.

"Well, that was an animated little discussion," Francione smiles as we walk back up to his office. Despite his break with the animal law community, he does have one big thing in common with its leader, ALDF founder Joyce Tischler. Both realize the power of using pets to push their message. "Dogs and cats are a wonderful teaching vehicle," Francione says. "Everyone in that room either has a dog or a cat, or has had a dog or cat. These people have deep emotional attachments. And now I'm saying to them, 'These animals shouldn't exist.' It horrifies them. They get more passionate than during any other lecture I give. But it also makes them think."

So is Francione just pushing buttons to get a rise out of people? He swears he isn't. He means every word he says. But even he has a hard time coming to grips with the implications of his arguments. "Look, we live in a society of tremendous alienation," he says, his voice softening for the first time. "We're becoming atomized in a way that human beings have never been before. We've sacrificed our friends for Twitter followers. We have security warnings everywhere keeping us in a constant state of worry about a terrorist threat. If you look around and you're not horribly depressed, there's something wrong with you. We *need* cats and dogs right now. They're the only source of unconditional, nonjudgmental love in our lives. They're the only real Christians left."

Francione doesn't expect his philosophy of animal rights to catch on anytime soon. "I'm aware I'm in a world where everything is aligned against the things I believe in," he says. "Human rights, animal rights—you can't separate the two. I've never fought for these social justice issues with the idea that I'm going to win. I don't think it has to do with winning. But I'm going to be fighting till the day I die." Even if the world miraculously comes around to his point of view, pets, he says, will still be with us for a while. "In another fifty years, we won't have animal agriculture the way we have it now. As a result of health, ethics, and environmental concerns, many of us will look at animal products the way we look at smoking cigarettes today. But we'll still have cats and dogs. They'll be the last thing to go."

Thinking about Jasper and Jezebel, I'm inclined to agree with Francione about at least one thing: we need our cats and dogs more than ever before. There's little I wouldn't do for my pets. But that doesn't include abolishing them to solve their existential crisis. Surely there must be another way. On the final leg of my journey, I went in search of a solution.

TWELVE

The Road Ahead

Nearly two years after I began my quest to explore our changing relationship with cats and dogs, I find myself back where I started: Indiana. I'm not at Wolf Park but rather seventy miles to the southeast, waiting outside a hotel in downtown Indianapolis. I'm not here to figure out where our companion animals came from; I'm here to figure out where they're going. Dogs and cats have reached a critical juncture in their social evolution: as they inch toward personhood, we must decide whether to embrace them as fellow members of society or limit them to being mere pets. I've come back to Indiana to figure out if this decision is even in our hands. Just how much control do we have over the status of cats and dogs?

It's a cloudy Saturday morning in mid-June, and the air is already muggy. A tan minivan pulls up outside the hotel, and the passenger door opens. I climb inside. In the driver's seat is Lisa Tudor, slight, in her early fifties, with blonde hair tied back in a short ponytail. She's wearing glasses, jean shorts, and a gray T-shirt sporting the word "IndyFeral." A dark blue tattoo runs up the inside of her left wrist: four characters in a Chinese script. There are no seats in the back of the van, just a tattered blanket laid over the floor, a few jugs of water, and a couple of large yellow plastic tubs filled with dry cat food. The car smells a bit like urine, and Tudor apologizes for the odor. She's not used to transporting human passengers.

We're headed to the Indiana State Fairgrounds a few miles away. As we drive through downtown, water sloshes in the back, and worn-out brakes squeal with the grind of metal on metal. Stores and office buildings eventually give way to tree-lined residential streets, and then we reach our destination: a flat, 250-acre expanse of dirt and asphalt covered with pavilions and parking lots. It's a ghost town. We've arrived between a gun-and-knife expo and a Shriner's convention, and the only people about are a few men in overalls, scooping up horse dung and baling hay. We drive a curved road that hugs the outside of a racetrack, passing a half dozen long, white horse stables, and pull up to a wood structure with a peaked green roof and white paint peeling from its exterior. A sign above its giant doors reads "Community Barn." Tudor and I get out of the van and walk inside.

It's dark in the barn. The only light comes from the two cavernous openings at either end. Horses fidget in plywood stalls, seven deep on each side. Wheelbarrows and brooms are propped up against the wall. Electric fans buzz but do little to move the pungent air. When my eyes adjust, I gaze up at the loft above the stalls, and that's when I spot them: four pairs of glowing yellow eyes blinking down at me. I step forward, and they disappear into the darkness. I glimpse a lanky black cat ducking behind a mound of hay. This is as close as they're going to let me get. Like the gray wolves I visited a couple of years back, these animals want nothing to do with people. Spooky. Frightened. Wild. They might as well be a different species from the felines that share our homes. And yet they may hold the key to the future of our relationship with cats and dogs.

Crossing Boundaries

Thousands of years after cats became domesticated, they conquered the world. Fleeing the collapse of ancient Egypt, they hitched rides on Greek ships and spread throughout Europe. There, their travels nearly ended, thanks to Pope Gregory IX and the mass executions that followed. But cats eventually rebounded and broached new territory. Today, they're found everywhere on earth, from the coldest mountains to the hottest deserts, from the United States to China, from Greenland to sub-Antarctic islands—hundreds of millions of them. And yet not all felines are created equal. For every pampered house cat, another lives on the street, killing rodents, scavenging garbage, fleeing humans. Wildcats are still among us; we just call them ferals.

Somewhere between 16 and 80 million homeless cats inhabit the United States alone. (Feral dogs are largely a thing of the past in America, due to early concerns about rabies and livestock, which led to tough leash laws and crackdowns on wandering mutts.) Some have been outside for generations, so wild they might as well be squirrels or raccoons. Others are former house cats, lost or abandoned, trying to make their way in an unfriendly world. Most live short lives. They starve. They freeze. They're hit by cars. And yet they keep breeding. A single male and female can give rise to hundreds of cats in just a few years, all born to suffer. Humane societies to the rescue, right? Wrong.

The world created by Henry Bergh didn't last long. He had founded the American Society for the Prevention of Cruelty to Animals in 1866 to protect domestic creatures and give them the most humane life possible. So when New York, plagued by packs of roving dogs, asked him to take over the city's pounds, he refused. He knew the work would involve euthanizing animals, and he didn't think a humane society should be in the killing business. He also worried that such an enterprise would drain his fledgling organization of the time and resources it needed to fight cruelty on the streets. His decision was prescient. In 1894, just a few years after he died, the ASPCA agreed to run New York's pounds, and its mission changed dramatically. By 1910, it was killing the vast majority of cats and dogs that came through its doors—tens of thousands per year— and humane organizations across the country followed suit. What little remained of Bergh's original dream had devolved into executing animals as humanely as possible. Drowning was replaced with gassing, and gassing with lethal injection, but the carnage continued. By the early 1970s, more than 23 million cats and dogs—one-fifth of the nation's pets—were dying every year in shelters, some run by the city, some by humane organizations. The very word "shelter" had lost its protective meaning; these weren't places of refuge—they were pits of death.

Feral cats fared the worst. They were rounded up like any other stray animal, but their temperament obviated any chance for adoption. A pickup by animal control was a certain death sentence. Worse, until 2006, the Humane Society of the United States actually supported the extermination of feral cats, believing it more merciful than letting them remain on the streets. If humane organizations weren't so bogged down by the day-to-day grind of shelter work, they could have done more for homeless animals—another of Bergh's fears realized—but not until the 1960s did they begin exploring ways to curb the killing, such as pushing spay/neuter. Even then, little attention was paid to ferals. And so the cats kept breeding—and dying.

Not everyone turned a blind eye. As early as the 1950s, a few small groups in England began caring for homeless cats: feeding them, trapping them, getting them neutered, then returning them outdoors. A decade later, a British model named Celia Hammond helped popularize the effort, known as trap-neuter-release. By 1980, she was reporting that she had observed hundreds of colonies of street cats whose numbers had stabilized or declined. TNR crossed the pond in 1990, when a Washington, DC, group calling itself Alley Cat Allies—today, the nation's largest cat advocacy organization—introduced the movement to the United States. It's now practiced throughout the world, from Qatar to the Galapagos, and in hundreds of American cities. Some groups care for just a handful of cats. IndyFeral looks after nearly 200,000.

Lisa Tudor was not a cat person. She surprised me with this fact on our drive to the fairgrounds. Born and raised in Indianapolis, "we mostly had dogs growing up," she said. She didn't become interested in the homeless cat issue until 2001, when the *Indianapolis Star* published a lengthy investigation of the city's animal sheltering operations. In a disturbing portrait of a system broken by poor management and misplaced priorities, the paper found that in 2000, the city's two main shelters—the municipal Animal Care and Control and the private Humane Society—had euthanized about 22,000 cats and dogs, a large fraction of them puppies and kittens. "When it comes to killing unwanted dogs and cats," the paper stated, "few cities are as deadly as Indianapolis." Tudor was floored. "They printed these really graphic pictures of barrels of animals that had been euthanized," she told me. "I had no idea how many were being killed. I was like, 'Why isn't somebody doing something?'"

She was volunteering at a low-cost spay/neuter clinic at the time. Named the Foundation Against Companion-Animal Euthanasia, it catered to low-income families that couldn't otherwise afford to fix and vaccinate their pets. But what about all of the animals that didn't belong to a family? The *Indianapolis Star* investigation clued Tudor in to an entire population FACE couldn't do anything about. "We were getting a lot of phone calls from people feeding feral cats and wondering how to help them," she told me, but FACE didn't have the resources to assist. So Tudor took matters into her own hands. One day, a call came in about a cat that was hanging around a Church's Chicken fast-food restaurant not far from the clinic. Tudor drove over and found a feline living near a dumpster, her long white hair blackened with grime and hopelessly matted. "Every year she has kittens," the employees told her, "and every year they die." She couldn't approach the cat—her eyes went black and her ears flattened when Tudor came close—so she set out a raccoon trap and hoped for the best. When she came by the next day, the cat was in the cage. Tudor took her to FACE to be spayed and vaccinated, then returned her to the lot and told the employees to set out regular food and water. "A month later, the cat looked 100 percent better," she said. Tudor was hooked.

Part of it may have been her life as a social worker. In addition to her efforts at FACE, Tudor had spent the past fifteen years helping people with autism and other mental disabilities assimilate into the workplace. She'd talk to employers and fellow employees, trying to assuage concerns. "People who had never been around these types of people before were scared," she told me. "They thought they were slow, that they were child abusers or violent. I tried to get them to look beyond the disability and see the person underneath." Tudor felt the same way when she began to encounter feral cats. Here were animals trying to make their way in the world, yet feared and misunderstood by those around them. "These cats are the victims," she said. "They've been dumped on the street, yet they're still able to survive. And for that, people want to kill them."

Tudor began taking every call that came into FACE about homeless cats. She soon found she couldn't help them all, at least not by herself. So she banded together with a few other volunteers and a veterinarian she knew and formed IndyFeral in 2002. She had no idea what she was doing. Her limited knowledge of TNR came from a few pamphlets Alley Cat Allies had printed, and she didn't know anything about running her own operation. "I went out and bought *Nonprofits for Dummies* and read it chapter by chapter," she laughed. Resources were also a problem. IndyFeral volunteers had to beg for pet food and borrow traps, and they scavenged dumpsters for old pieces of wood they could use to build winter shelters. Tudor quit her social work job and applied for grants and donations. "I just took that leap and prayed that in two years there'd be enough money to keep paying me."

IndyFeral didn't just survive; it thrived. As Tudor and her followers fanned out into the community, feeding and trapping, others joined the cause. "There were a lot of people out there who wanted an alternative to killing cats," she said. By the end of the group's first year, it was managing more than four hundred colonies and had neutered hundreds of felines. Today, it's one of the largest TNR operations in the country, with thirty volunteers who have worked with more than 3,000 "caretakers"—people in the community who manage their own colonies of feral cats. The group has neutered more than 30,000 animals and, together with FACE, has helped reduce cat intake into the city's shelters by 37 percent and euthanasia by 72 percent. That's only the beginning.

The four cats I spot in the Community Barn aren't the only ones that call the fairgrounds home. Not by a long shot. Tudor estimates there are as many as thirty felines on the property, possibly more. Most have been dumped here. Owners get kittens, don't neuter them, then abandon them when they begin to spray or yowl. Others don't want to deal with expensive medical problems. "People see the barns and assume someone will take care of them," Tudor says. "They just kick the cat to the curb."

We exit the other side of the barn and come upon a mountain range of hay spanning an asphalt lot. A black-and-white cat pokes his head out from one of the smaller piles. I'm surprised when he saunters over and rubs against my leg. "He must be a former house cat," Tudor says. "You could never touch a true feral." Give him time, however, and he'll be no different from the shadows I spotted in the barn. That's the thing about cats: there's still a lot of wild left in them, and they can access it when they need to. A cat born on the street that doesn't interact with humans in its first twelve weeks becomes as feral as its ancestors. So do erstwhile house cats left to their own devices for too long. The only difference is that house cats can come back; give them a bit of love and attention, and they'll remember who they are. True ferals, on the other hand, are forever lost to the wild. The distinction doesn't matter to most shelters. Overcrowded conditions give former pets little time to show their true colors. When a homeless feline comes through the doors, it almost never leaves alive.

That's why places like the fairgrounds are so important. At least out here, cats have a fighting chance. Tudor and her allies do everything a shelter is supposed to do—feed, neuter, and care for animals—without the threat of lethal injection. They even provide medical treatment. This guy in the hay, for example, is missing fur on the back of his head and at the base of his tail. Tudor tells me he has a flea allergy, and that she'll be by later to give him some medication. Others will get vaccines and dental work. "All of them get ongoing care after we neuter them," she says. "It's not like we're throwing them back out here and abandoning them." Perhaps that's why these days TNR stands for "trap-neuter-return," not "release." Tudor's group isn't surrendering these animals to the wild; it's restoring them to an area where it will look after them. "People think these cats live short, miserable lives," says Tudor. "Well if nobody's looking out for them, that's the case. They'll live two years. But we've seen cats ten, twelve, thirteen years old. They're dying of cancer and kidney failure, not starvation." These animals don't need a shelter; IndyFeral has turned the entire outdoors into a humane society.

As we prepare to leave, a white van pulls up, and a heavyset woman and her husband climb out. The woman waves to Tudor and walks over to a rectangular wire trap, about the size of a gym bag, tucked into the bushes next to one of the stables. She returns, lugging something heavy. A brown tabby snarls inside. "This is a new one!" she says to Tudor; it's not missing the tip of its left ear, the universal sign that it's been TNR'd. The woman is one of the many caretakers IndyFeral works with. She's set out a few more traps around the fairgrounds, and she and her husband hop back in the van to check on them. "We'll see you this afternoon," says Tudor. I'm curious to find out what happens next to the tabby. But first we have a few more stops to make.

After the fairgrounds, Tudor and I drive to a neighborhood about ten minutes from downtown. It's not exactly the nicest part of the city. Dilapidated homes, some abandoned, squat on dirt lots overgrown with weeds. Cars are missing windows. No one seems to be around. "I wouldn't come here at night," she says.

Tudor calls this place "the Boulevard." IndyFeral started coming here in 2007, back when she got a call that an elderly woman was feeding twenty cats in her backyard. "I came over and it was like, 'Oh my God. A cat explosion ready to happen,'" she says. The rest of the neighborhood wasn't any better. "There were cats everywhere. At least seventy-five of them. People were poisoning them, siccing dogs on them. It was your worst nightmare." Tudor and her volunteers consolidated the felines, setting up small wooden shelters and feeding stations at a few locations, then neutered them. Today, there are only twenty left. Unlike at the fairgrounds, almost no one dumps here, so IndyFeral has a real chance of eventually getting that number down to zero. "This is a place where TNR is definitely working," she says.

We drive around to check on a few of the residents. Our first stop is a small white house standing on cinderblocks. As we step out of the van, two cats emerge from beneath the home, a large black tom and a long-haired gray with nubs for ears. "That's from frostbite," Tudor tells me. "For a while it was all male cats here. We called it the 'Homeless Men's Shelter,'" she smiles. Tudor grabs a jug of water and one of the large plastic tubs of dry cat food from the back of the van and hauls them over to a couple of blue plastic bowls that have been placed just under the house. She tosses out dirty water and replaces it with fresh. Then she scoops a couple of handfuls of the dry food into the other bowl. I'm reminded of tagging along with Charlotte and Ginnie in New Orleans, as they filled their own feeding stations to care for the animal orphans of Hurricane Katrina. For Tudor, these felines are orphans as well. She doesn't call them strays or ferals, but rather "community cats," a term that implies they're still members of society. "They're part of our community too," she says. "They're not typical, but why should they be disenfranchised? They're just a different kind of cat that requires a different kind of care."

Not everyone agrees. There are the poisoners and the dog siccers and those who tell IndyFeral volunteers not to bring those damn cats back after they've neutered them. There are the nature groups like the Wildlife Society and the American Bird Conservancy, which call street cats an invasive species that kills billions of birds and small mammals every year; they fight for ordinances that would criminalize TNR, fining caretakers for feeding the animals. Then there's the state and federal language that strips homeless cats of their very status as domestic creatures. Wyoming, for example, lists stray cats as "predatory animals," along with coyotes, skunks, and porcupines. A group of outdoor enthusiasts in Wisconsin lobbied in 2005 to reclassify free-roaming cats as an unprotected species and open up a hunting season on them. And the Occupational Safety and Health Administration groups feral felines with insects and rodents as "vermin" that may pose a danger to shipyard employees. House cats may be quasi-citizens, but their outdoor counterparts are illegal aliens.

After stopping at a couple more feeding stations, we leave the Boulevard and head north about five miles to Broad Ripple Village, a neighborhood of bushy trees and well-mowed lawns. We pull up to Tudor's place, a modest white home connected to a single-car garage via an enclosed breezeway. A bulky jet-black cat with golden eyes sits on the grass. "That's Boris," she says. "He's my foster failure."

We enter the breezeway with Boris in tow. A couple of cats dart from the enclosure into the bushes. Four more remain inside, lounging on blankets in the sun. Although skinnier, they look a lot like Boris, right down to the missing left ear tip. None of them have names, however. They're all street cats, part of a colony Tudor's been managing for six years. Like many caretakers, she noticed a few strays in her neighborhood and began feeding them in her backyard. "Pretty soon, my house became ground zero," she laughs. "When I'd drive home at night, you'd see them all running here. It was kind of embarrassing."

Boris sniffs my shoe, then hops up on a table in the breezeway and nuzzles against Tudor's hand. He comes from similar beginnings. Abandoned on the street, he was picked up by Animal Care and Control, which was going to euthanize him. He had three strikes against him: he had a massive laceration on his side, he seemed feral, and he was black. Even without the first two, he would have been virtually impossible to adopt out. "People have weird stereotypes and superstitions," Tudor says. (Some things never change.) Fortunately, Tudor's group had just started a program called Feral Freedom, which rescues cats slated for death at the municipal shelter. Tudor brought Boris to her headquarters, had him neutered and his ear clipped, and took him home as a foster to recover from his injuries. She was supposed to return him outside. But she grew attached. He came indoors. Now he's her cat.

That means, despite being biologically identical to the ferals, Boris is a different creature entirely. Tudor's simple gesture—opening her front

door—transformed him from wildlife into family member, from vermin
to quasi-citizen. It's the same with any pet we adopt from a shelter or
rescue from the street. In an instant they go from worthless to priceless.
And if we return them or abandon them, they lose everything all over
again. The only soul pets have is the one we give them.

Tudor and I finish the day at IndyFeral headquarters. As we pull up,
I have another flashback to New Orleans. Like ARNO, the makeshift
shelter I visited there, Tudor's operation is located in a warehouse in an
industrial part of the city. Made of brick and aluminum, the dirty beige
building is home to several businesses, each with a roll-up garage door in
the back. That's where the similarities end, however. Unlike at ARNO,
there's nothing here to advertise IndyFeral's presence. The garage door is
closed. There are no volunteers bustling around the property. And there
are no large signs—just a small note taped to the back door that lists the
hours of operation. "We try to keep a low profile," says Tudor, as we pull
into a parking lot in the back. "Otherwise people will abandon their cats
here like they do at the fairgrounds." To prove her point, she gestures to a
few small wooden shelters hidden in a clump of bushes behind the lot. Six
felines live here, all dumped. Tudor would prefer no one else join them.

Inside, the disparities with ARNO continue. Whereas the New Orleans warehouse was packed floor to ceiling with animals, food, and
supplies, IndyFeral's headquarters is largely empty. Just a few traps and
carriers line the shelves, and the place is dead quiet. The differences
are telling. ARNO is a shelter, home to cats and dogs rescued from the
street, waiting months or even years to find a home. IndyFeral is a way
station. Any animals that come here are just passing through. Their
shelter is outdoors.

In a few hours, things will look much different. On Saturday after-
noons caretakers drop off their cats for neutering. Tudor expects about
fifty felines to come through the doors today, including a few brought
by the woman we saw at the fairgrounds. Tomorrow morning, Tudor, a
couple of vets, and about ten volunteers will form an assembly line: the
cats will be sedated, given a physical, neutered, and vaccinated for rabies and distemper. They'll also be groomed and treated for fleas. Then
they'll be placed back in their traps. "It's like Grand Central Station,"

Tudor says. A couple of days from now, the caretakers will pick the cats up and return them to where they found them. Then other caretakers will set out new traps. And the process will begin again. Currently there are seven hundred felines on the waiting list.

IndyFeral's work is part of the No Kill movement. In the 1960s, US shelters began taking a hard look at how many animals they were euthanizing. But not until the late 1980s did some begin to wonder why they were killing at all. An idea formed that no healthy animal should be destroyed. Humane societies looked to the past, back to a time when their mission was to protect animals, not control their numbers. In 1994, San Francisco SPCA head Richard Avanzino (who won a 1980 court case to save a dog named Sido from being killed under the terms of her owner's will) successfully pushed the city to end the killing of healthy dogs and cats in its three shelters, making it a model for the nation. Today, more than five hundred cities and towns are No Kill or approaching No Kill. When they achieve that status, humane societies, freed of the draining work of animal control, can return to their original mission of ending cruelty. They can return to the vision of Henry Bergh.

It's not as easy as it sounds. Animals keep pouring into shelters, so humane societies have to find ways to stem the flow. That means aggressively pushing spay/neuter and ending breed discrimination so that pit bulls stay in their homes. Shelters must also increase adoption rates to avoid overcrowding. One strategy is to make them more pleasant places to visit: dank, dark pounds are out; brightly lit, furnished enclosures, like the sparkling Louisiana SPCA I visited in New Orleans, are in. The Louisiana SPCA is also doing something a lot of overcrowded shelters are: shipping its excess pets to humane societies in the Northeast, where spay/neuter programs have dramatically reduced intake. Others bring shelter pets to places people congregate, like malls and grocery stores, and plaster their pictures on PetFinder, an Internet site that has facilitated more than 20 million adoptions. People want these animals, the thinking goes. The supply just has to reach the demand.

Of course, no No Kill community is complete without a TNR program. Refusal to euthanize can't just end at the shelter door; it must extend to the streets beyond. That's why Tudor has been working her tail off for the past decade. When she isn't overseeing spay/neuter operations at the warehouse, she's out in the city, keeping tabs on hundreds of colonies, recruiting new caretakers, and pushing for legislation to help feral cats. In 2006, she got Indianapolis to adopt an ordinance that made it legal to care for colonies. "Before that, people could be fined," she says. "We were criminalizing compassion." And in 2012, IndyFeral came full circle with FACE, merging with the spay-neuter clinic it had branched off from in 2002. FACE has now opened its facilities to feral cats, allowing Tudor's group to double the number of surgeries it performs every year. "We're already eight hundred cats above last year," she says. When the two groups split, the city's shelters were killing 22,000 cats and dogs a year. Today that number is just 6,000.

Tudor thinks Indianapolis could be a No Kill city in as little as two years. "I'd love to see a day where there's only one cat available for adoption, and everyone wants it," she says. "The fewer cats, the more valued they will be." Such a world would grant cats and dogs—whether they're pets or strays, pampered or abandoned—the most important right of all: the right to life.

It's a vision that keeps Tudor going every day. As I stand off to the side, she flits around the warehouse, cleaning cages, prepping the surgery room, getting meals ready. Then she opens the garage door and sunlight floods in. She's ready to welcome the coming deluge. A few minutes later, a cab pulls up to take me to the airport. I've got one last question for Tudor, about the tattoo on her left arm. It's an Asian proverb, she says. "Don't give up your dream."

As I ride to the airport, I think about Boris again. This creature, once deemed worthless by society and the law, became one of the most treasured animals in our country simply because Lisa Tudor let him inside. In these pages, I've given the impression that cats and dogs have changed dramatically in the millennia since they became domesticated, that with each passing year, they've become more like family, more like people. That's not entirely true. Pets, as Boris shows, have barely changed at all. It is we who have changed. We set them on the path to personhood. We passed laws making them the most valued species in society. We opened the front door.

And that means we decide what happens next.

A New Status

I'm headed east on a Michigan highway somewhere between Grand Rapids and Lansing. Four lanes of asphalt cut a black stripe through the heart of the state's farmland: shaggy jungles of yellow corn, green carpets of soy, vast caramel fields of bending wheat. Signs of human habitation are sparse: a tractor supply store; a faded red barn; a farmhouse with a sagging roof, its slim silver silo glinting in the sun. "If the barns are bigger than the homes, that's a good sign," says the man driving. "That's a farmer who realizes what's important."

My guide is David Favre, sixty-five, wearing a plaid orange shirt and brown work pants. Round glasses rest on an oval face, and his short black hair has begun to gray, receding in front and disappearing on top. He speaks softly, but adamantly—the kind of person who grabs an audience's attention by turning the volume down. Favre (pronounced "favor") has been thinking about the legal status of animals for most of his life. He's one of the foremost experts on the topic, the overseer of the world's largest online collection of animal law articles. And he's thought a lot about cats and dogs. He was one of the first people I called when I began writing this book and the one I most looked forward to meeting.

Favre was born in South Carolina, just a few years after World War II. His dad was a military test pilot who died in a crash. Favre was eleven at the time, with three younger siblings. His mother eventually remarried—to another test pilot—and the family moved to Virginia, where his stepfather sold fighter jets to the air force. Growing up, Favre spent a lot of time outdoors, camping and Boy Scouting. As a teenager he got hooked on science fiction. *Dune* was one of his favorite books. He was taken with the way the environment drove the plot, how the scarcity of water on a desert planet dominated the lives and rituals of its inhabitants. "It showed how important ecosystems are. No one was really thinking about that at the time," he says. "Plus," he laughs, "it was a great read."

Favre entered college in 1964. Nothing really interested him, but he liked science and decided to major in chemistry. Vietnam was still raging when he graduated; rather than wait to be drafted, he enlisted in the army. He served two years but never went to Southeast Asia. "I had a lot of time to think about what I wanted to do with my life," he says. In 1970, while still a private first class, he heard about the first Earth Day. Rallies around the country were to channel the frustrations of a burgeoning environmental movement, protesting everything from factory smoke to the dumping of toxic waste. Favre's degree in chemistry allowed him to understand the impact of pollution as few others did, and he got it into his head to get the army involved. "I wrote a letter to the local commander to see if he would spare a few trucks and cranes to haul garbage from the Colorado River, near where I was stationed," he tells me. "Well, that got some pretty weird looks. My drill sergeant just shook his head."

Favre left the army, and the environmental movement continued to gain steam, but he wasn't interested in joining the demonstrations. "I knew that to really make a difference, I needed to get involved in the legal system," he says. So he enrolled at William and Mary Law School in Williamsburg, Virginia. There, he took the university's first course in environmental law—the textbook, he says, was "just a hodgepodge of newspaper clippings"—and helped found the school's first environmental law student group. He graduated in 1973, got married, and formed an environmental law practice with one of his classmates. "We were going to save the world," he smiles. But saving the world didn't pay the bills, and Favre soon began teaching an extension course in environmental law at a nearby air force base. In 1976, he became a professor at the Detroit College of Law (now the Michigan State University College of Law), where he's been ever since.

Favre was teaching property law and environmental law, but by the late 1970s, he had begun to think beyond the environment. Instead, he began to think about the animals that inhabited it. In 1979, he penned the first law article on wildlife rights, arguing that deer, elephants, and other animals be granted legal personhood. He even proposed a constitutional amendment that would accord these creatures the right to a natural life, free from hunting and human encroachment. (He's since moderated his views. "I was a bit naïve and audacious," he smiles.) Like his letter to the army, the article generated little interest. "It was silence," he says. But it did catch the attention of a small group of lawyers calling itself Attorneys for Animal Rights. In 1981, the group's founder, Joyce

Tischler, invited Favre to the world's first conference on animal law, held in New York City. There, Favre met Tischler, Steven Wise, and a number of other lawyers trying to build a legal movement that would confer more rights to animals. "It was the first time people were starting to talk about this stuff," he says. "What they were saying made sense to me."

Still, Favre maintained his focus on wildlife. While the rest of the group, now called the Animal Legal Defense Fund, focused on pets and farm and research animals, he traveled the world, working to help countries like Malawi and Senegal develop antipoaching laws. He also wrote the first law book on CITES, the Convention on International Trade in Endangered Species, a multilateral treaty designed to protect threatened plants and animals. Favre's interest in wildlife wasn't the only thing that separated him from the rest of ALDF. Although he would serve on the organization's board for more than twenty years, he gradually became disillusioned with the idea of personhood for animals. He wanted to develop his own philosophy of animal rights. He thought he had a better way.

We turn south off the interstate onto a two-lane highway bordered by trees. Crops give way to pastures, and farmhouses become more frequent, connected to civilization by black power lines that regularly branch off the main road. In the distance, white smoke rises from the thin chimney of an ethanol plant; its giant steel tanks tower on the skyline like a small city, converting corn to fuel. Favre points out a factory farm just off the road. He estimates its giant tan warehouses are filled with a half million hens. If it's anything like the worst operations, the animals are packed tight in cramped cages, pumping out egg after egg while trying to avoid being cannibalized by the other birds. "There was a fire in a factory similar to this one that killed 800,000 chickens," he says. "And the quote from the owner was, 'Thank goodness nobody was hurt.' That's typical of the way a lot of people view animals: They aren't beings."

After a few miles, the highway forks off onto a smaller road and we head east again. Farmhouses become bungalows; pastures turn into grassy lawns. Soon we're on Main Street in a town called Vermontville, stretching just a few blocks in either direction. Men saw wood in front yards; clothes hang on lines. Favre gestures to a red-brick structure that looks like a church. "That's the old opera house," he says, built at the turn of the twentieth century. "Your universe could be so small back then and still be cultured." Two of Favre's children went to high school here, but the population has shrunk since then. The grocery has closed down. The young people have moved away. "This place is just barely hanging on," he says.

We exit town, and the farmhouses and pastures reappear. Cows graze in open fields. Favre turns onto a dirt road that rises and falls with the contours of land, sloping down to the nearby Thornapple River. Green fields of alfalfa surround us on all sides. "This is Amish country," he says. Many of his neighbors don't use electricity. "Sometimes you'll see them in carriages driving down this road."

We pull into a curved driveway and park in a circle of gravel. An open shed to our left contains about a hundred bales of hay and a driving lawnmower. To our right is Favre's house, large and L-shaped, sporting light brown vinyl siding and bright white window frames. Sitting by the front door is an old cat: mostly white with some black and brown splotches, he squints his right eye and moves stiffly as we approach, following us inside. "Come on in, Hans," Favre says in a high-pitched voice. The living room is spacious, with high ceilings and a large flat-panel TV. A digital photo frame sits on the kitchen counter, flashing pictures of his family. A radio transmitter on the roof provides the Wi-Fi; a satellite dish, the channels. "The guy down the road doesn't have a phone," he laughs, "but my roof looks like the top of an aircraft carrier." Favre's wife, Marty, stands in the kitchen. She's in her early sixties, wearing jeans and a plaid short-sleeved shirt, and her gray hair is pulled back tightly into a small ponytail. She greets me and leads me to a guestroom upstairs, where I unload my stuff. Favre pokes his head in a few minutes later. "You ready?" he says. He's itching to show me the farm.

Favre's farm sits on one hundred acres, two-thirds of it open field. He purchased the property fifteen years ago; thirty miles west of his university, it ensures that his thinking about animals is more than an academic pursuit. The land spills out in front of us as we walk out the door. Straight ahead, a meadow, bounded by maple and walnut trees on either side, stretches beyond the horizon. The vista behind us is open too, giving Favre and Marty an unobstructed view of every sunrise and sunset. Yellow and orange flowers blossom among rocks and shrubs. Canada

Geese honk overhead, their brown-gray feathers silhouetted against a baby blue sky. Favre takes it all in as if seeing it for the first time. His inner Boy Scout is right at home in this semi-tamed wilderness. "This is all our land, everything you see," he says. "We used to be campers, but we've lost that urge. We live on the best campsite in the world."

The farm hasn't always looked like this. Favre and his wife have spent much of their time here transforming a once barren and weedy place into a pastoral haven. The previous owners had only planted corn, which maximized profits but was terrible for the land. Nothing was growing; there weren't even insects. "It was a desert," Favre says. For the first ten years, he and Marty rotated soybean and wheat to restore nutrients to the soil. "It's taken a lot of time for us to get the earth back to the living thing it's supposed to be." A vegetable garden off to our left is just one of the beneficiaries; thick heads of broccoli burst out of the ground, ripe tomatoes pull on their vines, orange peppers glow in the sunlight. Farther ahead is a pond, encircled by cattails and the gilded petals of marsh marigolds. Goldfish glide beneath the surface; dragonflies buzz over it. A few frogs squat by the water's edge. "When we moved here, this whole thing was nothing but dirt," Favre says. "Now it's an entire ecosystem." I'm reminded of *Dune*.

It wouldn't be a farm, of course, without animals, and there are plenty of them: eighty sheep, thirty chickens, twelve turkeys, and six llamas. Wire fences attached to wood posts checkerboard the land, giving the creatures their own space. Some of the fences date back to the property's inception in the 1860s. They also give the place its name: Fence Row Farm.

We first visit the llamas, hanging out in a large gray barn carpeted with hay. They strike a comical pose with their jutting underbites, bow-legs, and swerved necks. A black male tries to entice a shaggy white female to come over, nibbling at the ground as if he's found something tasty. "He's lying right now," says Favre. "He doesn't have anything for her. It's just like watching teenagers. It's sex and food." Hens peck about for sunflower seeds, some inside the barn, others farther afield, stretching their wings over open grass; they have free range of the property. "*This*," says Favre, drawing a sharp distinction with the factory farm we saw earlier, "is a pretty good life for a chicken."

We walk a dirt path to a tin shed with a slanted roof. Its patio is filled with turkeys that gobble as we approach. Favre opens a surrounding fence and herds the birds out, spreading his arms and nudging them toward open pasture. "Come on, guys!" he says in the same high-pitched voice he used with Hans. The turkeys follow us to a field of alfalfa, pecking at the ground for insects. Here, we run into a few Icelandic sheep, their frizzy mops of wool—chocolate, coffee, vanilla—making them look a bit like dirigibles with horns. "This is Misty; this is Nancy," Favre says. "Over there, that's one of our prize winners. She's one of our really smart ones." He invites me to come over and touch one of the dark-brown ewes. I run my hands across her coarse outer coat and burrow them into the soft fur underneath. "It's OK," Favre coos in the animal's ear. She wags her tail.

It was a conversation with one of these creatures that led Favre to reject one of the more extreme animal rights positions—the one espoused by Gary Francione and others that it's better for animals not to exist than to live as someone's property. In an essay he penned in 2005, Favre imagines chatting with a black ram named Jet. He asks the animal if he feels oppressed. The sheep responds that if anyone's oppressed, it's Favre and Marty, who haul water, build shelters, and plant new pastures, all for his sake. "All we do is eat, drink, chew our cud, and watch the girls," Jet says. "I like our life." Then Favre presses further, asking the ram if he objects to being property, if he'd rather not exist than be owned by someone. "You're kidding me, right?" snorts Jet. "Just because you have psychological issues doesn't mean I don't appreciate being alive."

We end our tour in a vast field of goldenrod. A breeze ripples through the tall stalks with their lemon tips, sending yellow waves crashing into a sea of green. I say it's beautiful, but Favre seems frustrated. He and Marty have created an Eden on this farm, forging a balance between humans and nature and of nature with itself. Wi-Fi fills the house; geothermal heat warms it. Electric fences keep coyotes out; yet Favre refuses to allow hunters to shoot them on his land. The sheep rotate from pasture to pasture so they don't overgraze, but they're kept out of places where wild birds are nesting. Each being is respected, and its interests are balanced against those of everyone else. The farm is a microcosm of what Favre would like to see in society as a whole. Today, however, in this field, the wild is overstepping its bounds. The goldenrod, an invasive species, is choking out the crops Favre has planted. But his sour mood doesn't last long. In the distance, we spot a pair of deer bounding across the field and into the woods beyond. Favre's smile returns.

As we make our way back to the house, we shed nature with every acre. We leave the deer and wild plants behind, then the domesticated farm animals, until finally we come upon Hans, waiting for us at the front door. Next to him, behind a white porch gate, stand two Great Pyrenees, fluffy white giants of dogs weighing in at one hundred pounds each. Of all the creatures we've seen, these three are the most prized. Their fur can't be sold, and their meat can't be eaten, but they have a value above all else. They are family. We have returned to civilization.

After the farm tour, Favre and I settle into his living room—he on a plaid recliner, me on a cushy brown couch—and Marty brings out veggies and dip from the kitchen. Hans croaks a meow at Favre's feet, and he picks the cat up and places him on his lap, stroking him as tufts of white fur waft into the air. He's one of four felines the couple owns, most abandoned nearby. "Anybody who lives in the country winds up with extra pets," Favre says. "People can't be bothered to neuter them."

As we chat, Favre begins to unspool his philosophy of animal rights. Life on the farm has given him a unique perspective on the topic. His Eden, it turns out, is not the one many animal advocates would envision. Here, humans are not on the same plane as earth's creatures—they are decidedly above it. "Some animal rights advocates say that we're all equal; that we shouldn't use animals because that's exploitation," he says. "I think the world is more complex than that."

Take eating meat. In a world of vegan bumper stickers and veggie conferences, Favre stands out. The chickens, the turkeys, even the sheep we met earlier—many will end up on his dinner plate. Favre may respect them as individuals, but he also respects them as food. It wasn't always so. When he and Marty first began populating the farm, they had no intention of consuming its inhabitants. Marty originally got the sheep as a hobby; she wanted to make things with wool and thought it would be fun to raise them. But one day about ten years ago, when Favre was away at an animal law conference in New Zealand, she noticed that one of the ram's horns had grown so close to his face that it was cutting into his skin. September was approaching, a prime time for "fly strike," when the insects lay their eggs inside infected tissue and the maggots eat the animal alive. "We could have had him put down by a vet, but there were eighty pounds of meat that would have gone to waste," says Marty. "That seemed disrespectful." Still, "that first bite was tough," she admits. "It was a gourmet treat!" pipes Favre.

It soon became clear that fly strike wasn't the only problem. Too many roosters led to violent cockfights; old sheep lost their teeth and became crippled with arthritis. "In the pet world, you keep the animal alive; you treat it like a human," says Favre. "But the farm experience brought me to a different place. Here, you're in the natural world. And guess what? Not everybody gets to live to eighty. The important thing is that they live well and that their death is as humane as possible."

For Favre it all boils down to something he calls "respectful use." Animals should be allowed to exercise the full capacity of their being. Sheep should graze; chickens should spread their wings. At the same time, we can use these creatures as long as we balance their interests with ours. When it comes to farm animals, that balance frequently tips in our favor. But we've given pets far more leeway. It's not enough that they be pampered. They also have many more rights than other animals: the right to be free from abuse, the right to go to a good home in a custody battle, the right to life. Favre goes beyond that, respecting the very essence of our companion animals' "doghood" and "cathood." Dogs should have jobs, for example; his Great Pyrenees patrol the farm at night, protecting livestock from predators. Terriers should run. Bloodhounds should track. (He's not a fan of teacup poodles, canines whose only function seems to be serving as fashion accessories.) Cats, meanwhile, should be allowed to hunt—even if that means infringing on the rights of other animals. "We see dead rats from time to time," he says. "As far as I'm concerned, that's the balance of nature." Every year, we respect our pets more. We put more stock in their interests, their rights. Yet Favre doesn't think we should turn them into people. He has something better in mind.

That conversation is going to have to wait until tomorrow. The sun is setting. Favre picks Hans up off his lap and places him gingerly on the floor. Then we head outside again. White clouds have turned lavender, and the first stars are beginning to prick the darkening sky. Favre corrals the sheep and turkeys back into their enclosures and latches the gates for the night. It turns out he's putting on a bit of a show for me. Marty's the one who usually does all of the farmwork. She rises at dawn, making the rounds to the various pens, spreading seed, herding the sheep, cutting hay with the tractor, and, when the need arises, delivering newborn lambs. Favre, consumed with his academic work, tends mostly to the pets.

We head back inside, where Marty has prepared a generous dinner of potatoes, beans, and, yes, lamb chops. She says grace, and we all close our eyes. I've finally grown accustomed to the tranquility of the place, a city boy comfortably out of his element. Then we hear the unmistakable sound of hunters in the distance. Gunshots pop in the night. "Well," I say, "at least that's one thing you guys have in common with Baltimore."

The next morning I rise at the humane hour of 8:00 a.m. I'm awakened not by the crowing of roosters but rather by the barking of dogs. Today, it seems, will be all about pets. I meander down to the kitchen, where Marty has set out tea, scones, and fresh cantaloupe. When we've finished eating, Favre and I take the crumbs outside. The sky is a clear blue dome, and the treetops dissolve in bright sunlight. We enter a chicken coop he and Marty have converted from an old corncrib and dump the leftovers on the floor; the hens and roosters come flapping. Nothing on the farm is wasted. Marty walks past us on her way to let the sheep out.

We trek across a grass field, the blades still damp with dew, and take a seat on a pile of rocks nestled in a grove of walnut trees. Favre picks up where he left off the night before. His new thinking on the status of animals begins with a radical notion—radical at least among his peers: domestic animals should remain property. The designation, he says, isn't as regressive as it seems. For one, "property" implies an owner, someone responsible for the animal's well-being. "Think about Hans," he says. "If I free him from his status of property, where's he going to go? Who's going to look out for him? These animals depend on us for their care. I don't want to lose that." Without owners, pets are no better off than wildlife—or feral cats. Favre also notes that a lot has been accomplished within the property status, felony anticruelty laws being his favorite example. "You can still have rights without personhood," he says. "That was my intellectual breakpoint with everyone else. Some people say property can't have rights. Why? We make the law. There's nothing that says we can't do that."

Still, Favre isn't entirely comfortable with the word "property" alone, seeing as it also applies to toasters. So he's proposed a new legal status: living property. Think of it as a middle ground between property and personhood, an evolution rather than a revolution. The great thing about the term, he says, is that it gives lawmakers a clean slate. Rather than binding us to traditional definitions, "it will mean what we want it to mean. We can pour into it whatever rights we wish."

In a sense, we've been doing this for decades. We've taken two species of animal that are technically property and upgraded them with rights that should only be available to people. Cats and dogs have already blurred the line between property and person; Favre has just given it a name. He'd like to pour a few more rights in, however. He wants to see an end to the commercial sale of pets, for example. He doesn't think profit should enter into our relationship with beings that become our family members. Dogs and cats would only be gifted or adopted, and they would only go to stable homes, free of abuse. Speaking of abuse, though Favre is fond of current anticruelty laws, he doesn't think they are well enforced. When someone hurts a person, the government can go after the perpetrator, and the person himself can sue in court. Pets don't have this latter option; Favre says if they did, a lot more cruelty would be prosecuted, and a lot more cats and dogs would be removed from bad homes. A local humane society, perhaps now freed from the taxing work of animal control, could represent animals in court and provide a safe haven for them. Favre even thinks pets should be able to earn their own money, whether it be from a court settlement or a dog show. Thanks to the Uniform Trust Code, this is now possible.

Still, like any citizen, pets wouldn't have rights without responsibilities. A dog that sued could also be sued—and the money deducted from the same trust. "If you're in the system, you have to be in the system for more than one thing," says Favre. "It's only fair." One arena this might play out in is a dog bite case, in which a victim could file for monetary damages rather than seeking the death of the animal, assuming that animal had its own money. And as part of their responsibilities as fellow citizens, cats and dogs would have to "consent" to being neutered. Just like humans can't go around stealing without repercussion, pets can't breed out of control and expect society to clean up the mess. It's like life on the farm: everyone's interests must be balanced against those of everyone else.

Favre acknowledges that granting dogs and cats these extra rights will necessarily impinge on the rights of humans. A dog can't sue without a person being sued. A humane organization that takes your cat away weakens your property rights. But that's the way society has always advanced, he says. When blacks and women got more rights, they diluted the rights of those in power. Plantation owners lost their cheap labor; the white male vote counted less. Ultimately, however, the public decides that these sacrifices are worth it. Favre thinks it will be the same with pets. True, allowing cats and dogs into our inner circle will be a paradigm shift like no other. Citizenship has always been limited to human beings; admitting pets would break the species barrier for the first time in history. But as we consider changing the status of dogs and cats, we also consider what it means to be a person and what it means to be valued by society. And eventually, as we have in the past, we become better people. "It broadens the set of beings we have to show respect for," says Favre, "and that is a civilizing process."

I tell Favre that a lot of this—the adoption, the courtroom advocates, the granting of qualified rights and responsibilities—reminds me of our relationship with children. "It's a useful analogy," he smiles. "A child is legally recognized as a being, even though parents have a lot of leeway in how they exercise their responsibility. And if they fail, the court can step in and take the child away."

Indeed, the parallels between the rise of pets and the rise of children are uncanny. In the early nineteenth century, children were essentially the property of their parents. What few laws prevented them from abuse in the home or overwork in the factory were not enforced. A child's value at the time wasn't sentimental but rather market based, measured in terms of the income he or she brought home. A half century later, the Victorian era's culture of sentimentality sparked a social revolution, and reformers rose up to protect this most vulnerable segment of society. Foremost among them was a wealthy Manhattan socialite who helped create the world's first child protective agency—the New York Society for the Prevention of Cruelty to Children—less than a decade after he established something similar for animals. His name was Henry Bergh.

By the early twentieth century, judges had begun awarding noneconomic damages for mental pain and suffering and loss of companionship to the parents of slain children. Soon children would even have their own legal representation in court.

We've been treating cats and dogs like children for years. Favre just wants to formalize it. A new status for pets has been staring us in the face all along.

Favre and I get up after an hour of talking. My butt is sore, and my brain is full. He's promised to let me drive his tractor, and I take him up on it before I leave. The orange beast sits on a grassy hill next to a maple whose leaves have begun to turn yellow and red. A ewe follows us, a strand of alfalfa hanging from her mouth. Chickens cluck by in the distance. Whether or not Favre changes society, he's found his utopia here on this farm. He's created the world he wants to live in. As I climb aboard the tractor, I ask him how long he and Marty plan on staying here. "As long as we can," he says, wistfully surveying the landscape. "We have no interest in leaving."

The End of the Beginning

It's been a couple of months since I took my last trip for this book. I'm at home, going over my notes, revisiting the 10,000-year-old village of Shillourokambos. It was here, on the southern coast of the Mediterranean island of Cyprus, that early farmers stored grain in stone silos and kept livestock behind wood fences. It was also here that a French archaeologist named Jean-Denis Vigne made a surprising discovery. Digging beneath the foundation of an ancient home in 2001, he uncovered a shallow grave containing the skeleton of a human in the fetal position—and next to it, the remains of a young feline. The animal likely descended from creatures shipped to the village to combat rodents that had invaded its crops. And so began the domestication of the cat.

I'm struck by something Vigne told me: that the villagers of Shillourokambos had shipped in foxes for the same purpose. And yet only the cat became a pet. How is it that we've welcomed only cats and dogs as family members? The odds were certainly against them. There are millions of animals on earth, thousands of mammals, dozens of domesticates.

And yet we've embraced just two as part of our tribe. Were they the most adaptable of the bunch? Were they in the right place at the right time? Or were they just the only two animals willing to stick with us as we alternately deified and demonized them? Perhaps we were waiting for them, and they for us. Perhaps it was destiny.

David Favre spoke about dogs and cats civilizing us. I think that's true. We're a more humane society than we've ever been, more concerned about the plight of all creatures, whether they live on a factory farm or in our homes. In 2009, a Washington, DC, lawmaker considered making it illegal to kill rabbits, bats, and other wildlife, protecting them with the same laws that safeguard pets. In 2012, Southwest Airlines flew a late-blooming monarch butterfly across the country so it could reunite with its migrating companions. "Pets are the cutting edge," Favre told me. "They have the political muscle to make things change for all animals." And not just animals in the United States: China is embracing cats and dogs as companions in large numbers for the first time. India is home to the world's fastest-growing pet population. Where will these countries be in fifty years?

As much as pets have civilized us, however, I think they've also kept us wild. Of all the roles they play, the most important may be that of shaman. Instead of bridging the gap between our world and the spirit world, they serve as mediators between our asphalt jungle and the real one. All pets are a bit like feral cats, straddling the line between wild and domestic, person and beast. And because they can cross this boundary, they serve as a lifeline—perhaps the last lifeline—to our animal past. We don't just need them to comfort and play with us. We need them to remind us of who we are and where we came from. When we turn cats and dogs into people, we lose the animal part of ourselves. Is that something we're prepared to do?

I put down my notes and walk out my back door. It's a warm Sunday afternoon; the sun is high, and a slight breeze rustles the trees. I cross my yard, open the gate, and step out to the parking lot beyond. The mockingbirds are squawking, and I soon see why. Perched below them, at the base of a young oak tree, is Jasper. They're in little danger; he's yet to do more than chatter at them. He spots me and saunters over, rubbing against my leg and sitting at my feet. We both stare off into the distance. He wants to be out in the world, but he also wants to be here with me. I know I won't have him forever, but I have him now. So here we stand, two species drawn together over millennia, bonded by love and law. Who knows what the future will bring. For now, he has me, and I have him. My pet. My friend. My family.

Epilogue

O ne of the many highlights of writing this book was my visit with the Los Angeles Animal Cruelty Task Force, and not just because I got to hang out with a detective and a deputy district attorney. After a long day of canvassing crime scenes and scoping out the homes of suspected animal abusers, I collapsed onto my bed at a downtown hotel. The phone rang. It was my wife. She told me she was pregnant—with twins. I was overjoyed by the news; yet it forced me to confront a new mystery. I had been traveling the country to figure out how pets had become such an integral part of our families. Now I began to wonder how stable our relationship with cats and dogs really is. Do we stop treating our pets like fur babies once we give birth to human ones?

I worried that might be the case. Most of the animal advocates I met didn't have children. They had dedicated their lives to saving abused, orphaned, and maligned pets because they were especially close to their own pets. And I suspected they were especially close to their own pets because these animals *were* their kids. As Baltimore pit bull owner Jenine Gangi told me, "I'm fighting for my children and other people's children." What would happen if actual children entered the picture?

For me, the question is no longer hypothetical. Amelia and Juliet arrived in October 2012. Our cats—twins themselves—weren't sure what to make of the new additions. Jezebel sniffed them and then slunk down to the basement, where she moped for the better part of three months. Jasper was more understanding; he slept with them in their cribs on a few occasions and was especially drawn to them when they cried. Both cats know they're no longer the center of our attention. We spend less time with them, and they have two new competitors for our laps. But we've found plenty of room in our hearts for everyone. Jezebel still gets her nightly petting sessions. Jasper still gets his expensive kidney-friendly diet and yearly ultrasounds. We continue to take their pictures, call to ask about them when we go away, and spoil them rotten. They are, as they have always been, family. And that family is here to stay.

The tough part about completing a journey is that you begin to miss all the people you met along the way. I didn't have the time or money to make any return trips, so before this book went to publication, I called up everyone I visited for one final chat. It turns out my life isn't the only one that has changed.

Mietje Germonpré, who rediscovered the skull of what may be one of the earliest dogs, tells me that the field of canine domestication remains contentious. Experts continue to spar over just how, when, and where dogs first arose. Scientists, she says, are currently examining the DNA of ancient wolf bones in hopes of solving these mysteries once and for all. On the feline front, Carlos Driscoll, having settled the question of where cats came from, has moved on to figuring out how they became cats in the first place. Unlike dogs, whose appearance has changed dramatically since they descended from gray wolves, cats have mainly undergone a personality adjustment. Driscoll says he plans to set up an experiment akin to the one with the Siberian foxes, taming wildcats over many generations to get at the genes behind this personality shift—genes that could shed light on human maladies like depression and obsessive compulsive disorder.

Brian Hare is still a very busy man. In 2013 he took his studies at the Duke Canine Cognition Center global, cofounding a company called Dognition that allows owners to use online games and surveys to reveal the mental talents of their pups. The results feed into his current research, and he hopes the work—detailed in his new book, *The Genius of Dogs*—will help handlers better select and train seeing-eye dogs and military working dogs. He says more scientists are studying the canine mind than ever. One of the veterans, Marc Bekoff, tells me that some new observations he's made about how dogs play may help reveal the roots of reciprocity in humans. He's just finished his twenty-fifth book, *Why Dogs Hump and Bees Get Depressed*, which provides further insights into the emotional lives of all animals. And every week, he drives to the Boulder County Jail to teach his class. A couple of the inmates have gone on to work with animals after getting out; one is volunteering at a local humane society.

It took me two weeks to get Charlotte Bass Lilly on the phone. She remains as overcommitted as ever, working tirelessly to save the homeless pets of New Orleans. She's begun a fund-raising campaign to build a new shelter, more inviting and environmentally friendly than Animal Rescue New Orleans's current digs. Ginnie Baumann-Robilotta is still there, casting about for supplies and donations and keeping her feeding stations full. Meanwhile, Tana Barth has finally moved back into her former home, eight years after Katrina gutted it. The city, says Charlotte, is coming back to life, slowly but surely. Lisa Tudor's own pet rescue operation has also stayed in high gear. She estimates that thanks to the work of IndyFeral and the Foundation Against Companion-Animal Euthanasia, fewer than 5,000 cats and dogs will be euthanized in Indianapolis in 2013. She's convinced the city to modify its trap-neuter-return ordinance to allow her group to take more cats from the city's municipal shelter and return them outdoors, a move that could reduce euthanasia rates by half. She's also helping other counties to set up their own TNR programs and ordinances. Boris, she says, is doing well. To donate to either ARNO (animalrescueneworleans.org) or IndyFeral (indyferal.org), visit their websites.

Hector Sanchez remains "100 percent committed" to the LAPD's Animal Cruelty Task Force. He says the unit has the full support of the public, and he expects it to become a permanent fixture of the police department. He also notes that his officers are starting to use more cutting-edge techniques, like hair matching and DNA analysis, to track down animal abusers. Debbie Knaan still runs the Animal Cruelty Prosecution Program of the Los Angeles County District Attorney's Office. She's hoping to get a law passed that would mandate animal cruelty training for every cop in the state. The dog beheading case remains unsolved.

The animal law movement continues to grow. Joyce Tischler says that more law schools have added student chapters of the Animal Legal Defense Fund, and her organization's staff and pro bono network have expanded. "We're now doing five times as much litigation as we were ten years ago," she tells me. ALDF is currently trying to get other states to pass a version of the statute that allowed it to prosecute an animal hoarder in North Carolina. A painted portrait of Edgar, the Boston terrier Tischler rescued from that case, hangs in her bedroom.

Things have been mixed for pit bulls. The Maryland legislature made two attempts to effectively overturn the *Tracey v. Solesky* high court decision that labeled the breed "inherently dangerous," but lawmakers were unable to agree on a final bill. As a result, Jenine Gangi still fears that Armistead Gardens will evict her for owning Tank Girl and Baby Girl. Pauline Houliaras is trying to make sure that doesn't happen by reaching out to landlords and pressuring politicians. Her group, B-More Dog, still leads a pit bull march around Baltimore's Inner Harbor every month. Meanwhile, Kno, the pit bull put on trial in Georgia, was spared lethal injection when his lawyer was able to convince the court to move him to a New York animal sanctuary. As per the judge's ruling, the dog— who spent thirteen months in a shelter—must never be adopted, and he must be kept away from cats and children.

Lisa Phillips says her adopted military working dog, Rambo, is doing "fantastic." He just got fitted with a prosthetic leg and is learning to use it. She has started a new organization called Gizmo's Gift. Named after the first canine soldier she rescued, the group will help care for retired military dogs, as well as retired police dogs, airport security dogs, and border patrol dogs. She continues to push for legislation that would reclassify military working dogs as "canine members of the armed forces" instead of "equipment." Bill and Margaret Edwards are still bringing their therapy cats to nursing homes and Veterans Administration hospitals throughout New Jersey. Bill says they have begun teaching others to train their own cats to bring a "special joy" into the lives of the elderly and handicapped.

The American Veterinary Medical Association, the National Association for Biomedical Research, and various other animal-related industries continue to fight the pet personhood movement. Douglas Aspros is no longer the president of the AVMA, but he says he's as committed as ever to policy work. He's particularly interested in getting more women into leadership roles in the field. Gary Francione remains a thorn in the side of the animal law and animal rights movements. He's written a new book, *Eat Like You Care*, with his partner, Anna Charlton, which is packed with arguments about why readers should become vegan. The couple has added an additional dog to their pack, Duncan, a small black cockapoo found half starved on the streets of Newark. "He's our new member of the family," Francione says.

David Favre is consolidating all of his thoughts about the legal status of animals into a book, which he hopes to publish in the next couple of years. He's also organizing an international conference to explore how animals develop rights in other countries. The farm is treating him well. He and Marty have added a few more turkeys, and one of their sheep just took "Best in Show" at a local fiber festival. Eventually, he says, they'll scale back on the number of animals they care for—but they're not leaving anytime soon. Hans the cat is twelve years old now and feeling it; he spends most of his time indoors. A new feline showed up a couple of months ago. Favre and his wife have named him Zig (for a white zigzag pattern on his back), but they're still debating whether he'll be a barn or house cat. In the eyes of society, the outcome will make a world of difference.

A Brief History of Cats and Dogs

30,000 BC The earliest potential evidence for dog domestication, based on the skull of a wolflike canine, found in Goyet Cave in southern Belgium. Other evidence suggests dogs may have been domesticated thousands of years later.

10,000 BC An elderly human in Ain Mallaha in northern Israel is buried cradling a four-month-old puppy.

7500 BC A cat is buried with a human in a Neolithic village known as Shillourokambos on the southern coast of the Mediterranean island of Cyprus.

1950 BC Cats begin to appear in the art of ancient Egypt.

AD 200 Dogs are buried in Roman cemeteries with sentimental gravestones.

1233 Pope Gregory IX issues his *Vox in Rama*, which links felines to Satan and leads to the massacre of tens of millions of cats throughout Europe.

1500 Dogs begin to feature in scenes of domestic life in Renaissance art.

1637 René Descartes declares that animals are soulless machines, a doctrine that helps justify dog vivisection.

1822 The United Kingdom passes the first serious animal welfare law. Two years later, the world's first animal welfare organization, the Royal Society for the Prevention of Cruelty to Animals, is founded.

1866 Henry Bergh founds the American Society for the Prevention of Cruelty to Animals, America's first animal protection organization.

1880s Early flea and tick products begin to bring dogs indoors.

1893	Margaret Marshall Saunders pens *Beautiful Joe*, the "autobiography" of an abused dog who finds a loving home, one of the first told from a pet's perspective.
1894	A Baltimore judge rules that a cat is not property and thus can be stolen without repercussion.
1907	The vivisection of a dog at a London medical school sparks the Brown Dog Riots.
1929	The Seeing Eye, the first American guide dog school, is founded, ushering in an era of pets as assistance animals.
1942	Dogs for Defense begins training canines to go to war.
1947	Kitty litter is invented, helping turn cats into indoor pets.
1954	The Humane Society of the United States is founded.
1964	The Florida Supreme Court rules that pets are worth more than their market value.
1975	Peter Singer's *Animal Liberation* helps launch the modern animal rights movement.
1979	The Animal Legal Defense Fund is founded and campaigns for the rights of cats, dogs, and other animals in the legal system.
1990	The Americans with Disabilities Act requires hotels, restaurants, and other businesses to admit service animals, even if customers have allergies to or a fear of dogs.
1993	A wave of states begins adopting felony anticruelty laws; today, forty-nine states have such legislation.
1994	San Francisco ends the euthanasia of healthy dogs and cats in its three shelters, sparking the No Kill movement.
1998	Ádám Miklósi and Brian Hare publish studies showing that dogs can understand human pointing, an ability not seen in chimpanzees. The work prompts several more labs to begin studying the canine mind.
2000	Stanley and Linda Perkins's legal battle over their dog, Gigi, becomes one of the most expensive pet custody battles in US history.
2000	Boulder, Colorado, becomes the first city to use the term "guardian," in addition to or instead of "owner," in its pet-related ordinances. Nineteen other cities and one state follow suit.
2000	The Uniform Trust Code allows owners to leave money to their companion animals after they die.

2004   The largest veterinary malpractice damages in US history are awarded: $39,000 for the death of a dog.

2009   Suffolk County, New York, creates America's first animal abuser registry.

2012   The Maryland Court of Appeals rules that pit bulls are "inherently dangerous."

2013   Lackland Air Force Base unveils the US Military Working Dog Teams National Monument to honor the service of canine soldiers.

Acknowledgments

They say if you're going to write a book, write about something you enjoy. I've been fortunate to do that. I've also been fortunate to have the help of a lot of talented people.

First, I want to thank PublicAffairs for taking a chance on a different kind of pet book. I particularly want to thank Brandon Proia, for shepherding the book through its early stages and for his support and encouragement, and Ben Adams, who guided me the rest of the way and helped make a good book even better with his patience and perceptive edits. My agent, Jim Hornfischer, is the reason I got to work with Brandon and Ben at all; he believed in my idea from the beginning and helped shape my proposal until it was everything I hoped it could be.

If you enjoyed a historical anecdote in this book, chances are my stellar research assistant, Charlotte Stenberg, helped dig it up. The countless hours she spent in the library and in front of the computer helped guide me through thousands of years of human history and seemingly just as many languages. Without her, this book would have taken twice as long to write and would have been half as fun to read. I also want to thank two other researchers, Celia Turner and Margaret Fraser, who assisted with a variety of smaller projects.

I owe a huge debt to my mentor and former boss at *Science*, Colin Norman, who took time out of his retirement to read my book in full and offer incredibly helpful edits. I'm also grateful to a couple of other *Science* colleagues. Martyn Green helped set up my website (www.davidhgrimm. com) and keeps it running and looking beautiful, and Eli Kintisch provided advice and encouragement throughout the writing of this book.

I visited a lot of people for this book, and I'm indebted to everyone mentioned in its chapters, who gave so generously of their time. I also spoke to a lot of people not mentioned, who assisted with a wealth of background information. I'm especially thankful to David Favre, who, in addition to being a featured player, answered every one of my count-less e-mails and phone calls over the years.

I consulted several people about the history of cats and dogs. Don-ald Engels guided me through the rise and fall of cats in antiquity and reviewed my writing on the topic. Greger Larson assisted with technical advice on dog domestication and reviewed the relevant chapter. I also want to thank Robert Losey, Angela Perri, Juliet Clutton-Brock, Jen-nifer Leonard, Anna Kukekova, Phillip Howell, Salima Ikram, Ádám Miklósi, Robert Wayne, Lyudmilla Trut, Katherine Grier, Linda Kalof, Owen Lourie, Holly Jaycox, and Brian Casey.

Facts and figures regarding the current status of pets in society came from many folks. Stephen Zawistowski and Bernard Unti fielded numer-ous questions on the rise of the animal welfare movement and a variety of related issues. Also lending a hand were Randall Lockwood, Andrew Rowan, Rebecca Goldrick, David Kirkpatrick, Dennis Turner, James Serpell, Heather Case, John Bradshaw, and Merritt Clifton.

Law is not my specialty, and a number of people guided me through some very tricky concepts. Bruce Wagman helped me out immensely with tort law concepts and reviewed my chapter on the history of pets in the courtroom. I also had a lot of assistance from Adam Karp, Geordie Duckler, and Rebecca Huss. Other legal experts I consulted include Nancy Perry, Randy Turner, Paul Neuman, Renee Poirrier, Steve Ann Chambers, Steven Wise, Theresa Macellaro, Kristina Hancock, Barbara Gislason, Heidi Groff, Marcy LaHart, and Heidi Meinzer.

Help with the rise of the animal law movement and its current campaigns came from a number of sources, including Stephan Otto, Matthew Liebman, Pamela Frasch, Carter Dillard, Scott Heiser, Nicole Palotta, Lisa Franzetta, and Lise Harwin. I'm especially grateful to Chris Green, who provided an enormous amount of information on veterinary malpractice, animal-related legislation, and a variety of other topics.

A few individuals aided my research into the new roles and respon-sibilities of pets in society. Collen McGee helped arrange my visit to

Lackland Air Force Base. Karen Delise provided valuable historical information on pit bulls. Bill Kueser put me in touch with Bill and Margaret Edwards. Adam Kobek arranged my visit with Kno the pit bull, and David Ehsanipoor provided some background information on the case. In addition, Caroline Griffin assisted with information on animal-related issues in Baltimore.

I am indebted to Richard Cupp for giving me the lay of the land regarding the backlash against pet personhood. Also providing assistance were Adrian Hochstadt and Joan Miller.

Becky Robinson of Alley Cat Allies sent me useful information about feral cats and the No Kill shelter movement, as did Nathan Winograd. Laura Nirenberg helped me out with legal information regarding the status of these animals.

Thanks to my mom, Fern Rice, for helping to get me my first job at a veterinary clinic, and to her and the rest of my family, including my dad, Robert Rice, and brother, Jeff Grimm, for always believing in me. Thanks also to my in-laws, Susan and Herb Duffield, whose regular visits to our house to watch the kids allowed me to work overtime in the basement.

Lastly, I want to thank my wife, Amy Duffield, who first suggested I write a book—and then spent the next four years regretting it. A dedication alone doesn't come close to doing justice to everything she did to make all of this possible, from making sharp edits to putting up with my frequently insane travel schedule. Her help, love, and support are quite simply the reason this book exists.

Further Reading

I read a lot of books to write this one, but I found the following particularly helpful. I would highly recommend them to anyone interested in more information on these topics.

Anderson, Allen, and Linda C. Anderson. *Rescued—Saving Animals from Disaster: Life-Changing Stories and Practical Suggestions.* Novato, CA: New World Library, 2006. Fascinating tales from the animal rescue efforts in the aftermath of Hurricane Katrina.

Beers, Diane L. *For the Prevention of Cruelty: The History and Legacy of Animal Rights Activism in the United States.* Athens: Swallow Press/Ohio University Press, 2006. The most informative book I've read on the rise of the American animal welfare and animal rights movements.

Engels, Donald W. *Classical Cats: The Rise and Fall of the Sacred Cat.* London: Routledge, 1999. Wonderful history of cats in antiquity; lots of great information on Pope Gregory IX and his screed against cats.

Grier, Katherine C. *Pets in America: A History.* Chapel Hill: University of North Carolina Press, 2006. A fascinating look at the rise of dogs and cats (and other pets) in the United States; worth it for the pictures alone.

Jones, Susan D. *Valuing Animals: Veterinarians and Their Patients in Modern America.* Animals, History, Culture Series. Baltimore: Johns Hopkins University Press, 2003. Highly informative history of the veterinary profession in the United States.

Kalof, Linda. *Looking at Animals in Human History.* London: Reaktion Books, 2007. A look at our changing relationship with a variety of animals in antiquity and beyond.

Lemish, Michael G. *War Dogs: A History of Loyalty and Heroism.* 1st pbk. ed. Washington, DC: Brassey's, 1999. A fascinating history of canines in combat.

Podberscek, Anthony L., Elizabeth S. Paul, and James Serpell. *Companion Animals and Us: Exploring the Relationships Between People and Pets.* Cambridge: Cambridge University Press, 2000. On the treatment of pets in ancient and modern cultures.

Shiley, Mike, dir. *Dark Water Rising: The Truth About Hurricane Katrina Animal Rescues.* Shidog Films, 2006. The most informative and harrowing film I've seen on the pet rescue operations in the aftermath of Hurricane Katrina; not for the faint of heart.

Sources

Introduction

The section on Alex the dog is drawn from Lawrence Buser, "Dog, 13, Focus of Custody Dispute," *Commercial Appeal*, May 7, 2007; Lawrence Buser, "Parents to Share Deceased Son's Dog—Court Now Shifts Focus to Man's $2 Million Estate," *Commercial Appeal*, May 8, 2007; Stephanie Francis Ward, "Canine Case Is Doggone Tough: Tennessee Lawyer Is Guardian to Pet Caught in a Custody Battle," ABA *Journal eReport*, May 18, 2007; court records.

Chapter 1: The Pet Republic

Information on St. Francis of Assisi and Blessing of the Animals ceremonies is drawn from Marc Bekoff, *Encyclopedia of Animal Rights and Animal Welfare* (Santa Barbara, CA: Greenwood Press, 2010); J. Baird Callicott and Robert Frodeman, *Encyclopedia of Environmental Ethics and Philosophy* (Detroit: Macmillan Reference USA, 2009); Isadora Wilkenfeld, coordinator of cathedral programming and communications, Cathedral of St. John the Divine, personal communication; Kathleen Walker-Meikle, *Medieval Pets* (Rochester, NY: Boydell Press, 2012).

The section on pet-related statistics is drawn from the following sources: American Veterinary Medical Association, "U.S. Pet Ownership Demographics Sourcebook (2012)," https://www.avma.org/KB/Resources/Statistics /Pages/Market-research-statistics-US-Pet-Ownership-Demographics -Sourcebook.aspx; American Pet Products Association, "Pet Industry Market Size & Ownership Statistics," http://www.americanpetproducts.org/press _industrytrends.asp; Jonathan Berr, "Pet Ownership Falls in Hard Times," *MSN Money*, November 14, 2012; "The Harris Poll #70, June 10, 2011,"

www.harrisinteractive.com/NewsRoom/HarrisPolls/tabid/447/ctl/Read
Custom%20Default/mid/1508/ArticleId/814/Default.aspx; Cindy Hall and
Bob Laird, "Risking It All for Fido," *USA Today*, June 24, 1999; James A.
Serpell and Elizabeth S. Paul, "Pets in the Family: An Evolutionary Perspec-
tive," in *The Oxford Handbook of Evolutionary Family Psychology*, Catherine
Salmon and Todd K. Shackelford. Oxford Library of Psychology (New York:
Oxford University Press, 2011), xvii; 11th annual American Animal Hospi-
tal Association Survey (https://www.aahanet.org/Library/PetOwnerSurvey
.aspx); 2013/2014 American Pet Products Manufacturers Association Pet
Owner Survey (http://www.americanpetproducts.org/pubs_survey.asp); Tim
Devaney, "Perks on Rise for Pet Owners," *Washington Times*, November 12,
2009; "Fortune 500 Firms Offer Pet Insurance," *Investor's Business Daily*,
September 23, 2013; Paul Mann, "How the Rich Pamper Their Pets," *Forbes*,
January 15, 2008.

Chapter 2: Wolves and Wildcats

The passages on Edouard Dupont and the Goyet Cave are based on Francois
Stockmans, *Notice sur* Édouard *François Dupont* (Bruxelles: Académie Royale
de Belgique, 1965); François Stockmans, "Dupont, (Édouard-François)," in *Bi-
ographie Nationale*, t. 37 (Bruxelles : Établissements Émile Bruylant, 1971), col.
255–261; Edouard Dupont, *Les temps préhistoriques en Belgique. L'homme pen-
dant les âges de la pierre dans les environs de Dinant-sur-Meuse* (Baillaire, 1872);
*Bulletins de l'Academie Royale des Sciences, des Lettres, et des Beaux-Arts de Bel-
gique* (Bruxelles: Academie Royale de Belgique, March 1869); Michel Tous-
saint, "Un couteau aménagé dans un radius humain protohistorique découvert
aux grottes de Goyet (Gesves, province de Namur, Belgique)," *Bulletin de la
Société Préhistorique Française* 102, no. 3 (2005): 625–637; Michel Tossiant,
Angelika Becker, and Philippe Lacroix, "Recherches 1997–1998 aux grottes
de Goyet a Gesves, province de Namur," *Natae Praehistoricae* 18 (1998):
33–44; "Obituary: Edouard Francois Dupont," *Geological Magazine* 8 (June
1911); M. Germonpré et al., "Fossil Dogs and Wolves from Palaeolithic Sites
in Belgium, the Ukraine and Russia: Osteometry, Ancient DNA and Stable
Isotopes," *Journal of Archaeological Science* 36 (2009): 473–490; David Wescott
and Society of Primitive Technology, *Primitive Technology: A Book of Earth Skills*
(Salt Lake City, UR: Gibbs Smith Publisher, 1999), 248; Mikhail V. Sablin,
and Gennady A. Khlopachev, "The Earliest Ice Age Dogs: Evidence from
Eliseevichi 1," *Current Anthropology* 43 (2002): 795–799; Mietje Germonpré
(Royal Belgian Institute of Natural Sciences), personal communications.

The passages on Darwin and dog genetics are based on Charles Darwin, *The Variation of Animals and Plants Under Domestication* (New York: O. Judd & Company, 1868); Robert Wayne (UCLA), personal communication; C. Vilà and J. A. Leonard, "Canid Phylogeny and Origin of the Domestic Dog," in *The Genetics of the Dog*, ed. E. A. Ostrander and A. Ruvinsky. 2nd ed. (Wallingford, UK: CABI international, Oxon, 2012); B. M. Vonholdt et al., "Genome-Wide SNP and Haplotype Analyses Reveal a Rich History Underlying Dog Domestication," *Nature* 464 (2010): 898–902.

The passages on wolf domestication are drawn from József Topál et al., "Attachment to Humans: A Comparative Study on Hand-Reared Wolves and Differently Socialized Dog Puppies," *Animal Behaviour* 70 (2005); E. Kubinyi, Z. Virányi, and Á Miklósi, "Comparative Social Cognition: From Wolf and Dog to Humans," *Comparative Cognition and Behavior Reviews* 2 (2007): 26–46; Raymond Coppinger and Lorna Coppinger, *Dogs: A Startling New Understanding of Canine Origin, Behavior, and Evolution* (New York: Scribner, 2001).

The passages on Dmitri Belyaev and the fox farm experiments are based on L. N. Trut et al., "To the 90th Anniversary of Academician Dmitry Konstantinovich Belyaev (1917–1985)," *Russian Journal of Genetics* 43 (2007): 717–720; Lyudmila N. Trut, "Early Canid Domestication: The Farm-Fox Experiment: Foxes Bred for Tamability in a 40-Year Experiment Exhibit Remarkable Transformations That Suggest an Interplay Between Behavioral Genetics and Development," *American Scientist* 87 (1999): 160–169; *In Memory of D. K. Belyaev. Dmitrii Konstantinovich Belyaev: A Book of Reminiscences*, ed. V. K. Shumnyi et al. (Novosibirsk: Sib. Otd. Ros. Akad. Nauk, 2002).

The passages on early dogs are based on R. Y. Tito et al., "Brief Communication: DNA from Early Holocene American Dog," *American Journal of Physical Anthropology* 145 (2011): 653–657; Ofer Bar-Yosef and François Raymond Valla, *The Natufian Culture in the Levant*. Archaeological Series (Ann Arbor, MI: International Monographs in Prehistory, 1991); Simon J. M. Davis and François R. Valla, "Evidence for Domestication of the Dog 12,000 Years Ago in the Natufian of Israel," *Nature* 276, no. 5688 (1978): 608–610; Megan Garber, "Humanity's Best Friend: How Dogs May Have Helped Humans Beat the Neanderthals," *Atlantic*, May 14, 2012.

The passages on the Scottish wildcat are based on David W. Macdonald and Andrew J. Loveridge, *Biology and Conservation of Wild Felids*. Oxford Biology Series (Oxford: Oxford University Press, 2010), xix, 471–491; Carlos Driscoll, personal communication; Mike Daniels (John Muir Trust, Scotland), personal communication; Steve Piper (Scottish Wildcat Association), personal communication.

The passages on the Neolithic era are based on Ofer Bar-Yosef, "The Natu-
fian Culture in the Levant, Threshold to the Origins of Agriculture" (PDF),
Evolutionary Anthropology 6, no. 5 (1998): 159–177; J.-D. Vigne et al., "The
Early Process of Mammal Domestication in the Near East: New Evidence
from the Pre-Neolithic and Pre-Pottery Neolithic in Cyprus," *Current Anthropology* 52, suppl. 4 (2011): S255–S271; F. Salamini et al., "Genetics and
Geography of Wild Cereal Domestication in the Near East," *Nature Reviews
Genetics* 3 (2002): 429–441; M. A. Zeder, "Domestication and Early Agriculture in the Mediterranean Basin: Origins, Diffusion, and Impact," *Proceedings
of the National Academy of Sciences USA* 105 (2008): 11597–11604.

The passages on cat domestication are based on C. A. Driscoll et al., "The
Near Eastern Origin of Cat Domestication," *Science* 317 (2007): 519–523;
J. D. Vigne et al., "Early Taming of the Cat in Cyprus," *Science* 304 (2004):
259; C. A. Driscoll, D. W. Macdonald, and S. J. O'Brien, "From Wild Animals to Domestic Pets, an Evolutionary View of Domestication," *Proceedings
of the National Academy of Sciences USA*, 106, suppl. 1 (2009): 9971–9978;
Jean-Denis Vigne (CNRS, Paris), personal communication.

The claim that cats are the world's most popular pet is based on personal
communications with Dennis Turner, director of the Institute for Applied
Ethology and Animal Psychology in Hirzel, Switzerland; Kurt Kotrschal, director of the Konrad Lorenz Research Station in Berlin, Germany; and John
Bradshaw, director of the Anthrozoology Institute at the University of Bristol
in the United Kingdom. This claim has also been made in *Scientific American*.

Chapter 3: The Rise of the Pet

The account of Princess Joan and the ravages of the Black Death came primarily from Norman F. Cantor, *In the Wake of the Plague: The Black Death and
the World It Made*. 1st Perennial ed. (New York: Perennial/HarperCollins,
2002), 29–53. Additional details about Princess Joan were drawn from Mary
Anne Everett Green, *Lives of the Princesses of England, from the Norman Con-
quest* (London: H. Colburn, 1849), 242–259. Additional details about the
Black Death came from Giovanni Boccaccio and G. H. McWilliam, *The De-
cameron*. 2nd ed. (London: Penguin Books, 1995), 4–15; George Christakos,
*Interdisciplinary Public Health Reasoning and Epidemic Modelling: The Case of
Black Death* (Berlin, London: Springer, 2005), chs. 3 and 5.

Details about Pope Gregory IX and witchcraft came from Eric John, *The
Popes: A Concise Biographical History*. 1st ed. (New York: Hawthorn Books,
1964), 227–228; John Demos, *The Enemy Within: 2,000 Years of Witch-Hunting*

in the Western World (New York: Viking, 2008), 14–43; Robert Darnton, *The Great Cat Massacre and Other Episodes in French Cultural History* (New York: Basic Books, 1999), xiii, 88–97; Carl Van Vechten, *The Tiger in the House*. New York Review Books Classics (New York: New York Review of Books, 2006), 68–69; Jeffrey Burton Russell, *Witchcraft in the Middle Ages* (Ithaca, NY: Cornell University Press, 1972), 158–165; Edward Peters, *Inquisition* (Berkeley: University of California Press, 1989), pp. vi.

Much of my information about ancient Egypt came from two excellent books: Donald W. Engels, *Classical Cats: The Rise and Fall of the Sacred Cat* (London: Routledge, 1999); Jaromír Málek, *The Cat in Ancient Egypt* (Philadelphia: University of Pennsylvania Press, 1997). Engels, *Classical Cats*, was also an invaluable source of information on ancient Greece, ancient Rome, and the Middle Ages. Additional information on ancient Egypt came from Naguib Kanawati and Alexandra Woods, *Beni Hassan: Art and Daily Life in an Egyptian Province* (Cairo: Supreme Council of Antiquities, 2010), 41–44; Herodotus, *The Histories* (New York: Barnes & Noble Classics, 2005); V. Linseele, W. Vanneer, and S. Hendrickx, "Evidence for Early Cat Taming in Egypt," *Journal of Archaeological Science* 34 (2007): 2081–2090.

Additional information on ancient Greece and ancient Rome came from N. B. Todd, "Cats and Commerce," *Scientific American* 237 (1977): 100–107; Liliane Bodson, "Motivations for Pet-Keeping in Ancient Greece and Rome," in *Companion Animals and Us: Exploring the Relationships Between People and Pets*, ed. Anthony L. Podberscek, Elizabeth S. Paul, and James Serpell (Cambridge: Cambridge University Press, 2000), 27–41; J. Mazzorin and A. Tagliacozzo, "Morphological and Osteological Changes in the Dog from the Neolithic to the Roman Period in Italy," in *Dogs Through Time: An Archaeological Perspective*, ed. S. J. Crockford, 141–161. BAR International Series 889 (Victoria, British Columbia: International Congress of the International Council for Archaeozoology, 2000).

Most of my information about the Brown Dog Riots came from Coral Lansbury, *The Old Brown Dog: Women, Workers, and Vivisection in Edwardian England* (Madison: University of Wisconsin Press, 1985), 3–25. I also gleaned details from H. Kean, "An Exploration of the Sculptures of Greyfriars Bobby, Edinburgh, Scotland, and the Brown Dog, Battersea, South London, England," *Society and Animals* 11, no. 4 (2003): 353–373; W. B. Gratzer, *Eurekas and Euphorias: The Oxford Book of Scientific Anecdotes* (Oxford: Oxford University Press, 2004), 186–191.

I based my accounts of Medieval hunting on Sophia Menache, "Hunting and Attachment to Dogs in the Pre-modern Period," in *Companion Animals*

and Us: Exploring the Relationships Between People and Pets, ed. Anthony L.
Podberscek, Elizabeth S. Paul, and James Serpell (Cambridge: Cambridge
University Press, 2000); Linda Kalof, *Looking at Animals in Human History*
(London: Reaktion Books, 2007), 42–60.

My passage on cats and dogs in Renaissance art drew primarily from Ed-
gar Peters Bowron, Bruce Museum, and Museum of Fine Arts Houston,
Best in Show: The Dog in Art from the Renaissance to Today (New Haven, CT:
Yale University Press in association with the Museum of Fine Arts Hous-
ton and Bruce Museum, 2006), 1–37; Simona Cohen, *Animals as Disguised
Symbols in Renaissance Art*. Brill's Studies in Intellectual History (Leiden:
Brill, 2008), 211–215; Kenneth Clark, *Animals and Men: Their Relation-
ship as Reflected in Western Art from Prehistory to the Present Day* (London:
Thames and Hudson, 1977), 45–66.

Information on René Descartes came from Richard A. Watson, *Cogito,
Ergo Sum: The Life of René Descartes*. Rev. pbk. ed. (Boston: David R. Godine,
2007), 3–19, 166–169; René Descartes, *The Philosophical Writings of Descartes*
(Cambridge: Cambridge University Press, 1984), 78–85, 111–113, 138–141,
316–319, 348–367.

Other passages relating to vivisection and animal cruelty came from Linda
Kalof, *Looking at Animals in Human History* (London: Reaktion Books, 2007),
ix, 124–136, 222; Tom Regan and Peter Singer, *Animal Rights and Human
Obligations*. 2nd ed. (Englewood Cliffs, NJ: Prentice Hall, 1989), 67–68;
Richard D. French, *Antivivisection and Medical Science in Victorian Society*
(Princeton, NJ: Princeton University Press, 1975), 15–35; Richard D. French,
Antivivisection and Medical Science in Victorian Society (Princeton, NJ: Prince-
ton University Press, 1975), 15–35; "Richard Martin 'Humanity Dick' (1754–
1834)," *History Today* 54 (June 2004); Royal Commission on Vivisection,
*Report of the Royal Commission on the Practice of Subjecting Live Animals to Ex-
periments for Scientific Purposes* (London: Printed by G. E. Eyre and W. Spottis-
woode, for H. M. Stationery Off., 1876); Rod Preece, *Awe for the Tiger, Love
for the Lamb: A Chronicle of Sensibility to Animals* (Vancouver: University of
British Columbia Press, 2002), 162–163; Paul S. White, *The Experimental Animal in Victorian Britain* (New York: Columbia University Press, 2005).

Writing about pets in the Victorian era and modern America would have
been nearly impossible without Katherine C. Grier's *Pets in America: A History* (Chapel Hill: University of North Carolina Press, 2006). Additional
information for this section came from Norine Dresser, "The Horse *Bar
Mitzvah*: A Celebratory Exploration of the Human-Animal Bond," in *Companion Animals and Us: Exploring the Relationships Between People and Pets*,

ed. Anthony L. Podberscek, Elizabeth S. Paul, and James Serpell (Cambridge: Cambridge University Press, 2000); Philip Howell, "A Place for the Animal Dead: Pets, Pet Cemeteries and Animal Ethics in Late Victorian Britain," *Ethics, Place and Environment* 5 (2002): 5–22; "A Dog's Costly Funeral," *New York Times*, August 15, 1888; Stanley Coren, *The Pawprints of History: Dogs and the Course of Human Events* (New York: Free Press, 2002); H. Donald Winkler, *Lincoln's Ladies: The Women in the Life of the Sixteenth President*. Rev. exp. ed. (Nashville, TN: Cumberland House, 2004), 165; Jennifer Levitz, "American Parents Going to the Dogs After Human Kids Leave the Nest," *Wall Street Journal*, May 7, 2010; Claude S. Fischer and Michael Hout, *Century of Difference: How America Changed in the Last One Hundred Years* (New York: Russell Sage Foundation, 2006), ch. 4.

Chapter 4: Canine Einsteins

The passages on theory of mind are drawn from my personal communications with Brian Hare and Evan MacLean (both of Duke University), as well as from a number of scientific papers, including M. A. Udell and C. D. Wynne, "A Review of Domestic Dogs' (*Canis familiaris*) Human-Like Behaviors: Or Why Behavior Analysts Should Stop Worrying and Love Their Dogs," *Journal of the Experimental Analysis of Behavior* 89 (2008): 247–261; Brian Hare, "From Nonhuman to Human Mind: What Changed and Why?" *Current Directions in Psychological Science* 16 (2007): 60–64; Victoria Wobber et al., "Breed Differences in Domestic Dogs' (*Canis familiaris*) Comprehension of Human Communicative Signals," *Interaction Studies* 10 (2009): 206–224; B. Hare et al., "The Domestication of Social Cognition in Dogs," *Science* 298 (2002): 1634–1636; B. Hare and M. Tomasello, "Human-Like Social Skills in Dogs?" *Trends in Cognitive Sciences* 9 (2005): 439–444; N. J. Emery and N. S. Clayton, "Comparative Social Cognition," *Annual Review of Psychology* 60 (2009): 87–113; B. Hare et al., "Social Cognitive Evolution in Captive Foxes Is a Correlated By-Product of Experimental Domestication," *Current Biology* 15 (2005): 226–230; A. Miklósi et al., "A Comparative Study of the Use of Visual Communicative Signals in Interactions Between Dogs (*Canis familiaris*) and Humans and Cats (*Felis catus*) and Humans," *Journal of Comparative Psychology* 119 (2005): 179–186; J. Kaminski et al., "Domestic Dogs Comprehend Human Communication with Iconic Signs," *Developmental Science* 12 (2009): 831–837.

The passages on Charles Darwin come largely from Emma Townshend's fascinating *Darwin's Dogs: How Darwin's Pets Helped Form a World-Changing*

Theory of Evolution. 1st Frances Lincoln ed. (London: Frances Lincoln, 2009). Details on George Romanes come from George John Romanes, *Animal Intelligence*. International Scientific Series 24 (New York: D. Appleton and Company, 1883). The passage on John Lubbock comes from John Lubbock, "Teaching Animals to Converse," *Nature* (1884): 216; J. F. M. Clark, "John Lubbock and Mental Evolution," *Endeavour* 22, no. 2 (1998): 44–47. The passage on C. Lloyd Morgan was based on C. Lloyd Morgan, *An Introduction to Comparative Psychology*. Contemporary Science Series (London: W. Scott Ltd., 1894), xiv, 1, 382. The material on Donald Griffin was drawn from Charles G. Gross, *Donald R. Griffin: 1915–2003: A Biographical Memoir by Charles G. Gross*. Biographical Memoirs 86 (Washington, DC: National Academies Press, 2005); D. R. Griffin and G. B. Speck, "New Evidence of Animal Consciousness," *Animal Cognition* 7 (2004): 5–18.

Much of my information on Marc Bekoff came from talking to the man himself. I also gleaned details from his books, primarily *The Emotional Lives of Animals: A Leading Scientist Explores Animal Joy, Sorrow, and Empathy—and Why They Matter* (Novato, CA: New World Library, 2007).

The passage on other canine emotion studies is drawn from Rachel Zelkowitz, "Dogs Have a Nose for Inequity," *Science*, December 8, 2008; J. W. Pilley and A. K. Reid, "Border Collie Comprehends Object Names as Verbal Referents," *Behavioral Processes* 86 (2011): 184–195; Helen Fields, "Is Your Dog Pessimistic?" *Science*, October 11, 2010; D. Custance, and J. Mayer, "Empathic-Like Responding by Domestic Dogs (*Canis familiaris*) to Distress in Humans: An Exploratory Study," *Animal Cognition* 15 (2012): 851–859.

The passage on Alexandra Horowitz is drawn from personal conversations, as well as from A. Horowitz, "Disambiguating the 'Guilty Look': Salient Prompts to a Familiar Dog Behaviour," *Behavioral Processes* 81 (2009): 447–452; A. C. Horowitz and M. Bekoff, "Naturalizing Anthropomorphism: Behavioral Prompts to Our Humanizing of Animals," *Anthrozoös* 20 (2007): 23–35; A. Horowitz, "Attention to Attention in Domestic Dog (*Canis familiaris*) Dyadic Play," *Animal Cognition* 12 (2009): 107–118.

Chapter 5: The Eye of the Storm

General information and color about Hurricane Katrina and the ensuing flooding comes from the following sources: National Oceanic and Atmospheric Administration facts and figures; Douglas Brinkley, *The Great Deluge: Hurricane Katrina, New Orleans, and the Mississippi Gulf Coast*. 1st ed. (New York: Morrow, 2006); Caroline Penry-Davey and Peter Chinn, dirs., "The

Storm That Drowned a City," *NOVA*, aired November 22, 2005; Spike Lee, dir., *When the Levees Broke: A Requiem in Four Acts* (HBO, 2006); Fritz Institute, "Hurricane Katrina: Perceptions of the Affected," 2006, http://www .fritzinstitute.org/PDFs/findings/HurricaneKatrina_Perceptions.pdf).

Fay Bourg's story is based on the following sources: Carmel Cafiero, "Carmel on the Case: Katrina Dog Gone," WSVN, August 4, 2009, http://www .wsvn.com/features/articles/carmelcase/MI127694; Carmel Cafiero, "Dog Gone," WSVN, November 2, 2006, http://www.wsvn.com/features/articles /carmelcase/MI96970/dog-gone; Kristin M. Thomas, "Where Is Hunter?" *Capital City Free Press*, November 4, 2006; Diane Allevato, former head of the Marin Humane Society, personal communication; Donna Dickerson, former chaplain at the San Antonio State Hospital and Texas Center for Infectious Disease, personal communication; Megan McNabb, "Pets in the Eye of the Storm: Hurricane Katrina Floods the Courts with Pet Custody Disputes," *Animal Law* 14 (2007): 71–108; postings on Petfinder.com, Nola. com, Katrina.com, and helpbringhunterhome.blogspot.com.

General information and color about Katrina pet rescues comes from the following sources: Allen Anderson and Linda C. Anderson, *Rescued—Saving Animals from Disaster: Life-Changing Stories and Practical Suggestions* (Novato, CA: New World Library, 2006); Mike Shiley, dir., *Dark Water Rising: The Truth About Hurricane Katrina Animal Rescues* (Shidog Films, 2006); Geralyn Pezanoski, *Mine* (Film Movement, 2009); Cathy Scott, *Pawprints of Katrina: Pets Saved and Lessons Learned* (Hoboken, NJ: Wiley, 2008); Leslie Irvine, *Filling the Ark: Animal Welfare in Disasters* (Philadelphia: Temple University Press, 2009); Wendi Jonassen, "7 Years After Katrina, New Orleans Is Overrun by Wild Dogs," *Atlantic*, August 2012; Francis Battista, cofounder, Best Friends Animal Society, personal communication.

Details of the passage of the Louisiana Pet Evacuation Bill and the bill itself are drawn from Ann M. Simmons, "Bill Maps a Pet Evacuation Route," *Los Angeles Times*, March 26, 2006; Michelle Buckalew, "Pet Owners Throw Their Support Behind Evacuation Bill Proposal," Best Friends Animal Society, April 19, 2006, http://bestfriends.org/News-And-Features /News/Pet-Owners-Throw-Their-Support-Behind-Evacuation-Bill -Proposal; Bob LaMendola, "He Fought, Survived the Storm," *South Florida Sun Sentinel*, September 10, 2005; Cathy Scott, *Pawprints of Katrina: Pets Saved and Lessons Learned* (Hoboken, NJ: Wiley, 2008); Dave Shiflett, "Dogs Abandoned in Storms Get in Their Licks," *South Florida Sun Sentinel*, November 26, 2005; Louisiana Act No. 615, passed in 2006 in regular session.

Details of the 109th US Congress come from Mike Allen, "Reid Calls Bush a 'Loser,'" *Washington Post*, May 7, 2005; David D. Kirkpatrick and Carl Hulse, "At Center of Senate Showdown, a Boxer Takes on a Surgeon," *New York Times*, May 15, 2005; Charles Babington, "House Rejects Iraq Pullout after GOP Forces a Vote," *Washington Post*, November 19, 2005; Norman Ornstein and Barry McMillon, "One Nation, Divisible," *New York Times*, June 23, 2005.

Chapter 6: The Protected Pet

The sections on Henry Bergh and the early American animal welfare movement are drawn primarily from Marion Lane and Stephen Zawistowski, *Heritage of Care: The American Society for the Prevention of Cruelty to Animals* (Westport, CT: Praeger Publishers, 2008). I also drew from C. C. Buel, "Henry Bergh and His Work," *Scribner's Monthly* (1879): 872–884, and from David Favre and Vivien Tsang, "The Development of the Anti-Cruelty Laws During the 1800's," *Detroit College of Law Review* (1993); Stephen Zawistowski, ASPCA, personal communications.

Depictions of nineteenth-century New York come from a variety of sources, including Joel A. Tarr, "Urban Pollution—Many Long Years Ago," *American Heritage Magazine* 22 (October 1971); Sarah Schmidt, "Digging into New York City's Trashy History," OnEarth, http://www.onearth.org /article/digging-into-new-york-citys-trashy-history, 2010; "The Dog-Catcher Abroad," *New York Times*, June 2, 1881; "Another Dog-Catcher in Trouble," *New York Times*, August 8, 1877; "Fatally Hurt by Automobile," *New York Times*, September 14, 1899; "Kills 77,607 Dogs and Homeless Cats," *New York Times*, July 6, 1908. The Charles Dickens quote comes from his *American Notes for General Circulation* (London: Chapman and Hall, 1842).

The section on the rise of the animal welfare movement in the twentieth century comes primarily from Diane L. Beers. *For the Prevention of Cruelty: The History and Legacy of Animal Rights Activism in the United States* (Athens: Swallow Press/Ohio University Press, 2006). I also drew from Bernard Oreste Unti, *Protecting All Animals: A Fifty-Year History of the Humane Society of the United States* (Washington, DC: Humane Society Press, 2004); Deborah J. Salem, Andrew N. Rowan, and Humane Society of the United States, *The State of the Animals II: 2003*. Public Policy Series (Washington, DC: Humane Society Press, 2003); Daniel Engber, "Pepper," *Slate*, December 22, 2009; Bernard Unti, HSUS, personal communications.

The section on the creation of felony cruelty laws is drawn from Andrew N. Rowan and Beth Rosen, "Progress in Animal Legislation: Measurement and

Assessment," *The State of the Animals III: 2005*. Public Policy Series (Washington, DC: Humane Society Press, 2005); Frank R. Ascione and Randall Lockwood, "Cruelty to Animals: Changing Psychological, Social, and Legislative Perspectives," in *The State of the Animals: 2001*. Public Policy Series (Washington, DC: Humane Society Press, 2001); personal communications with David Favre of the Michigan State University College of Law and Randall Lockwood of the ASPCA.

Chapter 7: My Cat Is Not a Toaster

I drew the details of the Baltimore cat burglar incident primarily from three articles in the *Baltimore Sun*: "Who Owns This Cat?" (December 18, 1894); "The Cat Is Hers!" (December 19, 1894); "That Canton Cat" (December 20, 1894).

I drew details of ancient laws from James B. Pritchard, *Ancient Near Eastern Texts Relating to the Old Testament*. 2nd ed. (Princeton, NJ: Princeton University Press, 1955); John Sassoon, *Ancient Laws and Modern Problems: The Balance Between Justice and a Legal System*. Pbk. ed. (Portland, OR: Intellect Books, 2005); Steven M. Wise, "The Legal Thinghood of Nonhuman Animals," *Environmental Affairs* 23, no. 3 (1996): 471–546, http://lawdigital commons.bc.edu/cgi/viewcontent.cgi?article=1334&context=ealr; Steven M. Wise, *Rattling the Cage: Toward Legal Rights for Animals* (Cambridge, MA: Perseus Books, 2000); Christopher D. Stone, *Should Trees Have Standing? Toward Legal Rights for Natural Objects* (Los Altos, CA: W. Kaufmann, 1974); Carl Van Vechten, *The Tiger in the House*. New York Review of Books Classics (New York: New York Review of Books, 2006); Sophia Menache, "Hunting and Attachment to Dogs in the Pre-modern Period," in *Companion Animals and Us: Exploring the Relationships Between People and Pets*, ed. Anthony L. Podberscek, Elizabeth S. Paul, and James Serpell (Cambridge: Cambridge University Press, 2000).

The section on William Blackstone is based on Albert W. Alschuler, "Rediscovering Blackstone," *University of Pennsylvania Law Review* 145 (1996): 1–55; William Blackstone et al., *Commentaries on the Laws of England: In Four Books, with an Analysis of the Work*. From the 21st London ed. (New York: Harper & Brothers, 1847).

My information on the variety of court cases mentioned in this chapter comes from the following sources: The case of the dog killed by the train in New Orleans is based on the 1897 US Supreme Court opinion *Sentell v. New Orleans & C. R. Co.* The case of the Pomeranian killed in San Francisco is based on the 1919 California District Court of Appeal opinion *Roos v. Loeser*. The passage about the legal status of cats in the early twentieth century comes from *Law Notes* (1916–1917), Edward Thompson Co. vol. 204. The case of the dog shot by the cat owner in Maine is based on three sources: the 1914 Maine Supreme Court opinion *Thurston v. Carter*; "The Cat," *Altoona Mirror*, June 1, 1915; "Dog and Cat Case," *Naugatuck Daily News*, March 27, 1914. The case of the man keeping eight cats in Kansas is based on the 1934 Kansas Supreme Court opinion *Smith v. Steinrauf*. The case of the man stealing a cat in California is based on the 1984 California Court of Appeals opinion *People v. Sadowski*. The battle over Gigi is based on Alex Roth, "It's a Dog-Eat-Dog Battle in Court for Pet Custody," *San Diego Union-Tribune*, May 29, 2000.

The case of the dog killed by the garbage man in Florida is based on two sources: the 1964 Florida Supreme Court opinion *La Porte v. Associated Independents, Inc.* and "Mental or Emotional Distress: Pigeonhole Recovery or Independent Tort?" 49 Minn. L. Rev. 763 (1964–1965). The case of the cat in the dog's casket in New York is based on the 1979 Civil Court of the City of New York case opinion *Corso v. Crawford Dog and Cat Hospital, Inc.* The case of the German shepherd that died at a New York kennel is based on the 1980 Civil Court of the City of New York opinion *Brousseau v. Rosenthal*. The case of the Indiana custody battle over the Boston bull terrier is based on the 1944 Appellate Court of Indiana opinion *Akers v. Sellers*. The Iowa custody battle over the dog named Georgetta is based on the 1984 Iowa Court of Appeals decision *In re Marriage of Stewart*. The case of the two Virginia men fighting over custody of a cat is based on court materials from the 1997 Arlington, Virginia, case *Zovko v. Gregory*, including court motions, affidavits, and judicial riders. Details also come from Brooke A. Masters, "Custody Battle over Cat Brings Out Claws," *Washington Post*, September 21, 1997. The case of the trust for the dog, Dick, is based on a passage in *Kentucky Law Journal* (1922–1923): 248–249. The case of the will for Roxy Russell is based on the 1968 California Supreme Court case opinion *In Re Estate of Russell*.

The passages on tort law are based on Pamela D. Frasch, *Animal Law in a Nutshell*. West Nutshell Series (St. Paul, MN: Thomson/West, 2011); Christopher D. Seps, "Animal Law Evolution: Treating Pets as Persons in Tort and Custody Disputes," *University of Illinois Law Review* (2010): 1339–1373; Geordie Duckler, "The Economic Value of Companion Animals: A Legal and Anthropological Argument for Special Valuation," *Animal Law* 8 (2002): 199–221.

The details of the T-Bo Act are based on "Canine Loss Spurs New Law," *State Legislatures* 26 (2000): 11; Richard Locker, "T-Bo Act 'Recognizes Pets as Living Things, Not Merely Property,'" *Commercial Appeal*, February 10, 2000. The details of similar acts are based on Elaine T. Byszewski, "Valuing Companion Animals in Wrongful Death Cases: A Survey of Current Court and Legislative Action and a Suggestion for Valuing Pecuniary Loss of Companionship," *Animal Law* 215 (2003): 215–241.

The *Los Angeles Times* article that estimates there has been a hundredfold rise in pet custody cases since 1990 is Sanjiv Bhattacharaya, "To Love, Honor and Belly-Scratch," *Los Angeles Times*, January 9, 2005.

Details of the petimony, restraining order, and alcoholic beverages cases are based on *Dickson v. Dickson* (Ark. Garland County Ch. Ct. Oct. 14, 1994); *In Re Marriage of Fore*, No. Dw 243974 (Minn. Dist. Ct. Jan. 9, 2001); "This Marriage Went to the Dogs, but the Beast Got the Best of It," *Houston Chronicle*, July 16, 1987.

The passage about pet custody legislation is drawn from T. Christopher Wharton, "Fighting Like Cats and Dogs: The Rising Number of Custody Battles over the Family Pet," *Journal of Law and Family Studies* 10 (2008): 433–442; P. J. Huffstutter, "Wisconsin Bill Outlines Rules for Pet Custody," *Seattle Times*, July 15, 2007.

The passages about best-interest strategies are based on Rebecca J. Huss, "The Pervasive Nature of Animal Law: How the Law Impacts the Lives of People and Their Animal Companions," *Valparaiso University Law Review* 43 (2008): 1131–1154; Tabby McLain, "Adapting the Child's Best Interest Model to Custody Determination of Companion Animals," *Journal of Animal Law* 6 (2010): 151–168.

The section on the pet guardian movement is based on personal communications with In Defense of Animals founder Elliot Katz; Elliot Katz, "The President's Message: I Am Not an Owner; He Was Not My Property," *In Defense of Animals* (Spring 1994): 2; Ryan Morgan, "Only in Boulder: A Home for Pet 'Guardians,'" *Boulder Daily Camera*, March 29, 2009.

Details of the Pet Ownership in Public Housing Law come from Taimie Bryant, David Cassuto, and Rebecca Huss, *Animal Law and the Courts: A Reader*. American Casebooks (St. Paul, MN: Thomson/West, 2008), 167–208; personal communications with Valparaiso University law professor Rebecca J. Huss.

The section on the history of trusts and trust law is based on Breahn Vokolek, "America Gets What It Wants: Pet Trusts and a Future for Its Companion Animals," *UMKC Law Review* (2008); Edward William Lane,

An Account of the Manners and Customs of the Modern Egyptians (London: Ward, Lock and Co., 1890); Carl Van Vechten, *The Tiger in the House*. New York Review of Books Classics (New York: New York Review of Books, 2006); Gerry W. Beyer, "Pet Animals: What Happens When Their Humans Die," *Santa Clara Law Review* 40 (2000): 617–676; Susan J. Hankin, "Not a Living Room Sofa: Changing the Legal Status of Companion Animals," *Rutgers Journal of Law and Public Policy* 4, no. 2 (2007): 314–410.

The section on the drafting of the Uniform Trust Code comes from personal communications with the code's drafter, University of Missouri Law School professor David English, and Steve Ann Chambers, director of philanthropy for the Humane Society Legislative Fund.

Chapter 8: Civil Rights for Pets

The section on John Quincy Adams and slavery is drawn from the following sources: Joseph Wheelan, *Mr. Adams's Last Crusade: John Quincy Adams's Extraordinary Post-Presidential Life in Congress*. 1st ed. (New York: PublicAffairs, 2008); John Quincy Adams and John Greenleaf Whittier, *Letters from John Quincy Adams to His Constituents to the Twelfth Congressional District in Massachusetts (Washington, 13 March, 1837)* (Boston: I. Knapp, 1837); David C. Frederick, "John Quincy Adams, Slavery, and the Disappearance of the Right to Petition," *Law and History Review* 9 (1991); Mary Beth Corrigan, "Imaginary Cruelties? A History of the Slave Trade in Washington, DC," *Washington History* 13 (Fall–Winter 2001–2002).

The section on Sido the dog is drawn from Frances Carlisle, "Destruction of Pets by Will Provision," *Real Property, Probate and Trust Journal* 16 (1981): 894–903; letter from Laurence Kessenick to Henry Mark Holzer, editor of the *Animal Rights Law Reporter*; reporter's transcript, *Smith v. Avanzino*, California Superior Court, June 17, 1980; Laurence W. Kessenick (Attorneys for Animal Rights), amicus brief, *In the Matter of the Estate of Mary Murphy* (1980).

The history of the Animal Legal Defense Fund is drawn from personal conversations with ALDF founder, Joyce Tischler, as well as from Joyce Tischler, "The History of Animal Law, Part I (1972–1987)," *Stanford Journal of Animal Law and Policy* 1 (2008); Joyce Tischler, "A Brief History of Animal Law, Part II (1985–2011)," *Stanford Journal of Animal Law and Policy* 5 (2012): 27–77; Richard L. Cupp Jr., "A Dubious Grail: Seeking Tort Law Expansion and Limited Personhood as Stepping Stones Toward Abolishing Animals' Property Status," *SMU Law Review* 60 (2007): 3–54. Tischler's law school article is Joyce S. Tischler, "Rights for Nonhuman Animals: A Guardianship Model for Dogs and Cats," *San Diego Law Review* 14 (1977): 484–506. The *New York Times* article is William Glaberson, "Legal Pioneers Seek to Raise Lowly Status of Animals," *New York Times*, August 18, 1999. The *Los Angeles Times* article is Richard Marosi, "Every Dog Has His Day in Court," *Los Angeles Times*, May 24, 2000.

The section on the NAACP is drawn from Charles J. Russo, *Encyclopedia of Education Law* (Thousand Oaks, CA: Sage Publications, 2008); Richard T. Schaefer, *Encyclopedia of Race, Ethnicity, and Society* (Los Angeles: Sage Publications, 2008); Kofi Lomotey, *Encyclopedia of African American Education*. A Sage Reference Publication (Los Angeles: Sage, 2010); Mark V. Tushnet, *The NAACP's Legal Strategy Against Segregated Education, 1925–1950* (Chapel Hill: University of North Carolina Press, 1987); Leland B. Ware, "Setting the Stage for *Brown*: The Development and Implementation of the NAACP's School Desegregation Campaign, 1930–1950," *Mercer Law Review* 52 (2001): 631–673.

The section on Dred Scott is drawn from Helen Taylor Greene, and Shaun L. Gabbidon, *Encyclopedia of Race and Crime* (Los Angeles: Sage, 2009).

The section on the Woodley case is drawn from Barry Yeoman, "Special Report: Operation Rescue," *O, the Oprah Magazine*, June 2009, as well as from personal communications with ALDF's head lawyer on the case, Bruce Wagman.

The section on Bob Barker is drawn from Taimie L. Bryant, "The Bob Barker Gifts to Support Animal Rights Law," *Journal of Legal Education* 60 (2010): 237–262.

Chapter 9: The Perils of Personhood

The case of Bartholomew Chassenée and the rats of Autun was drawn from the following sources: E. P. Evans, *The Criminal Prosecution and Capital Punishment of Animals* (London: W. Heinemann, 1906); Percy Allen, *Burgundy: The Splendid Duchy Studies and Sketches in South Burgundy* (New York: J. Pott & Company, 1912); Berriat-Saint-Prix, "Prosecutions Against Animals," *American Jurist and Law Magazine* 1 (1829); Walter Woodburn Hyde, "The Prosecution and Punishment of Animals and Lifeless Things in the Middle Ages and Modern Times," *University of Pennsylvania Law Review and American Law Register* 64 (1916): 696–730.

The sections on medieval animal trials in general were drawn from Piers Beirne, "A Note on the Facticity of Animal Trials in Early Modern Britain;

or, the Curious Prosecution of Farmer Carter's Dog for Murder," *Crime, Law and Social Change* 55 (2011); F. Galeron, *Statistique de l'arrondissement de Falaise* (Paris: Hachette Livre, 1826); P. G. Langevin, *Recherches historiques sur Falaise* (Brée l'Aîné, 1814); P. G. Langevin, *Supplement aux recherches historiques sur Falaise* (Brée l'Aîné, 1826); Ruth A. Johnston, *All Things Medieval: An Encyclopedia of the Medieval World* (Westport, CT: Greenwood, 2011); Jen Girgen, "The Historical and Contemporary Prosecution and Punishment of Animals," *Animal Law* 9 (2003): 97–133; Linda Kalof, *Looking at Animals in Human History* (London: Reaktion Books, 2007), ix.

Details of the Wesley Frye mauling were drawn from the Effingham County Sheriff's Office Incident Report of July 24, 2012; G. G. Rigsby, "Hearing for Pit Bull Postponed Until January," *Savannah Morning News*, October 24, 2012; personal communications with David Ehsanipoor, spokesman Effingham County Sheriff's Office, and Romie Currier, director of Effingham County Animal Control.

The section on Ming's Opera House was drawn from "Ming Opera House," Montana Government website, www.metnet.mt.gov/special/quarries %20from%20the%20gulch/htm/ming.shtml; "Ming's Opera House," Montana Cowboy Hall of Fame, http://www.montanacowboyfame.com/151001 /256159.html; "Uncle Tom's Cabin," *Daily Helena Independent*, August 8, 1882.

Much of the historical information on bloodhounds and other "demon dogs" besides the pit bull is drawn from Karen Delise's *The Pit Bull Placebo* (Anubis Publishing, 2007). Other sources include "Untitled," *Sullivan Democrat*, December 15, 1864; "Torn by Dogs," *Sullivan Democrat*, March 17, 1891.

The sections on the history of the pit bull are drawn from Karen Delise's *The Pit Bull Placebo* (Anubis Publishing, 2007); Scot Brown, David Brand, and D. Blake Hallanan, "Time Bombs on Legs," *Time*, July 27, 1987; E. M. Swift, "The Pit Bull Friend and Killer," *Sports Illustrated*, July 27, 1987; 2006 *Encyclopaedia Britannica* entries for "bull terrier," "bulldog," and "pit bull"; "Bulldog Kills Five-Year-Old," *Big Spring Herald Sun*, July 18, 1976; Michelle Green, "An Instinct for the Kill," *People Weekly*, July 6, 1987; J. J. Sacks, R. W. Sattin, and S. E. Bonzo, "Dog Bite–Related Fatalities from 1979 through 1988," *Journal of the American Medical Association* 262 (1989): 1489–1492; J. J. Sack et al., "Breeds of Dogs Involved in Fatal Human Attacks in the United States Between 1979 and 1998," *Journal of the American Veterinary Medical Association* 217 (2000): 836–840.

Details on Armistead Gardens were drawn from Antero Pietila, "Armistead Gardens Ready to Experiment," *Baltimore Sun*, August 3, 2004; "Last

Straw for Armistead Gardens," *Baltimore Sun*, August 3, 1993; Peter Hermann and Cheryl L. Tan, "10 Arrested in Raids in Armistead Gardens Police Aim to Break up Teen Drug Ring," *Baltimore Sun*, March 27, 1997; letter from Armistead Homes Corporation to Jenine Gangi (August 10, 2012), composed by Sharon F. Vick, president, Armistead Homes Corporation.

Details of the Dominic Solesky mauling and aftermath were drawn from two court cases—*Tracey v. Solesky* (Maryland Court of Special Appeals, April 5, 2011) and *Tracey v. Solesky* (Court of Appeals of Maryland, 2012)—and a series of *Towson Times* articles by Bryan P. Sears, including "Pit Bull Attack Injures Boy, 10," *Towson Times*, May 2, 2007; "Gardina Proposes Pit Bull Task Force," May 9, 2007; "Dog That Mauled Boy Will Be Euthanized," May 16, 2007; "Charges Could Follow Pit Bull Attack of Boys," June 6, 2007; "Animal Panel Avoids Mentioning Breeds," August 8, 2007; "Gardina Would Put Bite on Dogs That Bite a Lot," September 12, 2007. Other details came from Anthony Solesky's self-published e-book, *Dangerous by Default: Extreme Breeds* (2010); Anthony Solesky, personal communication.

Information on breed-specific legislation was drawn from Susan Hunter and Richard A. Brisbin Jr., "Panic Policy Making: Canine Breed Bans in Canada and the United States" (paper presented at the annual meeting of the Western Political Science Association, La Riviera Hotel, Las Vegas, Nevada, March 8, 2007); Karyn Grey, "Breed-Specific Legislation Revisited: Canine Racism or the Answer to Florida's Dog Control Problems?" *Nova Law Review* (2003); Pamela D. Frasch, *Animal Law in a Nutshell*. West Nutshell Series (St. Paul, MN: Thomson/West, 2011); Joan E. Schaffner, *An Introduction to Animals and the Law* (New York: Palgrave Macmillan, 2011); David Clouston, "Just a Little Pit," *Salina Journal*, September 2, 2009; Katie Barnett, Ledy VanKavage, and Lauren A. Gallagher, "The Fiscal Impact of Breed Discriminatory Laws at the Dawn of Doggy DNA," *Public Lawyer* (Summer 2010); Stefanie A. Ott et al., "Is There a Difference? Comparison of Golden Retrievers and Dogs Affected by Breed-Specific Legislation Regarding Aggressive Behavior," *Journal of Veterinary Behavior: Clinical Applications and Research* 3 (2008): 134–140; Deborah L. Duffy, Yuying Hsu, and James A. Serpell, "Breed Differences in Canine Aggression," *Applied Animal Behaviour Science* 114 (2008): 441–460; Stephanie Smith, club communications manager, American Kennel Club, personal communication; ASPCA position statement on breed-specific legislation (http://www.aspca .org/about-us/aspca-policy-and-position-statements/position-statement -on-breed-specific-legislation).

The passage on the Michael Vick case was drawn from Jim Gorant, *The Lost Dogs: Michael Vick's Dogs and Their Tale of Rescue and Redemption* (New York: Gotham Books, 2010); Rebecca J. Huss, "Lessons Learned: Acting as a Guardian/Special Master in the Bad Newz Kennels Case," *Animal Law Review* 15 (2008).

Chapter 10: Citizen Canine

Facts and figures about modern military working dogs and Lackland Air Force Base came from conversations with individuals I met at Lackland. Additional reporting came from conversations with Collen Mcgee (chief, public affairs, 37th Training Wing, Lackland) and the following articles: Patrick Quinn, "US Military Deaths in Afghanistan Hit 2,000 after 11 Years of War," Associated Press, September 30, 2012; Robert R. Milner, "Mighty Dogs of the Military," *Air Force Magazine*, February 2008; Josh Eells, "Dogs of War," *Texas Monthly*, November 2011; Eric P. Newcomer, "A Lesson for Paramedics: How to Treat Dogs Who Work in a War Zone," *New York Times*, July 13, 2012; Eric Talmadge, "Dog Surge Joins Troop Surge in Afghan War," *Army Times*, January 23, 2010; Austin Wright, "Bill to Help Canine Comrades in Arms," *Politico*, March 14, 2012; Alicia Dennis, "Healing the Dogs Who Serve," *People*, March 15, 2010; Robert R. Milner, "Mighty Dogs of the Military," *Air Force Magazine*, February 2008; Lisa Rogak, *The Dogs of War: The Courage, Love, and Loyalty of Military Working Dogs*. 1st ed. (New York: Thomas Dunne Books/St. Martin's Griffin, 2011), x.

The section on the history of military working dogs is drawn primarily from Michael G. Lemish, *War Dogs: A History of Loyalty and Heroism*. 1st pbk. ed. (Washington, DC: Brassey's, 1999). Additional reporting comes from "Stoicism, Tears Mark Adieux as Army Takes 17 D.C. Dogs," *Washington Post*, July 24, 1943.

The section on citizenship is drawn from Stephen David Kantrowitz, *More Than Freedom: Fighting for Black Citizenship in a White Republic, 1829–1889* (New York: Penguin Press, 2012), 514; Judith N. Shklar, *American Citizenship: The Quest for Inclusion*. The Tanner Lectures on Human Values (Cambridge, MA: Harvard University Press, 1991), 120; Richard Bellamy, *Citizenship: A Very Short Introduction*. Very Short Introductions (Oxford: Oxford University Press, 2008), 133; Bruce A. Wagman, Sonia Waisman, and Pamela D. Frasch, *Animal Law: Cases and Materials*. 4th ed. (Durham, NC: Carolina Academic Press, 2010), xli.

The section on service animals is drawn from John J. Ensminger, *Service and Therapy Dogs in American Society: Science, Law and the Evolution of Canine Caregivers* (Springfield, IL: Charles C. Thomas, 2010), xiv; Rebecca F. Wisch, "Table of State Assistance Animal Laws," Animal Legal Historical Center, 2012 (updated 2013), http://animallaw.info/articles/State%20 Tables/tbusassistanceanimals.htm; Elizabeth R. Blandon, "Reasonable Accommodation or Nuisance? Service Animals for the Disabled," *Florida Bar Journal* 75 (2001).

The section on Ape the police dog is drawn from Marc Santora and William K. Rashbaum, "F.B.I. Dog Is Killed in Raid on Hideaway," *New York Times*, March 14, 2013; Douglass Dowty, "FBI Police Dog Ape, Killed in Herkimer Shootings Raid, Buried in Virginia," *Post Standard*, March 18, 2013; "Honoring Officers Killed in 2013," Officer Down Memorial Page, http://www.odmp.org/search/year.

The section on the history and role of police dogs is drawn from Samuel G. Chapman, *Police Dogs in North America* (Springfield, IL: C. C. Thomas, 1990), xv; Burkhard Bilger, "Beware of the Dogs," *New Yorker*, February 27, 2012.

The section on court cases and laws involving police dogs is drawn from *Florida v. Harris* (US Supreme Court, 2013); *Florida v. Jardines* (US Supreme Court, 2013); *Dye v. Wargo* (US Court of Appeals, Seventh Circuit, 2001); Douglass Dowty, "State Senators Pass Bill to Toughen Penalty for Killing Police Animals," *Post Standard*, March 25, 2013; Federal Law Enforcement Animal Protection Act of 2000; Craig Scheiner, "'Cruelty to Police Dog' Laws Update," *Animal Law* 7 (2001): 141–144.

The section on therapy animals is drawn from Donald Altschiller, *Animal-Assisted Therapy*. Health and Medical Issues Today (Santa Barbara, CA: Greenwood, 2011), xiii; Brad Kollus, "A Calming Presence," *Cat Fancy*, May 2009; Bill Kueser, VP marketing, Pet Partners, personal communication; A. Berry et al., "Use of Assistance and Therapy Dogs for Children with Autism Spectrum Disorders: A Critical Review of the Current Evidence," *Journal of Alternative and Complementary Medicine* 19 (2013): 73–80; D. L. Wells, "Dogs as a Diagnostic Tool for Ill Health in Humans," *Alternative Therapies in Health and Medicine* 18 (2012): 12–17; Leslie A. Lyons, "Why Do Cats Purr?" *Scientific American*, April 3, 2006; K. Arhant-Sudhir, R. Arhant-Sudhir, and K. Sudhir, "Pet Ownership and Cardiovascular Risk Reduction: Supporting Evidence, Conflicting Data and Underlying Mechanisms," *Clinical and Experimental Pharmacology and Physiology* 38 (2011): 734–738.

The section on laws pertaining to therapy animals is drawn from Rebecca J. Huss, "No Pets Allowed: Housing Issues and Companion Animals," *Animal Law Review* 11, no. 69 (2005); Rebecca Huss, personal communication, July 13, 2012; text of the Americans with Disabilities Act of 1990; Fair Housing Amendments Act of 1988; Air Carrier Access Act of 1986.

The section on the erosion of our social connections is drawn from Sherry Turkle, *Alone Together: Why We Expect More from Technology and Less from Each Other* (New York: Basic Books, 2011), xvii; Stephen Marche, "Is Facebook Making Us Lonely?" *Atlantic*, May 2012; Eric Klinenberg, *Going Solo: The Extraordinary Rise and Surprising Appeal of Living Alone* (New York: Penguin Press, 2012), 273; US Census figures from 2010; Andrew Steptoe et al., "Social Isolation, Loneliness, and All-Cause Mortality in Older Men and Women," *Proceedings of the National Academy of Sciences USA* 110, no. 15 (2013): 5797–5801; Association of Religion Data Archives (ARDA); Jon Katz, *The New Work of Dogs: Tending to Life, Love, and Family*. 1st ed. (New York: Villard, 2003), xxiii; A. R. McConnell et al., "Friends with Benefits: On the Positive Consequences of Pet Ownership," *Journal of Personality and Social Psychology* 101 (2011): 1239–1252; N. Epley, J. Schroeder, and A. Waytz, "Motivated Mind Perception: Treating Pets as People and People as Animals," *Objectification and (De)Humanization* 60 (2013): 127–152.

Chapter 11: The Meowist Revolution

The section on Marc Bluestone's case is drawn from the following sources: Jean-Paul Renaud, "Jury Awards Dog Owner $39,000 in Malpractice Suit," *Los Angeles Times*, February 24, 2004; Jean-Paul Renaud, "Man Hopes to Take Big Bite Out of Vets over Dead Dog," *Los Angeles Times*, February 8, 2004; Larry Welborn, "Dog Owner Gets $39,000 in Vet Suit," *Orange County Register*, February 21, 2004; "California Dog Owner Awarded $39,000 in Veterinary Malpractice Suit," *JAVMA News*, April 15, 2004; Julie Scelfo, "Good Dogs, Bad Medicine?" *Newsweek*, May 20, 2001; Monte Morin, "Renowned O.C. Animal Hospital Prosecuted," *Los Angeles Times*, September 7, 2001; Dawn Fallik, "Vets Fear Costly Lawsuits in Future," *Philadelphia Inquirer*, July 26, 2004; Anita Hamilton, "Woof, Woof Your Honor," *Time*, December 13, 2004; Kate Coscarelli, "Man's Best Friends and Their Owners Getting Day in Court," *Seattle Times*, June 12, 2005; autobiographical posts on marcbluestone.net.

Details on the veterinary community's response to the Bluestone ruling are drawn from "Task Force on Legal Status of Animals Approved,"

JAVMA News, July 15, 2004; "Pros and Cons of Allowing Recovery of Non-Economic Damages (as Opposed to Punitive Damages) for Injuries to or Loss of Animals," AVMA, June 2005, https://www.avma.org/Advocacy /StateAndLocal/Pages/non-econo-damages.aspx?PF=1; Gerald L. Eichinger, "Veterinary Medicine: External Pressures on an Insular Profession and How Those Pressures Threaten to Change Current Malpractice Jurisprudence," *Montana Law Review* 67 (Summer 2006).

The section on the history of veterinary medicine is drawn largely from Susan D. Jones, *Valuing Animals: Veterinarians and Their Patients in Modern America*. Animals, History, Culture Series (Baltimore: Johns Hopkins University Press, 2003). This was supplemented with information from Joel A. Tarr, "Urban Pollution—Many Long Years Ago," *American Heritage Magazine* 22 (October 1971); Andrew Robichaud and Erik Steiner, "Trail of Blood: The Movement of San Francisco's Butchertown and the Spatial Transformation of Meat Production, 1849–1901," Stanford University Spatial History Lab, 2010, https://www.stanford.edu/group/spatialhistory/cgi-bin/site /pub.php?id=31; Susan J. Hankin, "Making Decisions About Our Animals' Health Care: Does It Matter Whether We Are Owners or Guardians?" *Stanford Journal of Animal Law and Policy* 2 (2009): 1–51; Laura Parker, "When Pets Die at the Vet, Grieving Owners Call Lawyers," *USA Today*, March 14, 2005.

The section on the complications of personhood for pets and the veterinary community's response is drawn from David Favre, "The Duty of Owners to Provide Veterinary Medical Care to Animals," in *Animal Law and the Courts: A Reader*, ed. Taimie Bryant, David Cassuto, and Rebecca Huss. American Casebooks (St. Paul, MN: Thomson/West, 2008); Christopher Green, "The Future of Veterinary Malpractice Liability in the Care of Companion Animals," *Animal Law* 10 (2004): 163–250; Adrian Hochstadt, assistant director, state legislative and regulatory affairs, AVMA, personal communications; *Goodby v. Vetpharm* (Supreme Court of Vermont, 2009); *Strickland v. Medlen* (Supreme Court of Texas, 2013).

The section on other industries' responses to personhood for dogs and cats is drawn from Sue Russell, "Animal Research's Changing Equation," *Pacific Standard*, December 19, 2011; Sue Russell, "When Extreme Animal Rights Activists Attack," *Pacific Standard*, November 23, 2012; Robert J. Hawkins, "Neuroscientists, Animal Activists Meet at Center," *San Diego Union-Tribune*, November 13, 2010; Joan Miller, legislative Information Liaison, Cat Fanciers' Association, personal communications; Richard L. Cupp Jr., "A Dubious Grail: Seeking Tort Law Expansion and Limited

Personhood as Stepping Stones Toward Abolishing Animals' Property Status," *SMU Law Review* 60 (2007): 3–54.

The section on the changing demographics of the veterinary profession are drawn from David Segal, "High Debt and Falling Demand Trap New Vets," *New York Times*, February 23, 2013.

The section on pets as social parasites is drawn from Colleen Curry, "Daughter 'Devastated' After Family Swept Away Saving Dog," ABC News, November 27, 2012; Jason Dearen, "Howard Kuljian Death: 'Sneaker Waves' Blamed for California Family's Tragic Drowning," Associated Press, November 27, 2012; John Archer, "Pet Keeping: A Case Study in Maladaptive Behavior," in *The Oxford Handbook of Evolutionary Family Psychology*, ed. Catherine Salmon and Todd K. Shackelford. Oxford Library of Psychology (New York: Oxford University Press, 2011), xvii.

The section on Gary Francione is drawn mostly from personal conversations with him. I supplemented this reporting with the following sources: Gary L. Francione, *Animals as Persons: Essays on the Abolition of Animal Exploitation* (New York: Columbia University Press, 2008), xv; Gary L. Francione, *Animals, Property, and the Law*. Ethics and Action (Philadelphia: Temple University Press, 1995), xviii; Gary L. Francione, *Introduction to Animal Rights: Your Child or the Dog?* (Philadelphia: Temple University Press, 2000), xxxviii; Gary L. Francione, *Rain Without Thunder: The Ideology of the Animal Rights Movement* (Philadelphia: Temple University Press, 1996); Gary Francione, "We're All Michael Vick," *Philadelphia Daily News*, August 22, 2007; Caroline Fraser, "The Raid at Silver Spring," *New Yorker*, April 19, 1993, 66–84.

Chapter 12: The Road Ahead

The history of the US shelter movement was drawn from Nathan J. Winograd, *Redemption: The Myth of Pet Overpopulation and the No Kill Revolution in America*. 1st ed. (Los Angeles, CA: Almaden Books, 2007); Deborah J. Salem, Andrew N. Rowan, and Humane Society of the United States, *The State of the Animals II: 2003*. Public Policy Series (Washington, DC: Humane Society Press, 2003), vii; Deborah J. Salem, Andrew N. Rowan, and Humane Society of the United States, *The State of the Animals: 2001*. Public Policy Series. 1st ed. (Washington, DC: Humane Society Press, 2001), v.

The sections on TNR are drawn largely from Ellen Perry Berkeley, *TNR Past, Present, and Future: A History of the Trap-Neuter-Return Movement*. 1st American ed. (Washington, DC: Alley Cat Allies, 2004); Bill Theobald and

Bonny Harris, "City Shelters Kill 22,000 in One Year," *Indianapolis Star*, October 14, 2001; Bill Theobald and Bonny Harris, "Inadequate Animal Care Violates Indianapolis Law," *Indianapolis Star*, October 15, 2001; Joan E. Schaffner, *An Introduction to Animals and the Law* (New York: Palgrave Macmillan, 2011); "Wisconsin Is No Place for Cat-Hunting, Governor Says," *USA Today*, April 13, 2005; "Occupational Safety and Health Standards for Shipyard Employment," US Department of Labor, https://www.osha.gov/pls/oshaweb/owastand.display_standard_group?p_toc_level=1&p_part_number=1915. I also received technical advice from Becky Robinson, president of Alley Cat Allies.

The section on the No Kill movement is drawn from Nathan J. Winograd, *Redemption: The Myth of Pet Overpopulation and the No Kill Revolution in America*. 1st ed. (Los Angeles, CA: Almaden Books, 2007), and personal conversations with Nathan J. Winograd.

The section on the changing status of children in society is drawn largely from Viviana A. Rotman Zelizer, *Pricing the Priceless Child: The Changing Social Value of Children* (New York: Basic Books, 1985).

Statistics about global pet ownership come from Theresa Bradley, "The Dog Index: What Man's Best Friend Tells Us About Global Economic Development," *Quartz*, November 13, 2012; Stephanie Wong, "Shanghai's New Dog Rules Mean One Best Friend per Household," *Bloomberg News*, February 24, 2011.

Index

Credit: Amy Duffield

David Grimm is a deputy news editor at *Science*, the world's largest journal of scientific research and science news. He is the recipient of the 2010 Animal Reporting Award from the National Press Club and has been featured in *The Best American Science and Nature Writing*. His work has appeared in *Science*, *US News & World Report*, *The Bark*, and the *Financial Times*. He teaches journalism at Johns Hopkins University and has a PhD in genetics from Yale. He lives in Baltimore with his wife, twin girls, and twin cats.

PublicAffairs is a publishing house founded in 1997. It is a tribute to the standards, values, and flair of three persons who have served as mentors to countless reporters, writers, editors, and book people of all kinds, including me.

I. F. STONE, proprietor of *I. F. Stone's Weekly*, combined a commitment to the First Amendment with entrepreneurial zeal and reporting skill and became one of the great independent journalists in American history. At the age of eighty, Izzy published *The Trial of Socrates*, which was a national bestseller. He wrote the book after he taught himself ancient Greek.

BENJAMIN C. BRADLEE was for nearly thirty years the charismatic editorial leader of *The Washington Post*. It was Ben who gave the *Post* the range and courage to pursue such historic issues as Watergate. He supported his reporters with a tenacity that made them fearless and it is no accident that so many became authors of influential, best-selling books.

ROBERT L. BERNSTEIN, the chief executive of Random House for more than a quarter century, guided one of the nation's premier publishing houses. Bob was personally responsible for many books of political dissent and argument that challenged tyranny around the globe. He is also the founder and longtime chair of Human Rights Watch, one of the most respected human rights organizations in the world.

•   •   •

For fifty years, the banner of Public Affairs Press was carried by its owner Morris B. Schnapper, who published Gandhi, Nasser, Toynbee, Truman, and about 1,500 other authors. In 1983, Schnapper was described by *The Washington Post* as "a redoubtable gadfly." His legacy will endure in the books to come.

Peter Osnos, *Founder and Editor-at-Large*